So I'm a
So What?

6

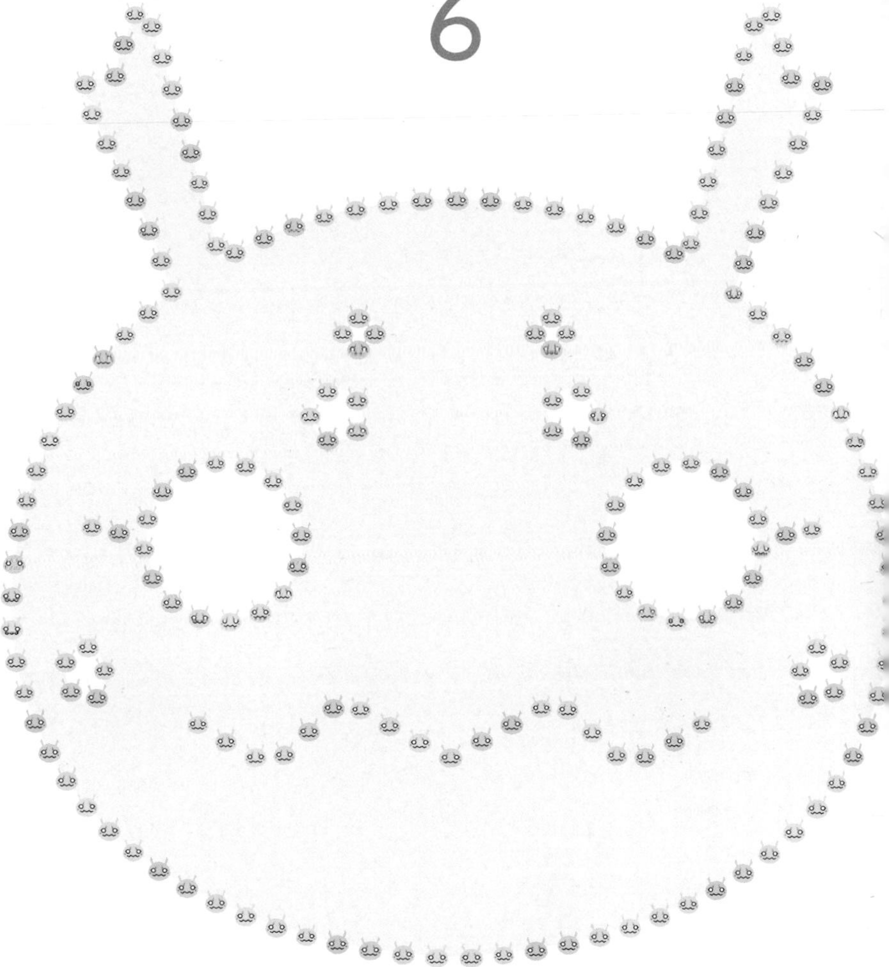

Art:
Asahiro Kakashi

Original Story:
Okina Baba

Character Design:
Tsukasa Kiryu

So I'm a Spider, So What?

CONTENTS

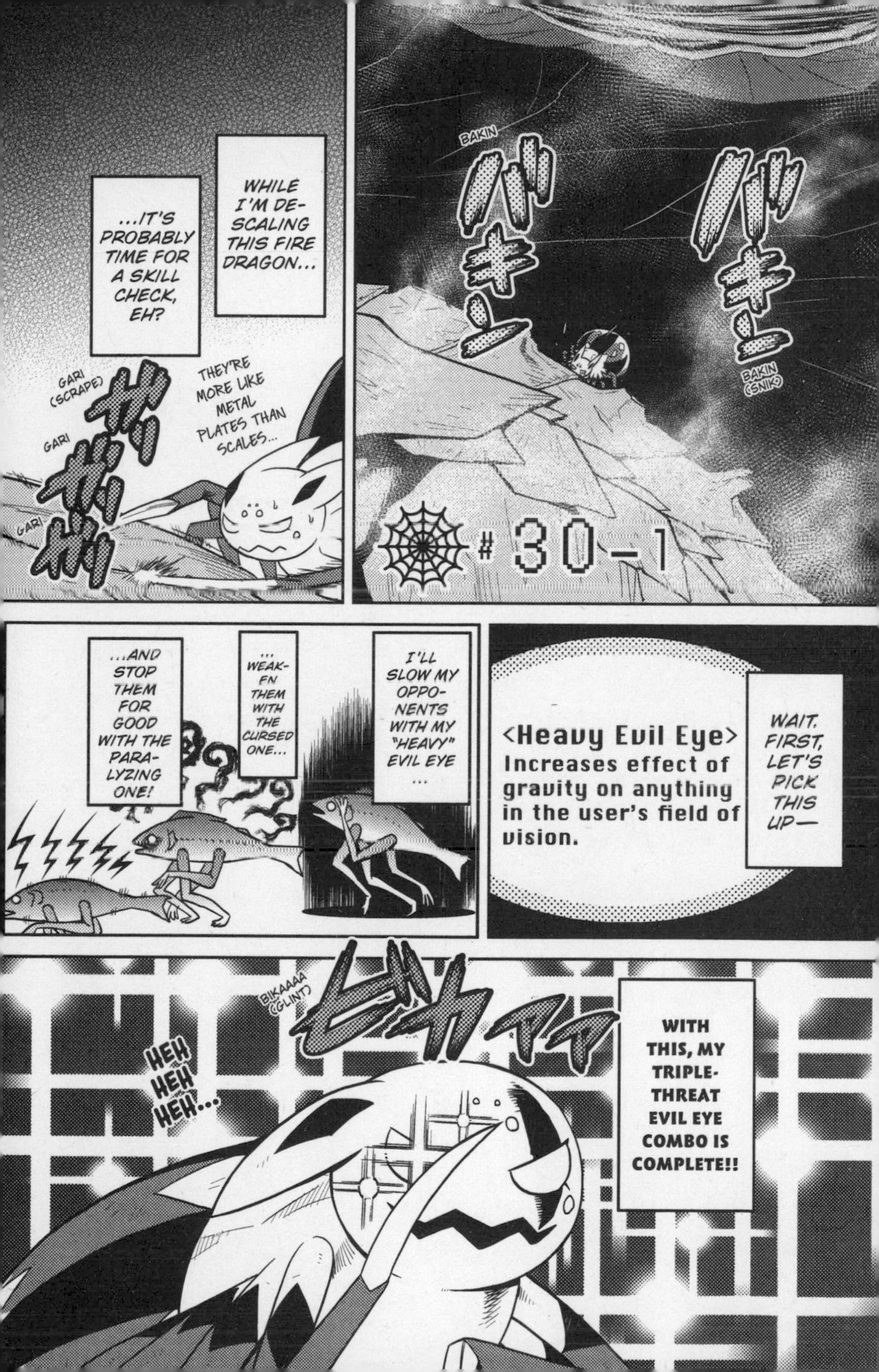
BAKIN
BAKIN (SNIK)
#30-1
WHILE I'M DE-SCALING THIS FIRE DRAGON...
...IT'S PROBABLY TIME FOR A SKILL CHECK, EH?
GARI (SCRAPE)
GARI
GARI
THEY'RE MORE LIKE METAL PLATES THAN SCALES...
WAIT. FIRST, LET'S PICK THIS UP—
<Heavy Evil Eye>
Increases effect of gravity on anything in the user's field of vision.
I'LL SLOW MY OPPONENTS WITH MY "HEAVY" EVIL EYE...
...WEAKEN THEM WITH THE CURSED ONE...
...AND STOP THEM FOR GOOD WITH THE PARALYZING ONE!
WITH THIS, MY TRIPLE-THREAT EVIL EYE COMBO IS COMPLETE!!
BIKAAAA (GLINT)
HEH HEH HEH...

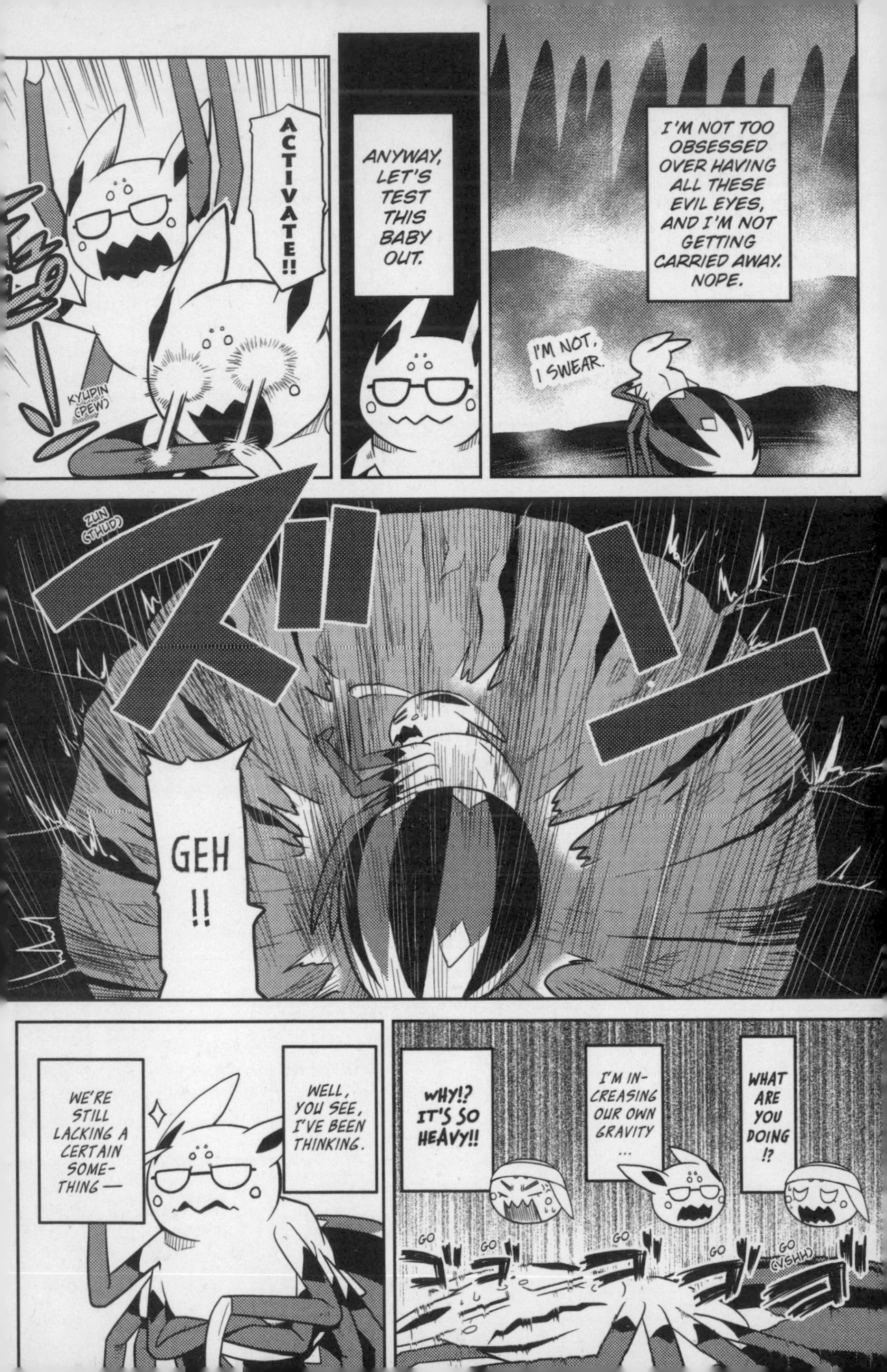
I'M NOT TOO OBSESSED OVER HAVING ALL THESE EVIL EYES, AND I'M NOT GETTING CARRIED AWAY. NOPE.
I'M NOT, I SWEAR.
ANYWAY, LET'S TEST THIS BABY OUT.
ACTIVATE!!
KYUPIN (PEW)
ZUN (THUD)
GEH !!
WHAT ARE YOU DOING !?
I'M IN-CREASING OUR OWN GRAVITY ...
WHY!? IT'S SO HEAVY!!
GO GO GO GO GO (VSHH)
WELL, YOU SEE, I'VE BEEN THINKING.
WE'RE STILL LACKING A CERTAIN SOME-THING—

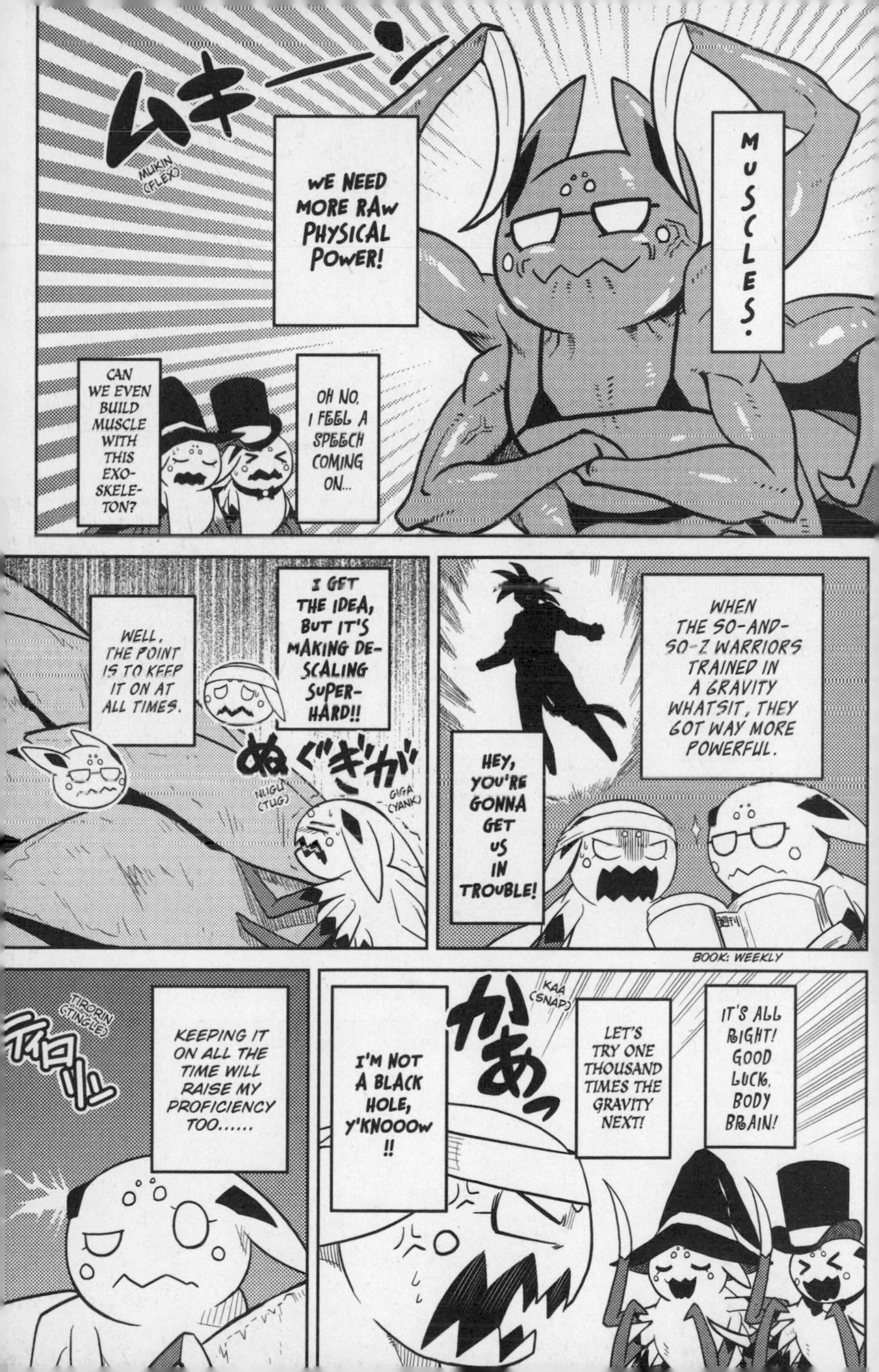
MUSCLES.
WE NEED MORE RAW PHYSICAL POWER!
ムキーン
MUKIN (FLEX)
OH NO, I FEEL A SPEECH COMING ON...
CAN WE EVEN BUILD MUSCLE WITH THIS EXO-SKELE-TON?
WHEN THE SO-AND-SO-Z WARRIORS TRAINED IN A GRAVITY WHATSIT, THEY GOT WAY MORE POWERFUL.
HEY, YOU'RE GONNA GET US IN TROUBLE!
BOOK: WEEKLY
I GET THE IDEA, BUT IT'S MAKING DE-SCALING SUPER-HARD!!
WELL, THE POINT IS TO KEEP IT ON AT ALL TIMES.
ぬぐぎが
NUGU (TUG)
GIGA (YANK)
IT'S ALL RIGHT! GOOD LUCK, BODY BRAIN!
LET'S TRY ONE THOUSAND TIMES THE GRAVITY NEXT!
かあっ
KAA (SNAP)
I'M NOT A BLACK HOLE, Y'KNOOOW!!
KEEPING IT ON ALL THE TIME WILL RAISE MY PROFICIENCY TOO......
ティロリン
TIRORIN (TINGLE)

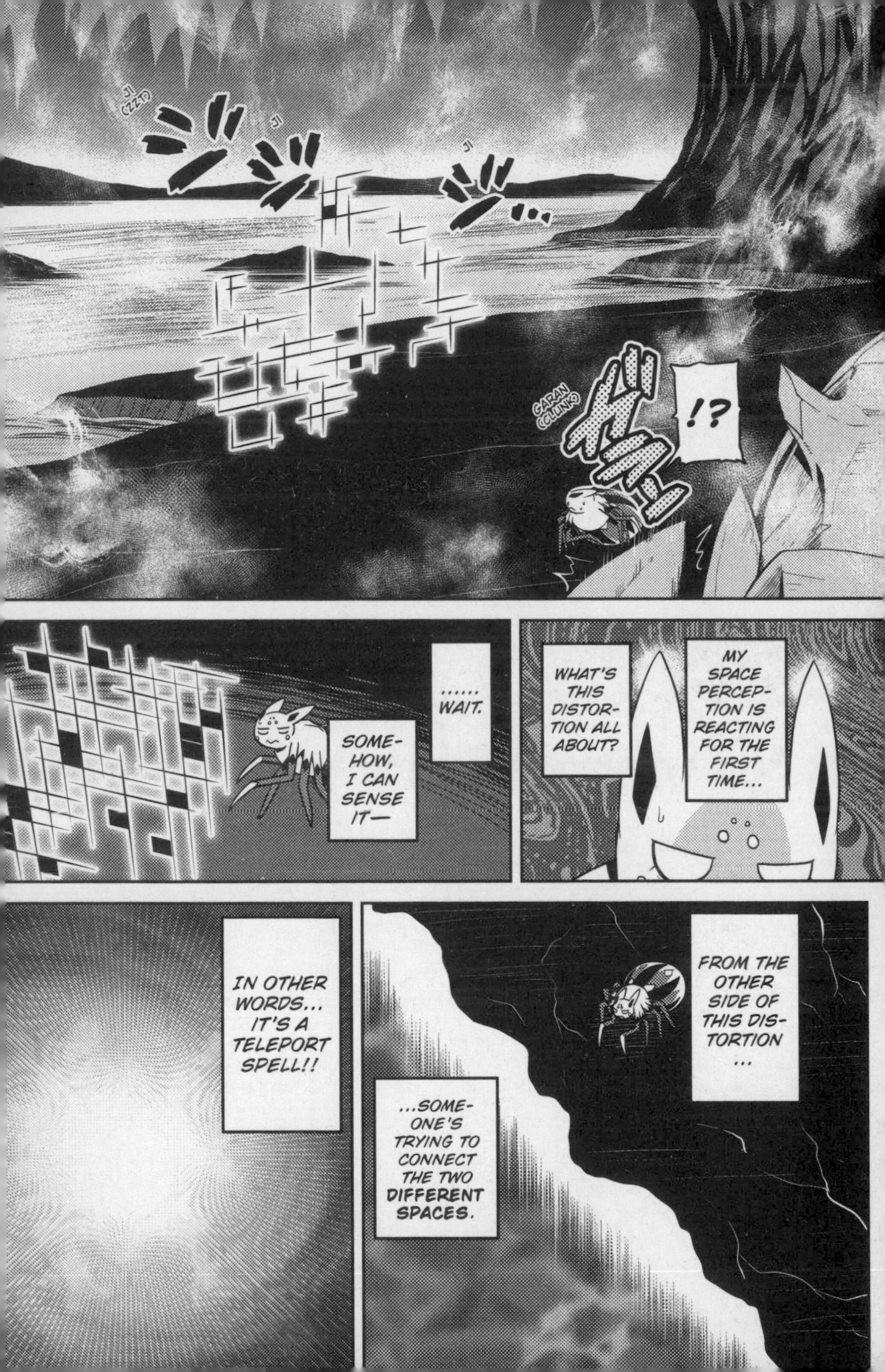
JI (ZZT)
JI
JI
GARAN (CLUNK)
!?
MY SPACE PERCEPTION IS REACTING FOR THE FIRST TIME...
WHAT'S THIS DISTORTION ALL ABOUT?
......WAIT.
SOMEHOW, I CAN SENSE IT—
FROM THE OTHER SIDE OF THIS DISTORTION...
...SOMEONE'S TRYING TO CONNECT THE TWO DIFFERENT SPACES.
IN OTHER WORDS... IT'S A TELEPORT SPELL!!

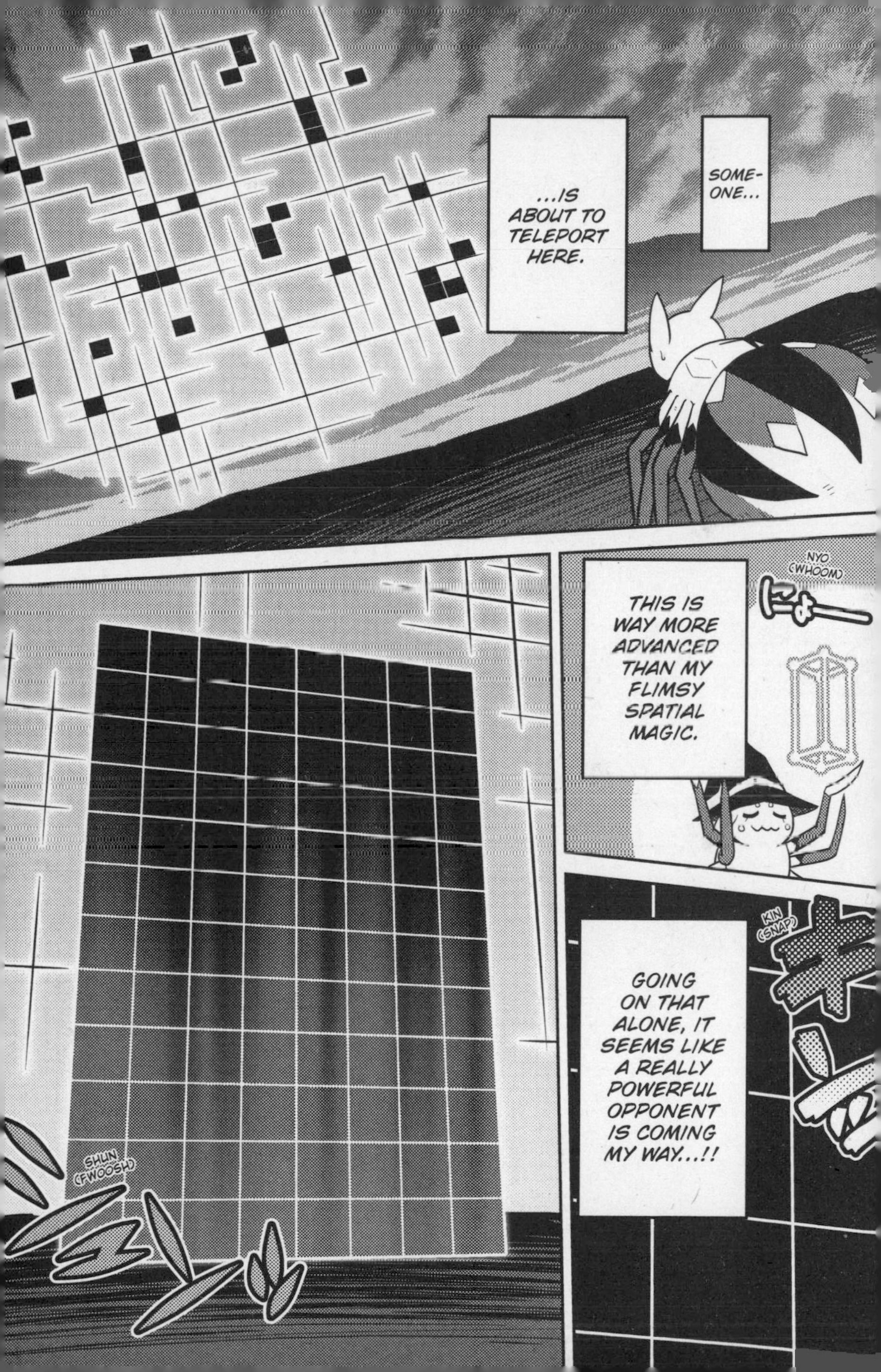
SOME-ONE...
...IS ABOUT TO TELEPORT HERE.
NYO (WHOOM)
THIS IS WAY MORE ADVANCED THAN MY FLIMSY SPATIAL MAGIC.
KIN (SNAP)
GOING ON THAT ALONE, IT SEEMS LIKE A REALLY POWERFUL OPPONENT IS COMING MY WAY...!!
SHUN (FWOOSH)

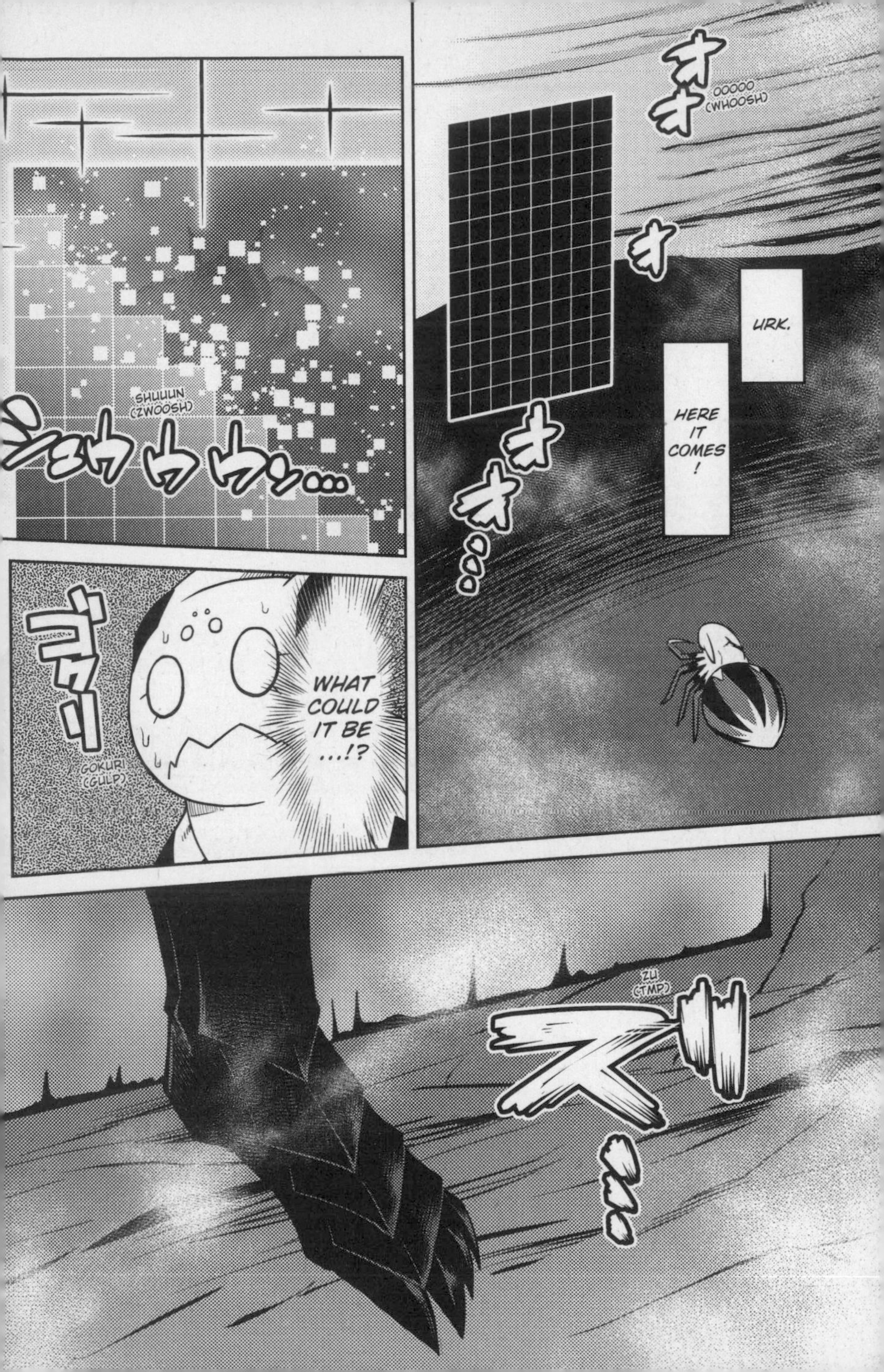
OOOOO (WHOOSH)
URK.
HERE IT COMES!
SHUUUN (ZWOOSH)
WHAT COULD IT BE ...!?
GOKURI (GULP)
ZU (TMP)

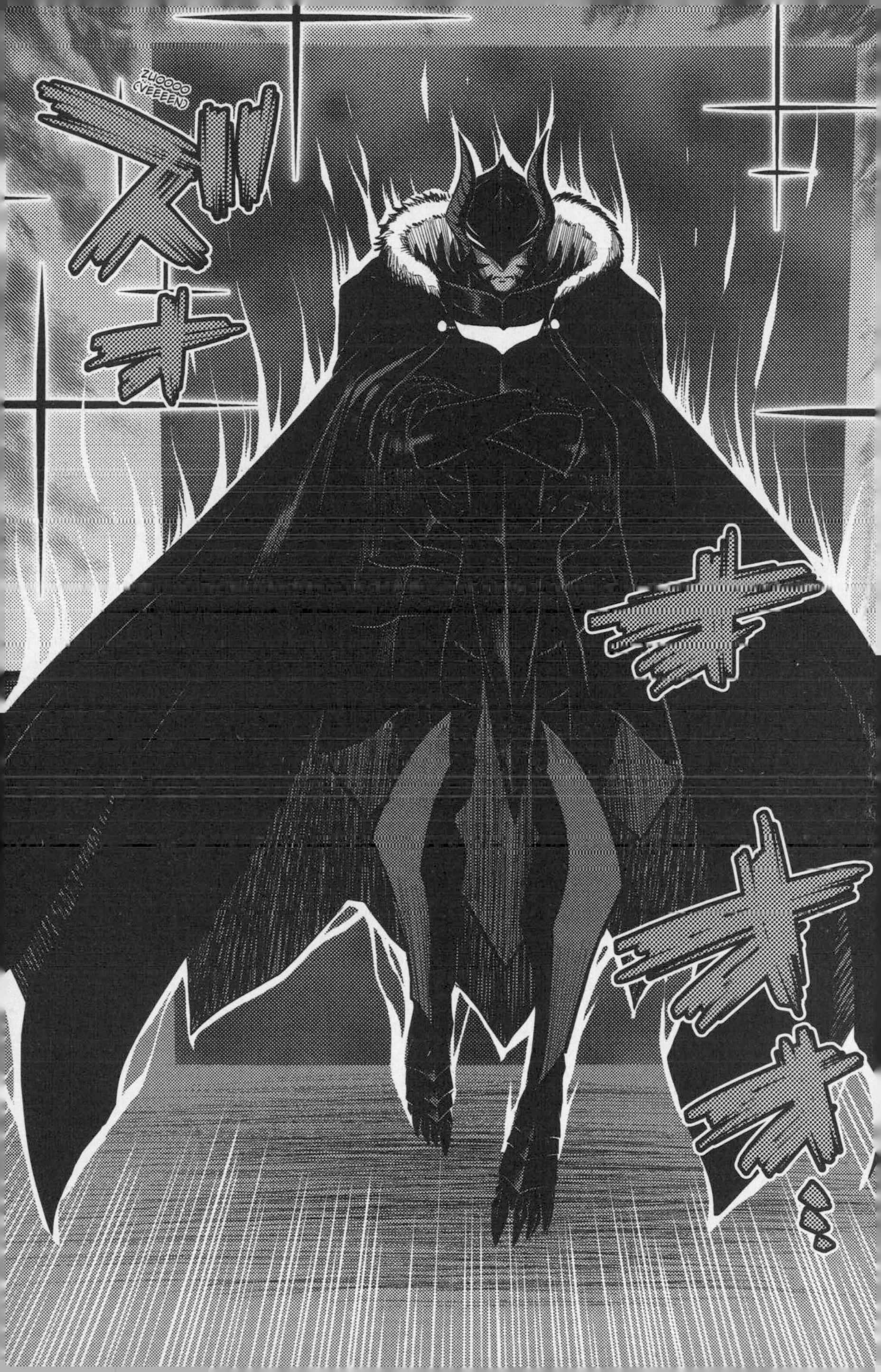
ズォオオ
ZUOOOO
(VEEEEN)

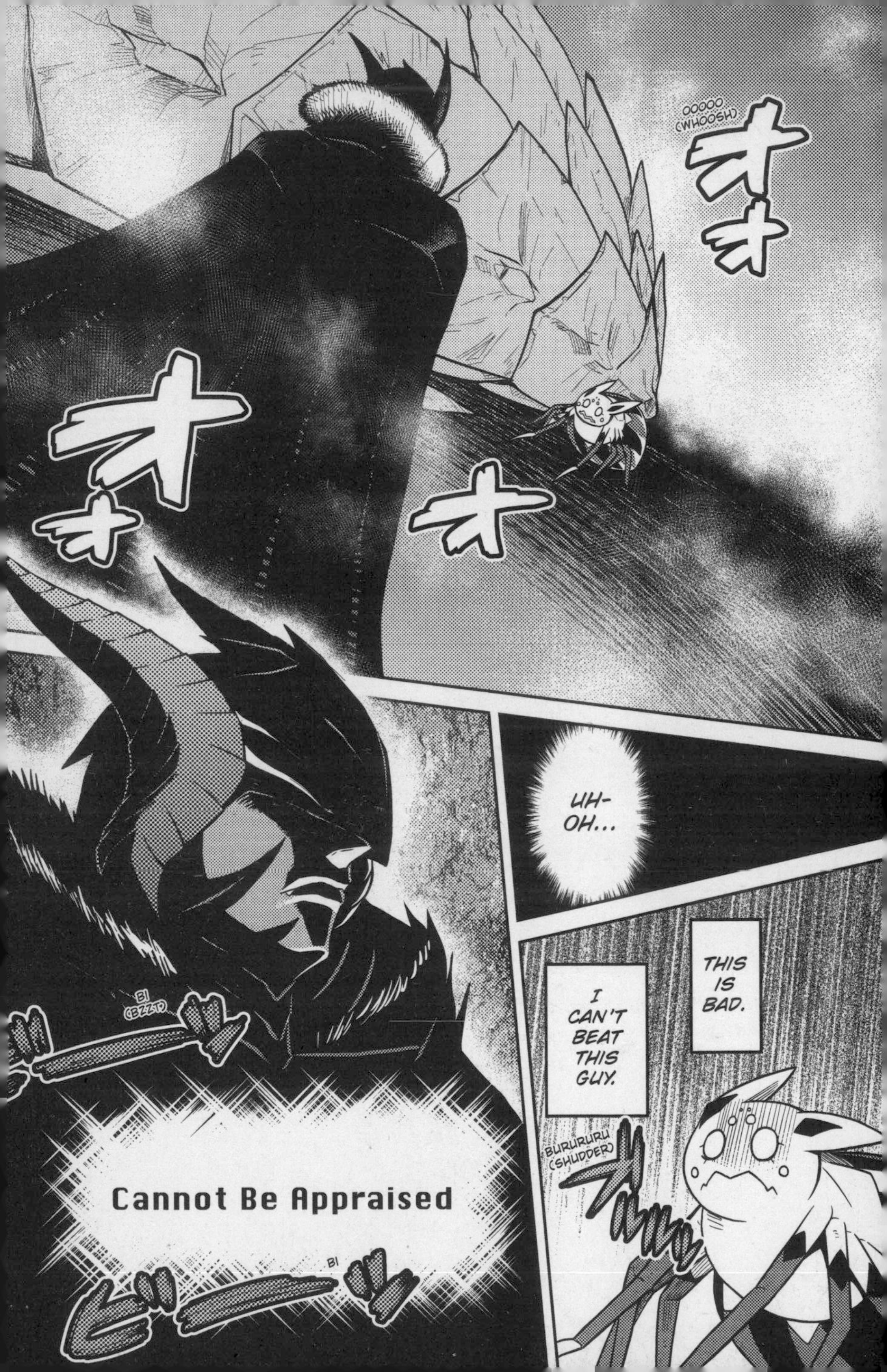
OOOOO
(WHOOSH)
UH-
OH...
THIS
IS
BAD.
I
CAN'T
BEAT
THIS
GUY.
BURURURU
(SHUDDER)
BI
(BZZT)
Cannot Be Appraised
BI

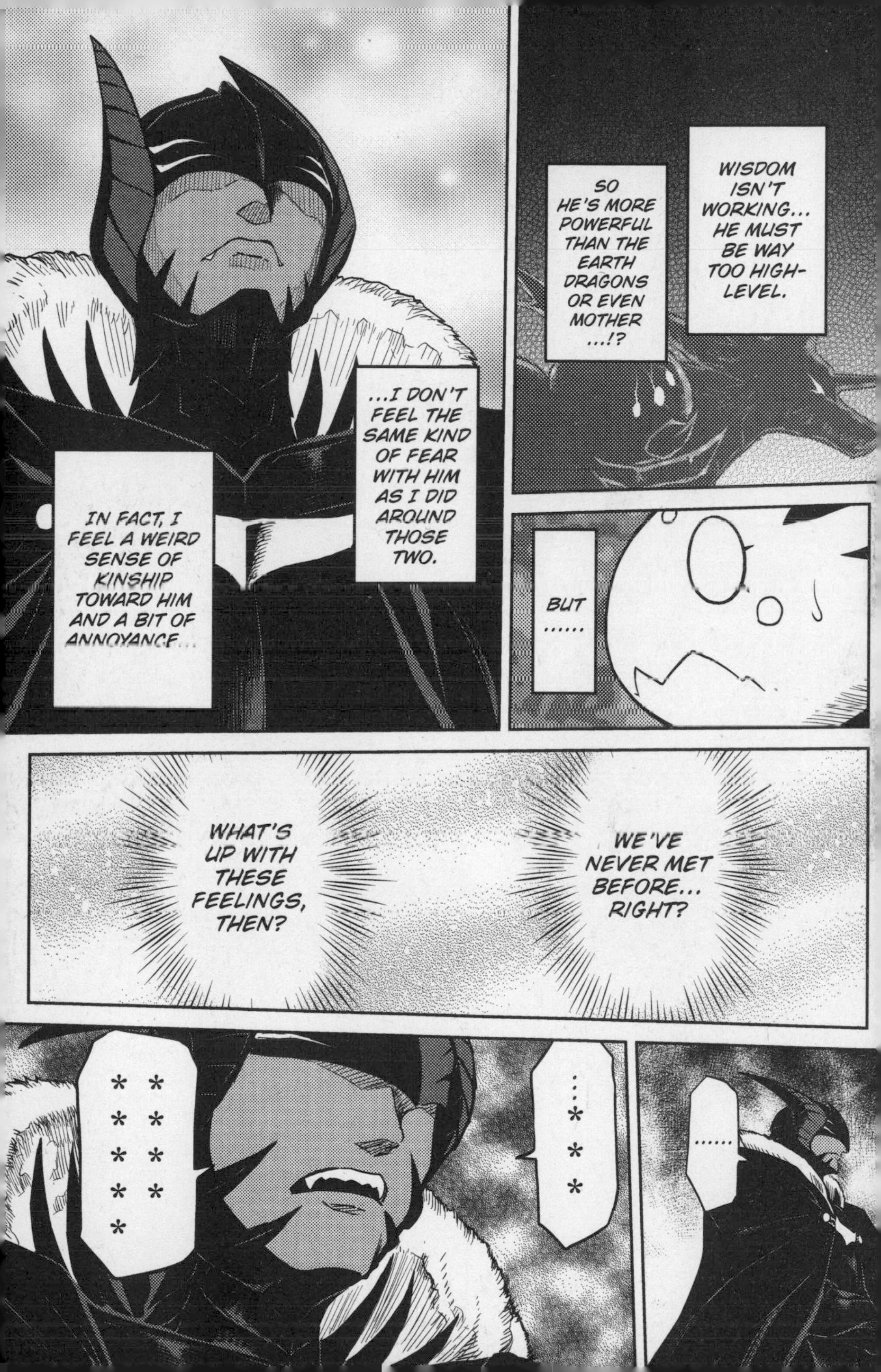
WISDOM ISN'T WORKING... HE MUST BE WAY TOO HIGH-LEVEL.
SO HE'S MORE POWERFUL THAN THE EARTH DRAGONS OR EVEN MOTHER ...!?
BUT ......
...I DON'T FEEL THE SAME KIND OF FEAR WITH HIM AS I DID AROUND THOSE TWO.
IN FACT, I FEEL A WEIRD SENSE OF KINSHIP TOWARD HIM AND A BIT OF ANNOYANCE...
WE'VE NEVER MET BEFORE... RIGHT?
WHAT'S UP WITH THESE FEELINGS, THEN?
......
...* * *
* * * * * * * * *

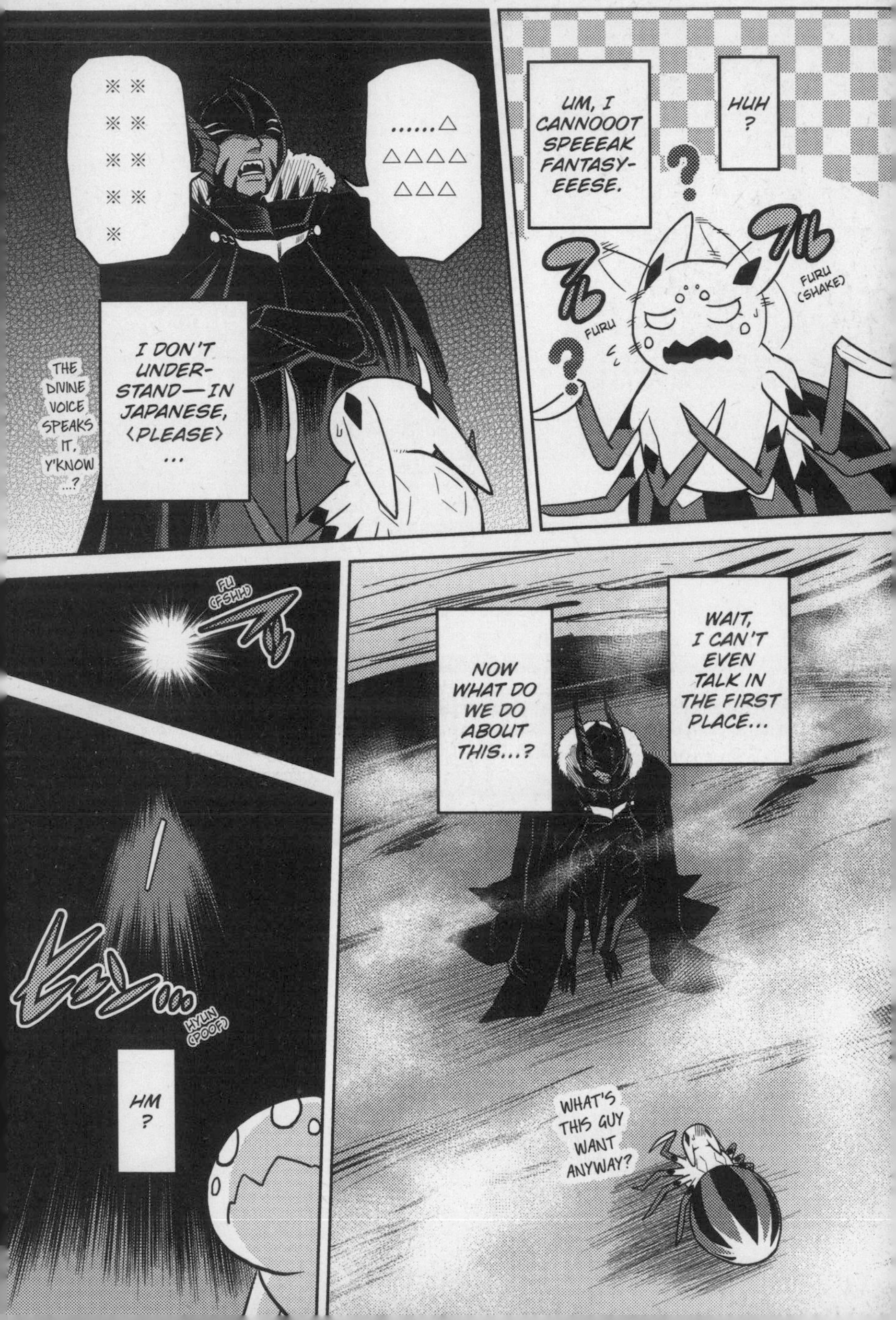
HUH ?
UM, I CANNOOOT SPEEEAK FANTASY-EEESE.
FURU (SHAKE)
FURU
※※※※※※※※※
......△ △△△△ △△△
I DON'T UNDER-STAND—IN JAPANESE, 〈PLEASE〉 ...
THE DIVINE VOICE SPEAKS IT, Y'KNOW ...?
WAIT, I CAN'T EVEN TALK IN THE FIRST PLACE...
NOW WHAT DO WE DO ABOUT THIS...?
WHAT'S THIS GUY WANT ANYWAY?
FU (FSHH)
HYUN (POOF)
HM ?

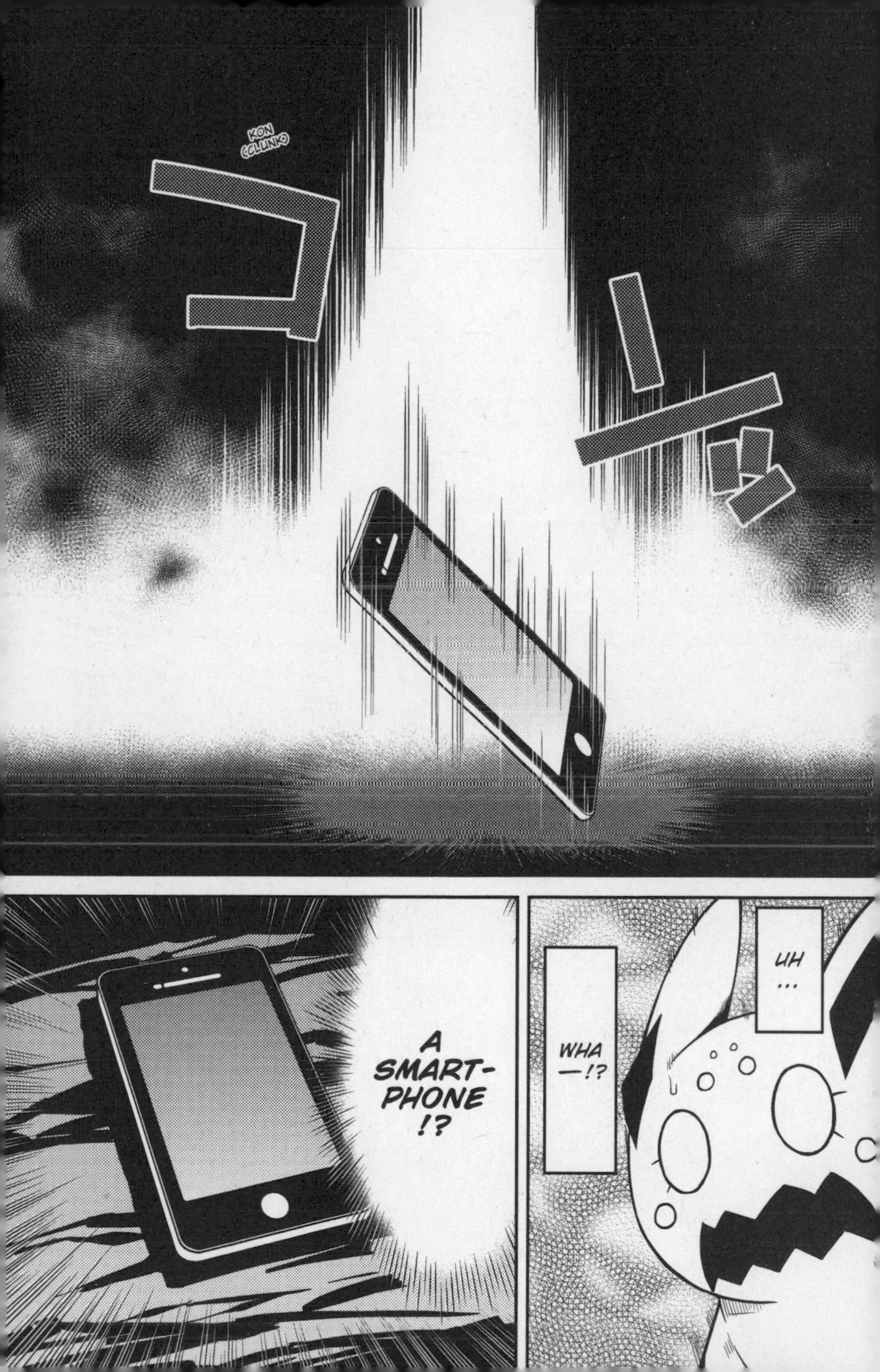
KON
(CLUNK)
コーン
UH
...
WHA
—!?
A
SMART-
PHONE
!?

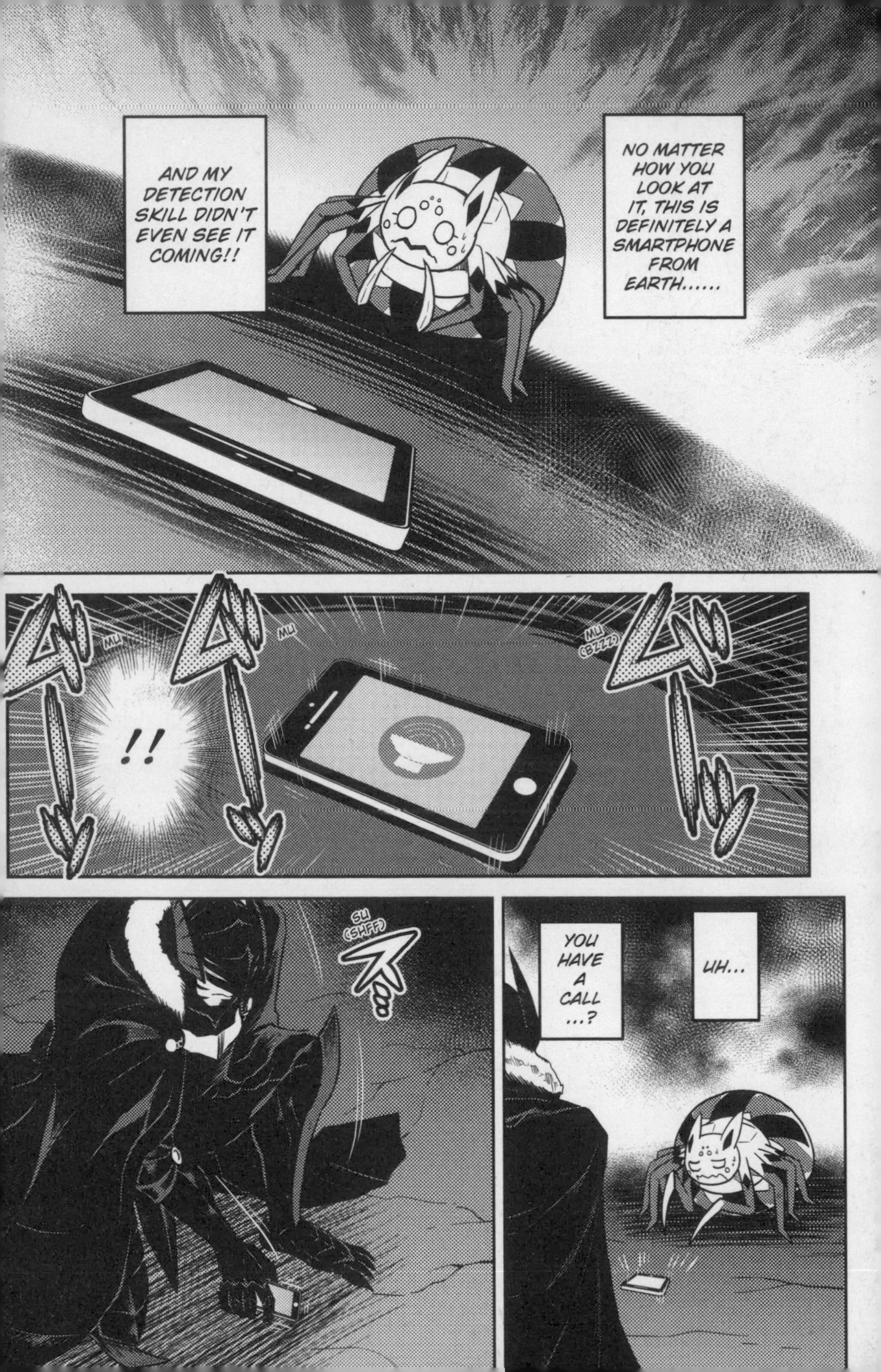

NO MATTER HOW YOU LOOK AT IT, THIS IS DEFINITELY A SMARTPHONE FROM EARTH......
AND MY DETECTION SKILL DIDN'T EVEN SEE IT COMING!!
MU (BZZZ)
MU
MU
!!
UH...
YOU HAVE A CALL ...?
SU (SHFF)

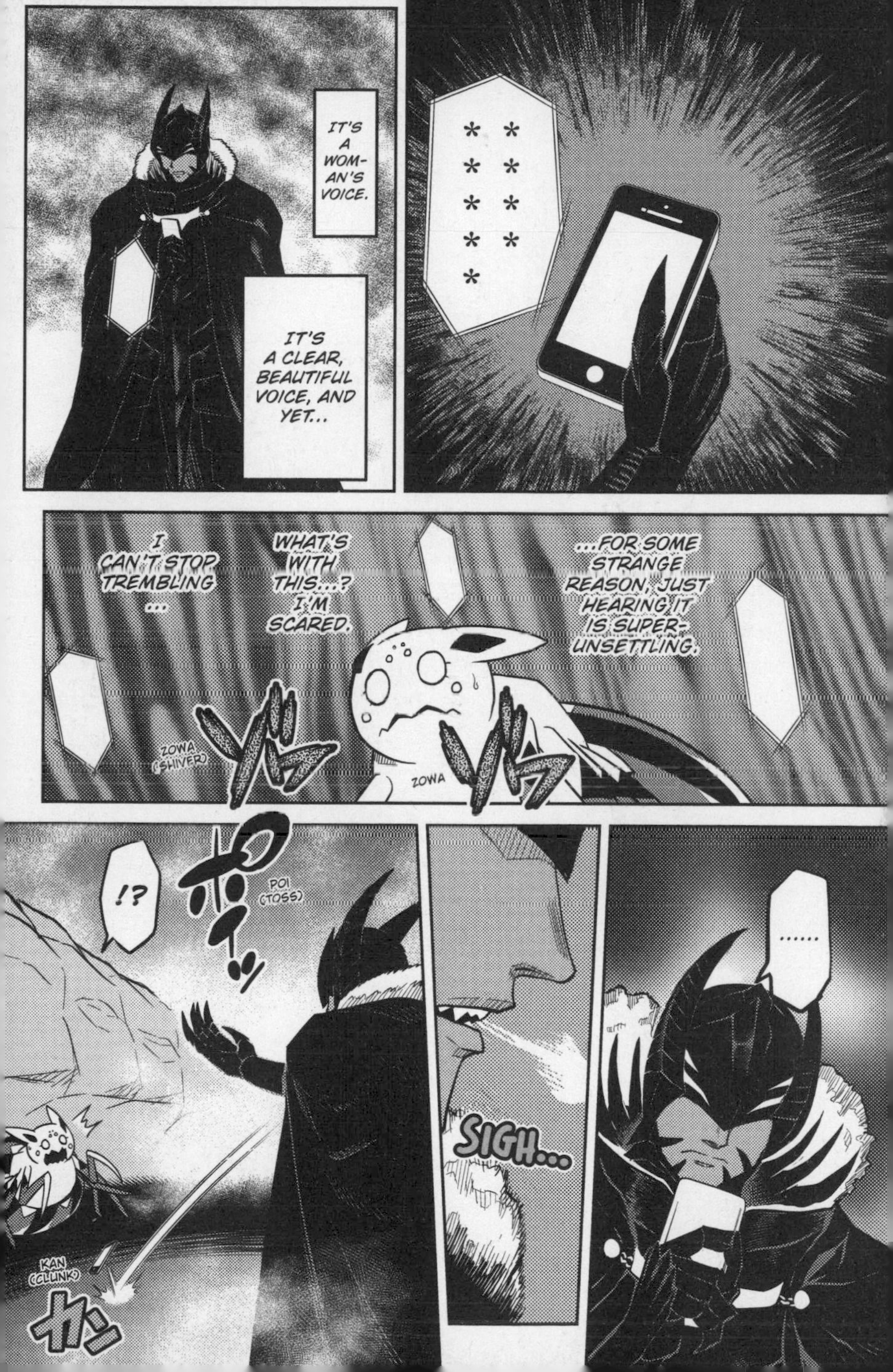
* * * * * * * * *
IT'S A WOMAN'S VOICE.
IT'S A CLEAR, BEAUTIFUL VOICE, AND YET...
...FOR SOME STRANGE REASON, JUST HEARING IT IS SUPER-UNSETTLING.
WHAT'S WITH THIS...? I'M SCARED.
I CAN'T STOP TREMBLING...
ZOWA
ZOWA (SHIVER)
......
SIGH...
!?
POI (TOSS)
KAN (CLUNK)

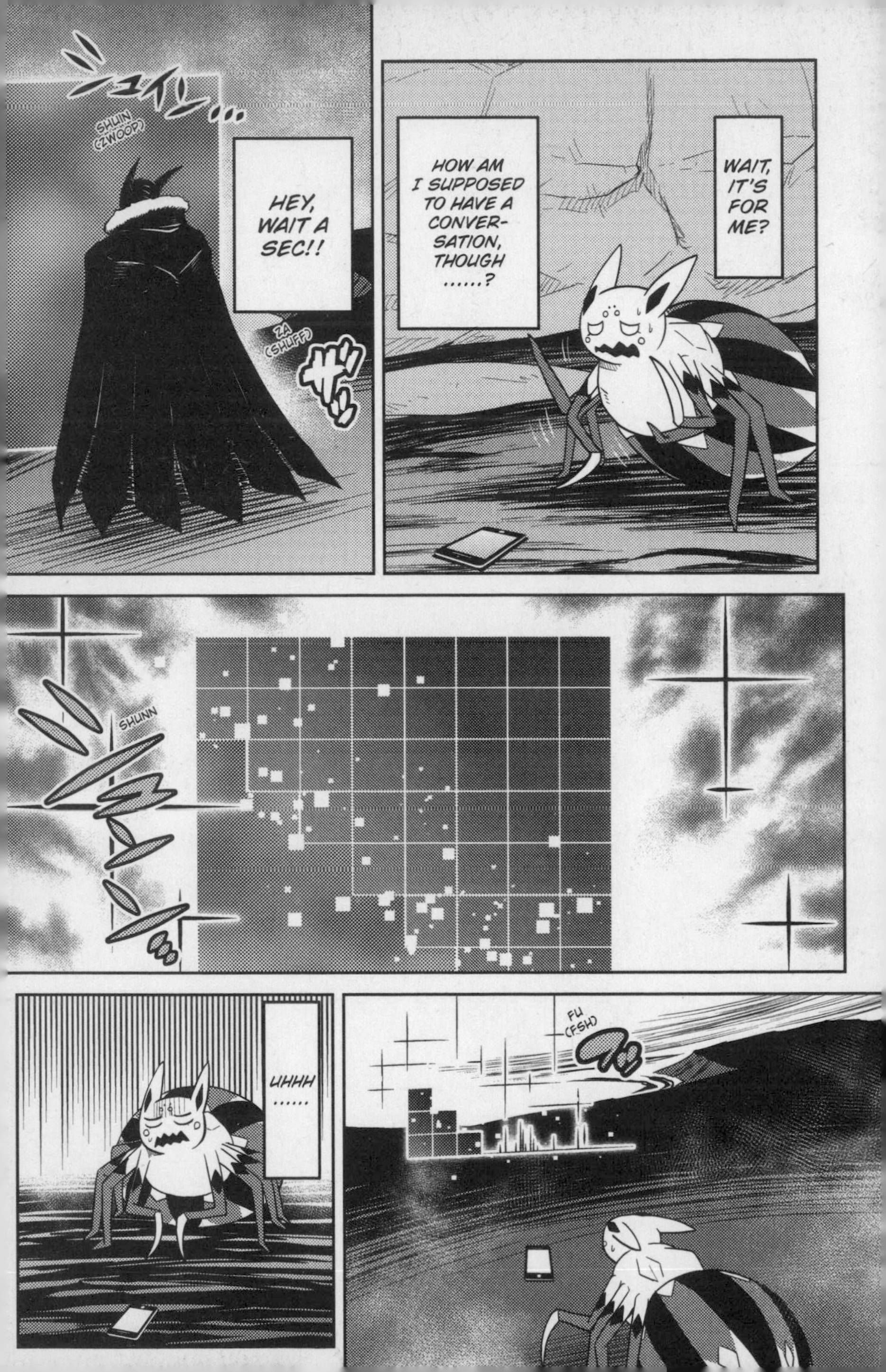
WAIT, IT'S FOR ME?
HOW AM I SUPPOSED TO HAVE A CONVER-SATION, THOUGH ......?
SHUIN (ZWOOP)
HEY, WAIT A SEC!!
ZA (SHUFF)
SHUNN
FU (FSH)
UHHH ......

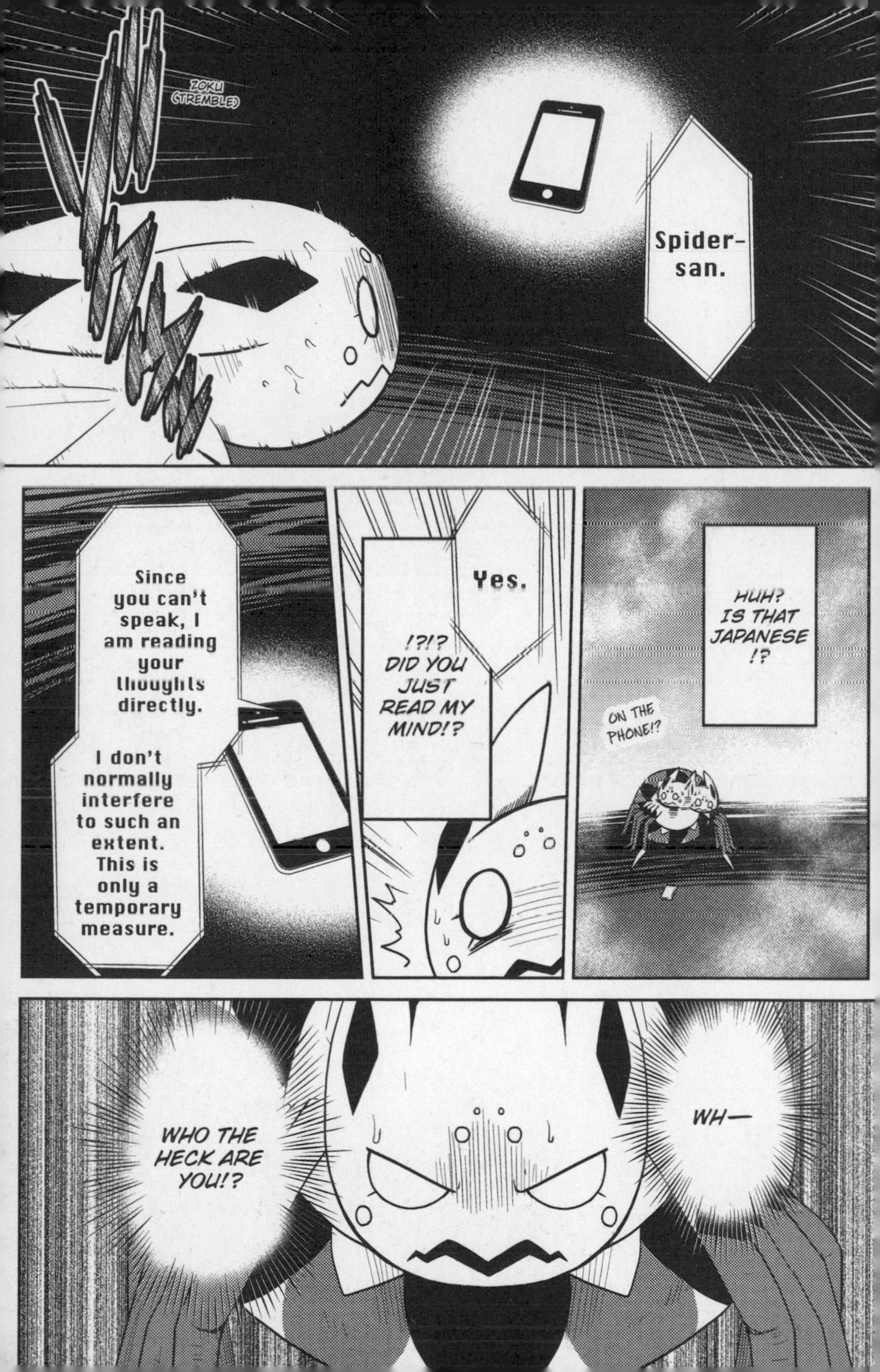
Spider-san.
ZOKU (TREMBLE)
HUH? IS THAT JAPANESE!?
ON THE PHONE!?
Yes.
!?!? DID YOU JUST READ MY MIND!?
Since you can't speak, I am reading your thoughts directly.
I don't normally interfere to such an extent. This is only a temporary measure.
WH—
WHO THE HECK ARE YOU!?

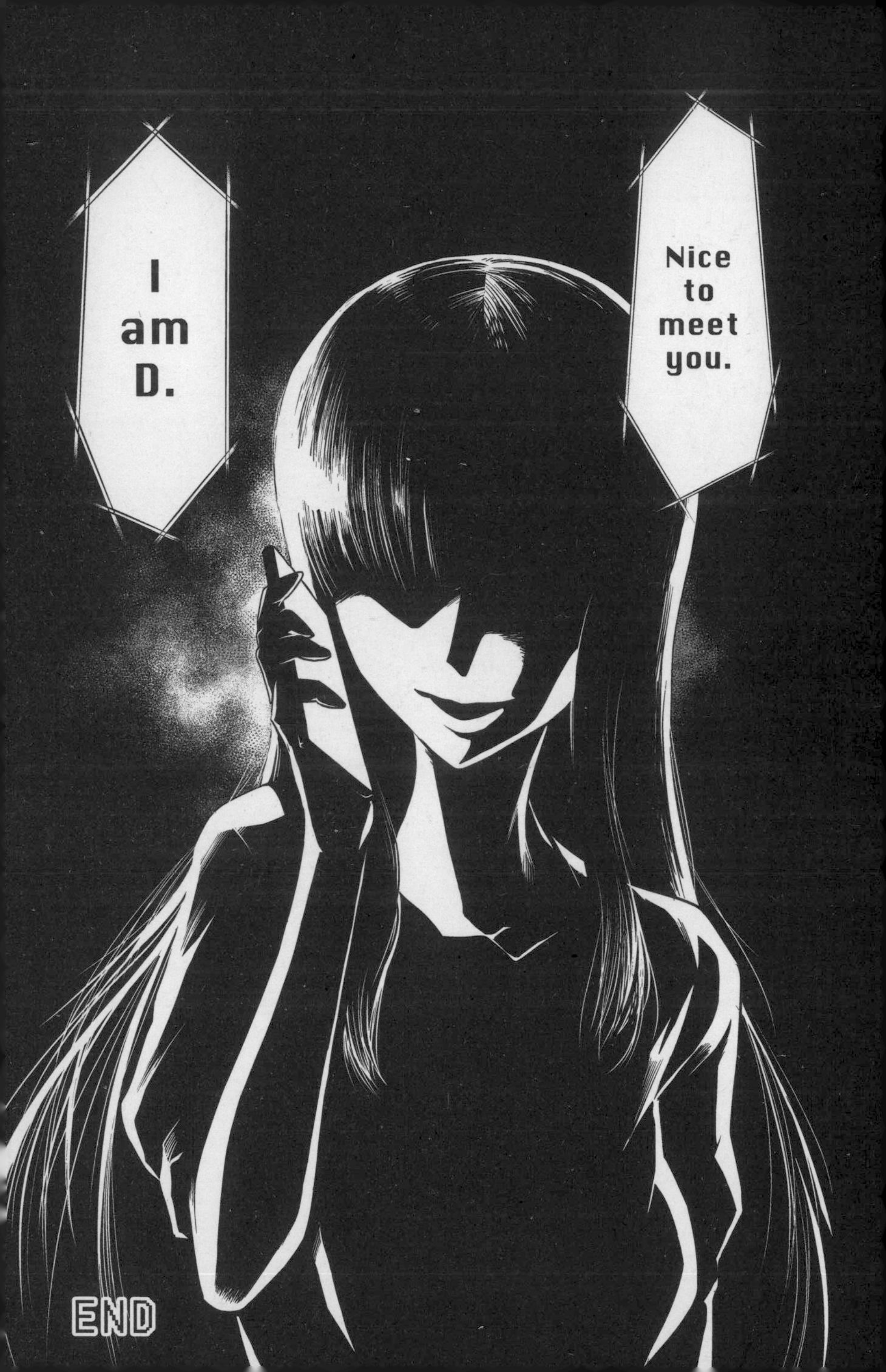
Nice to meet you.
I am D.
END

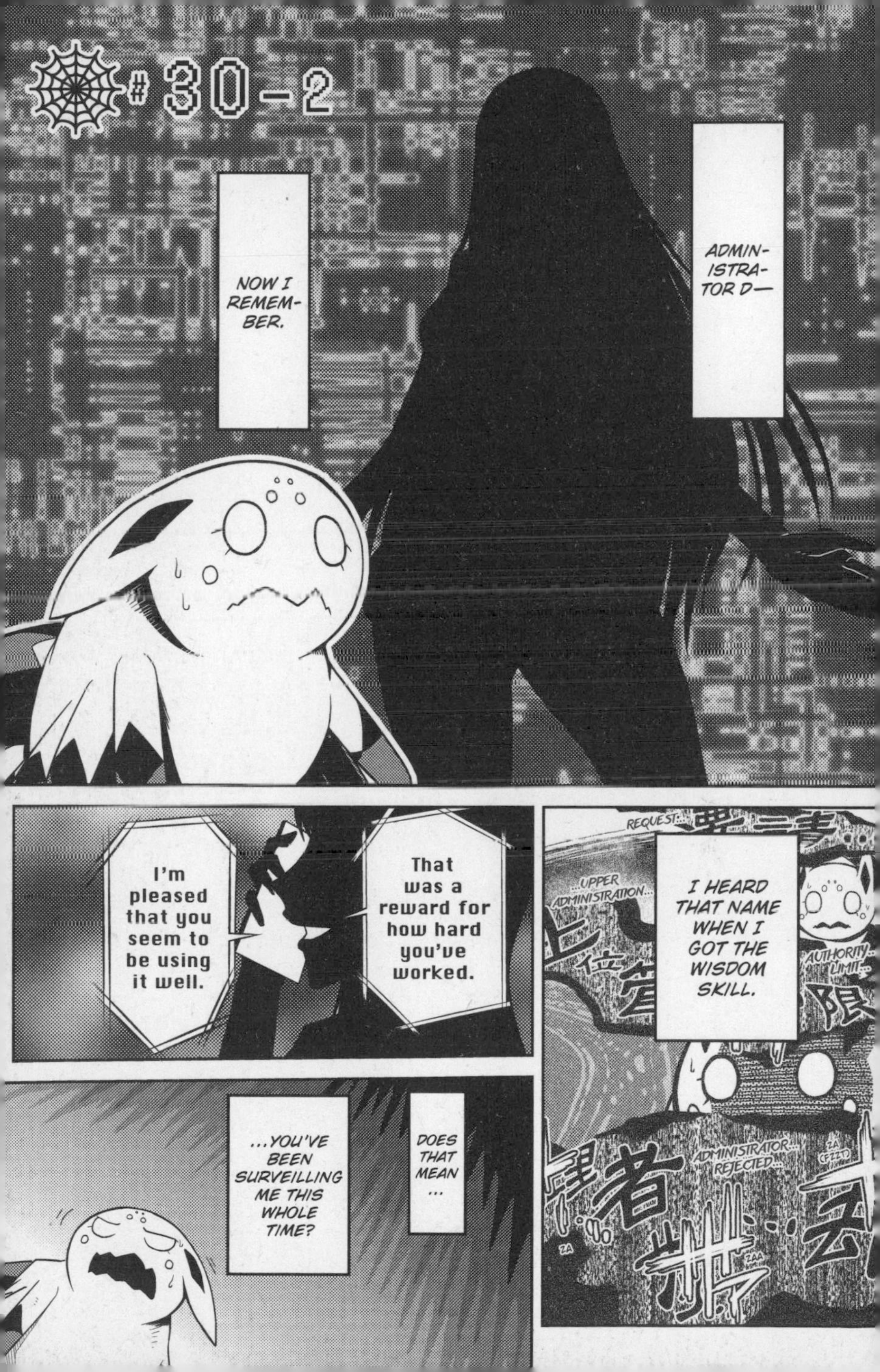

#30-2
ADMIN-ISTRA-TOR D—
NOW I REMEMBER.
REQUEST...
I HEARD THAT NAME WHEN I GOT THE WISDOM SKILL.
...UPPER ADMINISTRATION...
AUTHORITY... LIMIT...
ZA (FZZT)
ADMINISTRATOR... REJECTED...
ZAA
ZA
That was a reward for how hard you've worked.
I'm pleased that you seem to be using it well.
DOES THAT MEAN...
...YOU'VE BEEN SURVEILLING ME THIS WHOLE TIME?

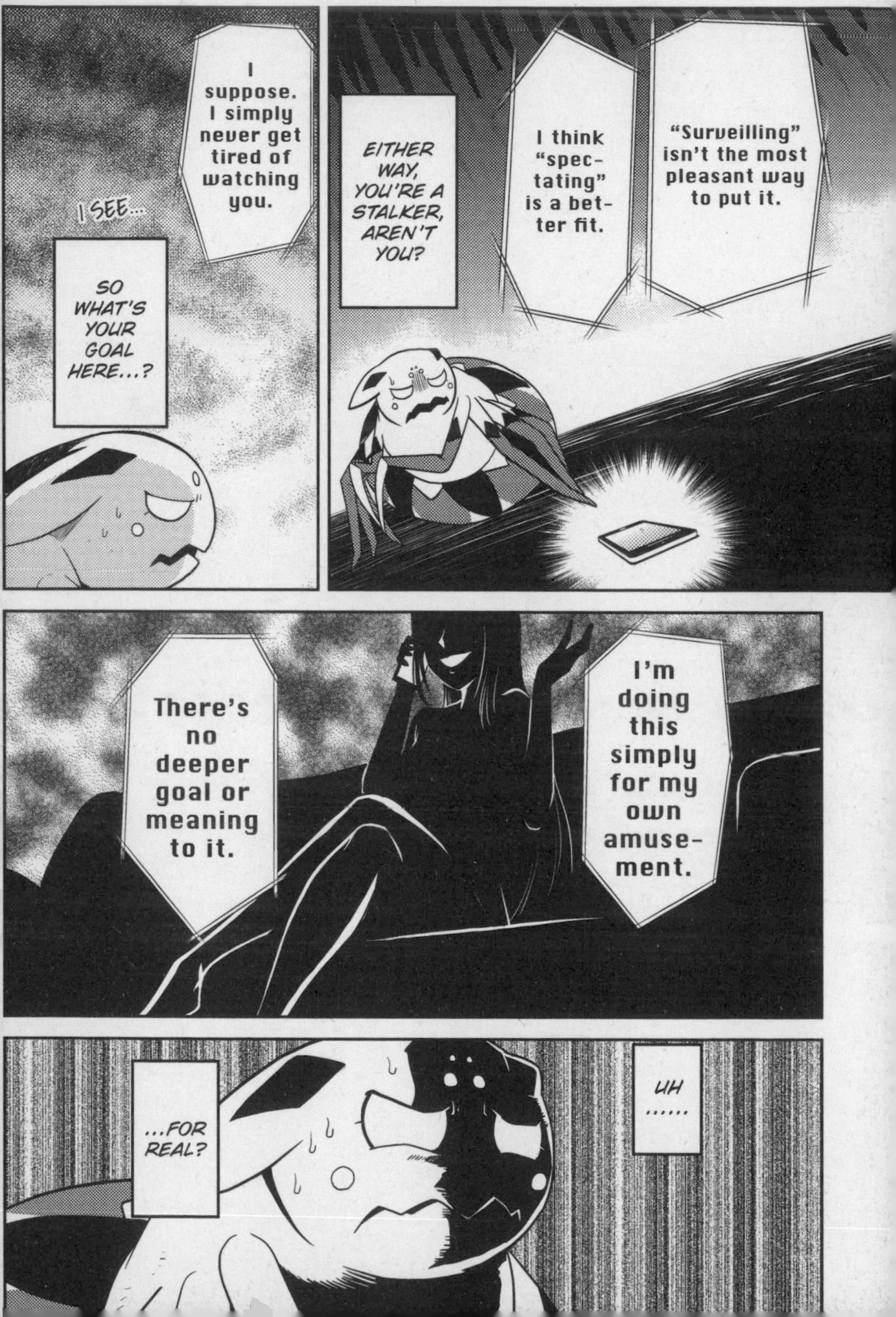

"Surveilling" isn't the most pleasant way to put it.
I think "spec-tating" is a bet-ter fit.
EITHER WAY, YOU'RE A STALKER, AREN'T YOU?
I suppose. I simply never get tired of watching you.
I SEE...
SO WHAT'S YOUR GOAL HERE...?
I'm doing this simply for my own amuse-ment.
There's no deeper goal or meaning to it.
UH ......
...FOR REAL?

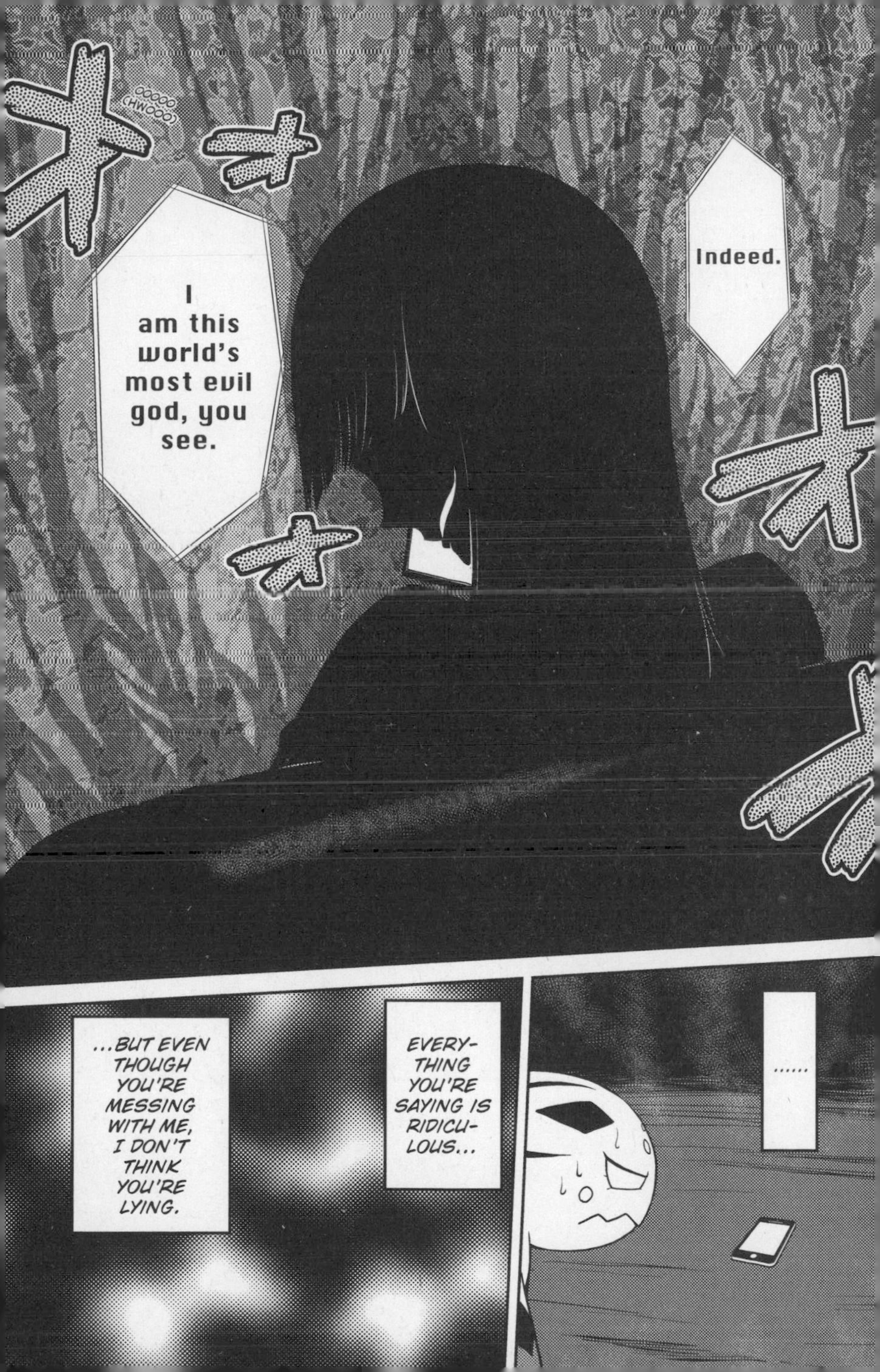
Indeed.
OOOOO (HWOOO)
I am this world's most evil god, you see.
......
EVERY-THING YOU'RE SAYING IS RIDICU-LOUS...
...BUT EVEN THOUGH YOU'RE MESSING WITH ME, I DON'T THINK YOU'RE LYING.

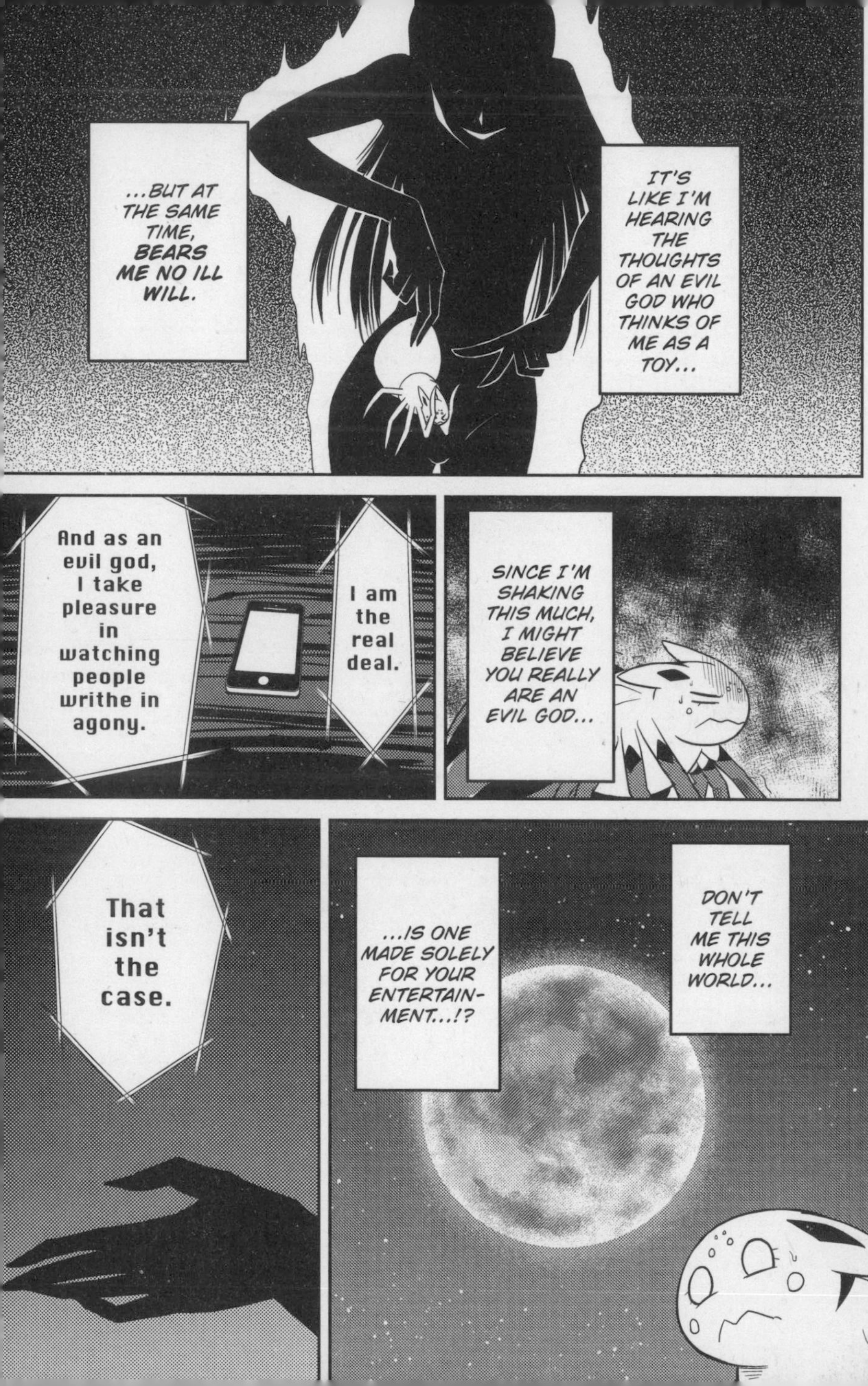
IT'S LIKE I'M HEARING THE THOUGHTS OF AN EVIL GOD WHO THINKS OF ME AS A TOY...
...BUT AT THE SAME TIME, BEARS ME NO ILL WILL.
SINCE I'M SHAKING THIS MUCH, I MIGHT BELIEVE YOU REALLY ARE AN EVIL GOD...
I am the real deal.
And as an evil god, I take pleasure in watching people writhe in agony.
DON'T TELL ME THIS WHOLE WORLD...
...IS ONE MADE SOLELY FOR YOUR ENTERTAIN-MENT...!?
That isn't the case.

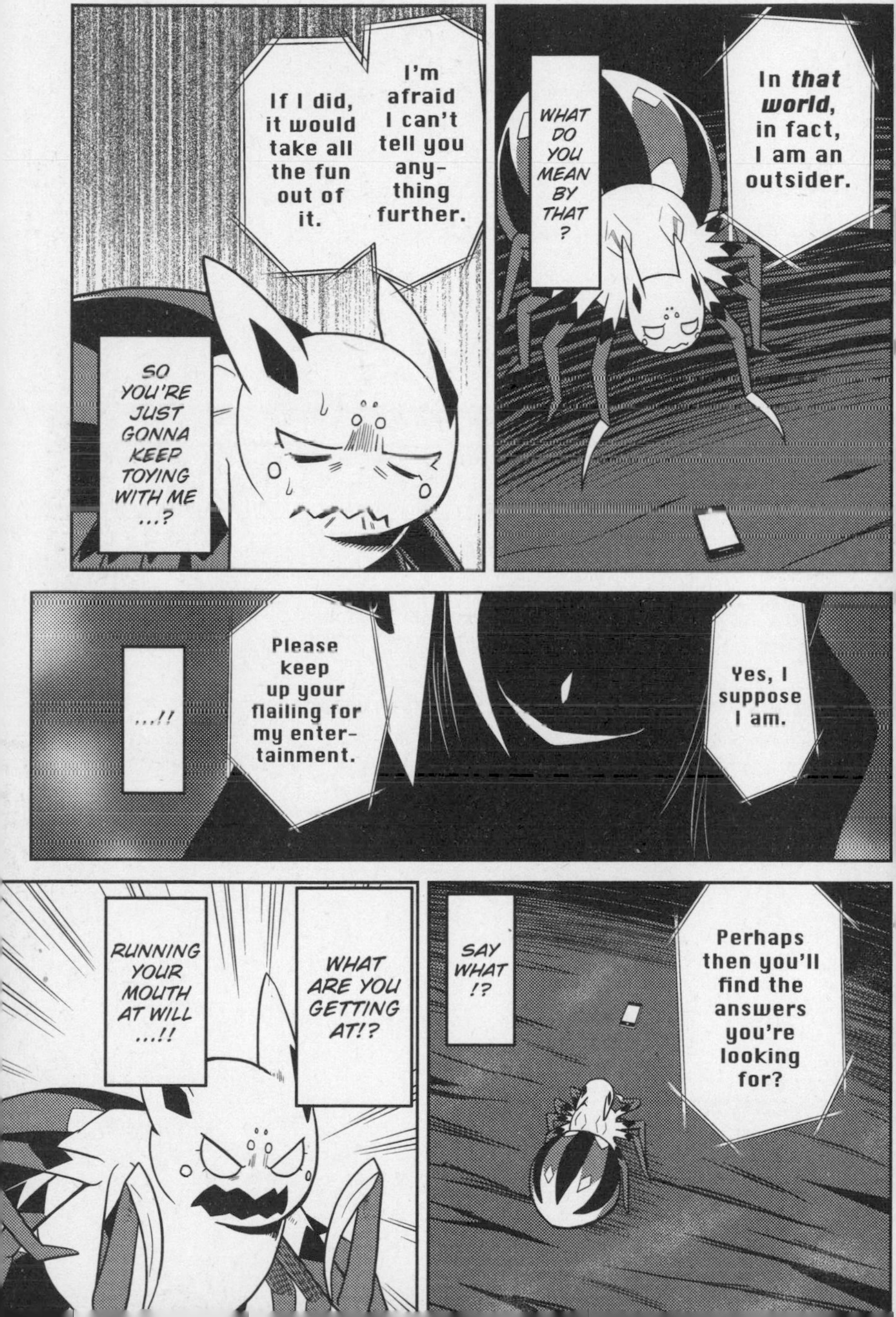
In *that world*, in fact, I am an outsider.
WHAT DO YOU MEAN BY THAT?
I'm afraid I can't tell you any-thing further.
If I did, it would take all the fun out of it.
SO YOU'RE JUST GONNA KEEP TOYING WITH ME ...?
Yes, I suppose I am.
Please keep up your flailing for my enter-tainment.
...!!
Perhaps then you'll find the answers you're looking for?
SAY WHAT !?
WHAT ARE YOU GETTING AT!?
RUNNING YOUR MOUTH AT WILL ...!!

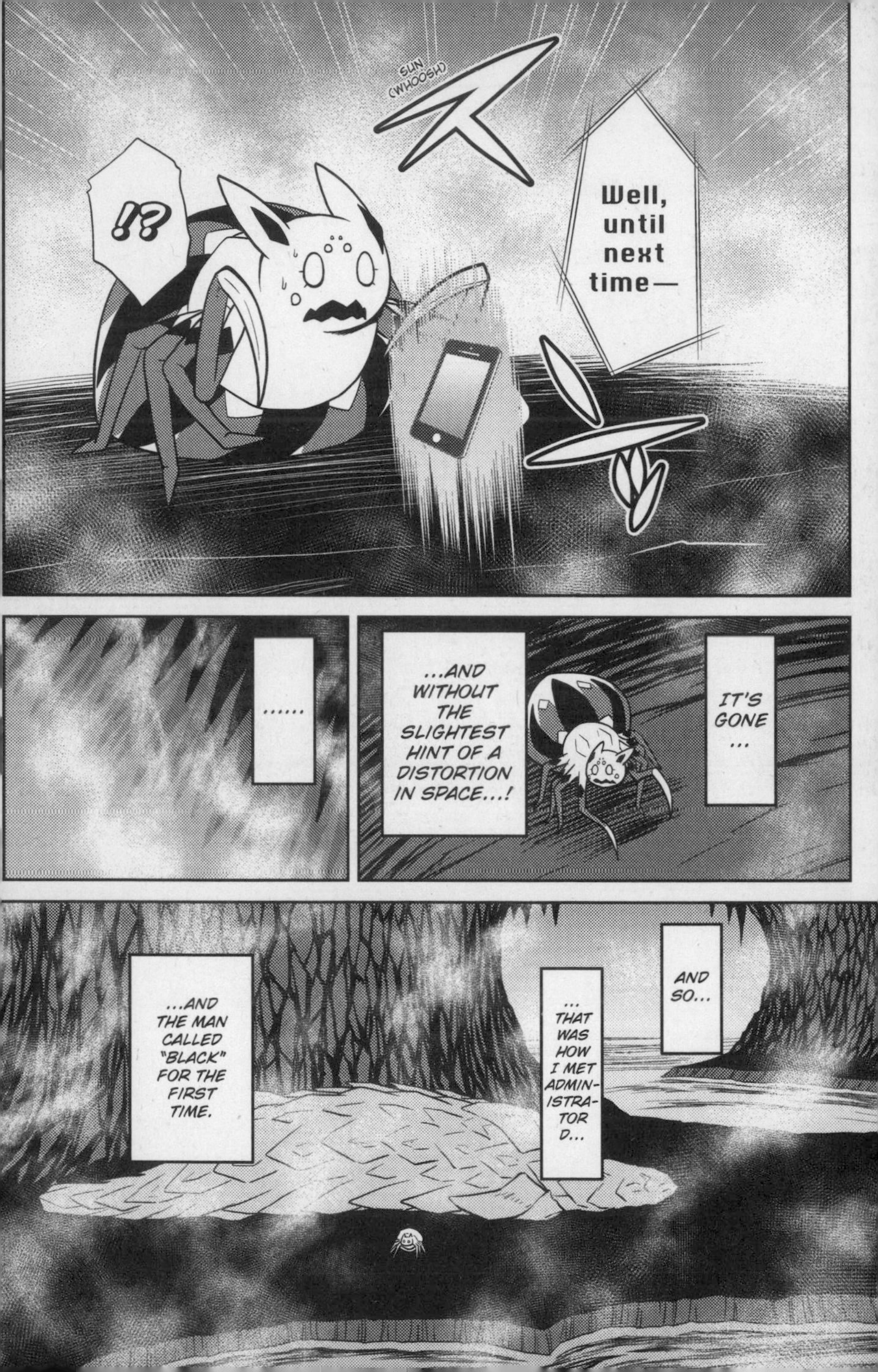
Well, until next time—
SUN (WHOOSH)
!?
IT'S GONE...
...AND WITHOUT THE SLIGHTEST HINT OF A DISTORTION IN SPACE...!
......
AND SO...
...THAT WAS HOW I MET ADMINISTRATOR D...
...AND THE MAN CALLED "BLACK" FOR THE FIRST TIME.

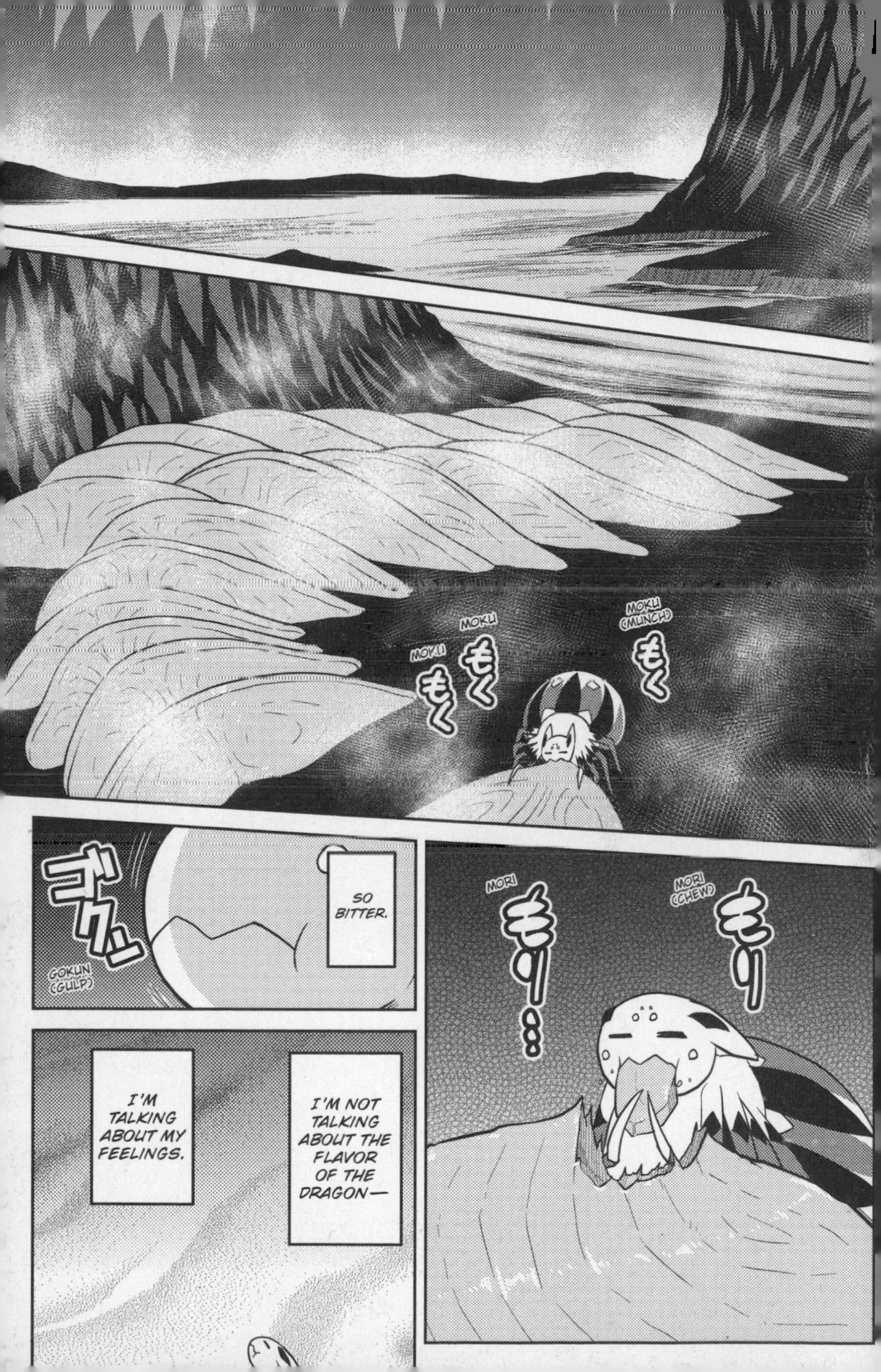
もく
MOKU (MUNCH)
もく
MOKU
もく
MOKU
もり
MORI (CHEW)
もり…
MORI
ゴクン
GOKUN (GULP)
SO BITTER.
I'M NOT TALKING ABOUT THE FLAVOR OF THE DRAGON—
I'M TALKING ABOUT MY FEELINGS.

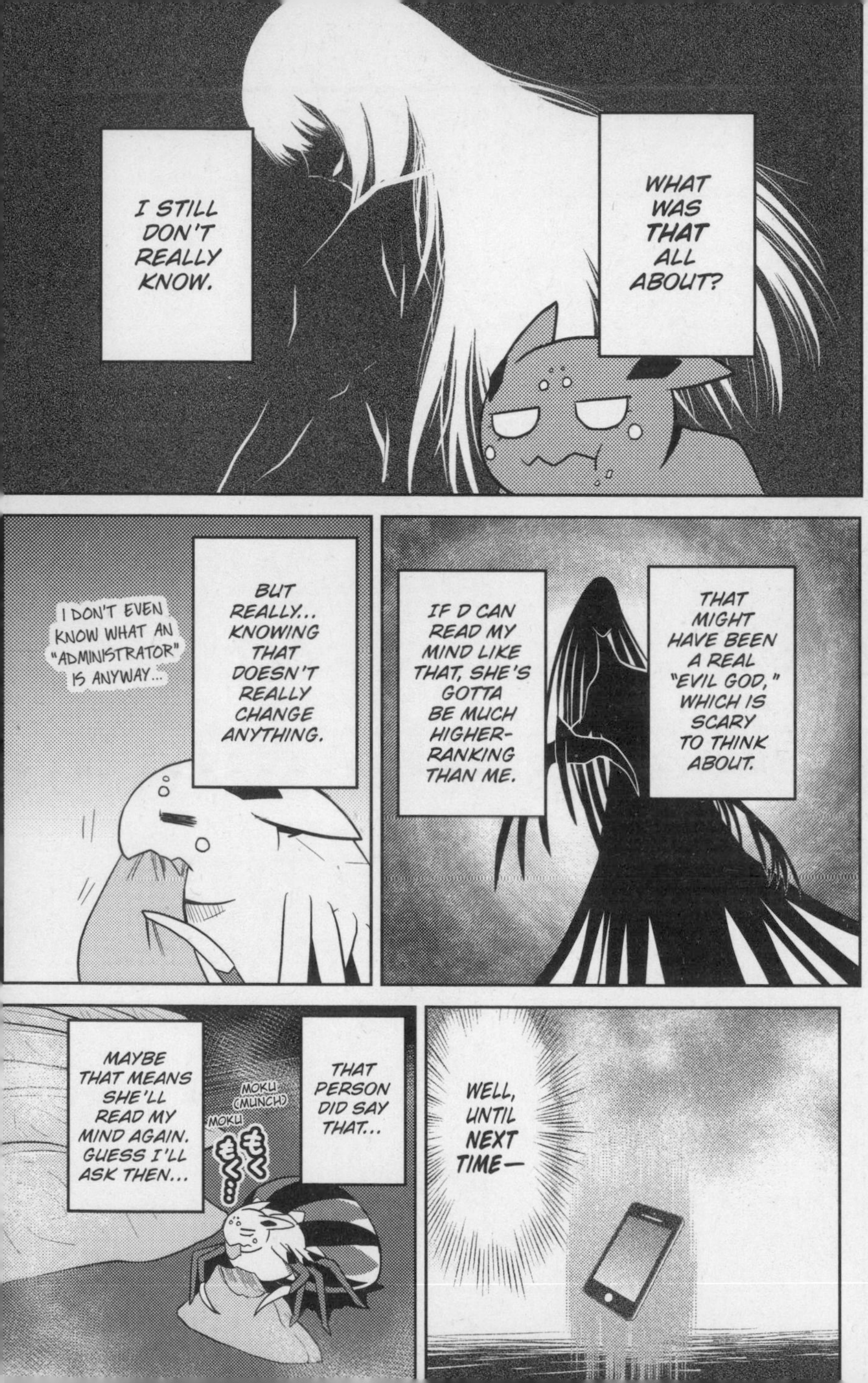
WHAT WAS THAT ALL ABOUT?
I STILL DON'T REALLY KNOW.
THAT MIGHT HAVE BEEN A REAL "EVIL GOD," WHICH IS SCARY TO THINK ABOUT.
IF D CAN READ MY MIND LIKE THAT, SHE'S GOTTA BE MUCH HIGHER-RANKING THAN ME.
BUT REALLY... KNOWING THAT DOESN'T REALLY CHANGE ANYTHING.
I DON'T EVEN KNOW WHAT AN "ADMINISTRATOR" IS ANYWAY...
WELL, UNTIL NEXT TIME—
THAT PERSON DID SAY THAT...
MAYBE THAT MEANS SHE'LL READ MY MIND AGAIN. GUESS I'LL ASK THEN...
MOKU (MUNCH)
MOKU
もくもく...

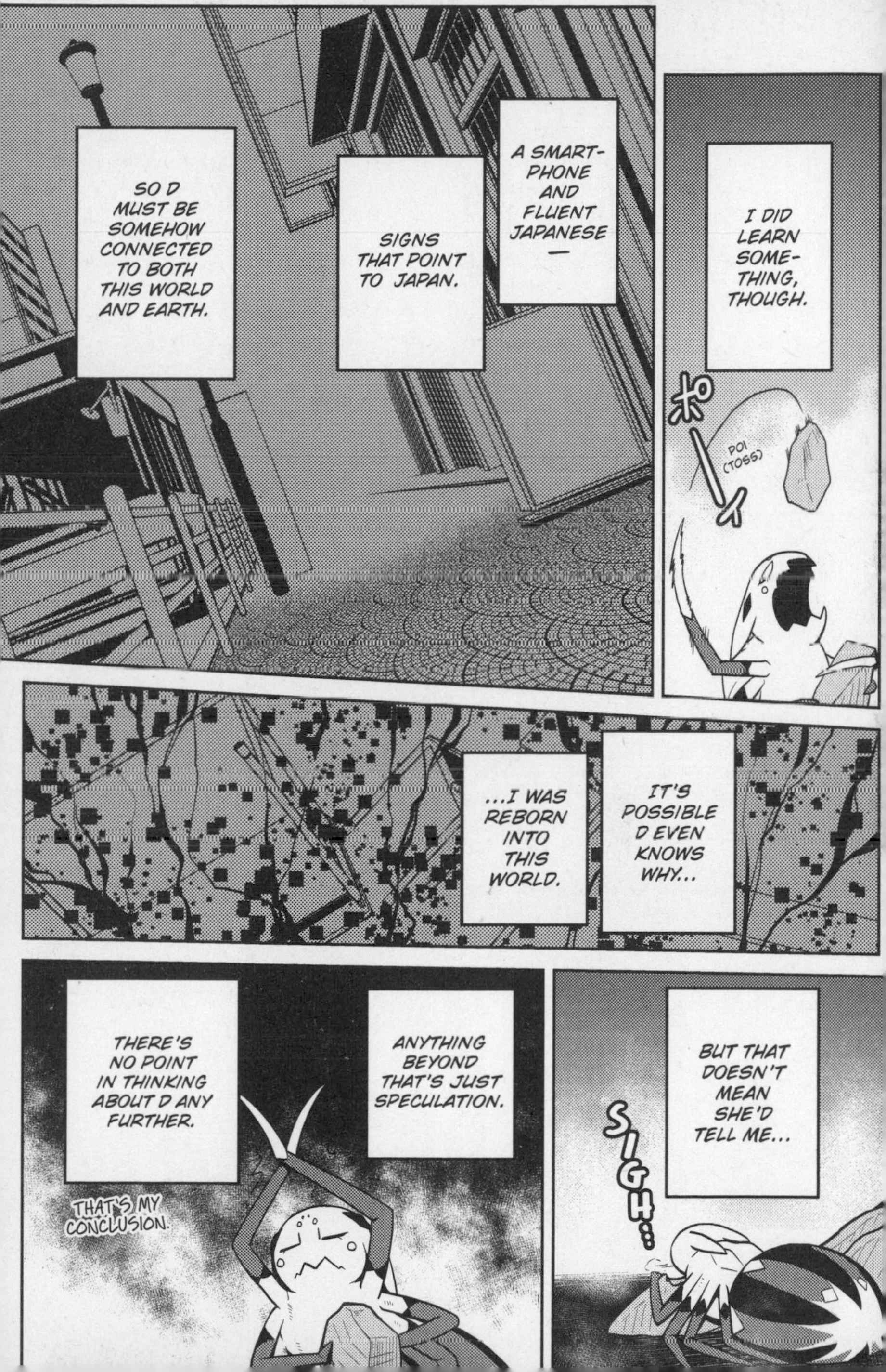
I DID LEARN SOMETHING, THOUGH.
ポイ
POI (TOSS)
A SMARTPHONE AND FLUENT JAPANESE—
SIGNS THAT POINT TO JAPAN.
SO D MUST BE SOMEHOW CONNECTED TO BOTH THIS WORLD AND EARTH.
IT'S POSSIBLE D EVEN KNOWS WHY...
...I WAS REBORN INTO THIS WORLD.
BUT THAT DOESN'T MEAN SHE'D TELL ME...
SIGH...
ANYTHING BEYOND THAT'S JUST SPECULATION.
THERE'S NO POINT IN THINKING ABOUT D ANY FURTHER.
THAT'S MY CONCLUSION.

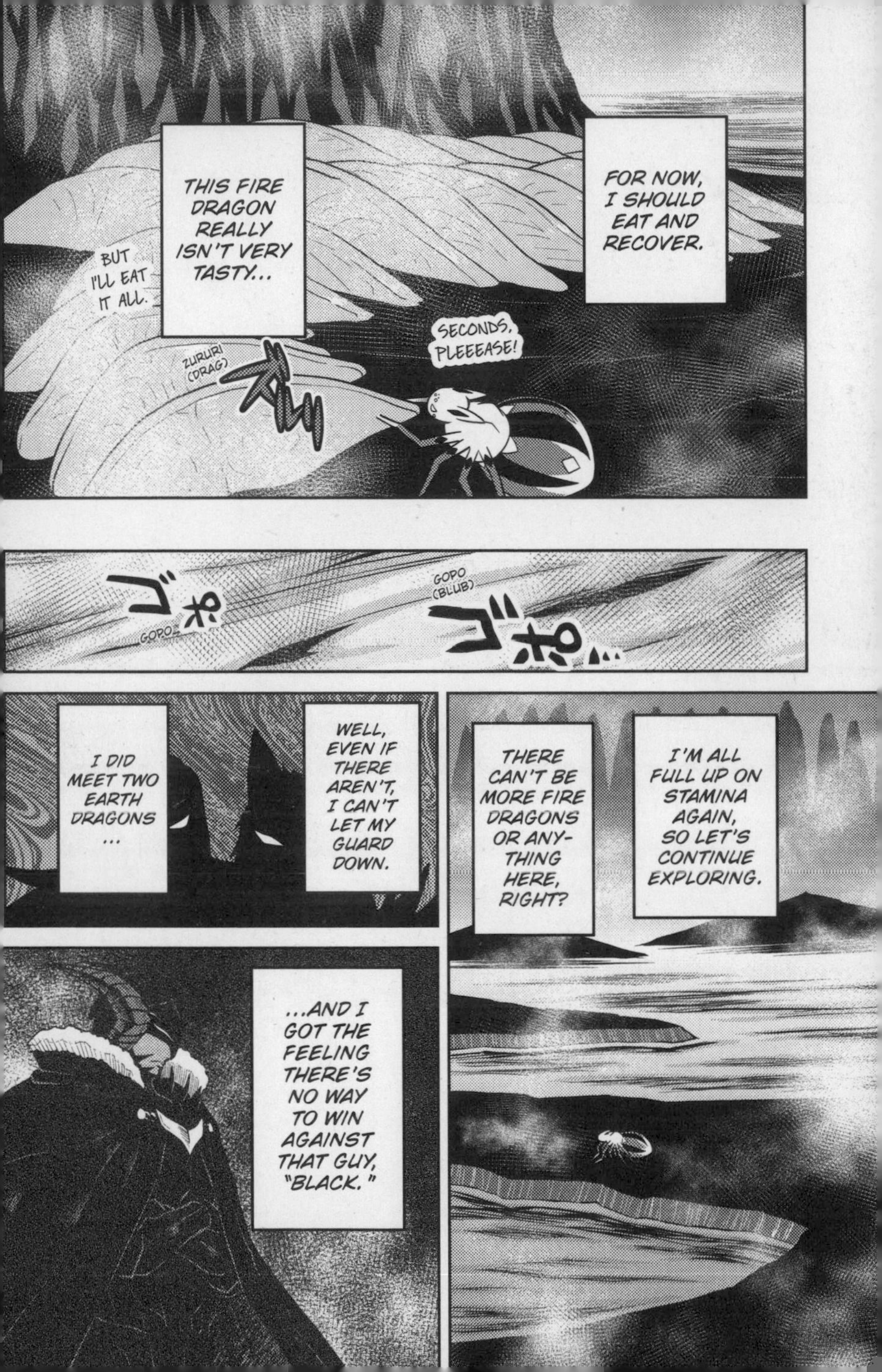
FOR NOW, I SHOULD EAT AND RECOVER.
THIS FIRE DRAGON REALLY ISN'T VERY TASTY...
BUT I'LL EAT IT ALL.
SECONDS, PLEEEASE!
ZURURI (DRAG)
GOPO (BLUB)
GOPO
I'M ALL FULL UP ON STAMINA AGAIN, SO LET'S CONTINUE EXPLORING.
THERE CAN'T BE MORE FIRE DRAGONS OR ANY-THING HERE, RIGHT?
WELL, EVEN IF THERE AREN'T, I CAN'T LET MY GUARD DOWN.
I DID MEET TWO EARTH DRAGONS ...
...AND I GOT THE FEELING THERE'S NO WAY TO WIN AGAINST THAT GUY, "BLACK."

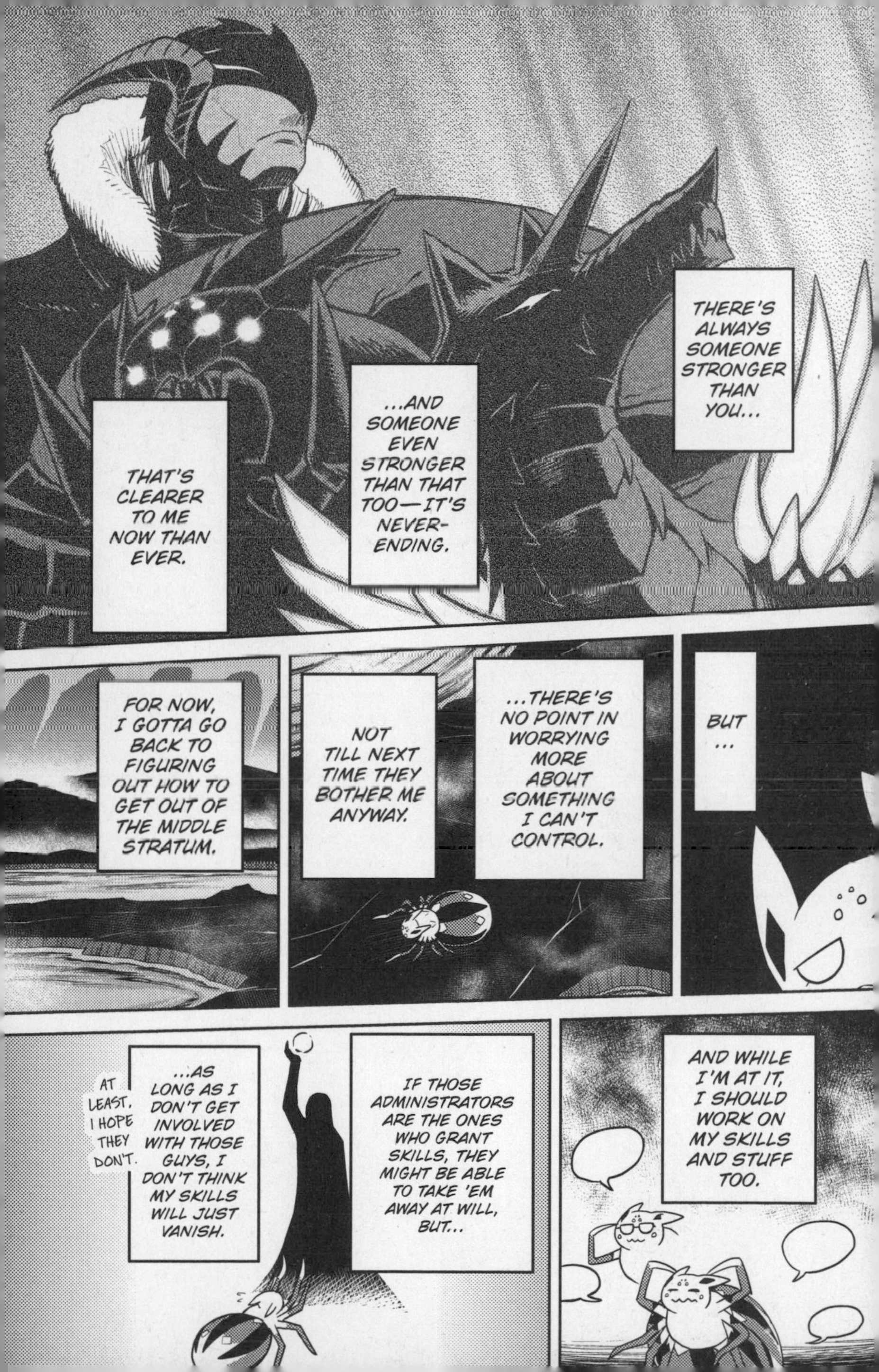
THERE'S ALWAYS SOMEONE STRONGER THAN YOU...
...AND SOMEONE EVEN STRONGER THAN THAT TOO—IT'S NEVER-ENDING.
THAT'S CLEARER TO ME NOW THAN EVER.
BUT...
...THERE'S NO POINT IN WORRYING MORE ABOUT SOMETHING I CAN'T CONTROL.
NOT TILL NEXT TIME THEY BOTHER ME ANYWAY.
FOR NOW, I GOTTA GO BACK TO FIGURING OUT HOW TO GET OUT OF THE MIDDLE STRATUM.
AND WHILE I'M AT IT, I SHOULD WORK ON MY SKILLS AND STUFF TOO.
IF THOSE ADMINISTRATORS ARE THE ONES WHO GRANT SKILLS, THEY MIGHT BE ABLE TO TAKE 'EM AWAY AT WILL, BUT...
...AS LONG AS I DON'T GET INVOLVED WITH THOSE GUYS, I DON'T THINK MY SKILLS WILL JUST VANISH.
AT LEAST, I HOPE THEY DON'T.

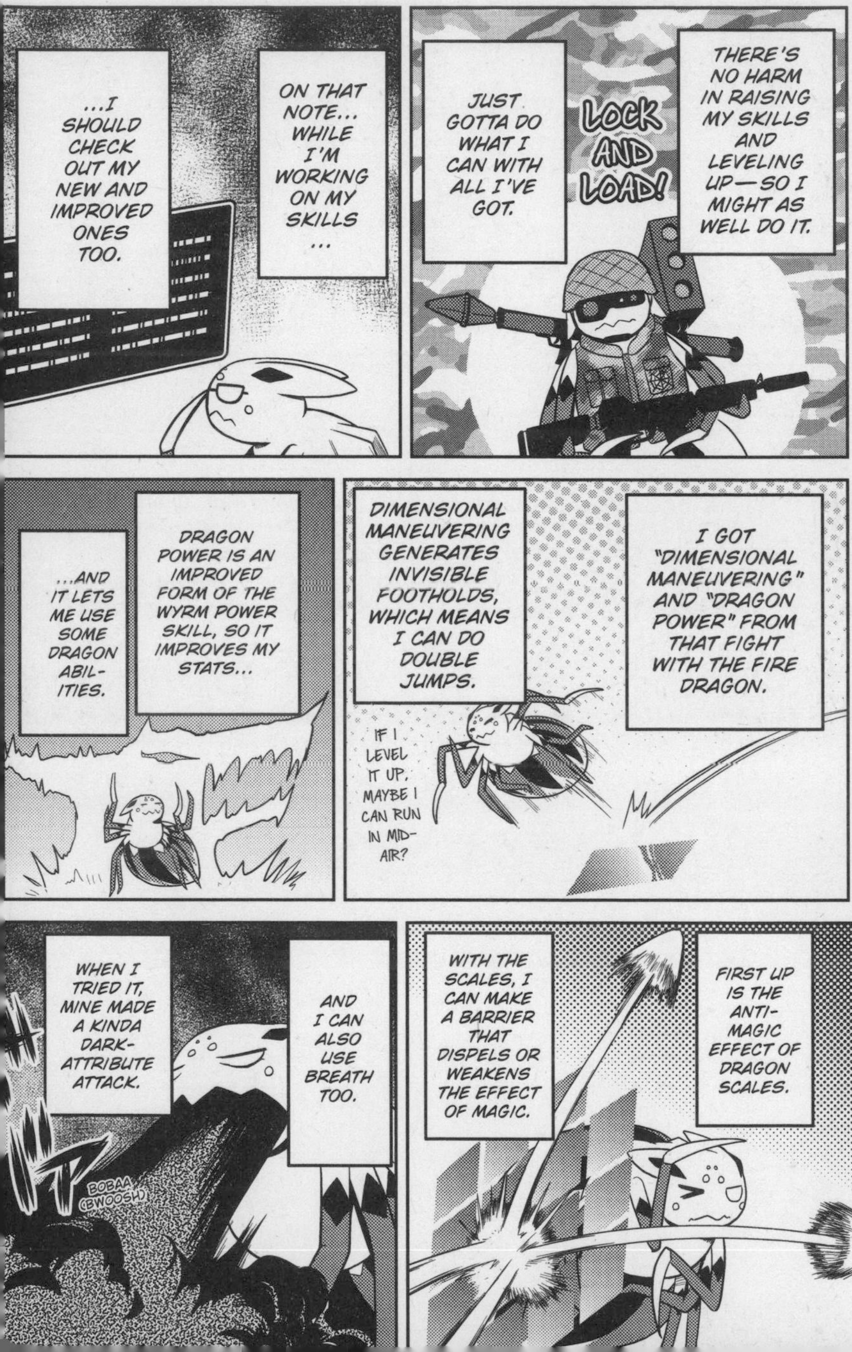
THERE'S NO HARM IN RAISING MY SKILLS AND LEVELING UP—SO I MIGHT AS WELL DO IT.
LOCK AND LOAD!
JUST GOTTA DO WHAT I CAN WITH ALL I'VE GOT.
ON THAT NOTE... WHILE I'M WORKING ON MY SKILLS...
...I SHOULD CHECK OUT MY NEW AND IMPROVED ONES TOO.
I GOT "DIMENSIONAL MANEUVERING" AND "DRAGON POWER" FROM THAT FIGHT WITH THE FIRE DRAGON.
DIMENSIONAL MANEUVERING GENERATES INVISIBLE FOOTHOLDS, WHICH MEANS I CAN DO DOUBLE JUMPS.
IF I LEVEL IT UP, MAYBE I CAN RUN IN MID-AIR?
DRAGON POWER IS AN IMPROVED FORM OF THE WYRM POWER SKILL, SO IT IMPROVES MY STATS...
...AND IT LETS ME USE SOME DRAGON ABIL-ITIES.
FIRST UP IS THE ANTI-MAGIC EFFECT OF DRAGON SCALES.
WITH THE SCALES, I CAN MAKE A BARRIER THAT DISPELS OR WEAKENS THE EFFECT OF MAGIC.
AND I CAN ALSO USE BREATH TOO.
WHEN I TRIED IT, MINE MADE A KINDA DARK-ATTRIBUTE ATTACK.
BOBAA (BWOOSH)

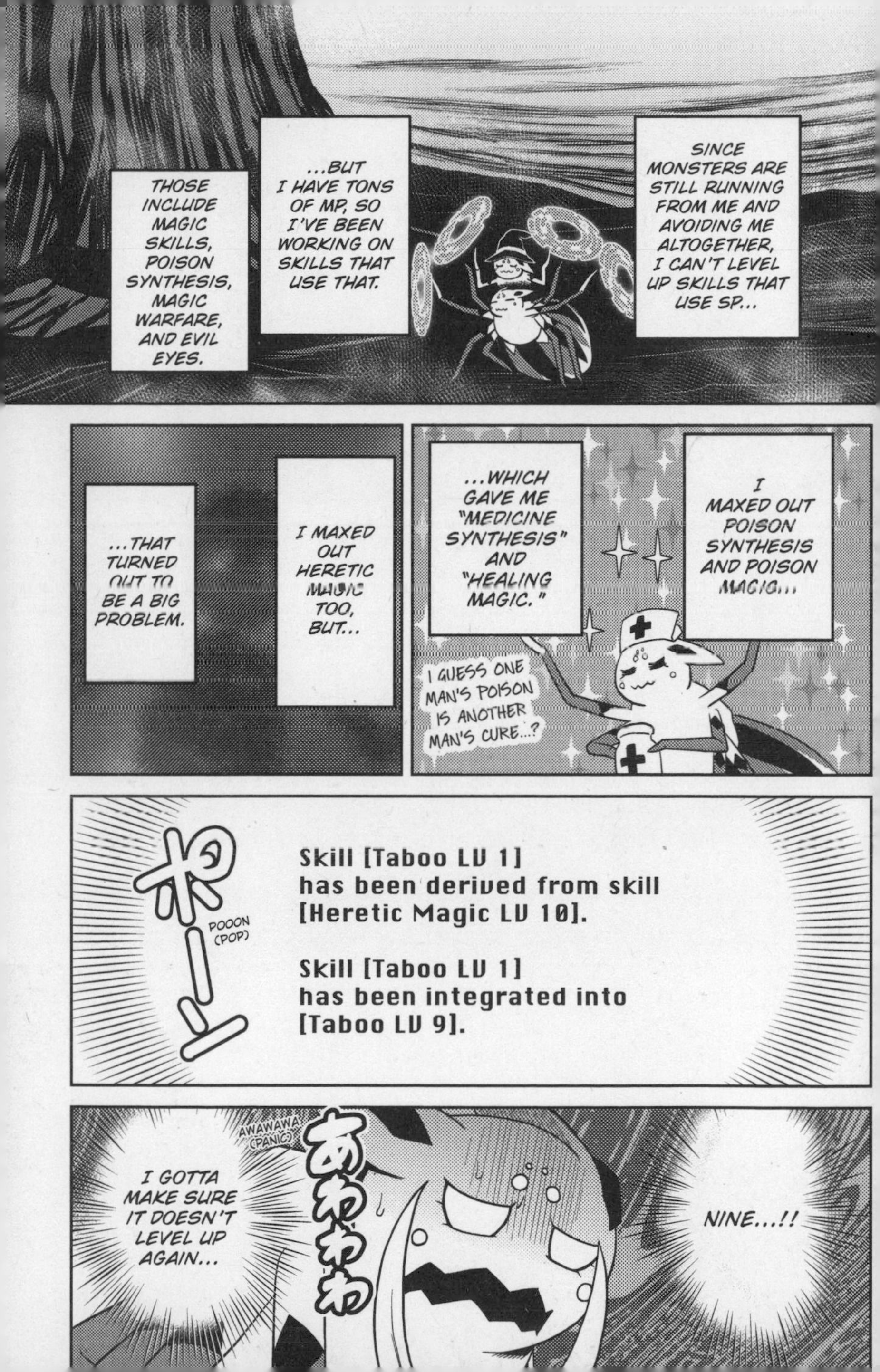
SINCE MONSTERS ARE STILL RUNNING FROM ME AND AVOIDING ME ALTOGETHER, I CAN'T LEVEL UP SKILLS THAT USE SP...
...BUT I HAVE TONS OF MP, SO I'VE BEEN WORKING ON SKILLS THAT USE THAT.
THOSE INCLUDE MAGIC SKILLS, POISON SYNTHESIS, MAGIC WARFARE, AND EVIL EYES.
I MAXED OUT POISON SYNTHESIS AND POISON MAGIC...
...WHICH GAVE ME "MEDICINE SYNTHESIS" AND "HEALING MAGIC."
I GUESS ONE MAN'S POISON IS ANOTHER MAN'S CURE...?
I MAXED OUT HERETIC MAGIC TOO, BUT...
...THAT TURNED OUT TO BE A BIG PROBLEM.
Skill [Taboo LV 1] has been derived from skill [Heretic Magic LV 10].
Skill [Taboo LV 1] has been integrated into [Taboo LV 9].
ポーン
POOOON (POP)
NINE...!!
あわわわ
AWAWAWA (PANIC)
I GOTTA MAKE SURE IT DOESN'T LEVEL UP AGAIN...

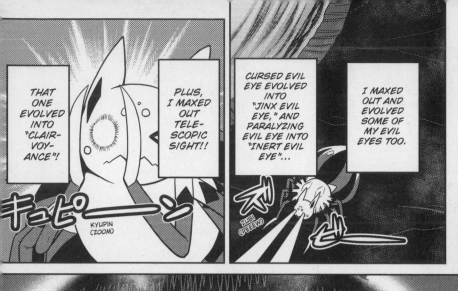

I MAXED OUT AND EVOLVED SOME OF MY EVIL EYES TOO.
CURSED EVIL EYE EVOLVED INTO "JINX EVIL EYE," AND PARALYZING EVIL EYE INTO "INERT EVIL EYE"...
ZUBI (PEEEW)
PLUS, I MAXED OUT TELE-SCOPIC SIGHT!!
THAT ONE EVOLVED INTO "CLAIR-VOY-ANCE"!
KYUPIN (ZOOM)
CLAIR-VOYANCE DOESN'T LET ME SEE ANYWHERE IN THE WORLD LIKE I'D HOPED.
IT JUST HAS BETTER RANGE AND CAN SEE THROUGH WALLS, BUT—
!?
NOW...
...I SEE SOME-THING IN THE DISTANCE......

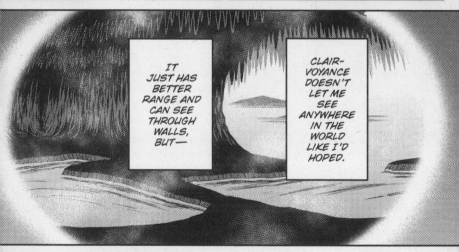

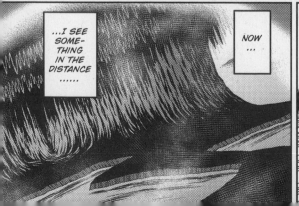

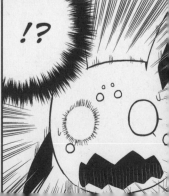

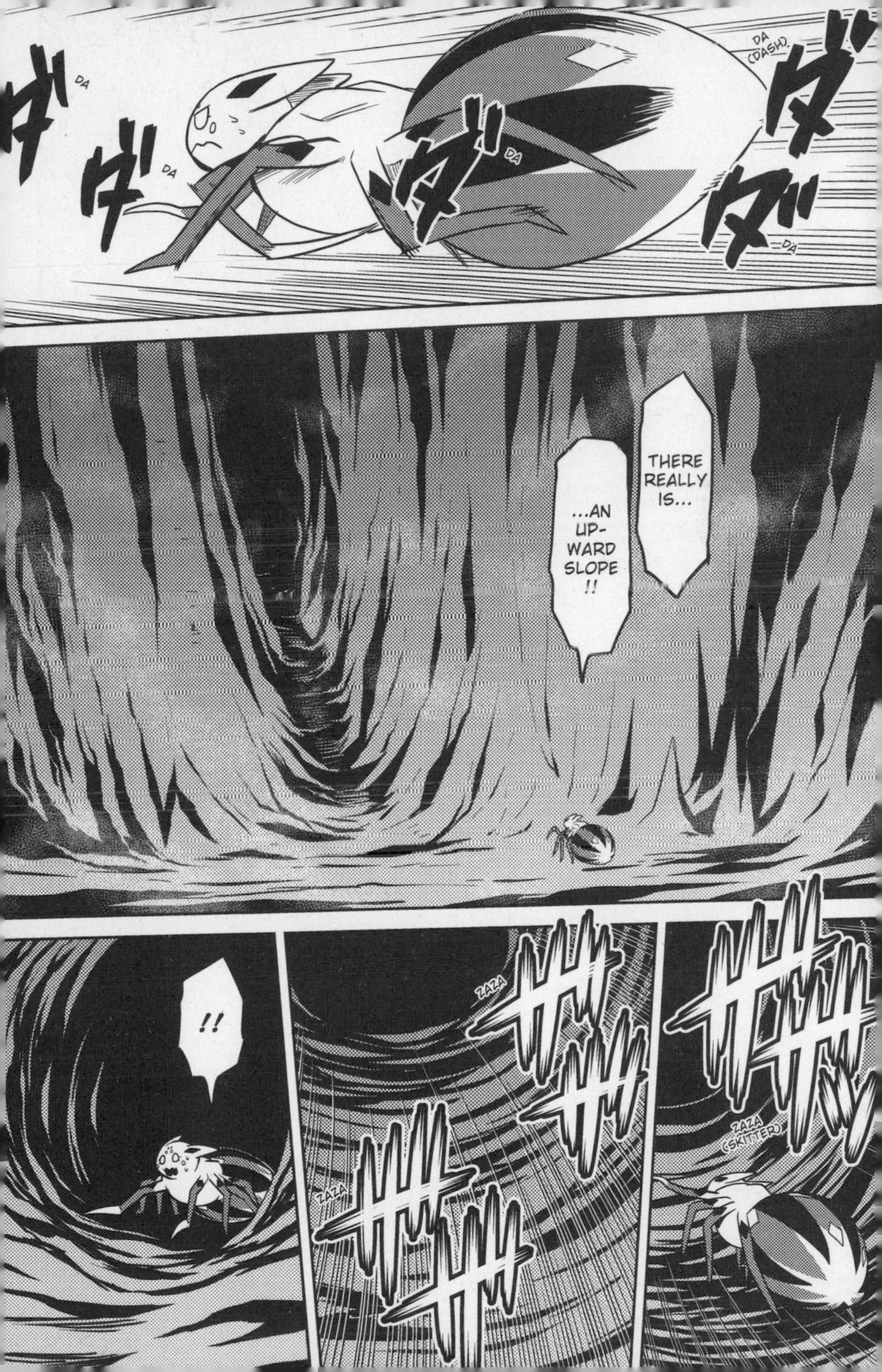
DA (DASH)
DA
DA
DA
DA
THERE REALLY IS...
...AN UP-WARD SLOPE !!
ZAZA (SKITTER)
ZAZA
ZAZA
!!

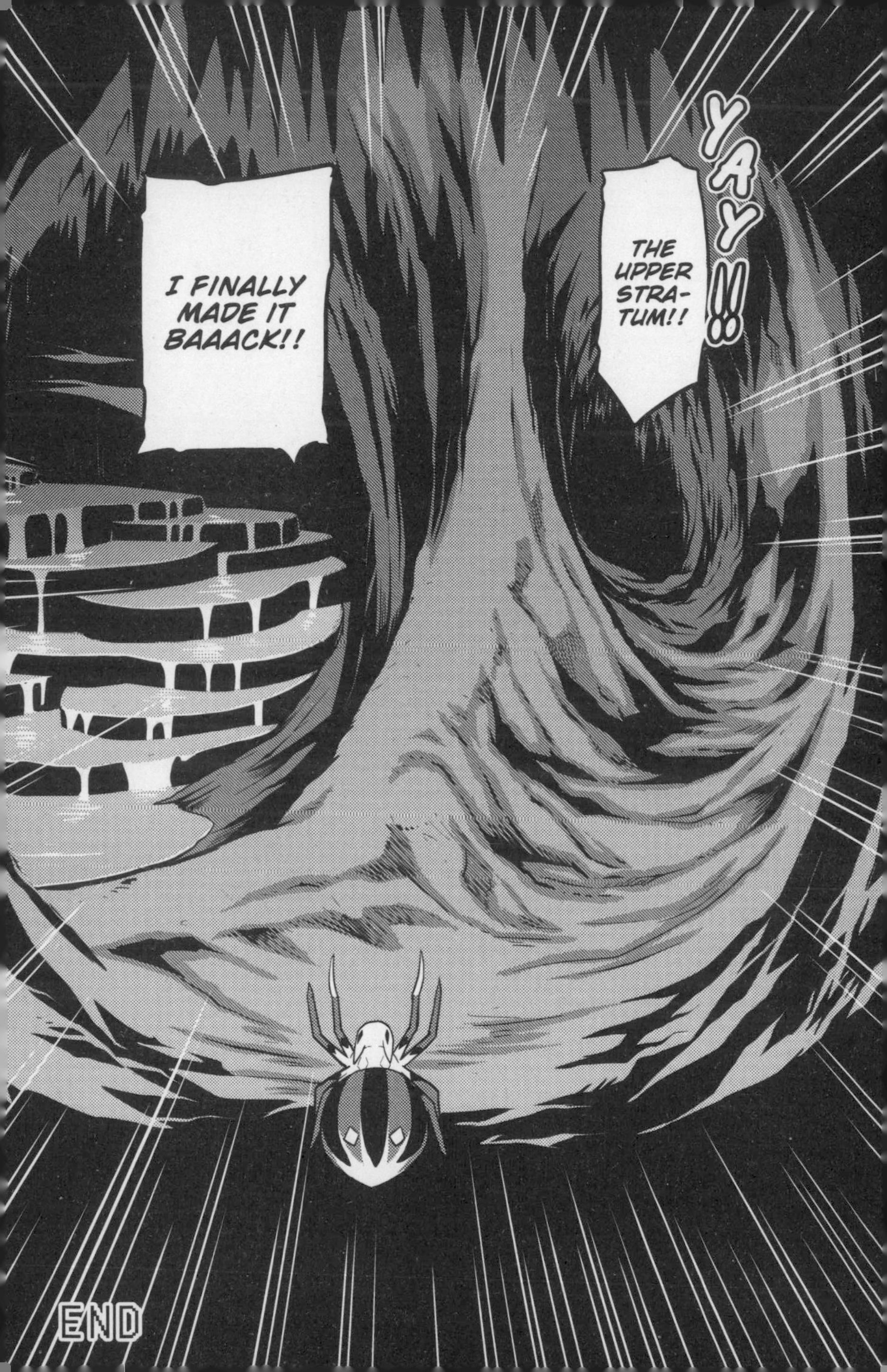
YAY!!
THE UPPER STRA-TUM!!
I FINALLY MADE IT BAAACK!!
END

So I'm a Spider, So What?

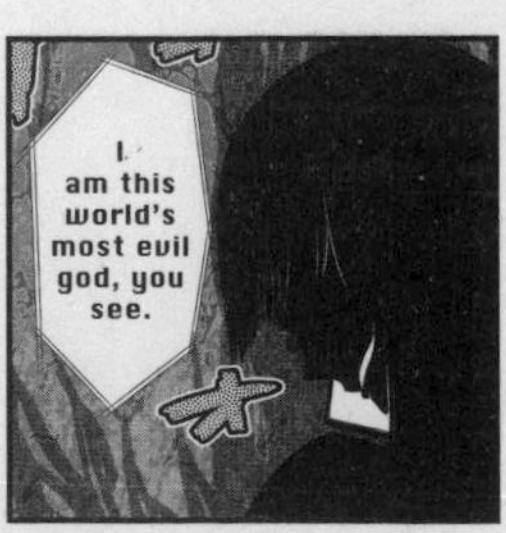
I am this world's most evil god, you see.

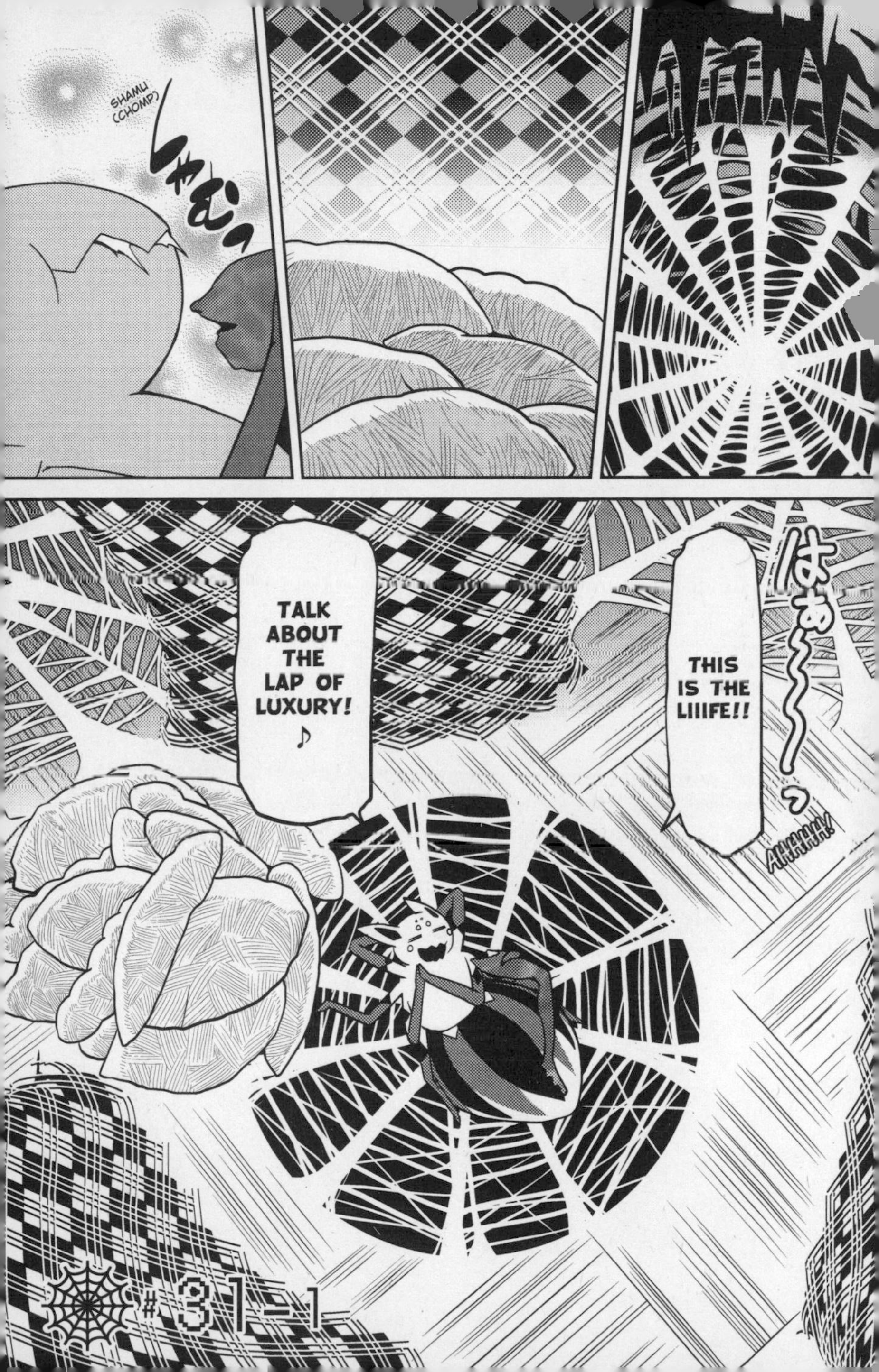
しゃむっ
SHAMU (CHOMP)
はあ～～～っ
AHHHHH!
THIS IS THE LIIIFE!!
TALK ABOUT THE LAP OF LUXURY! ♪
#31-1

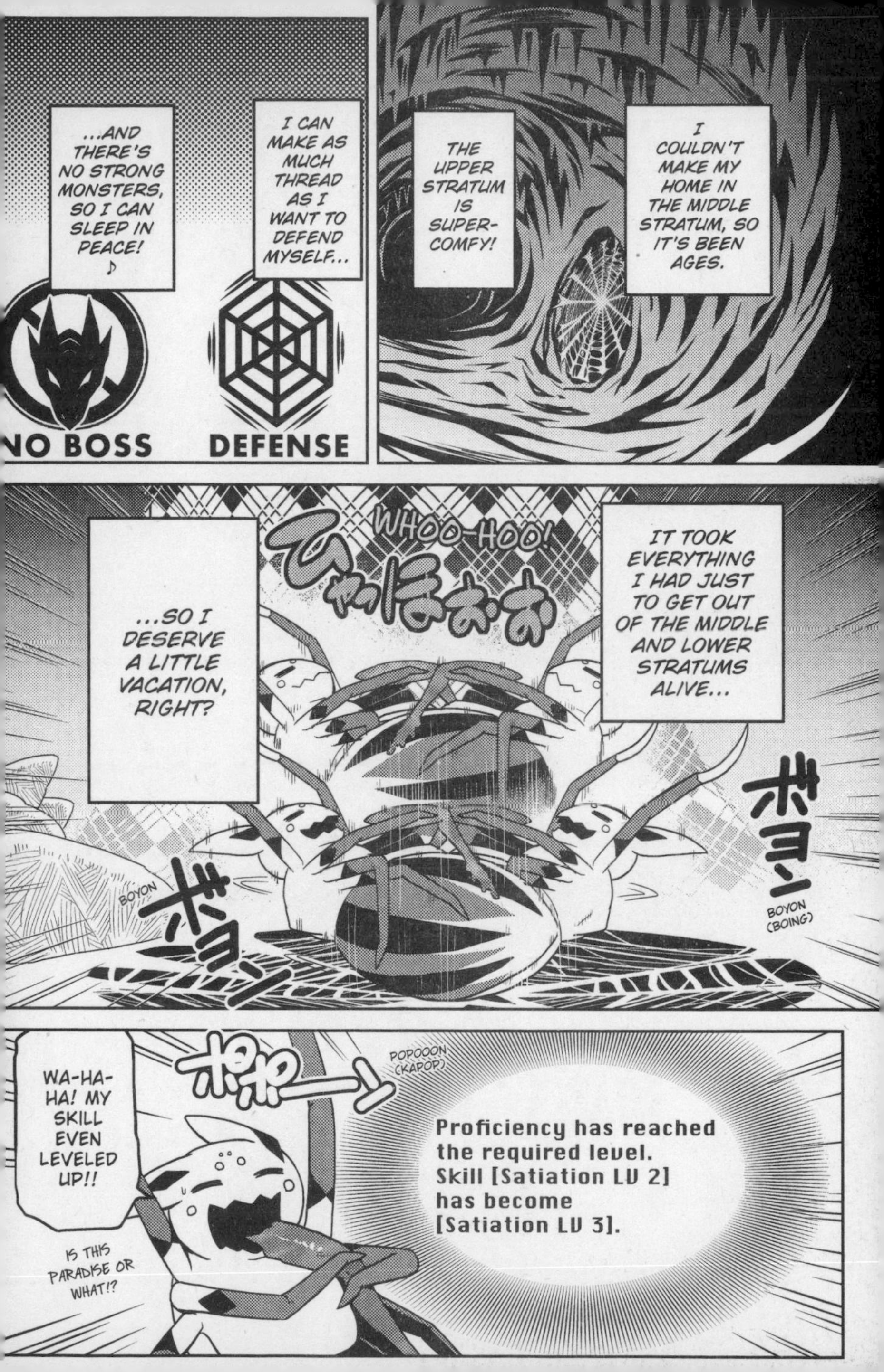
I COULDN'T MAKE MY HOME IN THE MIDDLE STRATUM, SO IT'S BEEN AGES.
THE UPPER STRATUM IS SUPER-COMFY!
I CAN MAKE AS MUCH THREAD AS I WANT TO DEFEND MYSELF...
DEFENSE
...AND THERE'S NO STRONG MONSTERS, SO I CAN SLEEP IN PEACE! ♪
NO BOSS
IT TOOK EVERYTHING I HAD JUST TO GET OUT OF THE MIDDLE AND LOWER STRATUMS ALIVE...
WHOO-HOO!
...SO I DESERVE A LITTLE VACATION, RIGHT?
BOYON (BOING)
BOYON
Proficiency has reached the required level. Skill [Satiation LV 2] has become [Satiation LV 3].
POPOOON (KAPOP)
WA-HA-HA! MY SKILL EVEN LEVELED UP!!
IS THIS PARADISE OR WHAT!?

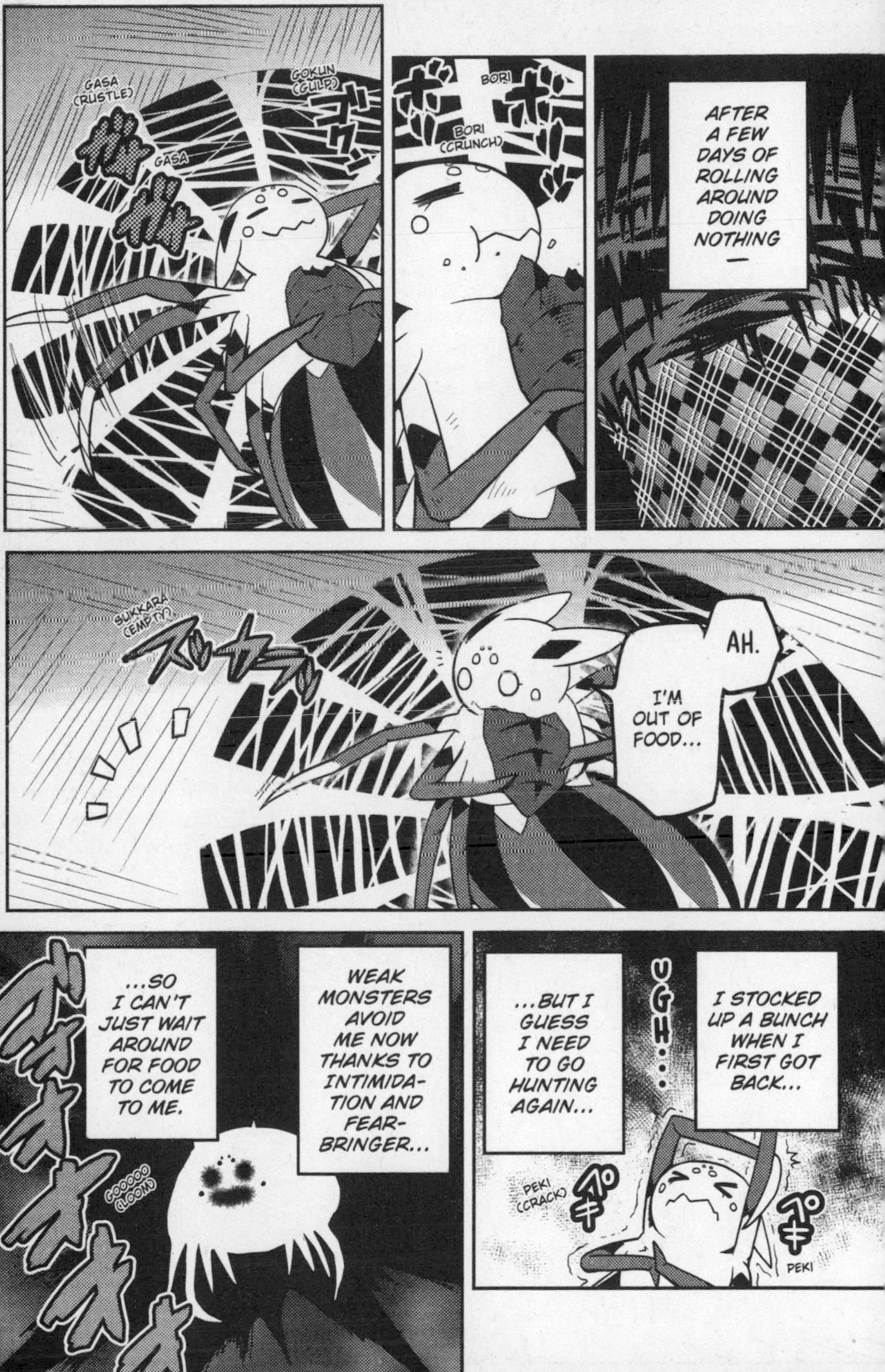
AFTER A FEW DAYS OF ROLLING AROUND DOING NOTHING —
BORI
BORI (CRUNCH)
GOKUN (GULP)
GASA (RUSTLE)
GASA
AH.
I'M OUT OF FOOD...
SUKKARA (EMPTY)
I STOCKED UP A BUNCH WHEN I FIRST GOT BACK...
UGH...
...BUT I GUESS I NEED TO GO HUNTING AGAIN...
PEKI (CRACK)
PEKI
WEAK MONSTERS AVOID ME NOW THANKS TO INTIMIDATION AND FEAR-BRINGER...
...SO I CAN'T JUST WAIT AROUND FOR FOOD TO COME TO ME.
GOOOOO (LOOM)

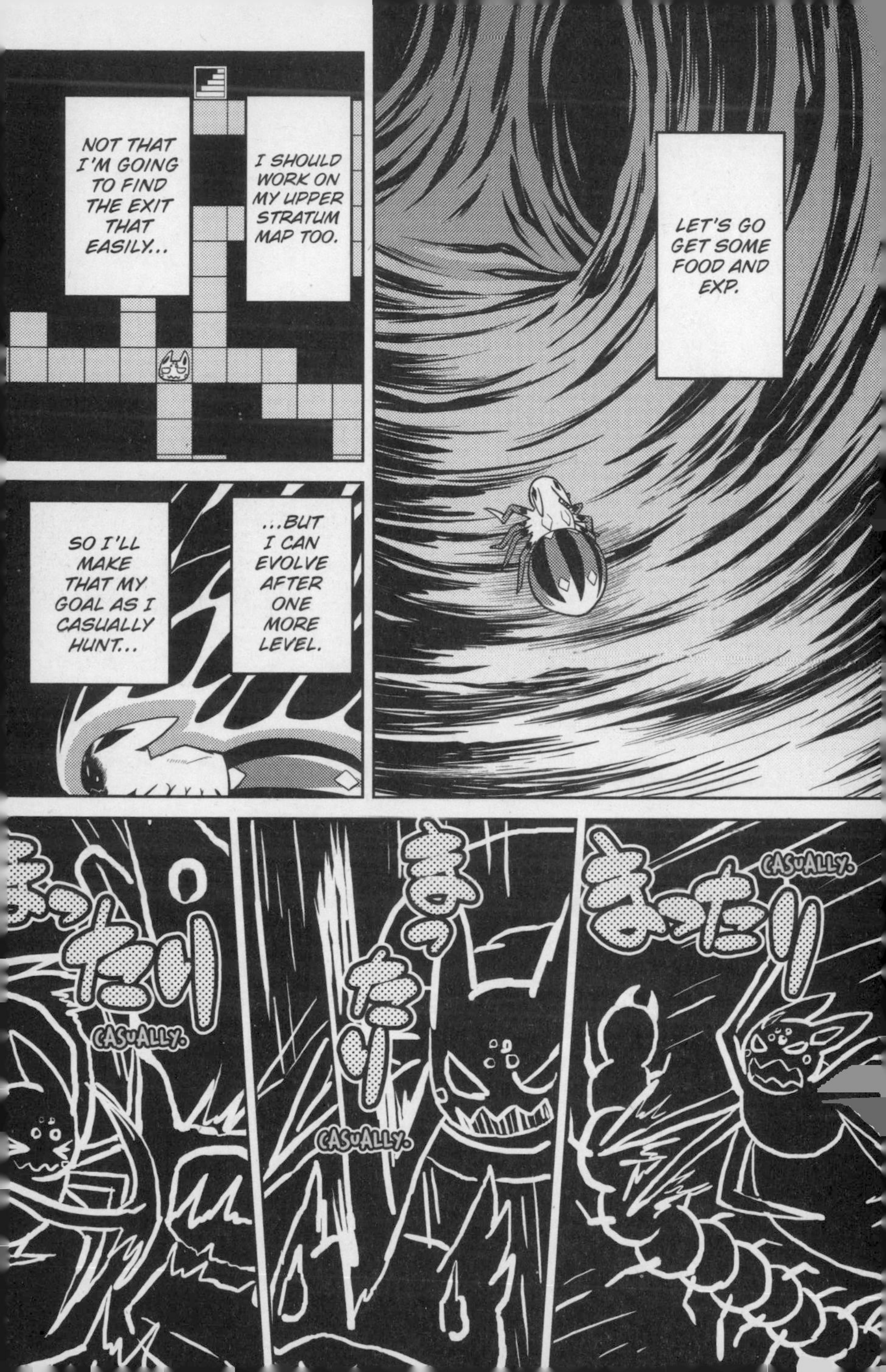
LET'S GO GET SOME FOOD AND EXP.
I SHOULD WORK ON MY UPPER STRATUM MAP TOO.
NOT THAT I'M GOING TO FIND THE EXIT THAT EASILY...
...BUT I CAN EVOLVE AFTER ONE MORE LEVEL.
SO I'LL MAKE THAT MY GOAL AS I CASUALLY HUNT...
まったり
CASUALLY.
まったり
CASUALLY.
まったり
CASUALLY.

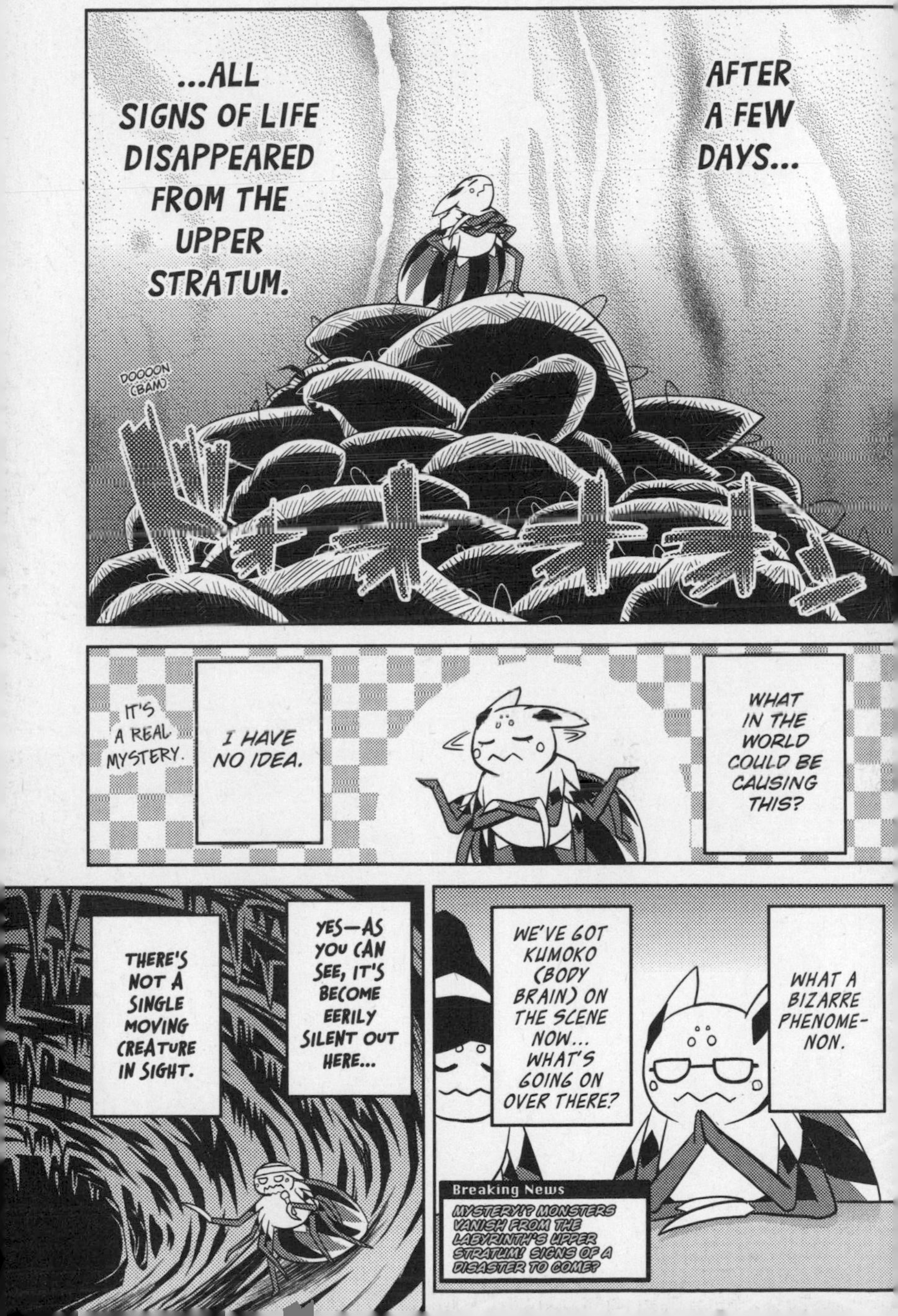
AFTER A FEW DAYS...
...ALL SIGNS OF LIFE DISAPPEARED FROM THE UPPER STRATUM.
DOOOON (BAM)
WHAT IN THE WORLD COULD BE CAUSING THIS?
I HAVE NO IDEA.
IT'S A REAL MYSTERY.
WHAT A BIZARRE PHENOME-NON.
WE'VE GOT KUMOKO (BODY BRAIN) ON THE SCENE NOW... WHAT'S GOING ON OVER THERE?
Breaking News
MYSTERY!? MONSTERS VANISH FROM THE LABYRINTH'S UPPER STRATUM! SIGNS OF A DISASTER TO COME?
YES—AS YOU CAN SEE, IT'S BECOME EERILY SILENT OUT HERE...
THERE'S NOT A SINGLE MOVING CREATURE IN SIGHT.

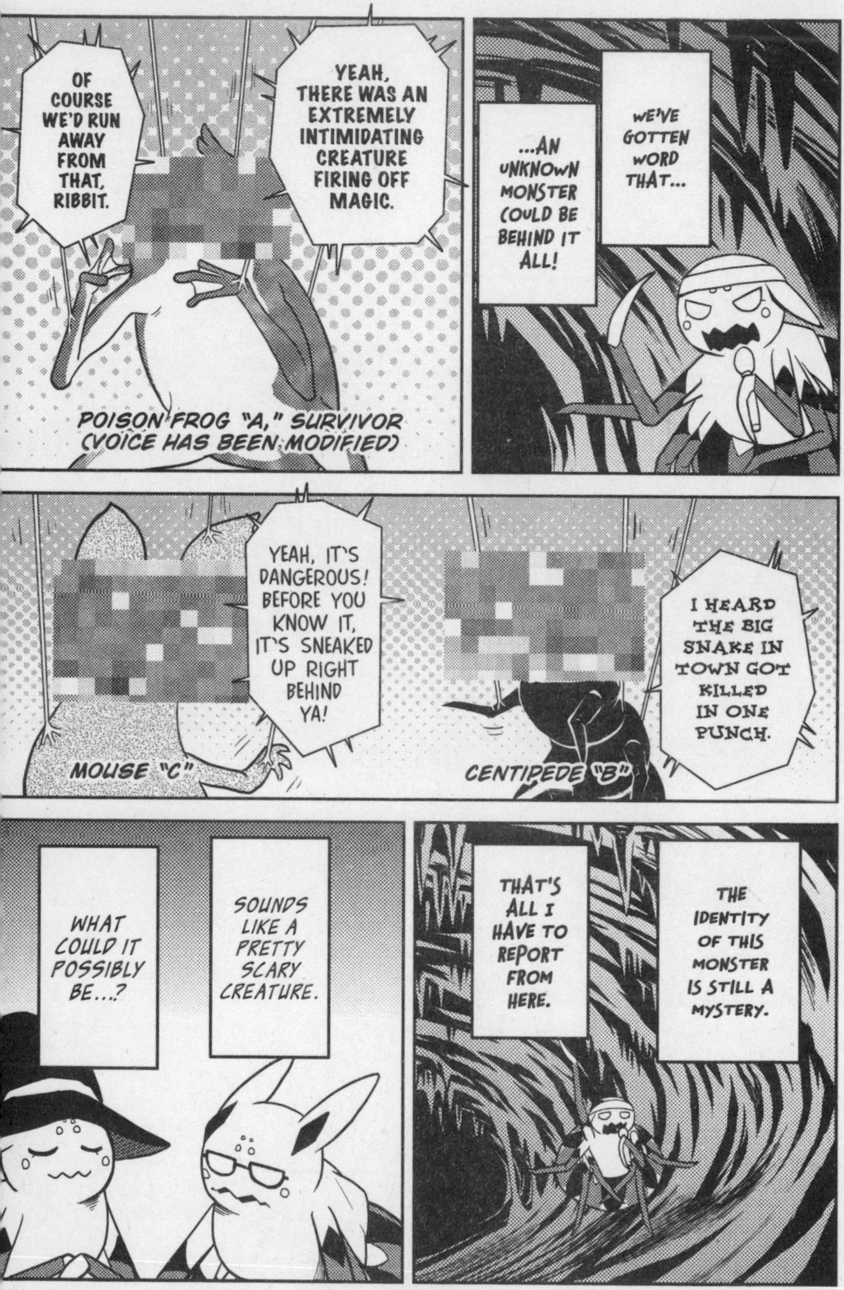
WE'VE GOTTEN WORD THAT...
...AN UNKNOWN MONSTER COULD BE BEHIND IT ALL!
YEAH, THERE WAS AN EXTREMELY INTIMIDATING CREATURE FIRING OFF MAGIC.
OF COURSE WE'D RUN AWAY FROM THAT, RIBBIT.
POISON FROG "A," SURVIVOR (VOICE HAS BEEN MODIFIED)
I HEARD THE BIG SNAKE IN TOWN GOT KILLED IN ONE PUNCH.
CENTIPEDE "B"
YEAH, IT'S DANGEROUS! BEFORE YOU KNOW IT, IT'S SNEAKED UP RIGHT BEHIND YA!
MOUSE "C"
THE IDENTITY OF THIS MONSTER IS STILL A MYSTERY.
THAT'S ALL I HAVE TO REPORT FROM HERE.
SOUNDS LIKE A PRETTY SCARY CREATURE.
WHAT COULD IT POSSIBLY BE...?

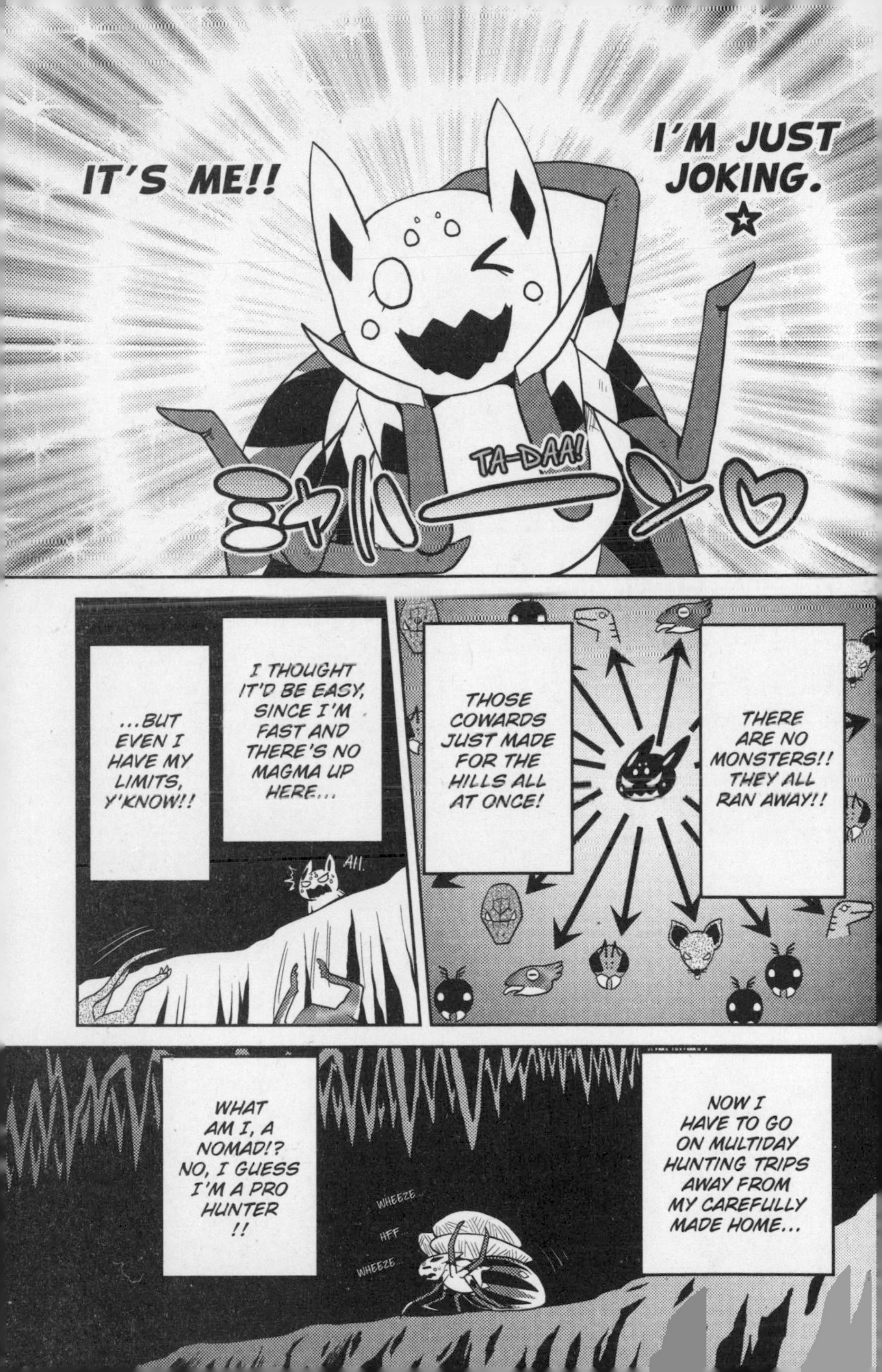
I'M JUST JOKING. ☆
IT'S ME!!
TA-DAA!
THERE ARE NO MONSTERS!! THEY ALL RAN AWAY!!
THOSE COWARDS JUST MADE FOR THE HILLS ALL AT ONCE!
I THOUGHT IT'D BE EASY, SINCE I'M FAST AND THERE'S NO MAGMA UP HERE...
...BUT EVEN I HAVE MY LIMITS, Y'KNOW!!
AH.
NOW I HAVE TO GO ON MULTIDAY HUNTING TRIPS AWAY FROM MY CAREFULLY MADE HOME...
WHAT AM I, A NOMAD!? NO, I GUESS I'M A PRO HUNTER !!
WHEEZE...
HFF...
WHEEZE...

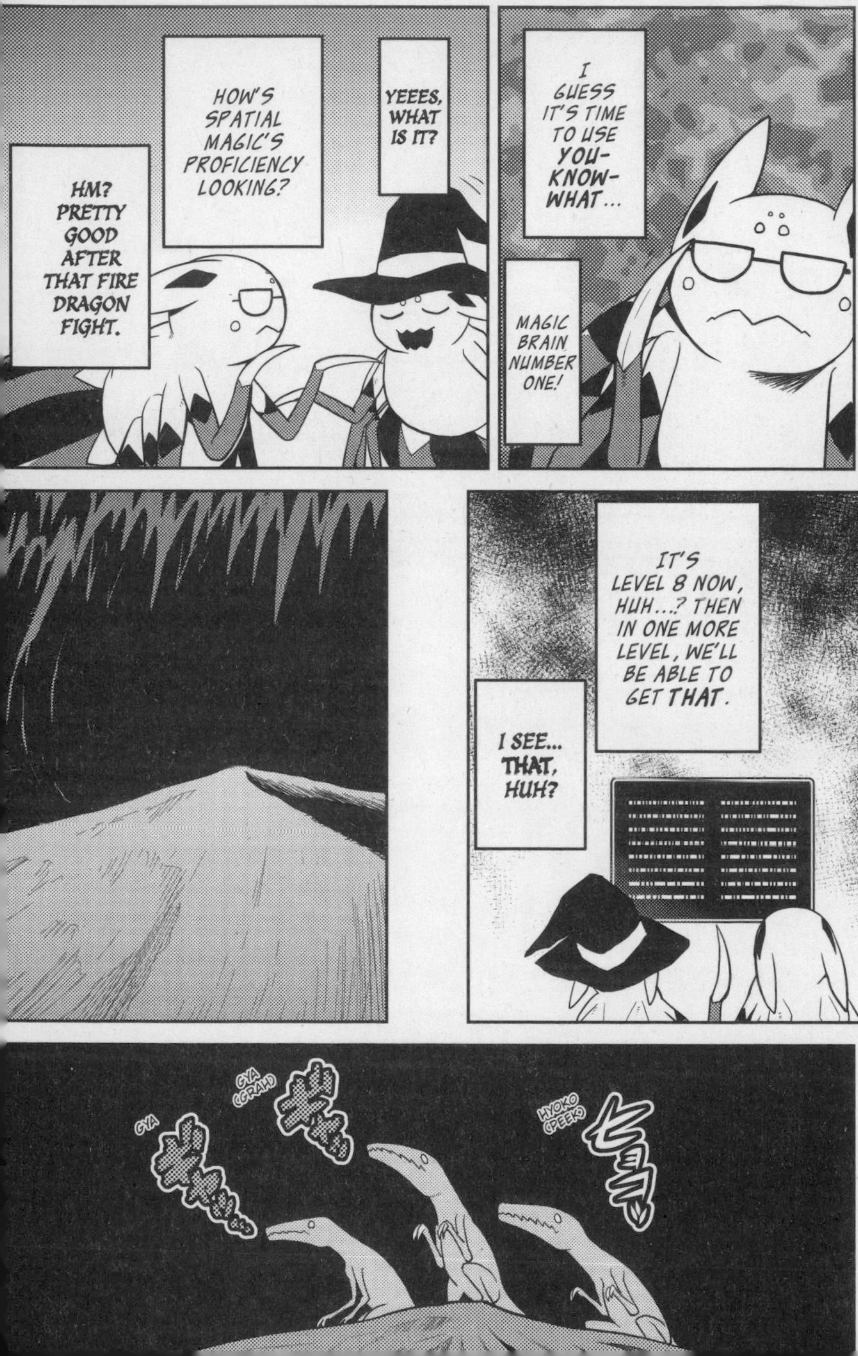
I GUESS IT'S TIME TO USE YOU-KNOW-WHAT...
MAGIC BRAIN NUMBER ONE!
YEEES, WHAT IS IT?
HOW'S SPATIAL MAGIC'S PROFICIENCY LOOKING?
HM? PRETTY GOOD AFTER THAT FIRE DRAGON FIGHT.
IT'S LEVEL 8 NOW, HUH...? THEN IN ONE MORE LEVEL, WE'LL BE ABLE TO GET THAT.
I SEE... THAT, HUH?
HYOKO (PEEK)
GYA (GRAH)
GYA

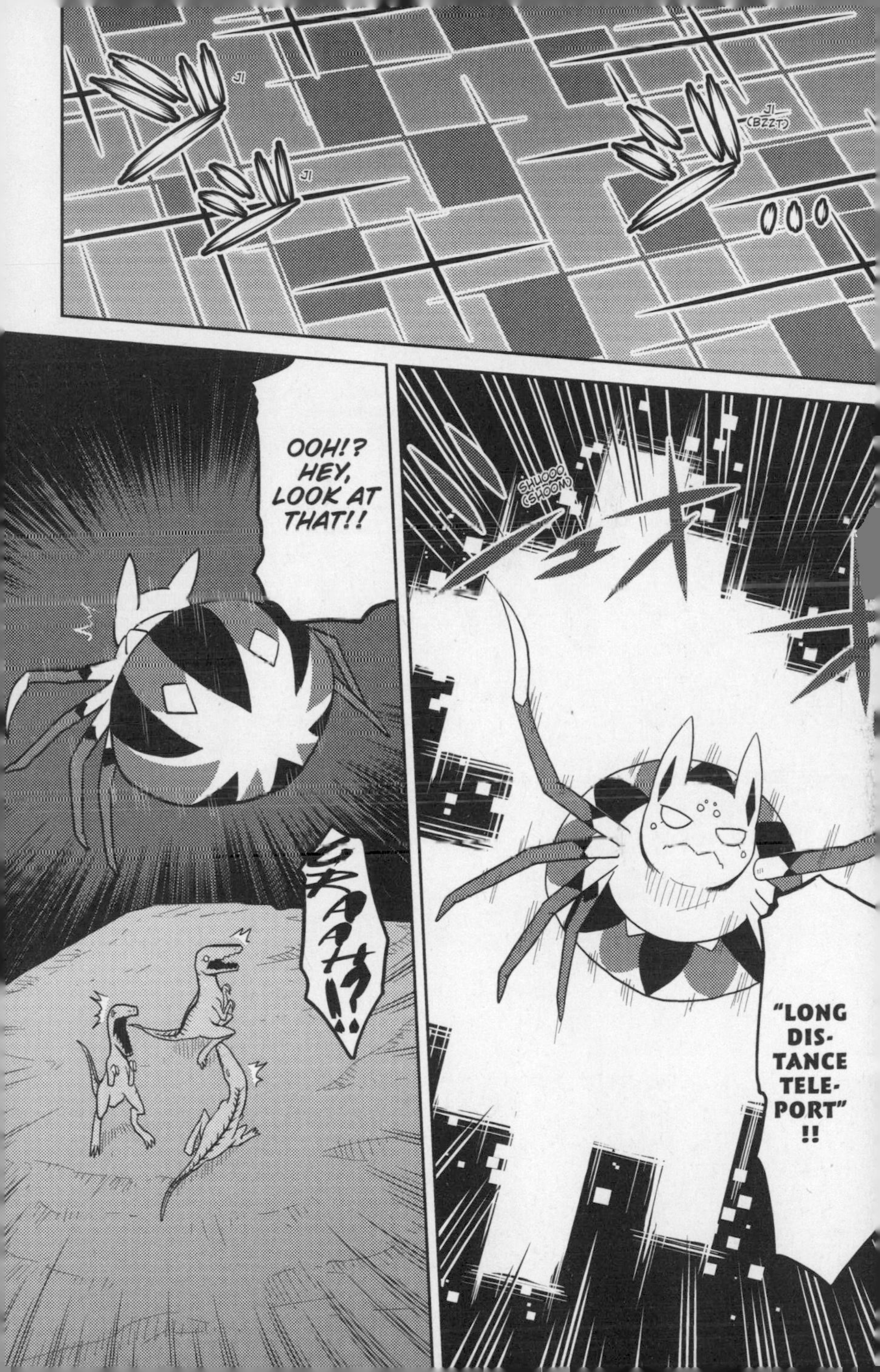
JI
(BZZT)
JI
JI
SHUOOO
(SHOOM)
"LONG DISTANCE TELEPORT"!!
OOH!? HEY, LOOK AT THAT!!

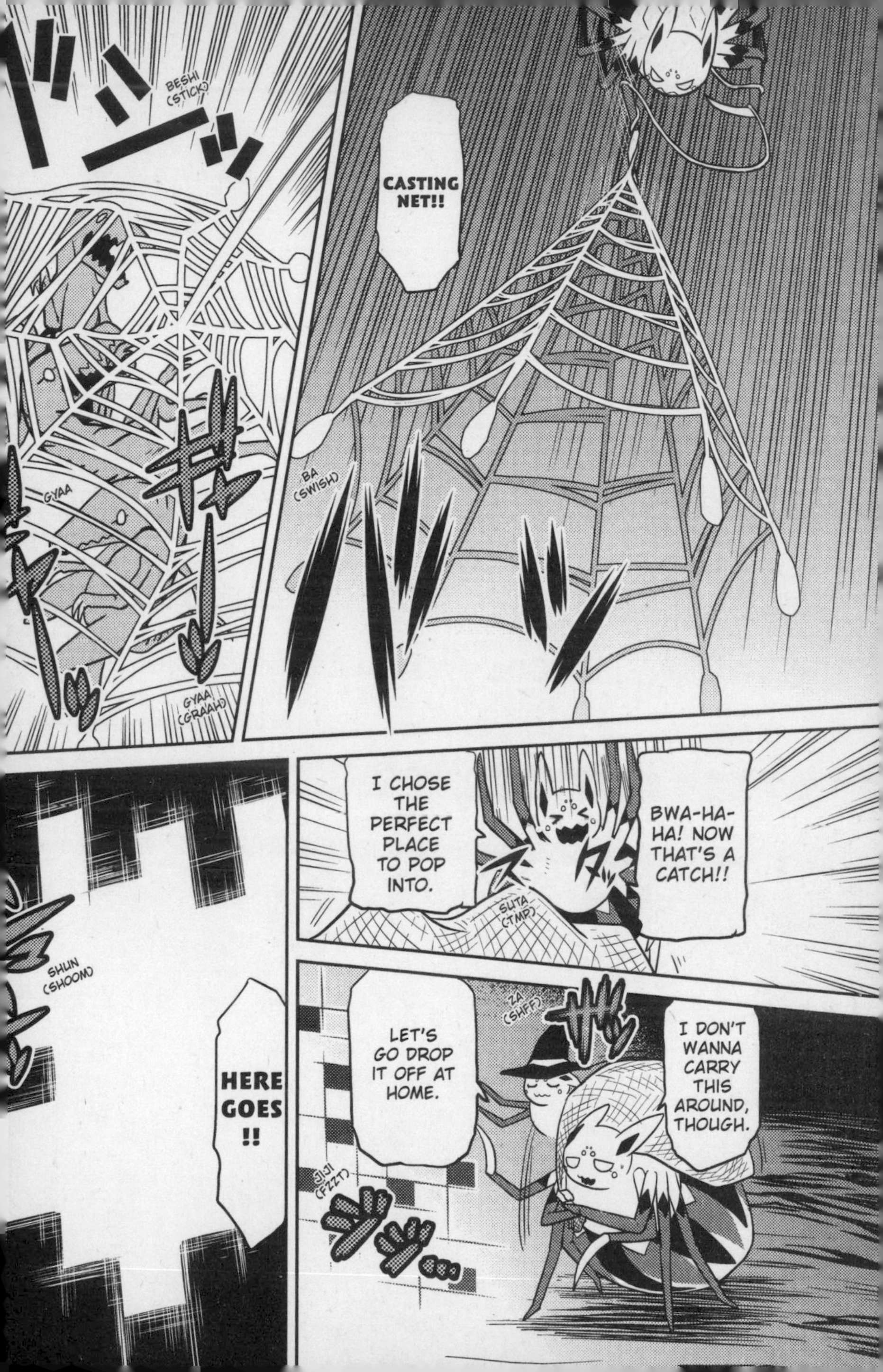
CASTING NET!!
BA (SWISH)
BESHI (STICK)
GYAA
GYAA (GRAAH)
BWA-HA-HA! NOW THAT'S A CATCH!!
I CHOSE THE PERFECT PLACE TO POP INTO.
SUTA (TMP)
I DON'T WANNA CARRY THIS AROUND, THOUGH.
ZA (SHFF)
LET'S GO DROP IT OFF AT HOME.
JIJI (FZZT)
SHUN (SHOOM)
HERE GOES!!

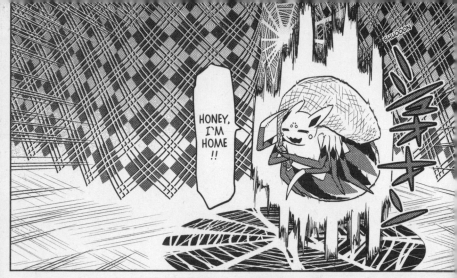

SHUOOON
HONEY, I'M HOME!!
POOON (POP)
<Long-Distance Teleport> Spatial Magic LV 9 spell. Instantly transports the user to anywhere they've been before.
THIS SPELL SOLVES THE FOOD PROBLEM.
I CAN JUST POP IN WHEREVER THERE MIGHT BE MUNSTERS AND GRAB WHAT I FIND!!
IT ONLY WORKS FOR PLACES I'VE BEEN TO BEFORE...
WALK
WALK
...BUT NOW I CAN EXPLORE WITHOUT WORRYING ABOUT THE TRIP BACK.
SHORTCUT
THESE MONSTERS ARE WIMPS COMPARED TO THE ONES IN MIDDLE AND LOWER STRATUMS.
SUPAN (SNAP)
WELL, I DON'T NEED TO WORRY ABOUT GETTING DONE IN, SO...
...LET'S LOOK FOR SOME BIGGER GAME!

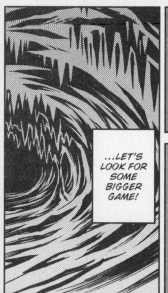

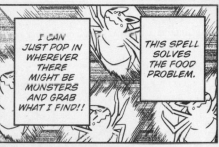

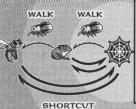

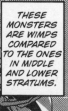

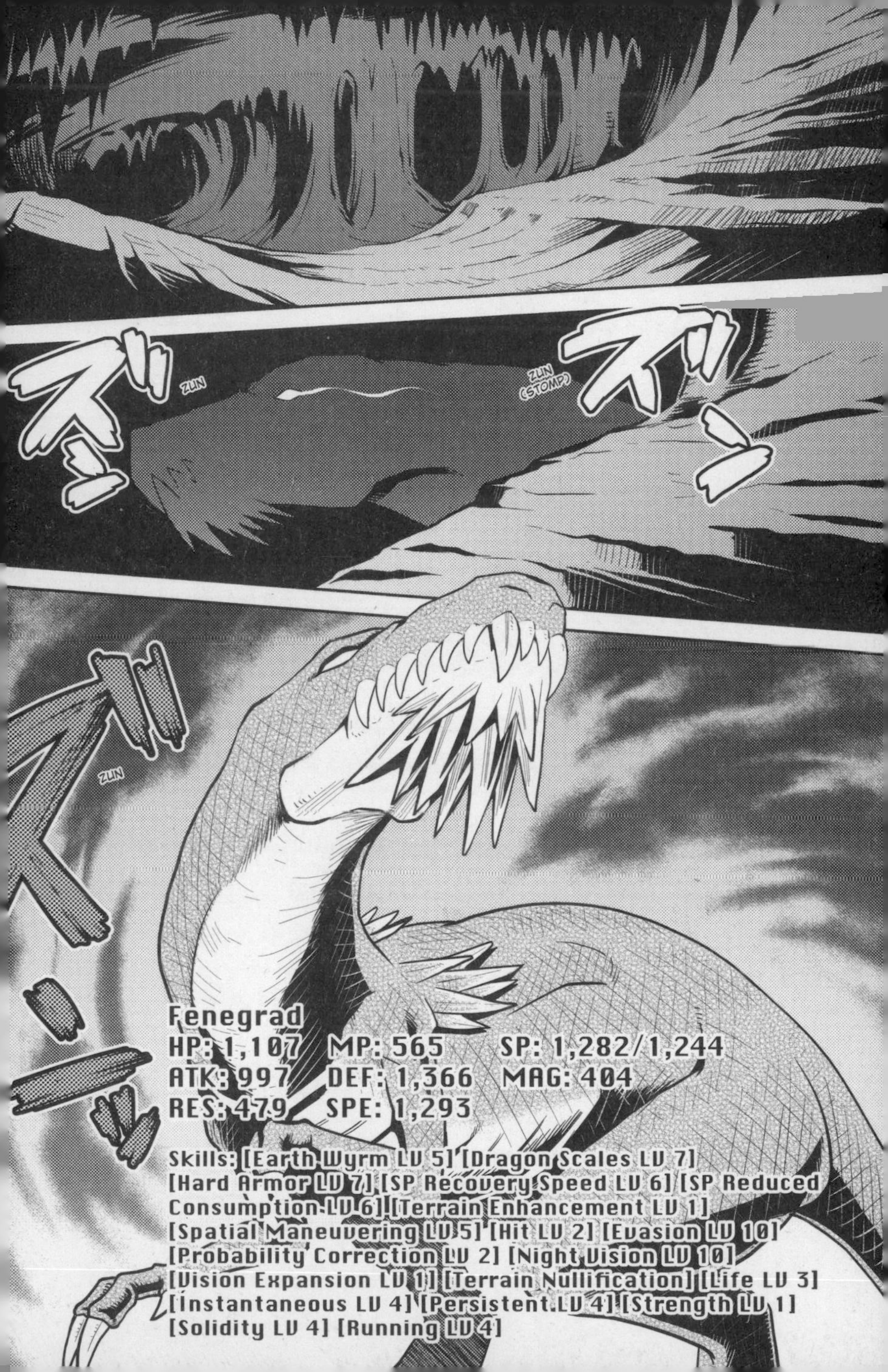
ZUN (STOMP)
ZUN
ZUN
Fenegrad
HP: 1,107 MP: 565 SP: 1,282/1,244
ATK: 997 DEF: 1,366 MAG: 404
RES: 479 SPE: 1,293
Skills: [Earth Wyrm LV 5] [Dragon Scales LV 7] [Hard Armor LV 7] [SP Recovery Speed LV 6] [SP Reduced Consumption LV 6] [Terrain Enhancement LV 1] [Spatial Maneuvering LV 5] [Hit LV 2] [Evasion LV 10] [Probability Correction LV 2] [Night Vision LV 10] [Vision Expansion LV 1] [Terrain Nullification] [Life LV 3] [Instantaneous LV 4] [Persistent LV 4] [Strength LV 1] [Solidity LV 4] [Running LV 4]

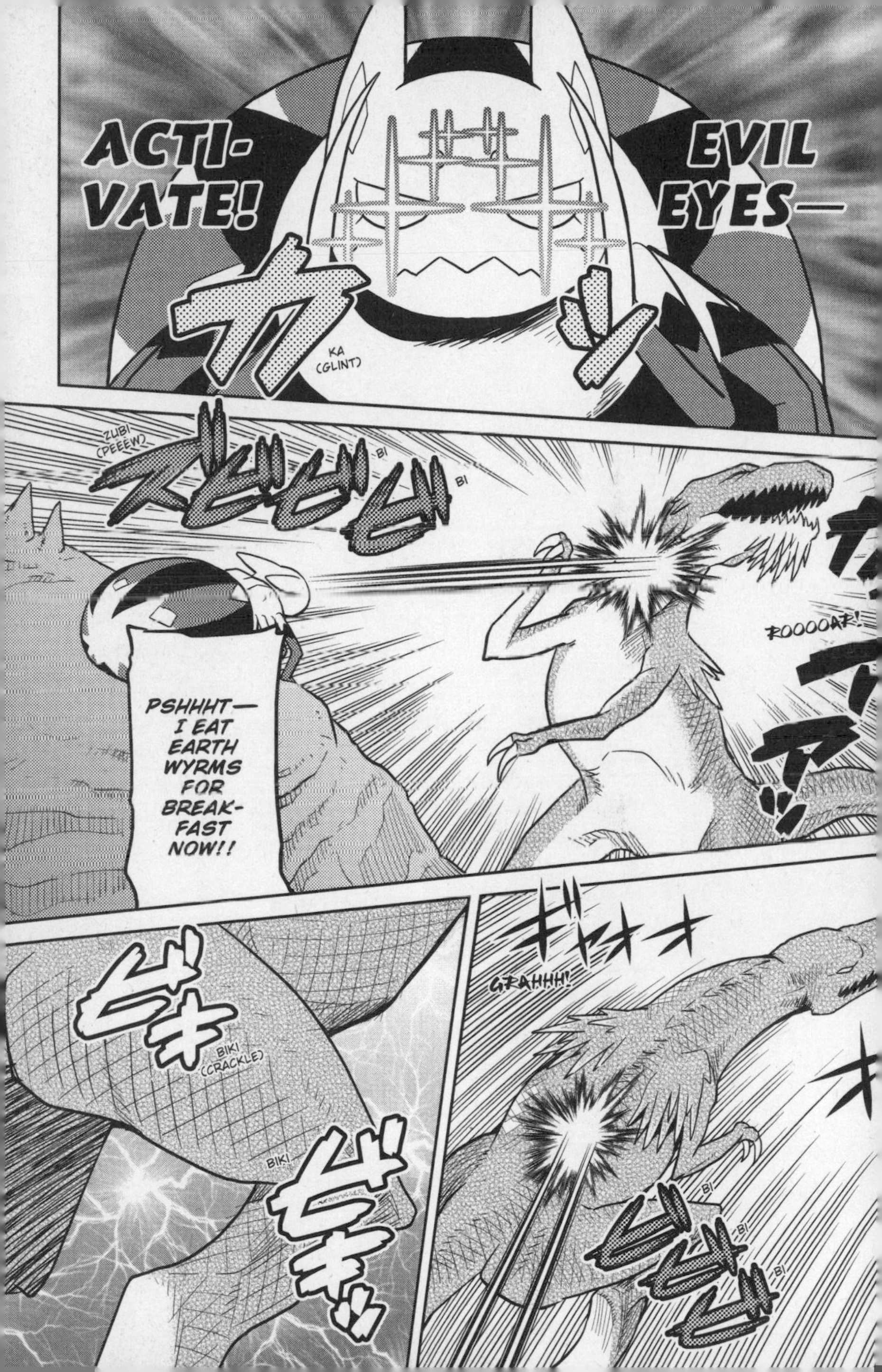
EVIL EYES—
ACTI-VATE!
KA (GLINT)
ZUBI (PEEEW)
BI
BI
ROOOOAR!
PSHHHT— I EAT EARTH WYRMS FOR BREAK-FAST NOW!!
GRAHHH!
BI
BI
BI
BIKI (CRACKLE)
BIKI

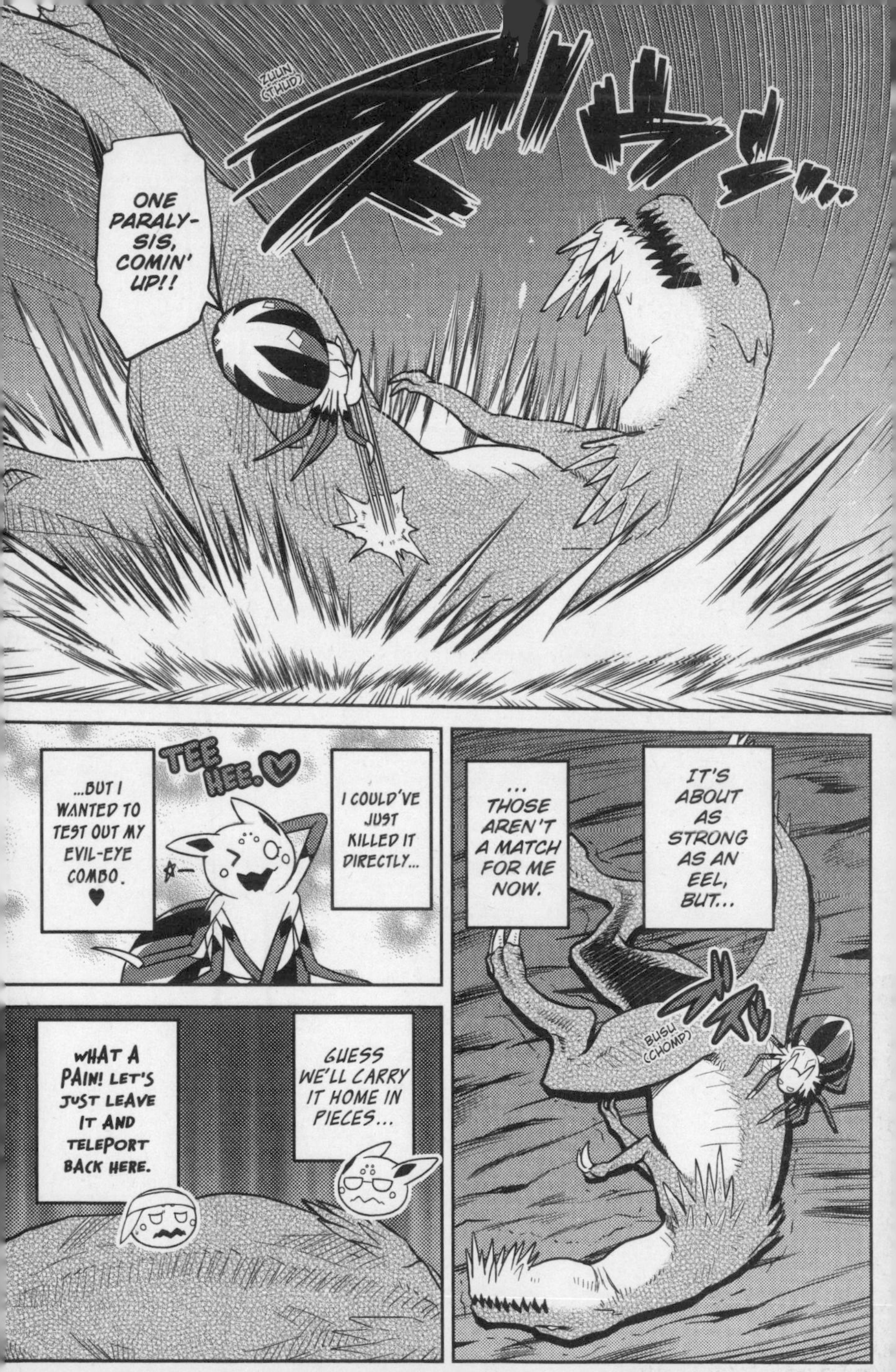
ZUUN (THUD)
ONE PARALYSIS, COMIN' UP!!
IT'S ABOUT AS STRONG AS AN EEL, BUT...
... THOSE AREN'T A MATCH FOR ME NOW.
BUSU (CHOMP)
I COULD'VE JUST KILLED IT DIRECTLY...
TEE HEE.♥
...BUT I WANTED TO TEST OUT MY EVIL-EYE COMBO. ♥
GUESS WE'LL CARRY IT HOME IN PIECES...
WHAT A PAIN! LET'S JUST LEAVE IT AND TELEPORT BACK HERE.

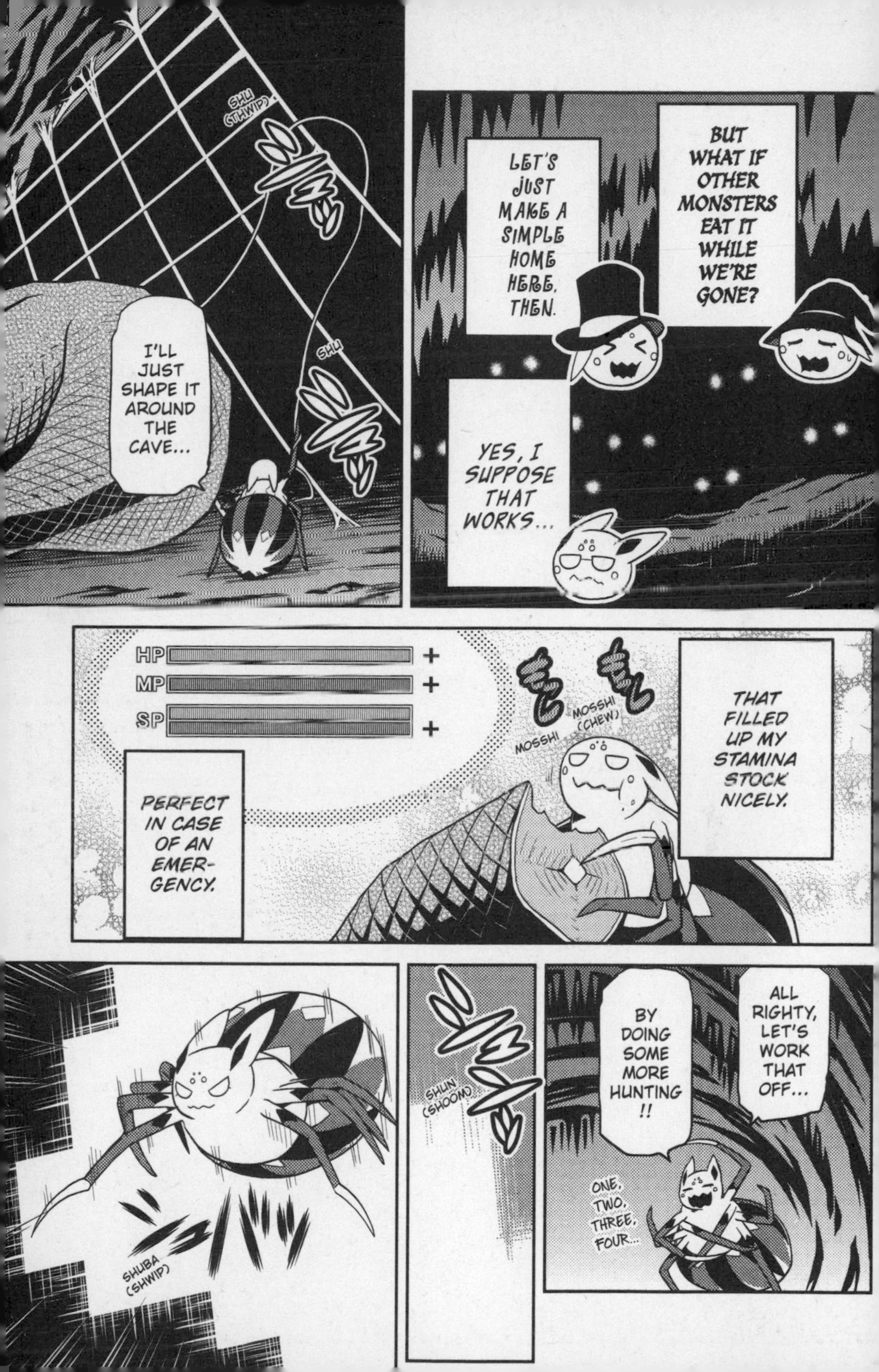
BUT WHAT IF OTHER MONSTERS EAT IT WHILE WE'RE GONE?
LET'S JUST MAKE A SIMPLE HOME HERE, THEN.
YES, I SUPPOSE THAT WORKS...
SHU (THWIP)
SHU
I'LL JUST SHAPE IT AROUND THE CAVE...
THAT FILLED UP MY STAMINA STOCK NICELY.
MOSSHI (CHEW)
MOSSHI
HP
MP
SP
PERFECT IN CASE OF AN EMERGENCY.
ALL RIGHTY, LET'S WORK THAT OFF...
BY DOING SOME MORE HUNTING!!
ONE, TWO, THREE, FOUR...
SHUN (SHOOM)
SHUBA (SHWIP)

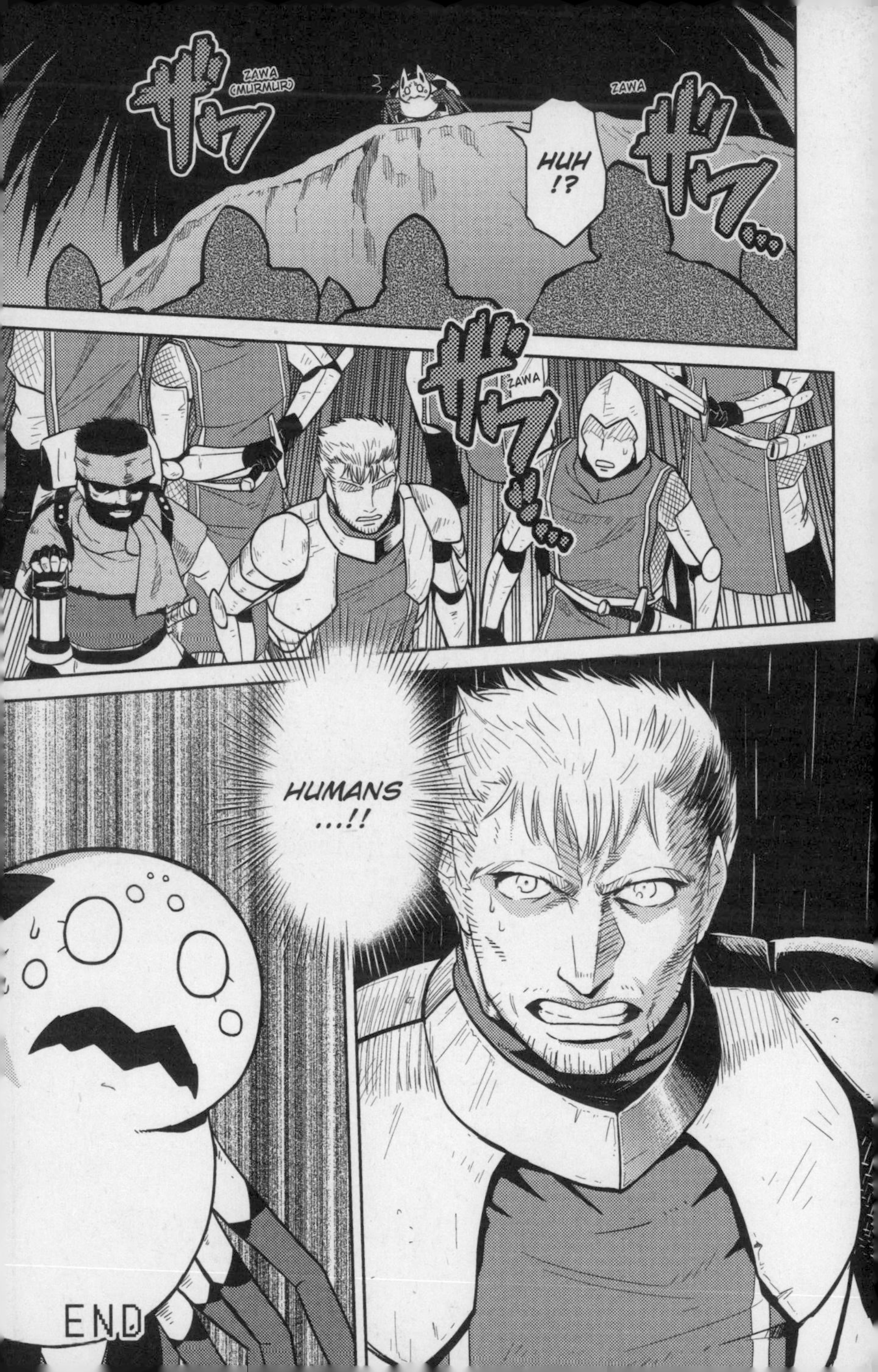
ZAWA
HUH !?
ZAWA (MURMUR)
ZAWA
HUMANS ...!!
END

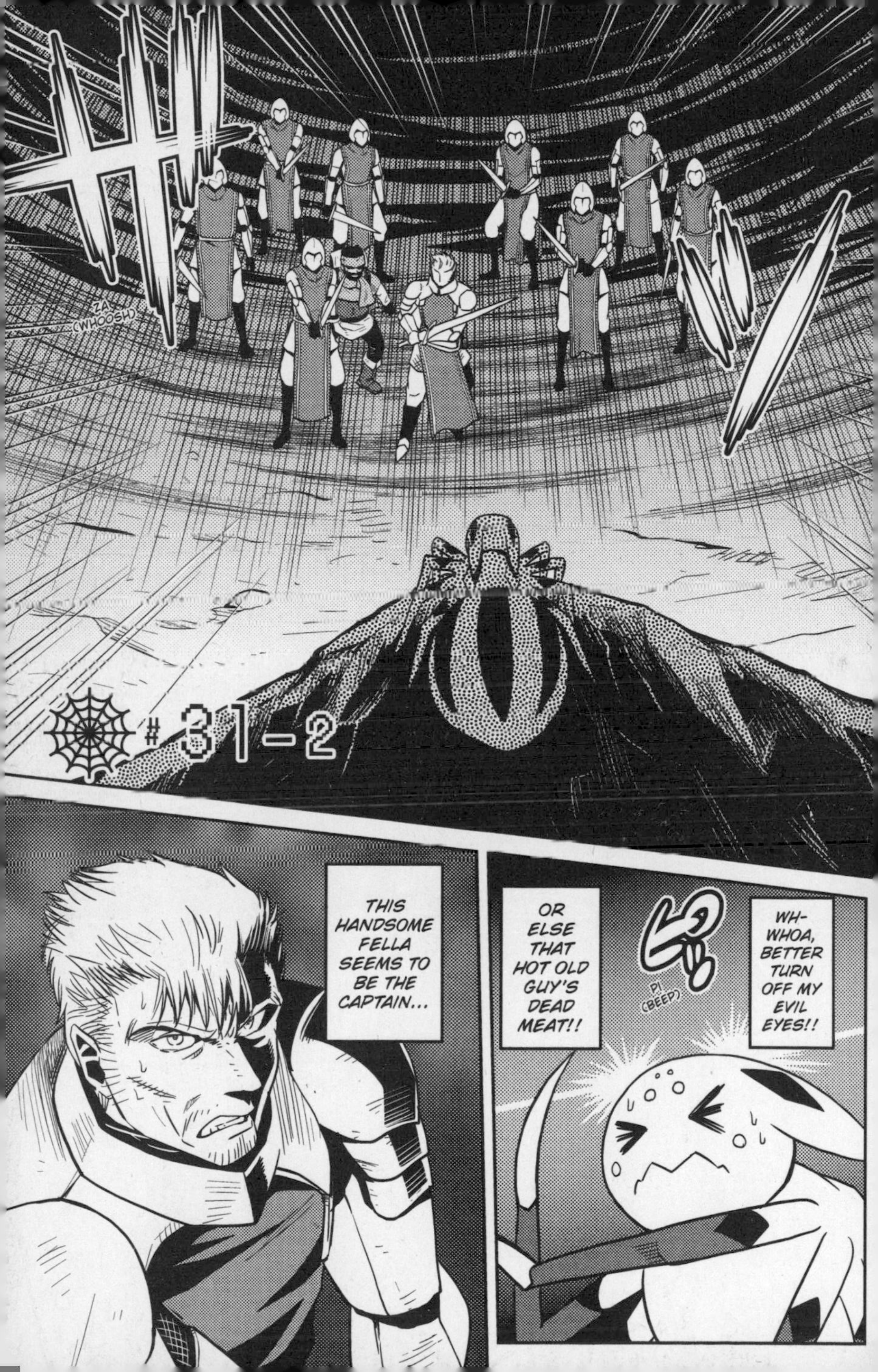
ZA (WHOOSH)
#31-2
WH-WHOA, BETTER TURN OFF MY EVIL EYES!!
PI (BEEP)
OR ELSE THAT HOT OLD GUY'S DEAD MEAT!!
THIS HANDSOME FELLA SEEMS TO BE THE CAPTAIN...

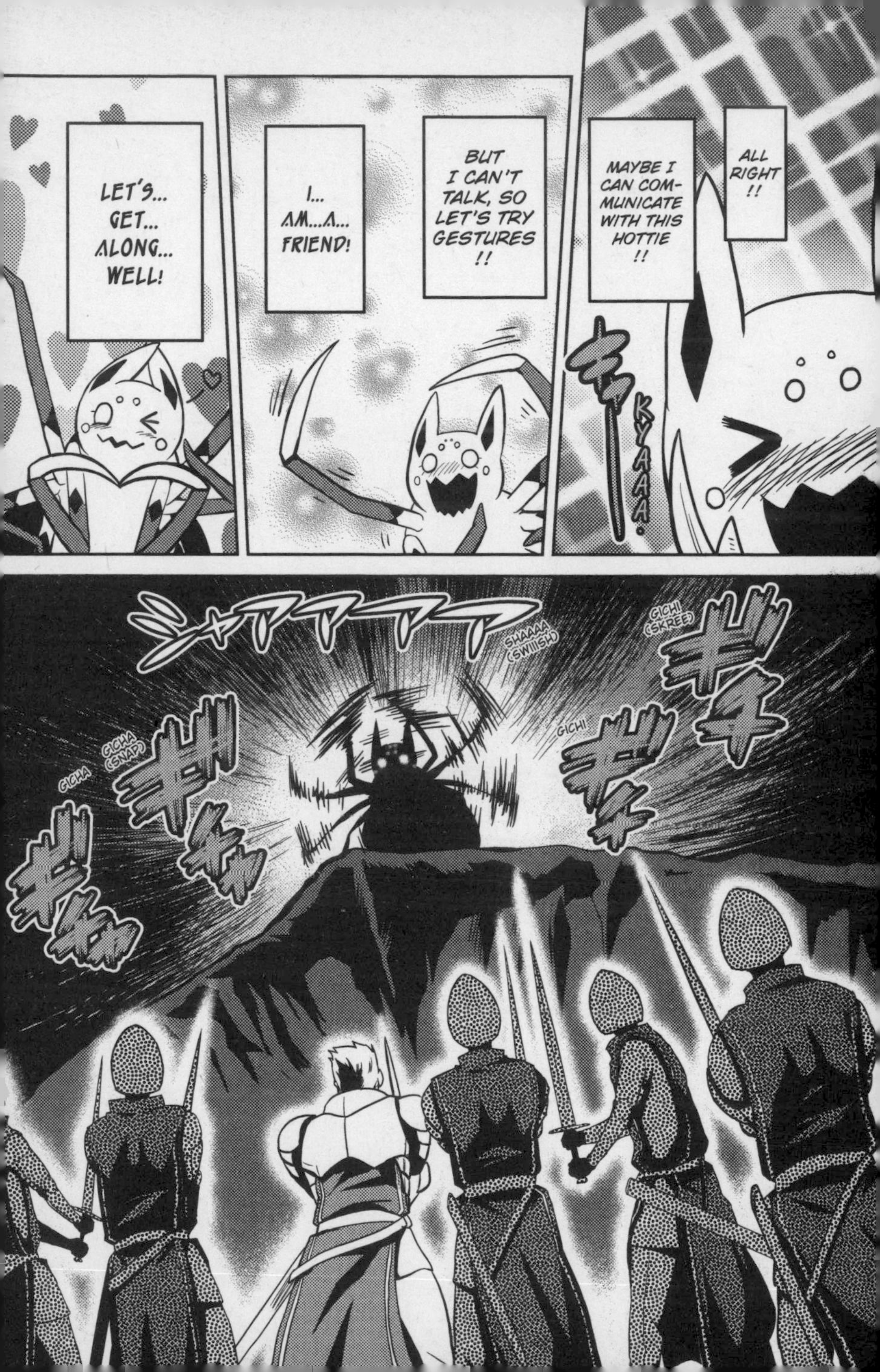
ALL RIGHT!!
MAYBE I CAN COM-MUNICATE WITH THIS HOTTIE!!
KYAAAA.
BUT I CAN'T TALK, SO LET'S TRY GESTURES!!
I... AM...A... FRIEND!
LET'S... GET... ALONG... WELL!
GICHI (SKREE)
GICHI
SHAAAA (SWIIISH)
GICHA (SNAP)
GICHA

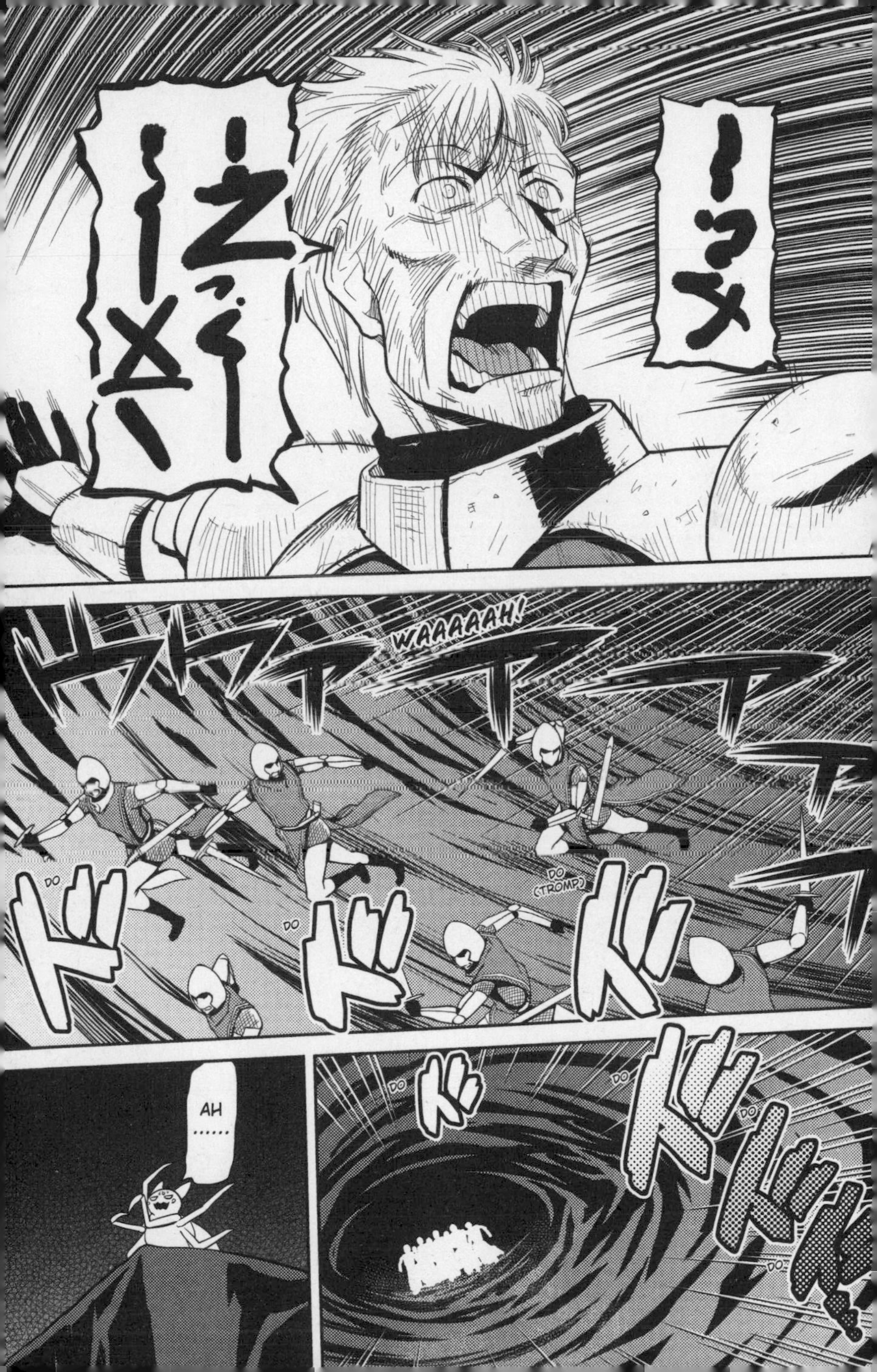
WAAAAAAH!
DO
DO
(TROMP)
DO
DO
DO
DO
AH
......

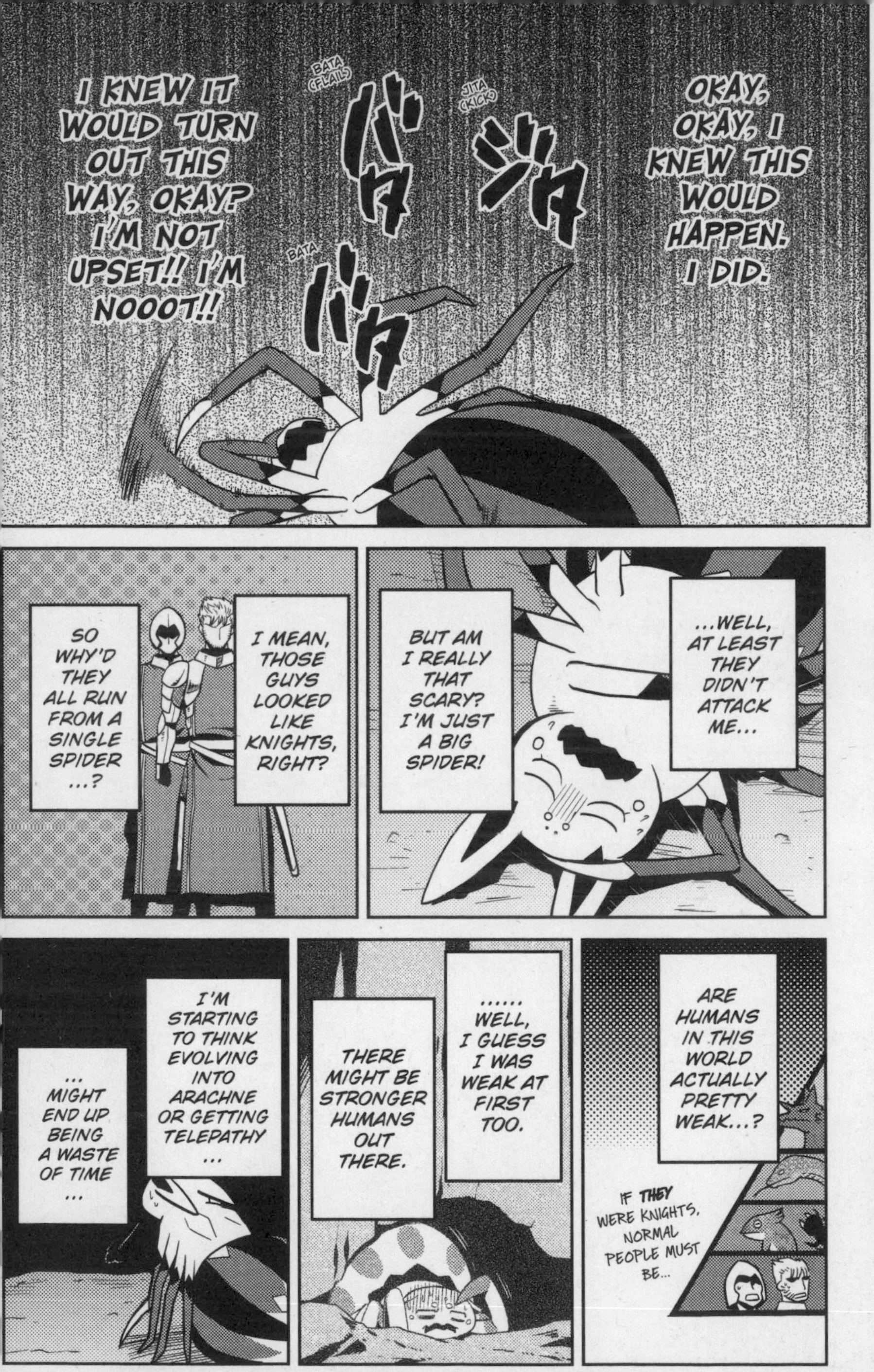
OKAY, OKAY, I KNEW THIS WOULD HAPPEN. I DID.
JITA (KICK)
BATA (FLAIL)
BATA
I KNEW IT WOULD TURN OUT THIS WAY, OKAY? I'M NOT UPSET!! I'M NOOOT!!
...WELL, AT LEAST THEY DIDN'T ATTACK ME...
BUT AM I REALLY THAT SCARY? I'M JUST A BIG SPIDER!
I MEAN, THOSE GUYS LOOKED LIKE KNIGHTS, RIGHT?
SO WHY'D THEY ALL RUN FROM A SINGLE SPIDER ...?
ARE HUMANS IN THIS WORLD ACTUALLY PRETTY WEAK...?
IF THEY WERE KNIGHTS, NORMAL PEOPLE MUST BE...
...... WELL, I GUESS I WAS WEAK AT FIRST TOO.
THERE MIGHT BE STRONGER HUMANS OUT THERE.
I'M STARTING TO THINK EVOLVING INTO ARACHNE OR GETTING TELEPATHY ...
... MIGHT END UP BEING A WASTE OF TIME ...

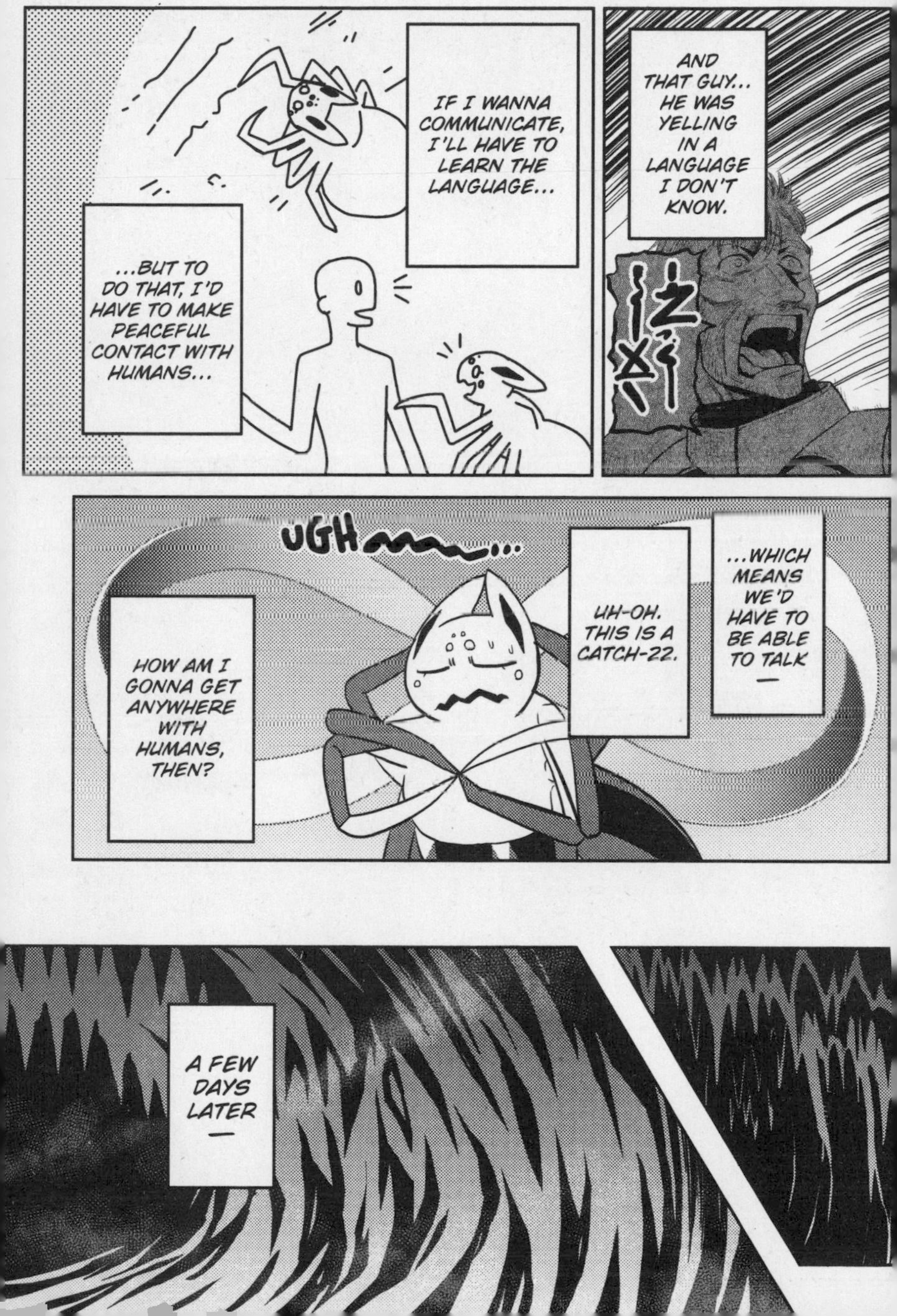
AND THAT GUY... HE WAS YELLING IN A LANGUAGE I DON'T KNOW.
IF I WANNA COMMUNICATE, I'LL HAVE TO LEARN THE LANGUAGE...
...BUT TO DO THAT, I'D HAVE TO MAKE PEACEFUL CONTACT WITH HUMANS...
...WHICH MEANS WE'D HAVE TO BE ABLE TO TALK —
UH-OH. THIS IS A CATCH-22.
UGH...
HOW AM I GONNA GET ANYWHERE WITH HUMANS, THEN?
A FEW DAYS LATER —

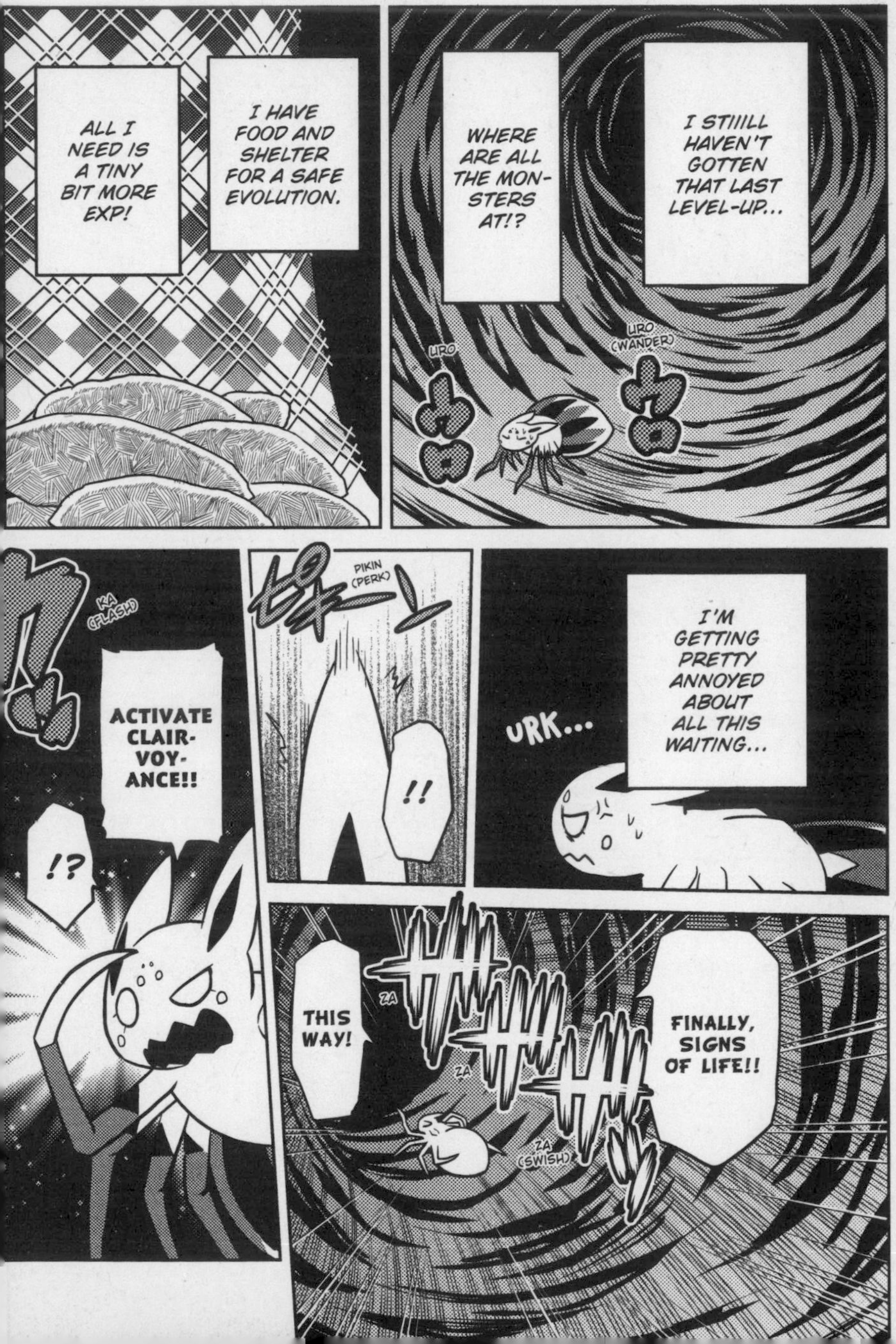
I STIIILL HAVEN'T GOTTEN THAT LAST LEVEL-UP...
WHERE ARE ALL THE MON-STERS AT!?
URO (WANDER)
URO
I HAVE FOOD AND SHELTER FOR A SAFE EVOLUTION.
ALL I NEED IS A TINY BIT MORE EXP!
I'M GETTING PRETTY ANNOYED ABOUT ALL THIS WAITING...
URK...
PIKIN (PERK)
!!
FINALLY, SIGNS OF LIFE!!
ZA
ZA
ZA (SWISH)
THIS WAY!
KA (FLASH)
ACTIVATE CLAIR-VOY-ANCE!!
!?

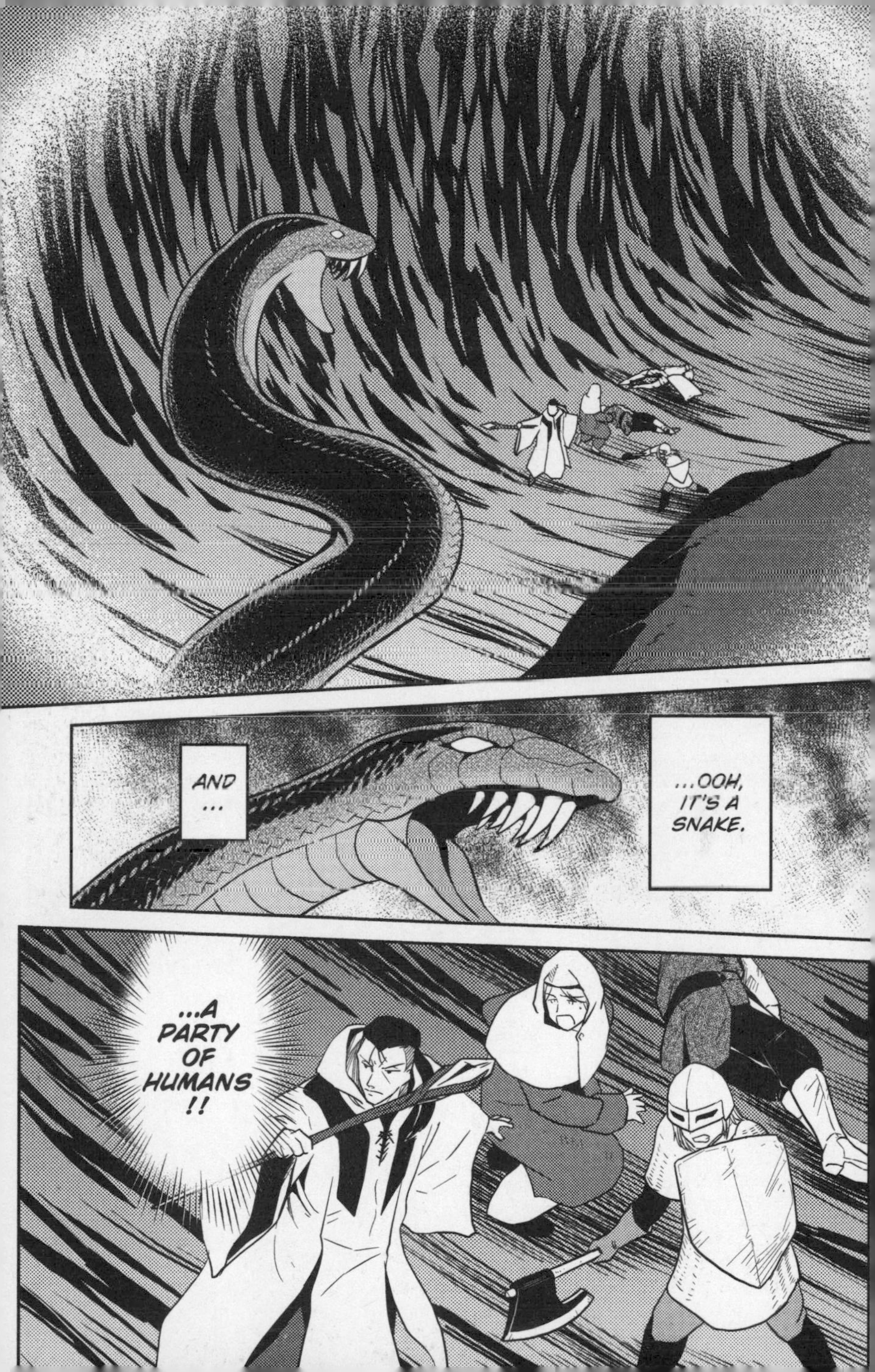
...OOH, IT'S A SNAKE.
AND ...
...A PARTY OF HUMANS!!

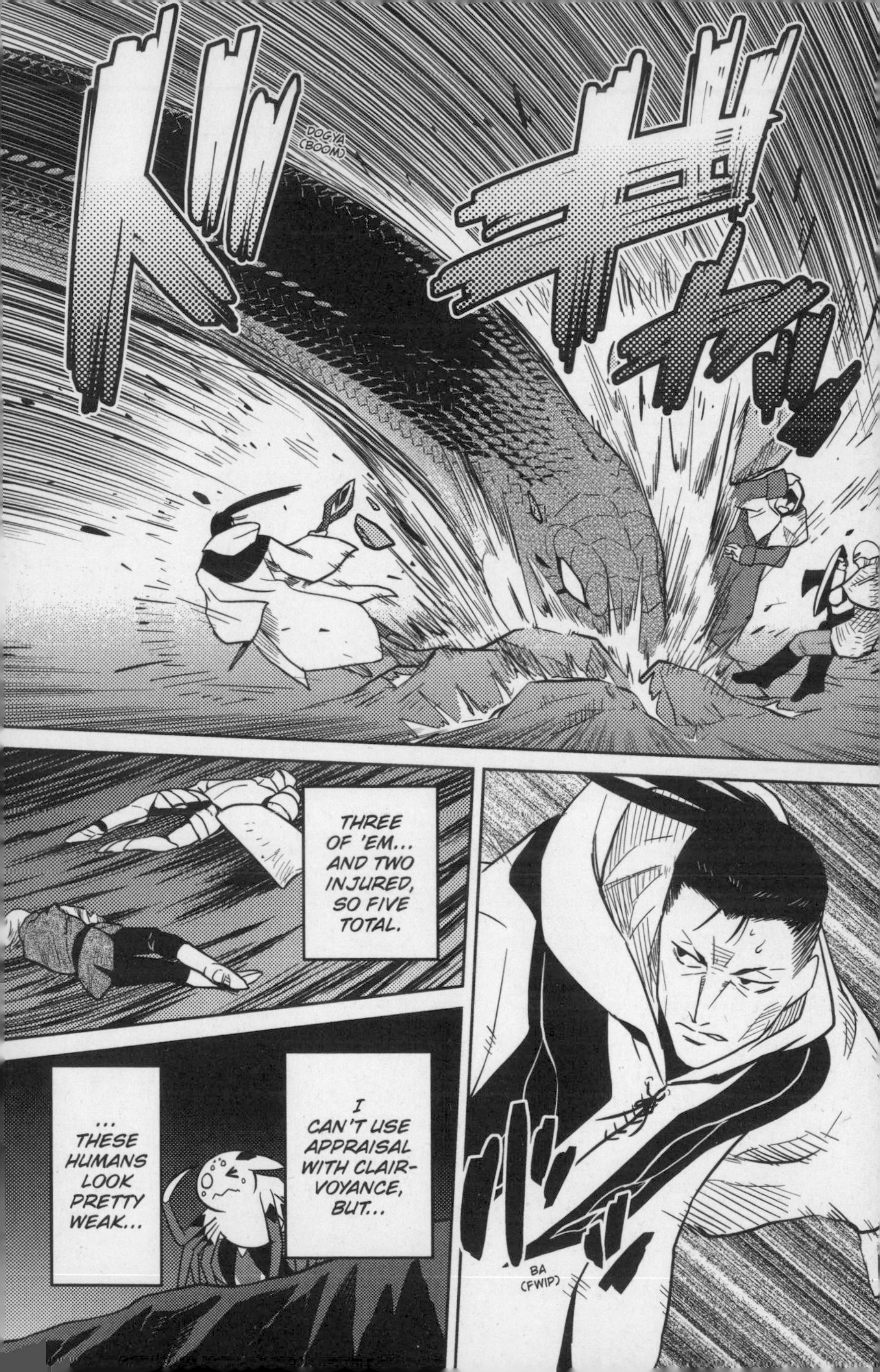
DOGYA (BOOM)
BA (FWIP)
THREE OF 'EM... AND TWO INJURED, SO FIVE TOTAL.
I CAN'T USE APPRAISAL WITH CLAIR-VOYANCE, BUT...
... THESE HUMANS LOOK PRETTY WEAK...

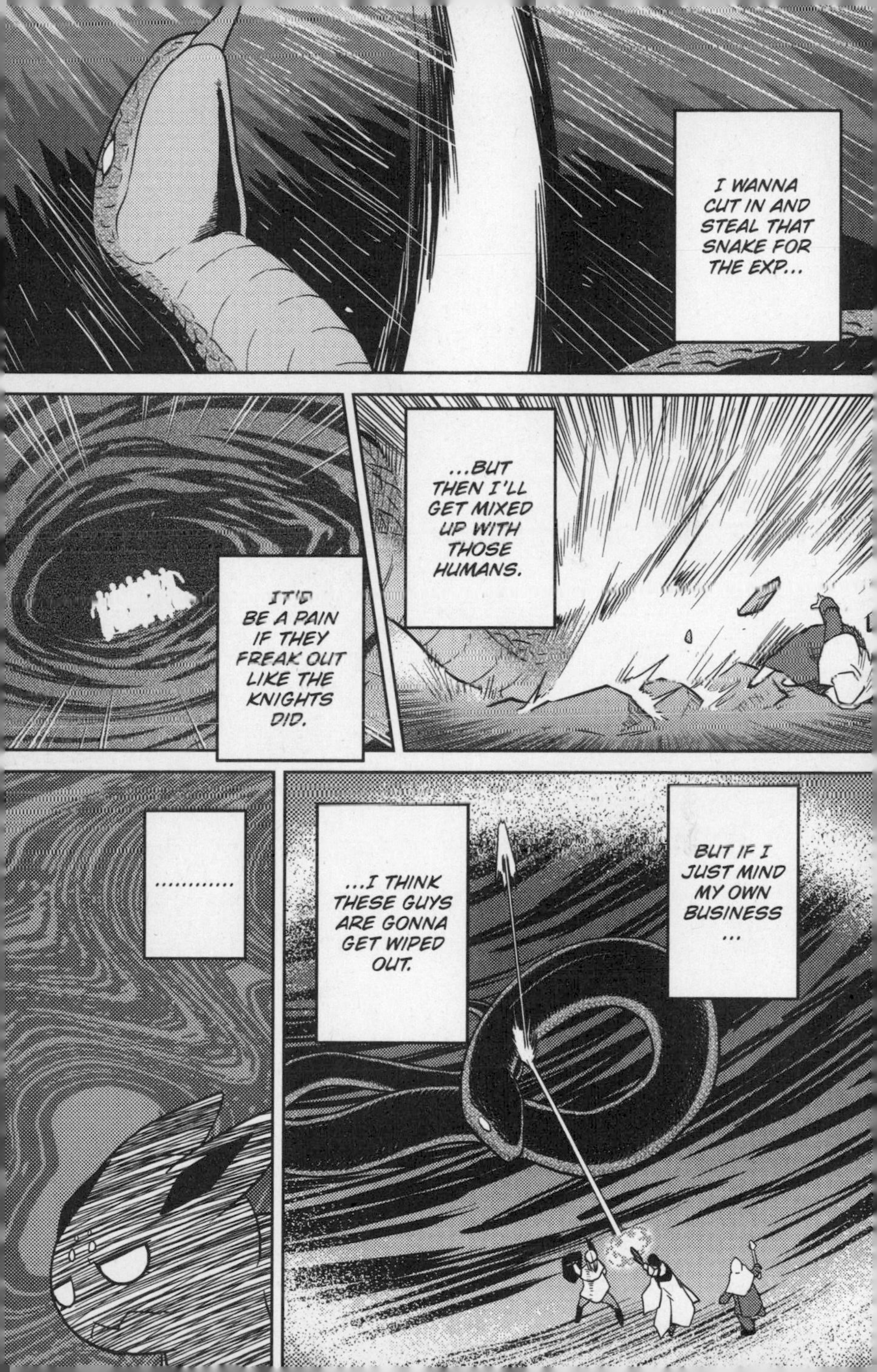
I WANNA CUT IN AND STEAL THAT SNAKE FOR THE EXP...
...BUT THEN I'LL GET MIXED UP WITH THOSE HUMANS.
IT'D BE A PAIN IF THEY FREAK OUT LIKE THE KNIGHTS DID.
BUT IF I JUST MIND MY OWN BUSINESS ...
...I THINK THESE GUYS ARE GONNA GET WIPED OUT.
....

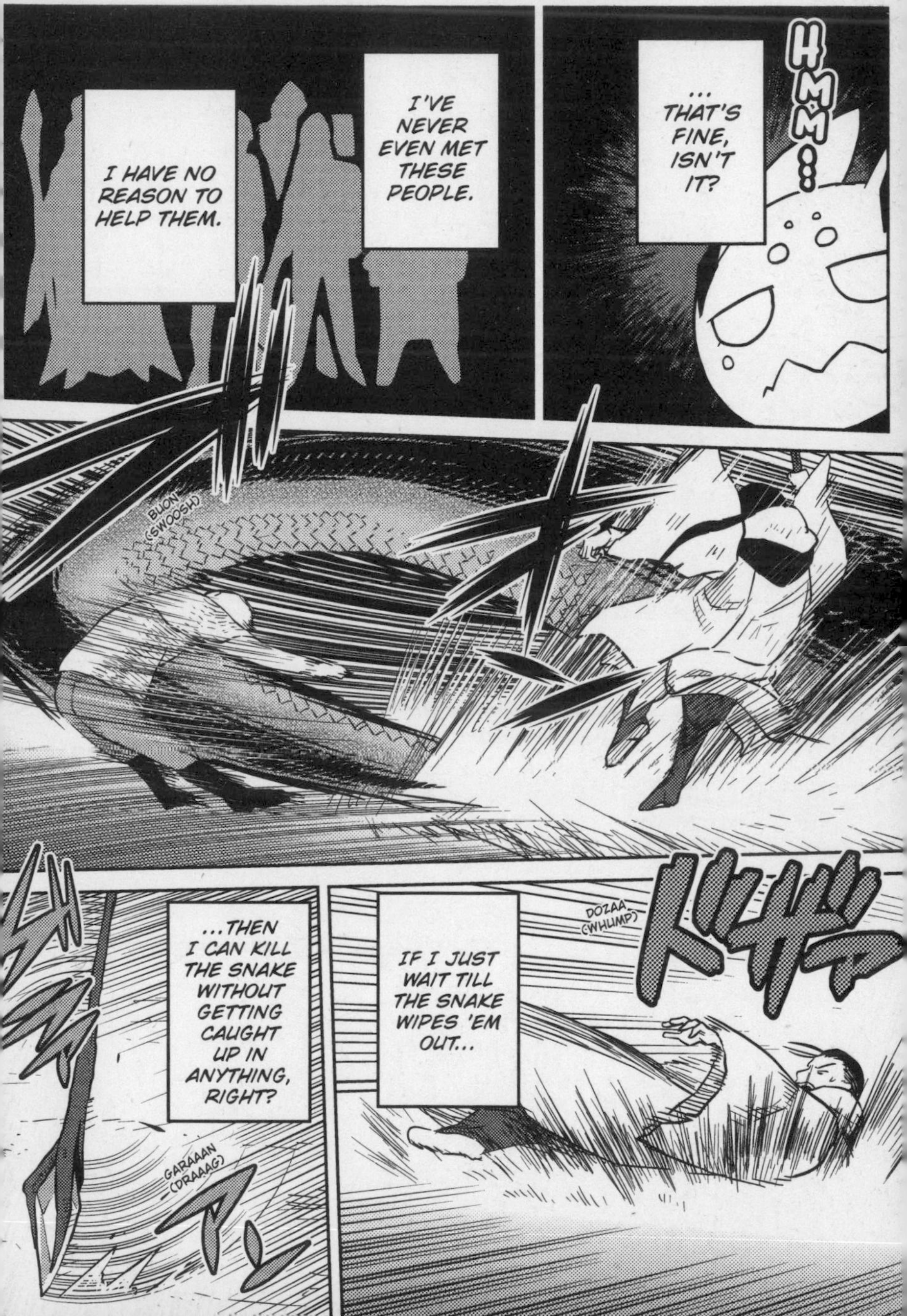
HMM...
...THAT'S FINE, ISN'T IT?
I'VE NEVER EVEN MET THESE PEOPLE.
I HAVE NO REASON TO HELP THEM.
BUON (SWOOSH)
DOZAA (WHUMP)
IF I JUST WAIT TILL THE SNAKE WIPES 'EM OUT...
...THEN I CAN KILL THE SNAKE WITHOUT GETTING CAUGHT UP IN ANYTHING, RIGHT?
GARAAAN (DRAAAG)

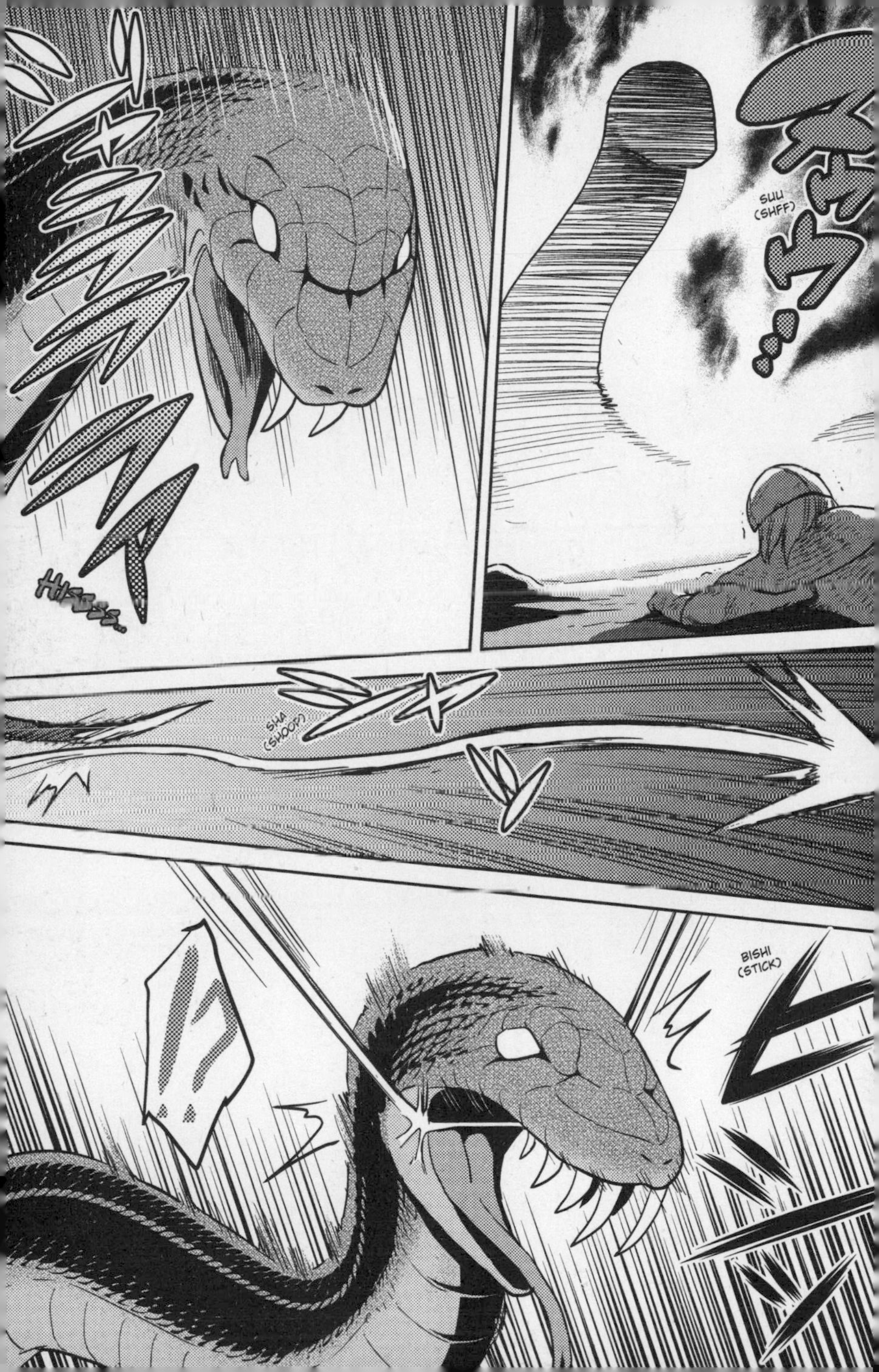
SUU
(SHFF)
HISSSS...
SHA
(SHOOP)
BISHI
(STICK)

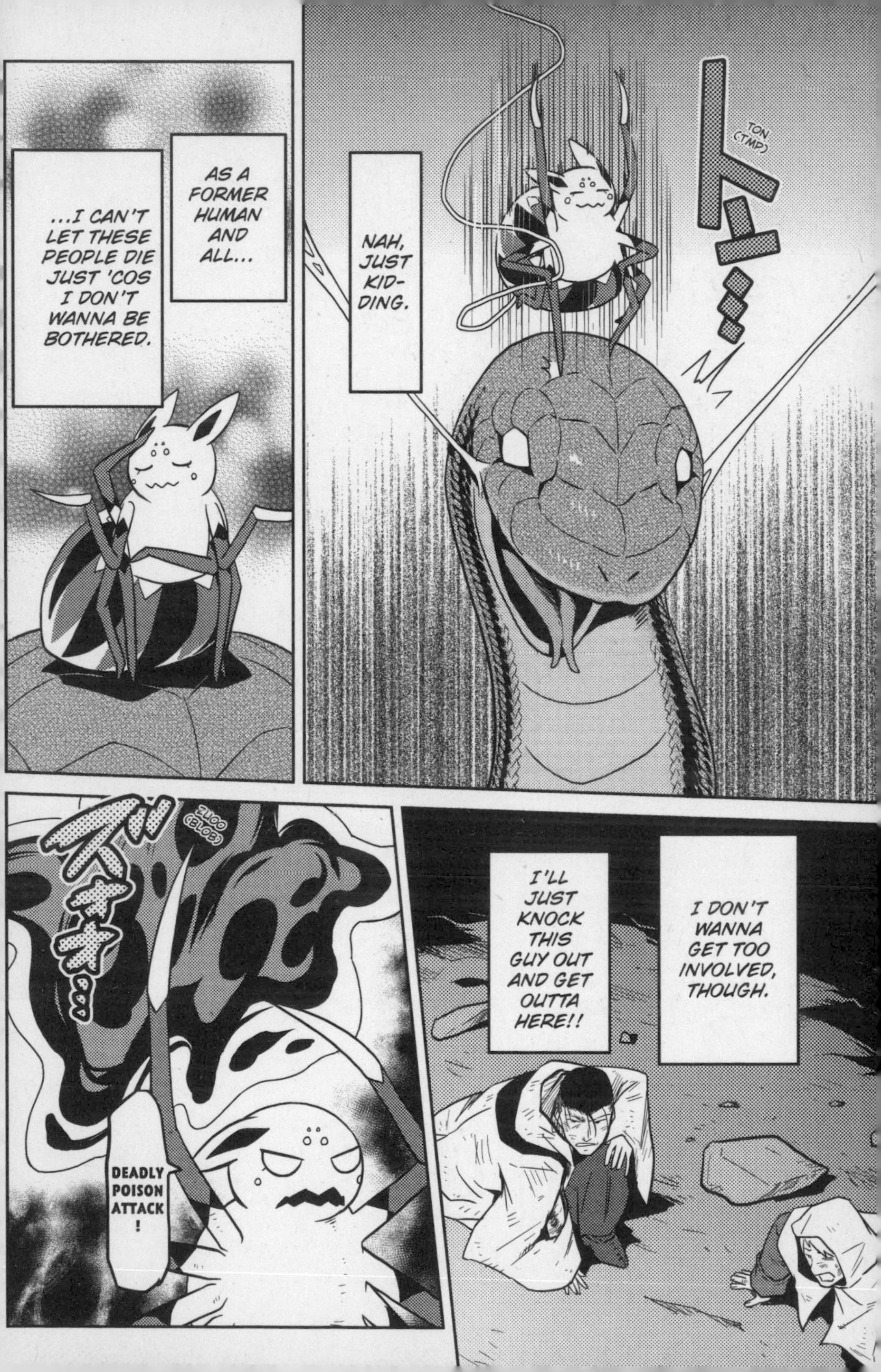
AS A FORMER HUMAN AND ALL...
...I CAN'T LET THESE PEOPLE DIE JUST 'COS I DON'T WANNA BE BOTHERED.
TON (TMP)
NAH, JUST KID-DING.
I DON'T WANNA GET TOO INVOLVED, THOUGH.
I'LL JUST KNOCK THIS GUY OUT AND GET OUTTA HERE!!
OOZ (BLOB)
DEADLY POISON ATTACK!

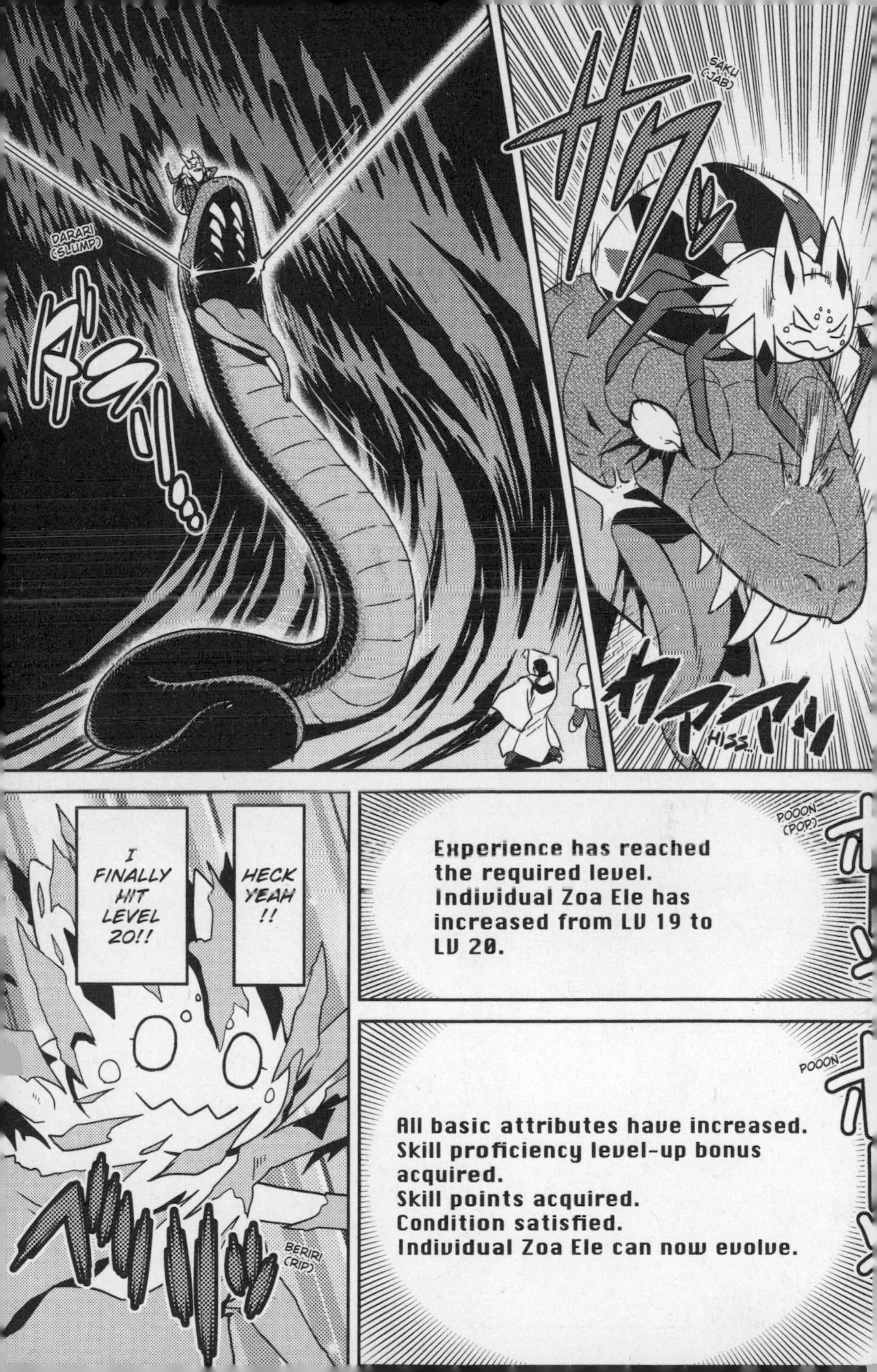
SAKU (JAB)
HISS
DARARI (SLUMP)
POOON (POP)
Experience has reached the required level. Individual Zoa Ele has increased from LV 19 to LV 20.
POOON
All basic attributes have increased.
Skill proficiency level-up bonus acquired.
Skill points acquired.
Condition satisfied.
Individual Zoa Ele can now evolve.
HECK YEAH!!
I FINALLY HIT LEVEL 20!!
BERIRI (RIP)

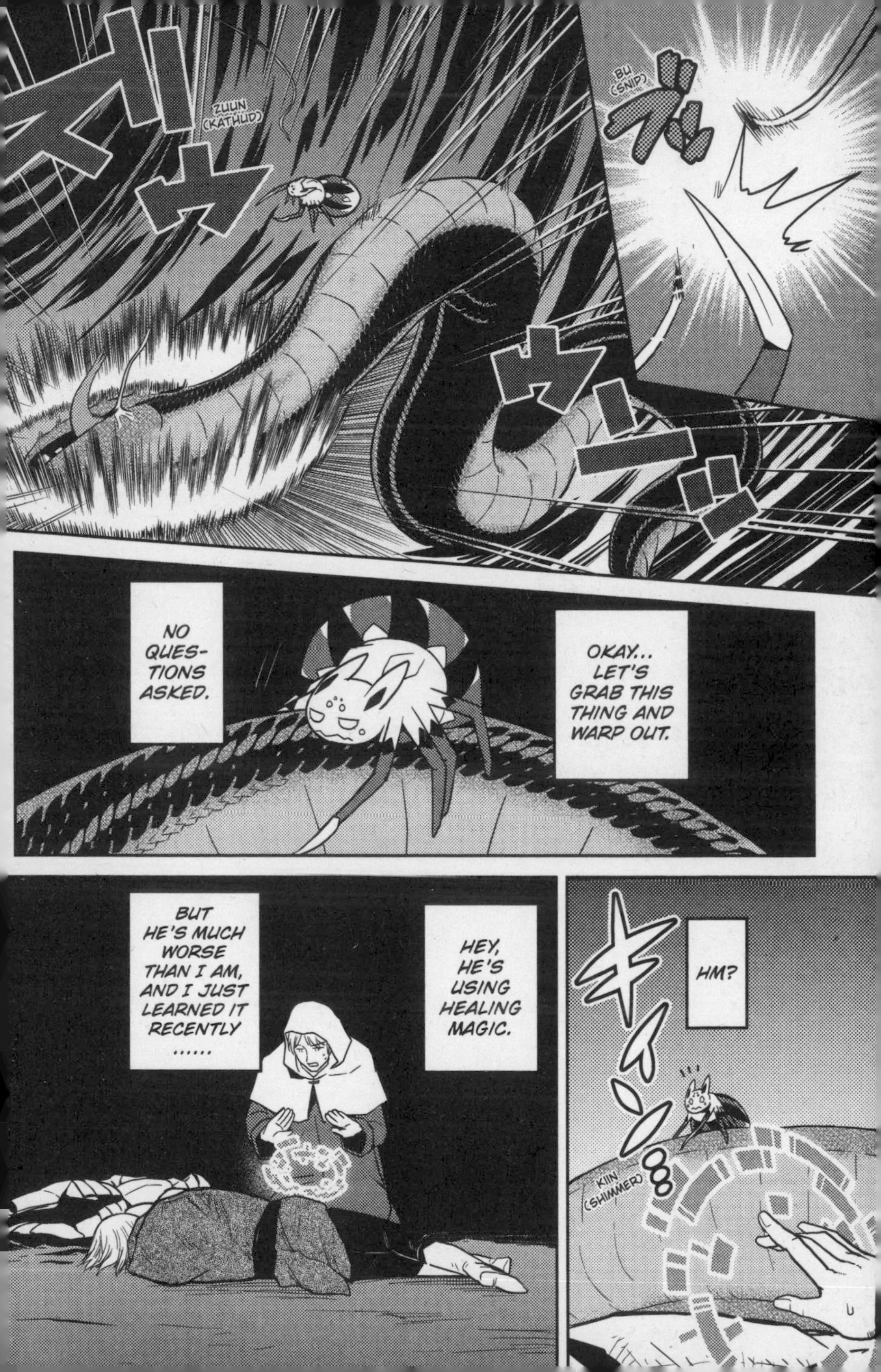
BU (SNIP)
ZUUN (KATHUD)
OKAY... LET'S GRAB THIS THING AND WARP OUT.
NO QUES-TIONS ASKED.
HM?
KIIN (SHIMMER)
HEY, HE'S USING HEALING MAGIC.
BUT HE'S MUCH WORSE THAN I AM, AND I JUST LEARNED IT RECENTLY ......

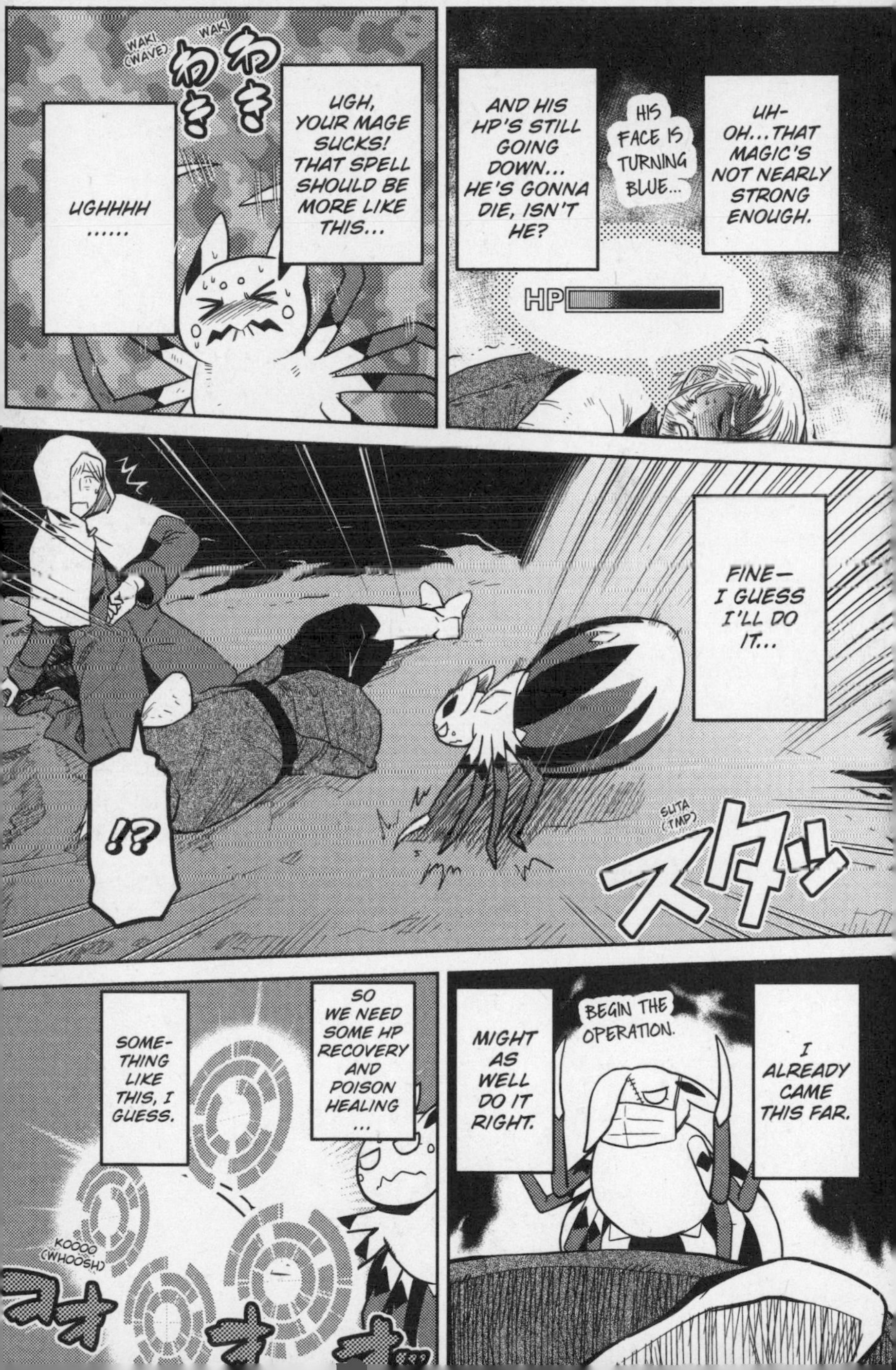
UH-OH...THAT MAGIC'S NOT NEARLY STRONG ENOUGH.
HIS FACE IS TURNING BLUE...
AND HIS HP'S STILL GOING DOWN... HE'S GONNA DIE, ISN'T HE?
HP
わきわき
WAKI WAKI (WAVE)
UGH, YOUR MAGE SUCKS! THAT SPELL SHOULD BE MORE LIKE THIS...
UGHHHH ......
FINE— I GUESS I'LL DO IT...
スタッ
SUTA (TMP)
!?
I ALREADY CAME THIS FAR.
BEGIN THE OPERATION.
MIGHT AS WELL DO IT RIGHT.
SO WE NEED SOME HP RECOVERY AND POISON HEALING...
SOMETHING LIKE THIS, I GUESS.
コオオオ
KOOOO (WHOOSH)

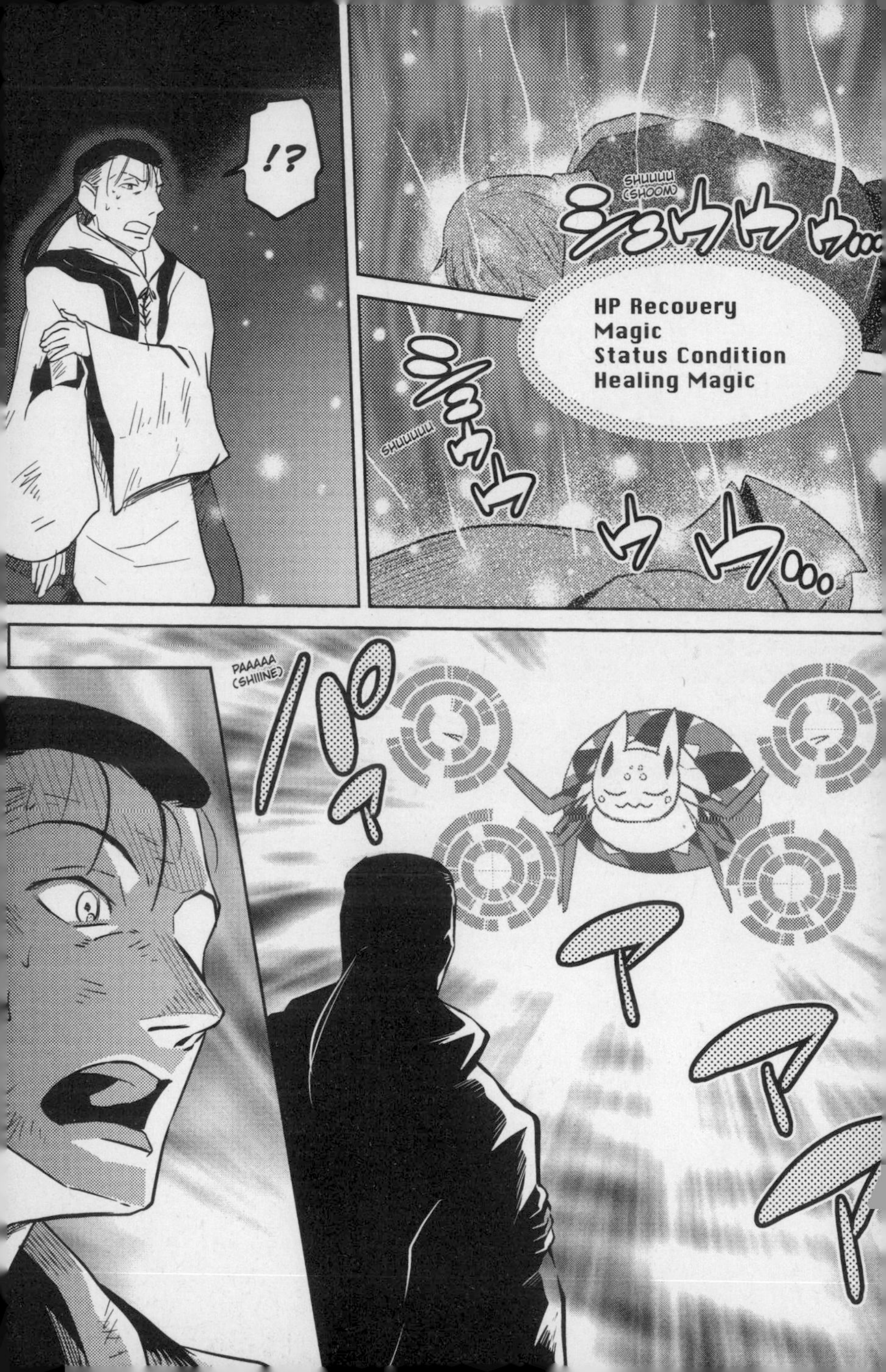
SHUUUU (SHOOM)
HP Recovery Magic
Status Condition Healing Magic
SHUUUUU
!?
PAAAAA (SHIIINE)

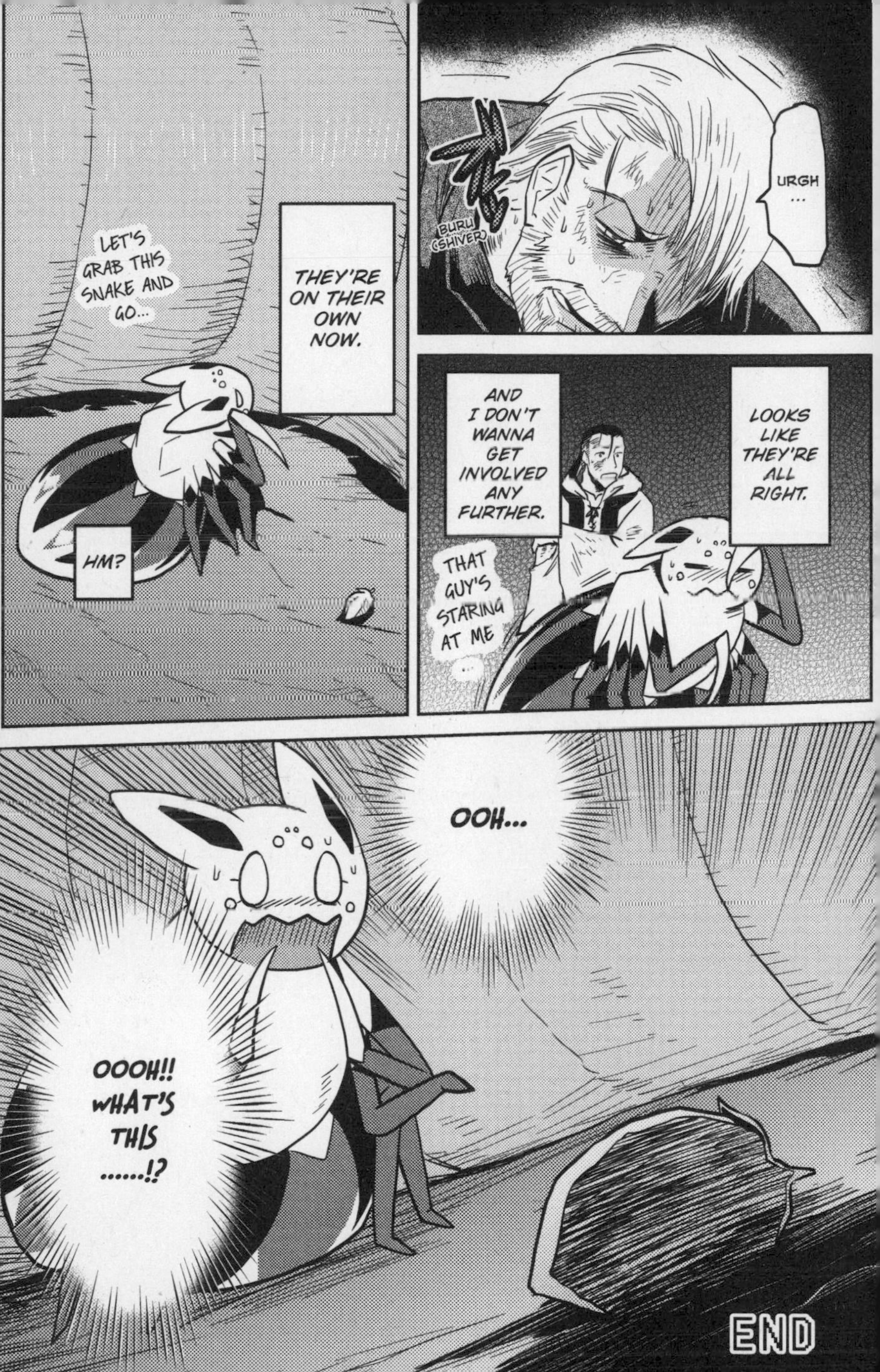
BURU (SHIVER)
URGH ...
LOOKS LIKE THEY'RE ALL RIGHT.
AND I DON'T WANNA GET INVOLVED ANY FURTHER.
THAT GUY'S STARING AT ME
...
THEY'RE ON THEIR OWN NOW.
LET'S GRAB THIS SNAKE AND GO...
HM?
OOH...
OOOH!! WHAT'S THIS ......!?
END

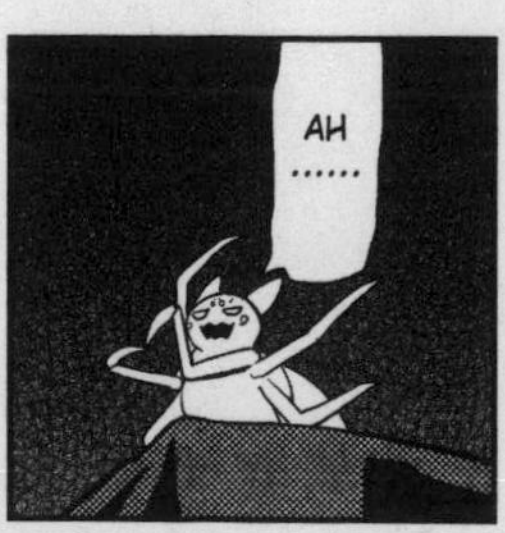
AH
......

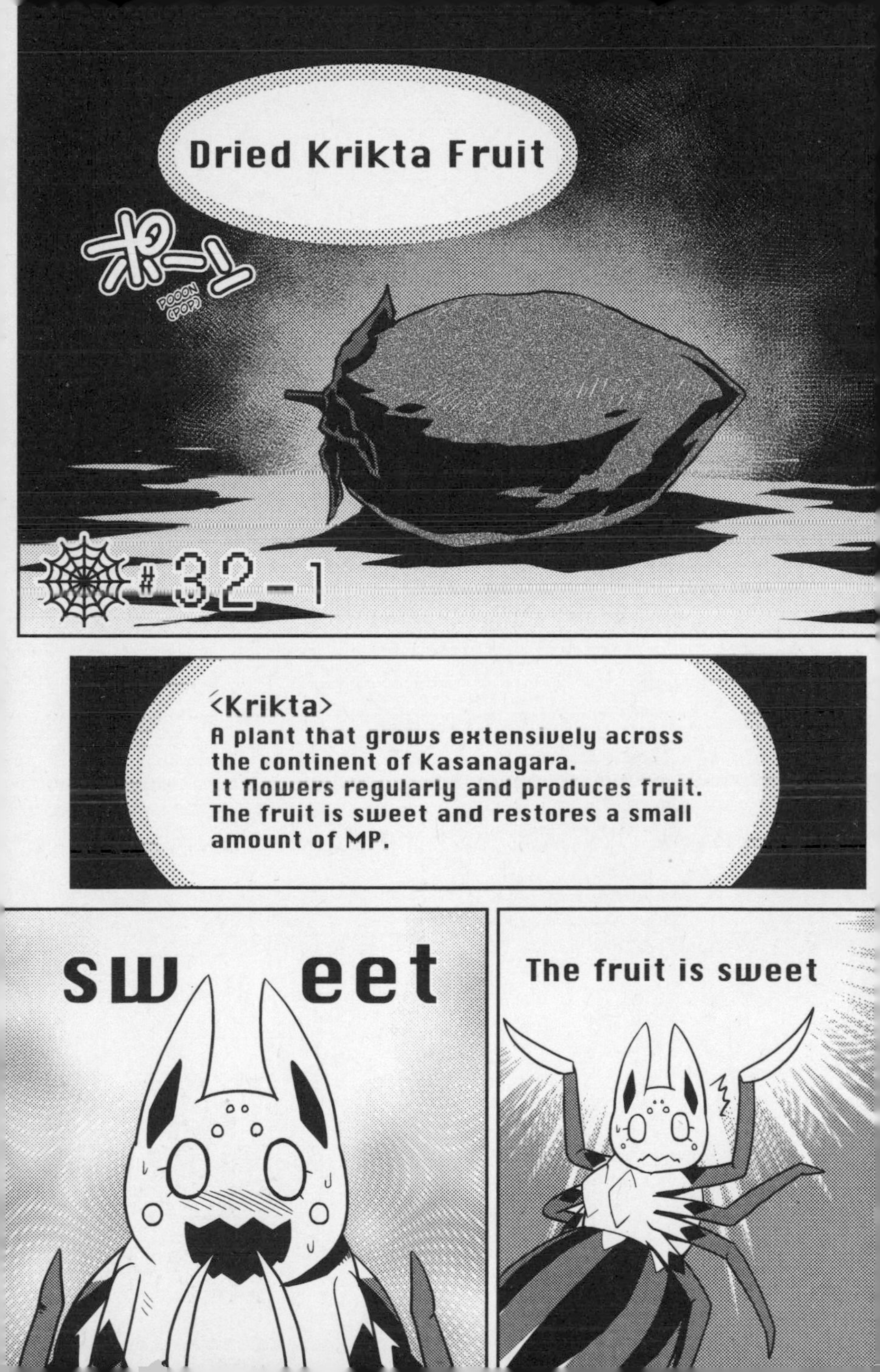
Dried Krikta Fruit
ポーン
POOON (POP)
#32-1
<Krikta>
A plant that grows extensively across the continent of Kasanagara.
It flowers regularly and produces fruit.
The fruit is sweet and restores a small amount of MP.
The fruit is sweet
sw eet

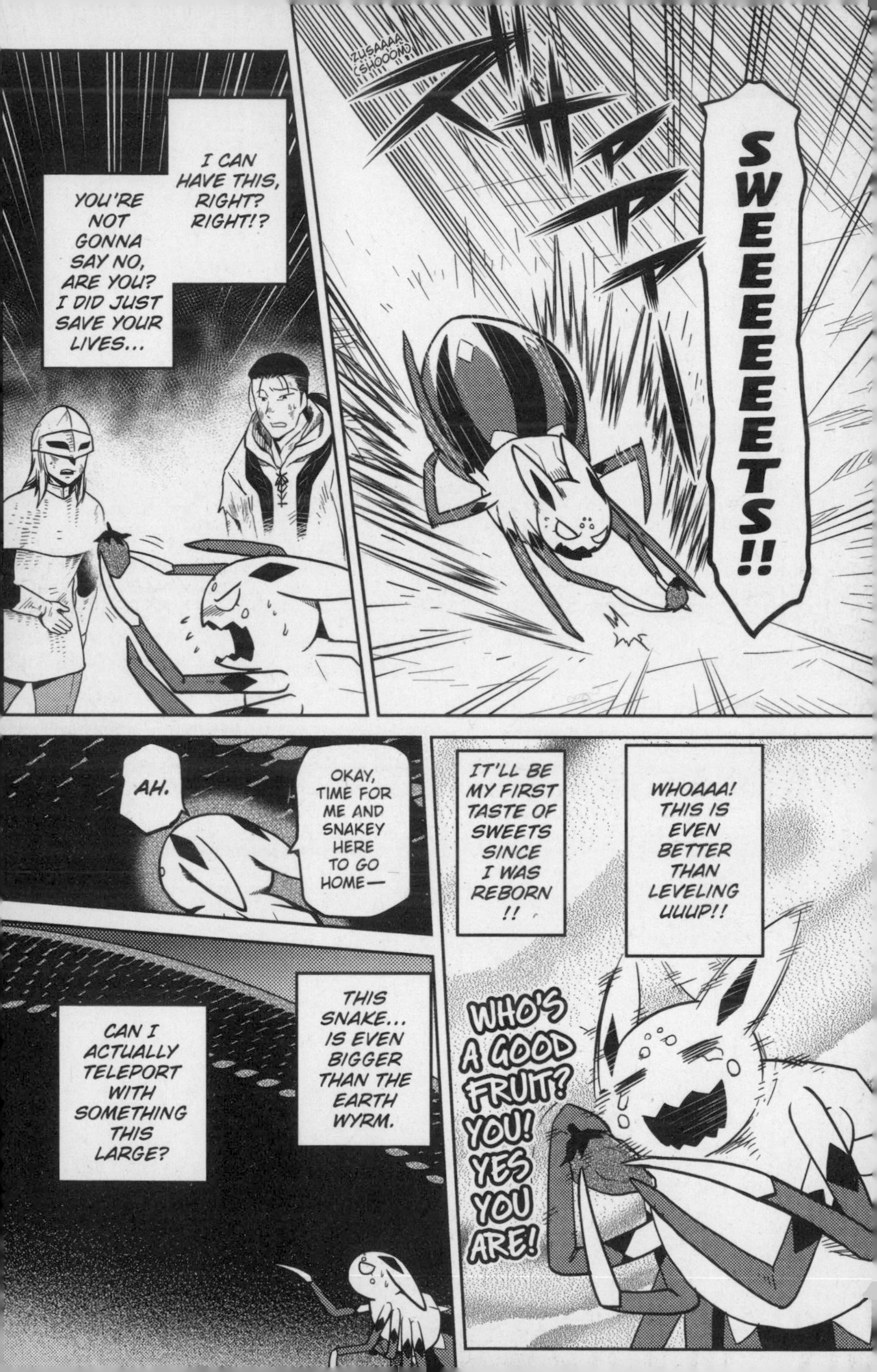
ZUSAAAA (SHOOOM)
SWEEEEEETS!!
I CAN HAVE THIS, RIGHT? RIGHT!?
YOU'RE NOT GONNA SAY NO, ARE YOU? I DID JUST SAVE YOUR LIVES...
WHOAAA! THIS IS EVEN BETTER THAN LEVELING UUUP!!
IT'LL BE MY FIRST TASTE OF SWEETS SINCE I WAS REBORN!!
WHO'S A GOOD FRUIT? YOU! YES YOU ARE!
OKAY, TIME FOR ME AND SNAKEY HERE TO GO HOME—
AH.
THIS SNAKE... IS EVEN BIGGER THAN THE EARTH WYRM.
CAN I ACTUALLY TELEPORT WITH SOMETHING THIS LARGE?

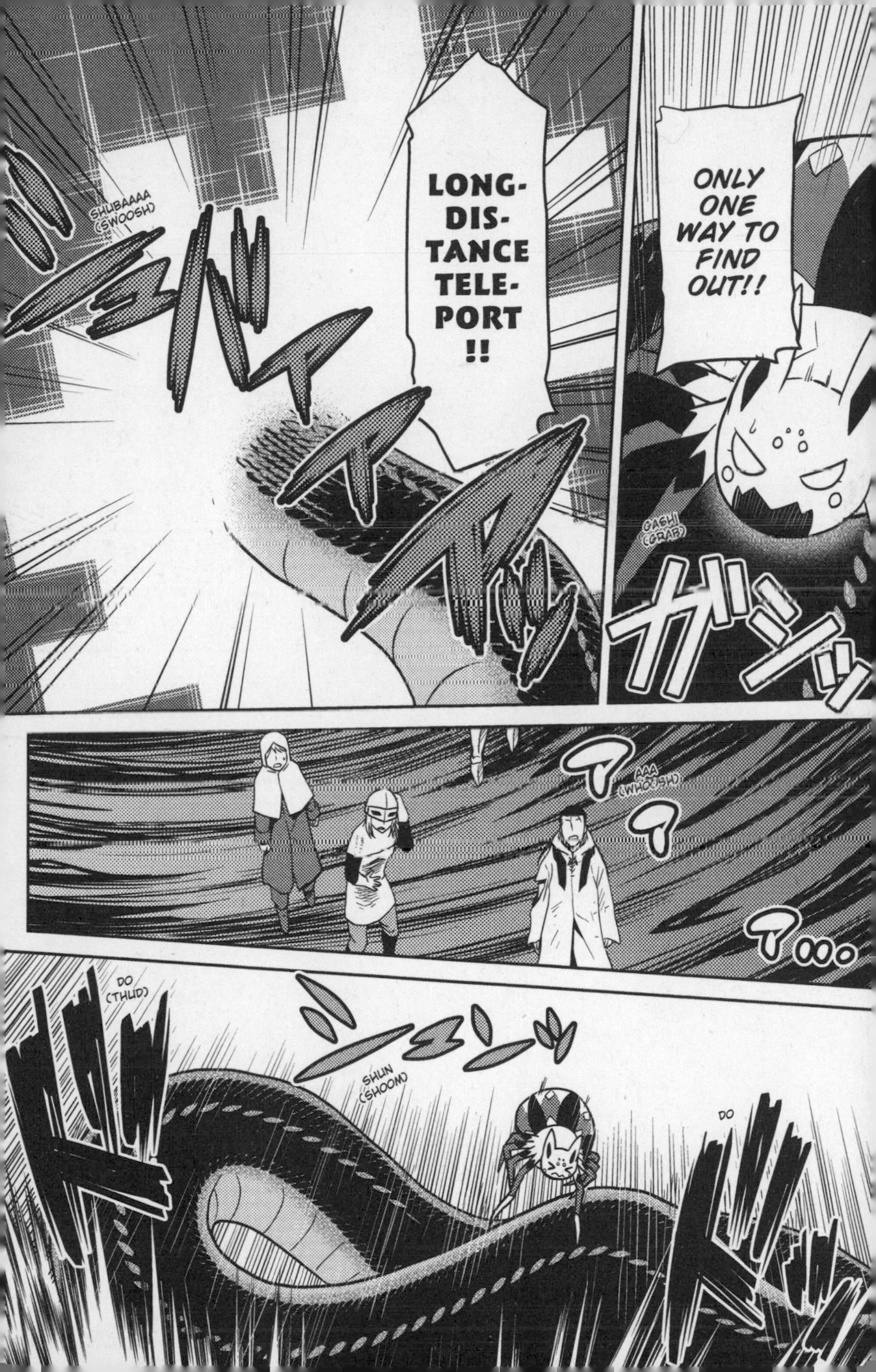
ONLY ONE WAY TO FIND OUT!!
GASHI (GRAB)
LONG-DISTANCE TELEPORT!!
SHUBAAAA (SWOOSH)
AAA (WHOOSH)
DO
SHUN (SHOOM)
DO (THUD)

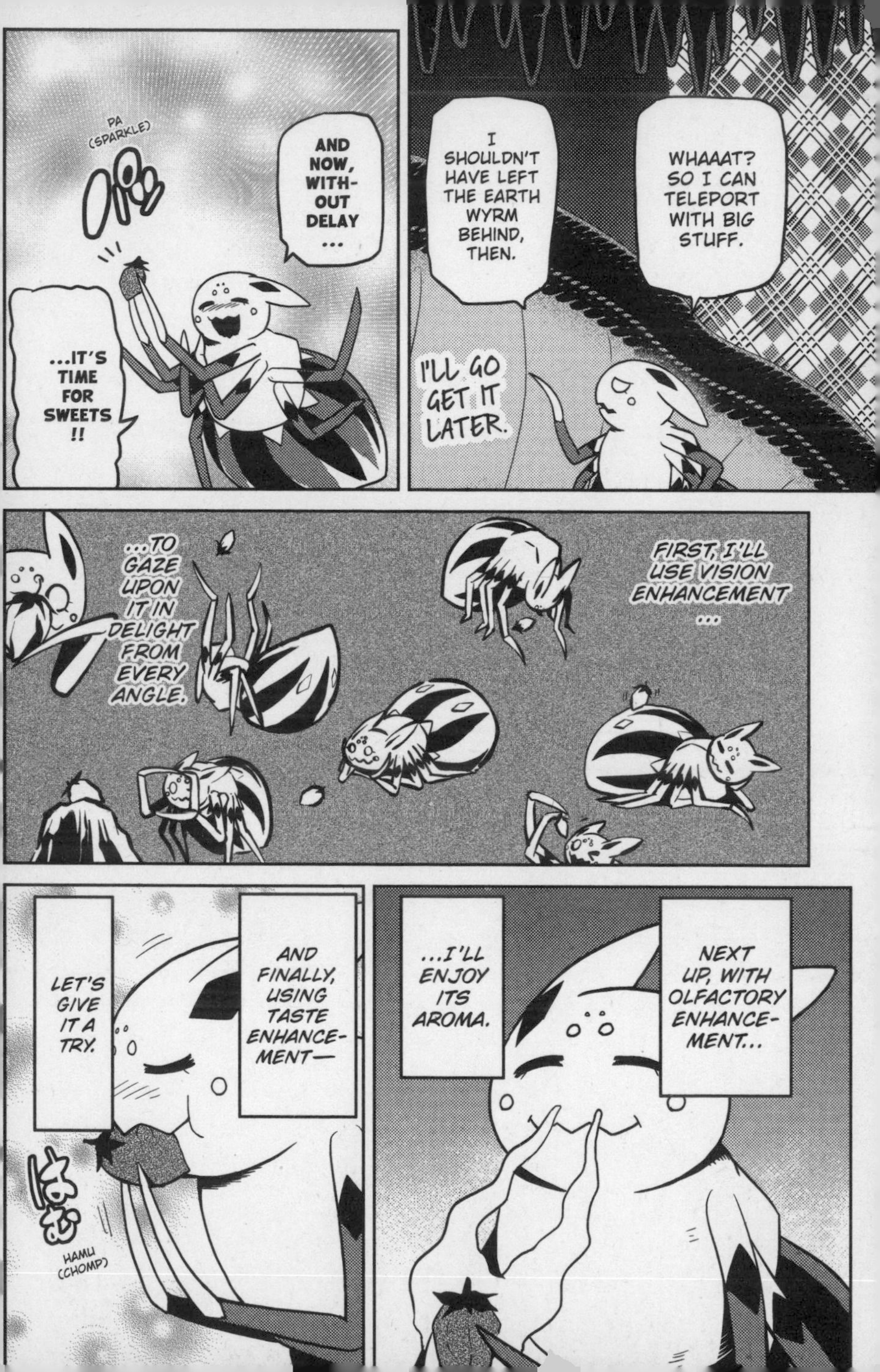
WHAAAT? SO I CAN TELEPORT WITH BIG STUFF.
I SHOULDN'T HAVE LEFT THE EARTH WYRM BEHIND, THEN.
I'LL GO GET IT LATER.
AND NOW, WITHOUT DELAY...
PA (SPARKLE)
...IT'S TIME FOR SWEETS!!
FIRST, I'LL USE VISION ENHANCEMENT...
...TO GAZE UPON IT IN DELIGHT FROM EVERY ANGLE.
NEXT UP, WITH OLFACTORY ENHANCEMENT...
...I'LL ENJOY ITS AROMA.
AND FINALLY, USING TASTE ENHANCEMENT—
LET'S GIVE IT A TRY.
HAMU (CHOMP)

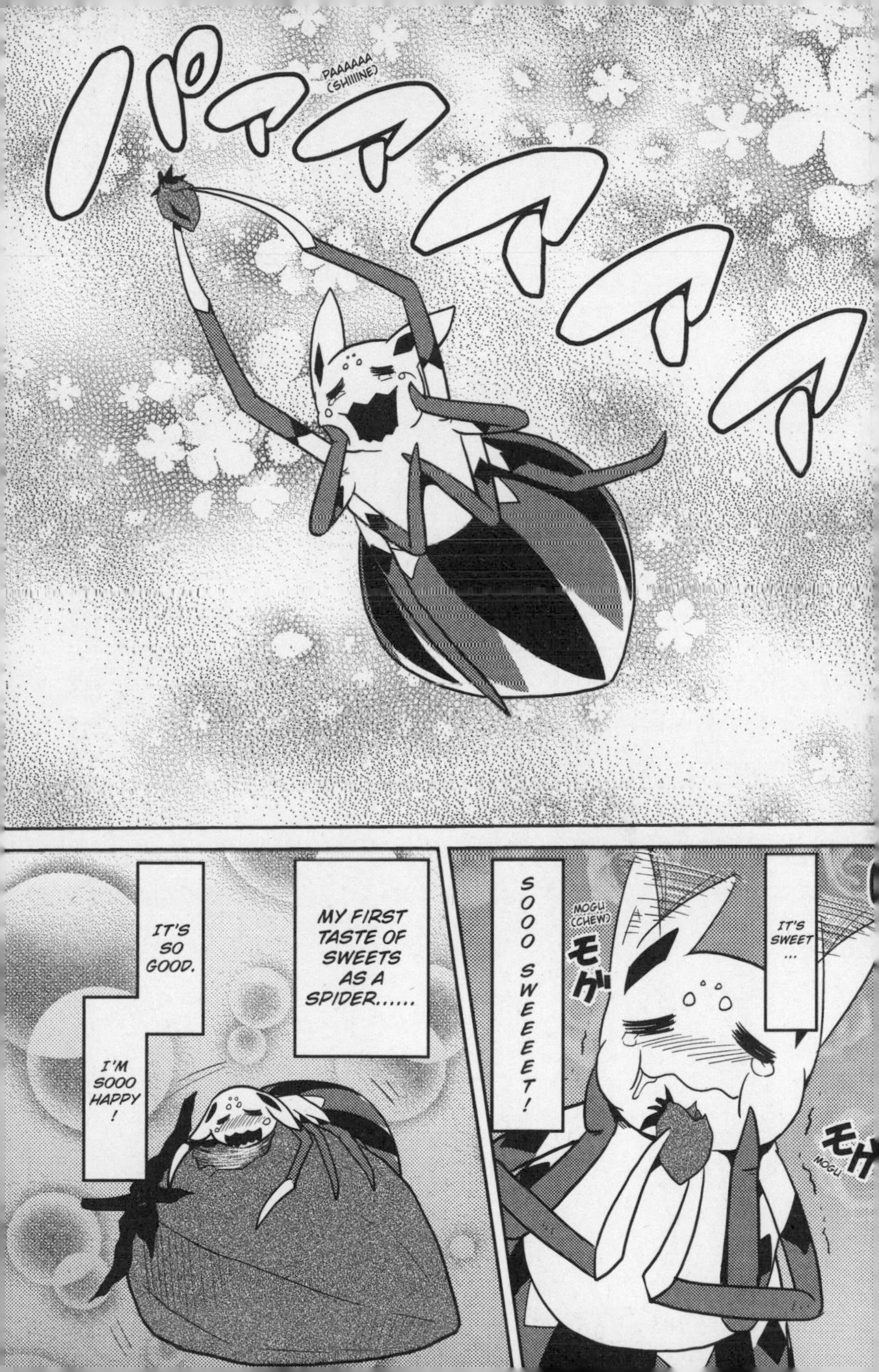
PAAAAAAA (SHIIIINE)
IT'S SWEET ...
MOGU (CHEW)
SOOO SWEEEEET!
MOGU
MY FIRST TASTE OF SWEETS AS A SPIDER......
IT'S SO GOOD.
I'M SOOO HAPPY!

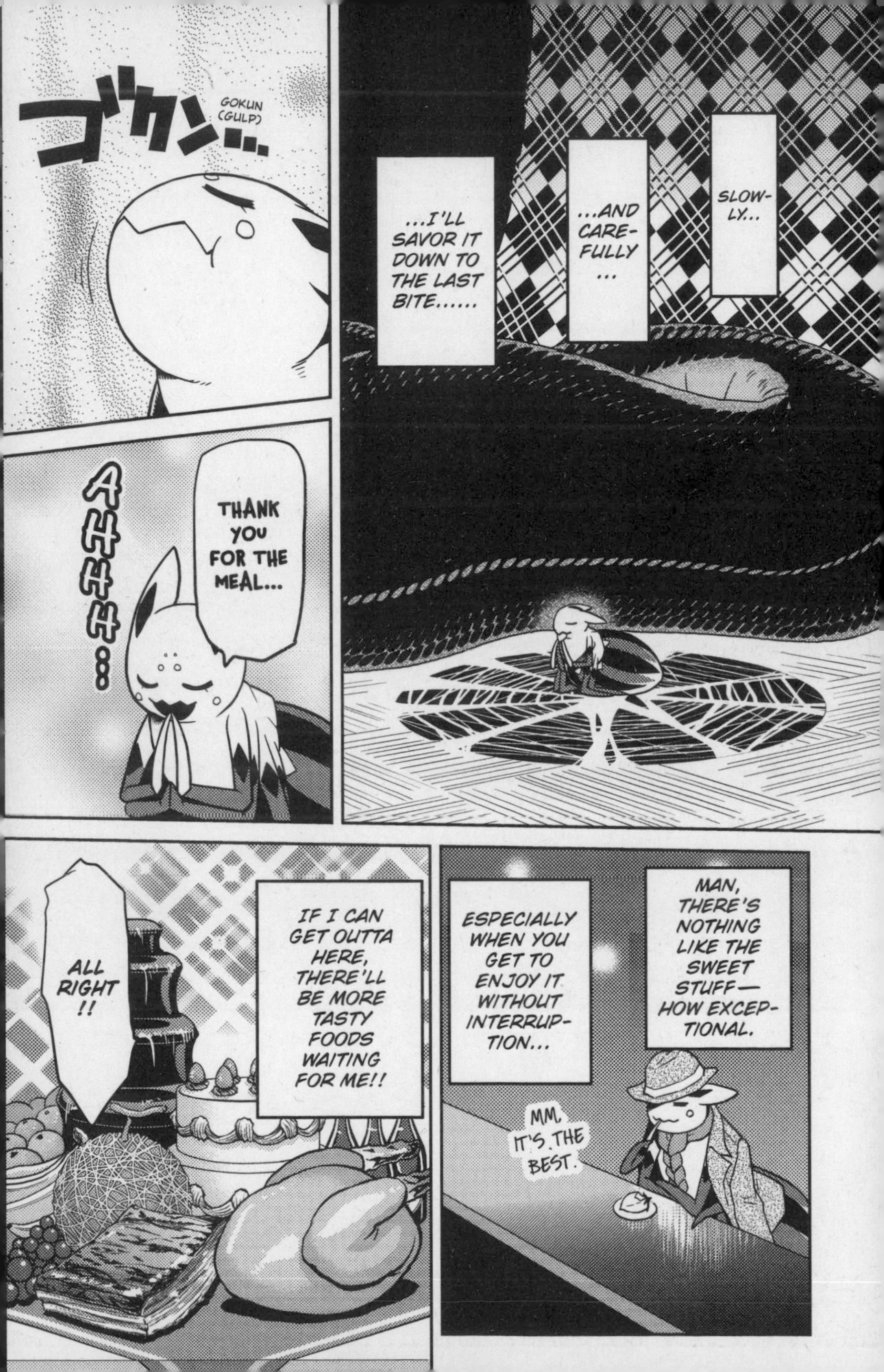
SLOW-LY...
...AND CARE-FULLY...
...I'LL SAVOR IT DOWN TO THE LAST BITE......
ゴクン...
GOKUN (GULP)
THANK YOU FOR THE MEAL...
AHHH...
MAN, THERE'S NOTHING LIKE THE SWEET STUFF— HOW EXCEP-TIONAL.
ESPECIALLY WHEN YOU GET TO ENJOY IT WITHOUT INTERRUP-TION...
MM. IT'S THE BEST.
IF I CAN GET OUTTA HERE, THERE'LL BE MORE TASTY FOODS WAITING FOR ME!!
ALL RIGHT!!

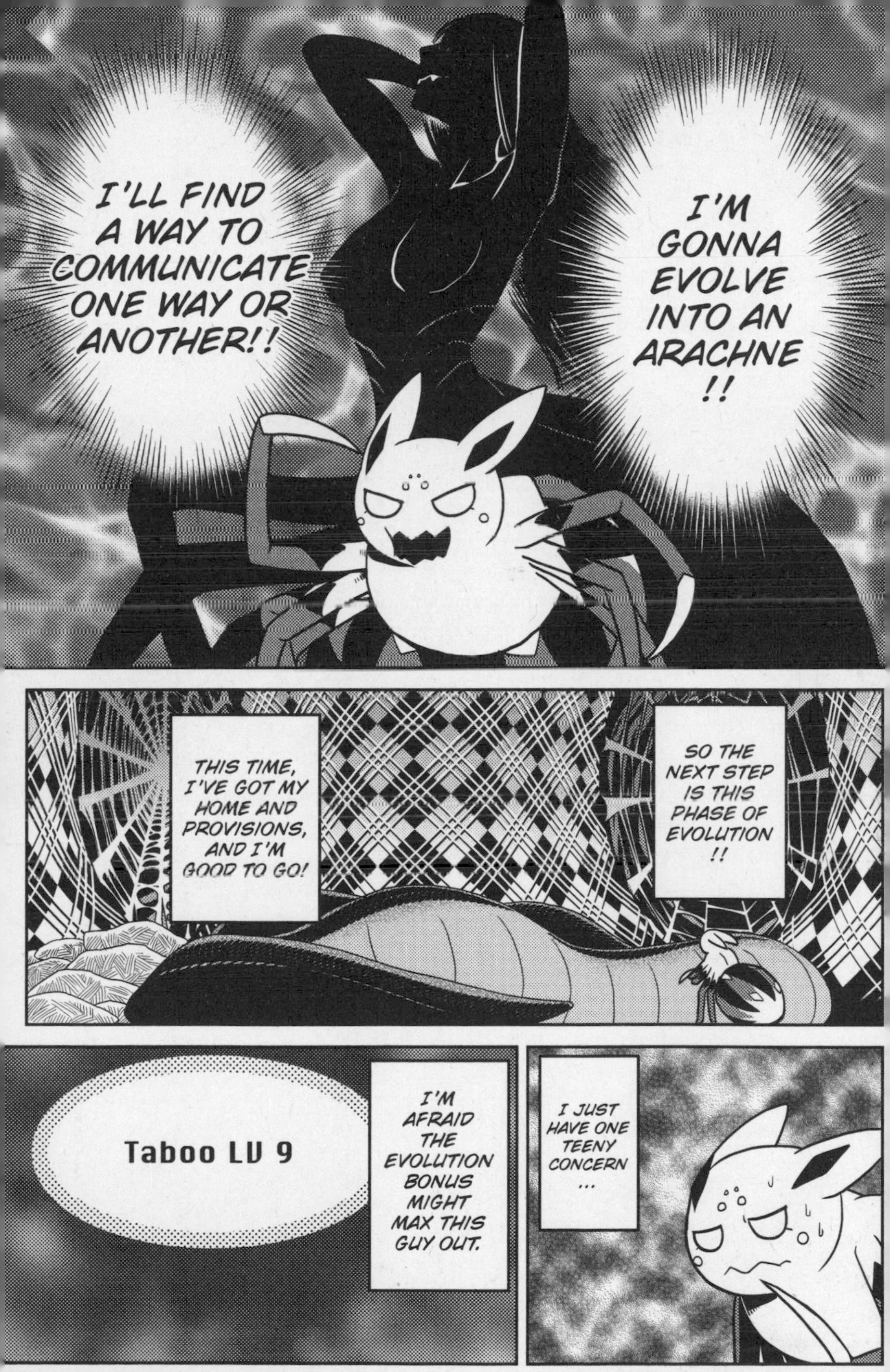
I'M GONNA EVOLVE INTO AN ARACHNE !!
I'LL FIND A WAY TO COMMUNICATE ONE WAY OR ANOTHER!!
SO THE NEXT STEP IS THIS PHASE OF EVOLUTION !!
THIS TIME, I'VE GOT MY HOME AND PROVISIONS, AND I'M GOOD TO GO!
I JUST HAVE ONE TEENY CONCERN ...
I'M AFRAID THE EVOLUTION BONUS MIGHT MAX THIS GUY OUT.
Taboo LV 9

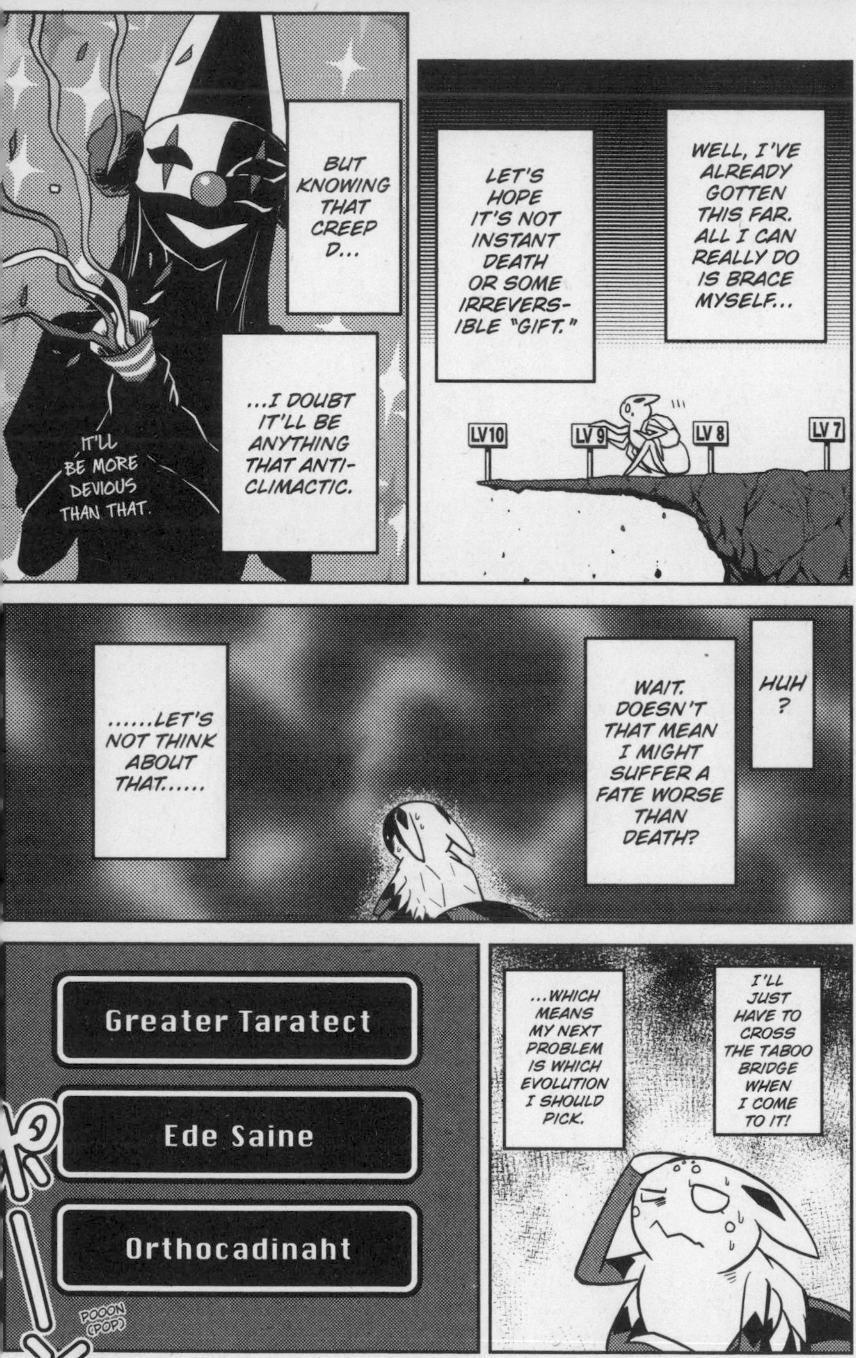

WELL, I'VE ALREADY GOTTEN THIS FAR. ALL I CAN REALLY DO IS BRACE MYSELF...
LET'S HOPE IT'S NOT INSTANT DEATH OR SOME IRREVERS-IBLE "GIFT."
LV 7
LV 8
LV 9
LV10
BUT KNOWING THAT CREEP D...
...I DOUBT IT'LL BE ANYTHING THAT ANTI-CLIMACTIC.
IT'LL BE MORE DEVIOUS THAN THAT.
HUH?
WAIT. DOESN'T THAT MEAN I MIGHT SUFFER A FATE WORSE THAN DEATH?
......LET'S NOT THINK ABOUT THAT......
I'LL JUST HAVE TO CROSS THE TABOO BRIDGE WHEN I COME TO IT!
...WHICH MEANS MY NEXT PROBLEM IS WHICH EVOLUTION I SHOULD PICK.
Greater Taratect
Ede Saine
Orthocadinaht
POOON (POP)

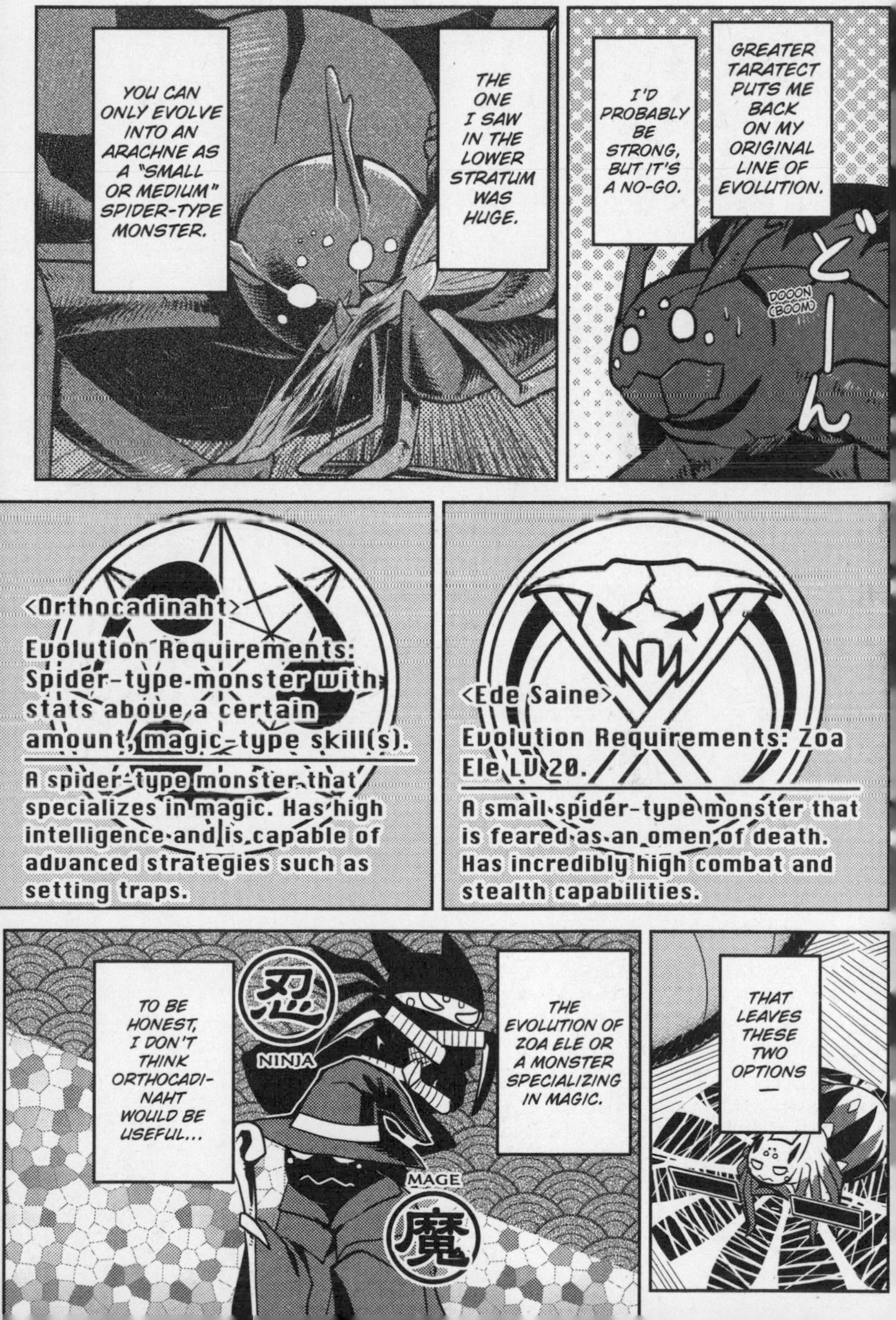
GREATER TARATECT PUTS ME BACK ON MY ORIGINAL LINE OF EVOLUTION.
I'D PROBABLY BE STRONG, BUT IT'S A NO-GO.
どーん
DOOON (BOOM)
THE ONE I SAW IN THE LOWER STRATUM WAS HUGE.
YOU CAN ONLY EVOLVE INTO AN ARACHNE AS A "SMALL OR MEDIUM" SPIDER-TYPE MONSTER.
<Ede Saine>
Evolution Requirements: Zoa Ele LV 20.
A small spider-type monster that is feared as an omen of death. Has incredibly high combat and stealth capabilities.
<Orthocadinaht>
Evolution Requirements: Spider-type monster with stats above a certain amount, magic-type skill(s).
A spider-type monster that specializes in magic. Has high intelligence and is capable of advanced strategies such as setting traps.
THAT LEAVES THESE TWO OPTIONS —
THE EVOLUTION OF ZOA ELE OR A MONSTER SPECIALIZING IN MAGIC.
忍
NINJA
MAGE
魔
TO BE HONEST, I DON'T THINK ORTHOCADINAHT WOULD BE USEFUL...

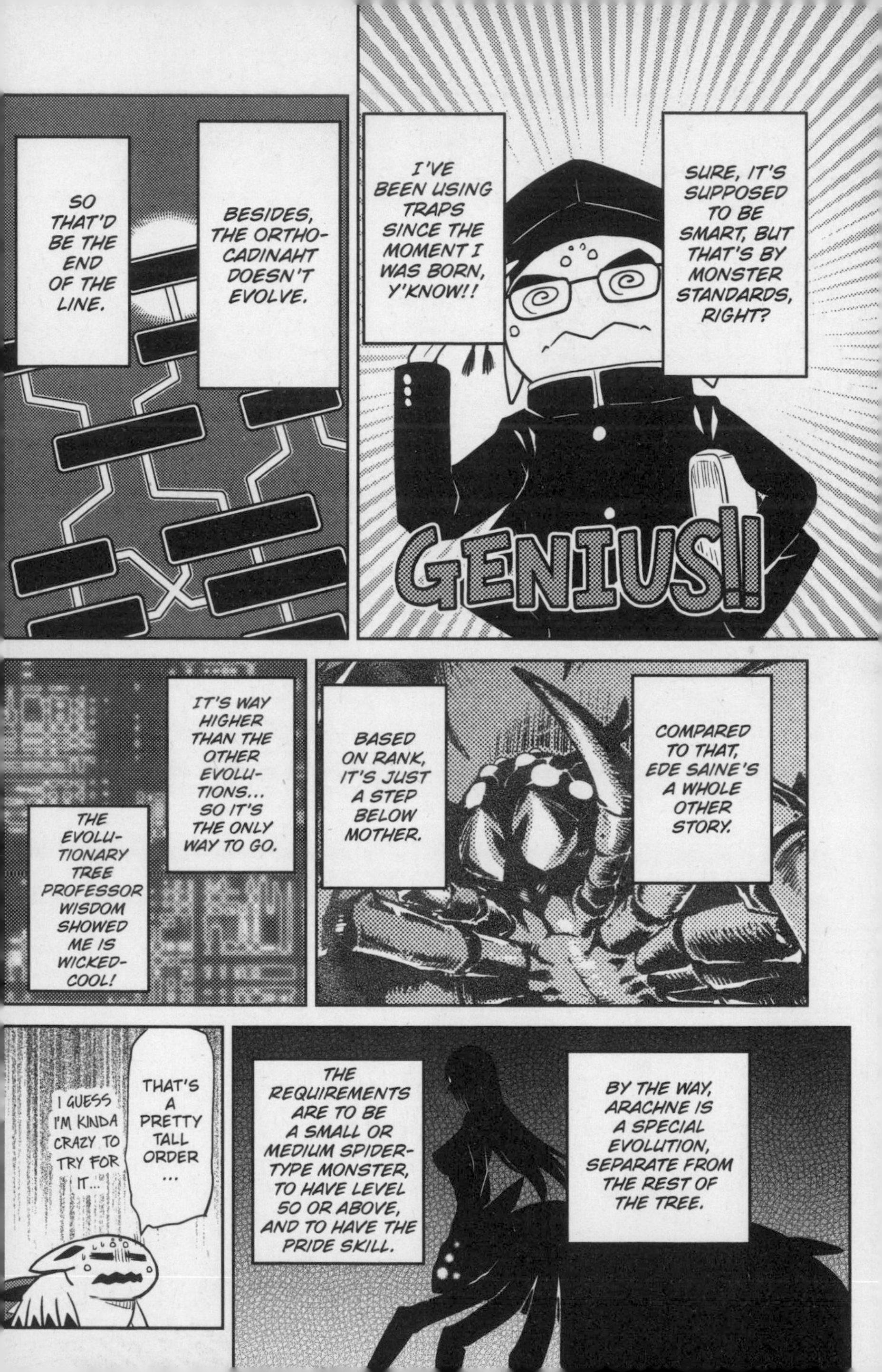
SURE, IT'S SUPPOSED TO BE SMART, BUT THAT'S BY MONSTER STANDARDS, RIGHT?
I'VE BEEN USING TRAPS SINCE THE MOMENT I WAS BORN, Y'KNOW!!
GENIUS!!
BESIDES, THE ORTHO-CADINAHT DOESN'T EVOLVE.
SO THAT'D BE THE END OF THE LINE.
COMPARED TO THAT, EDE SAINE'S A WHOLE OTHER STORY.
BASED ON RANK, IT'S JUST A STEP BELOW MOTHER.
IT'S WAY HIGHER THAN THE OTHER EVOLU-TIONS... SO IT'S THE ONLY WAY TO GO.
THE EVOLU-TIONARY TREE PROFESSOR WISDOM SHOWED ME IS WICKED-COOL!
BY THE WAY, ARACHNE IS A SPECIAL EVOLUTION, SEPARATE FROM THE REST OF THE TREE.
THE REQUIREMENTS ARE TO BE A SMALL OR MEDIUM SPIDER-TYPE MONSTER, TO HAVE LEVEL 50 OR ABOVE, AND TO HAVE THE PRIDE SKILL.
THAT'S A PRETTY TALL ORDER...
I GUESS I'M KINDA CRAZY TO TRY FOR IT...

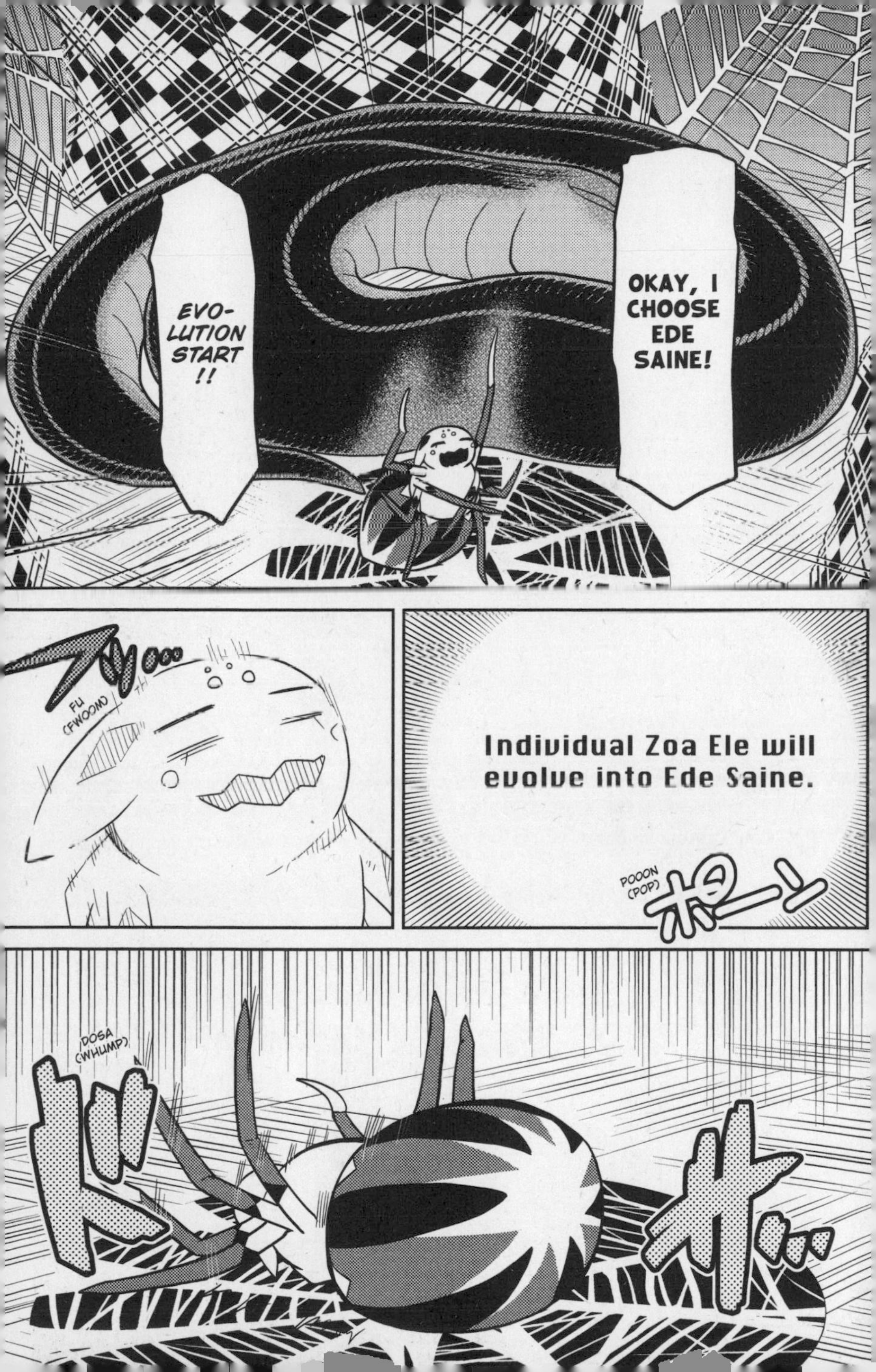
OKAY, I CHOOSE EDE SAINE!
EVO-LUTION START!!
Individual Zoa Ele will evolve into Ede Saine.
POOON (POP)
FU (FWOOM)
DOSA (WHUMP)

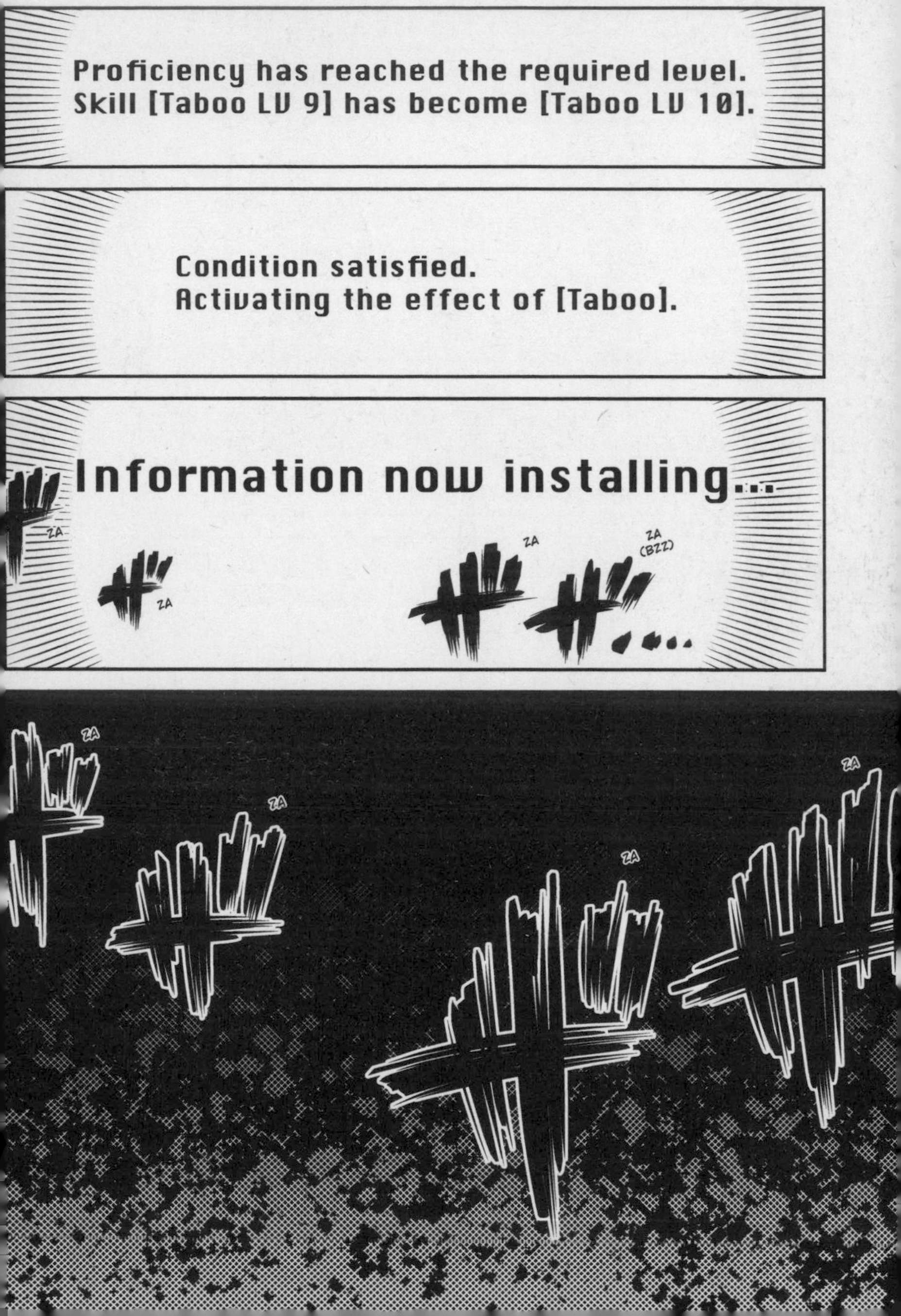
Proficiency has reached the required level.
Skill [Taboo LV 9] has become [Taboo LV 10].
Condition satisfied.
Activating the effect of [Taboo].
Information now installing...
ZA (BZZ)
ZA
ZA
ZA
ZA
ZA
ZA
ZA

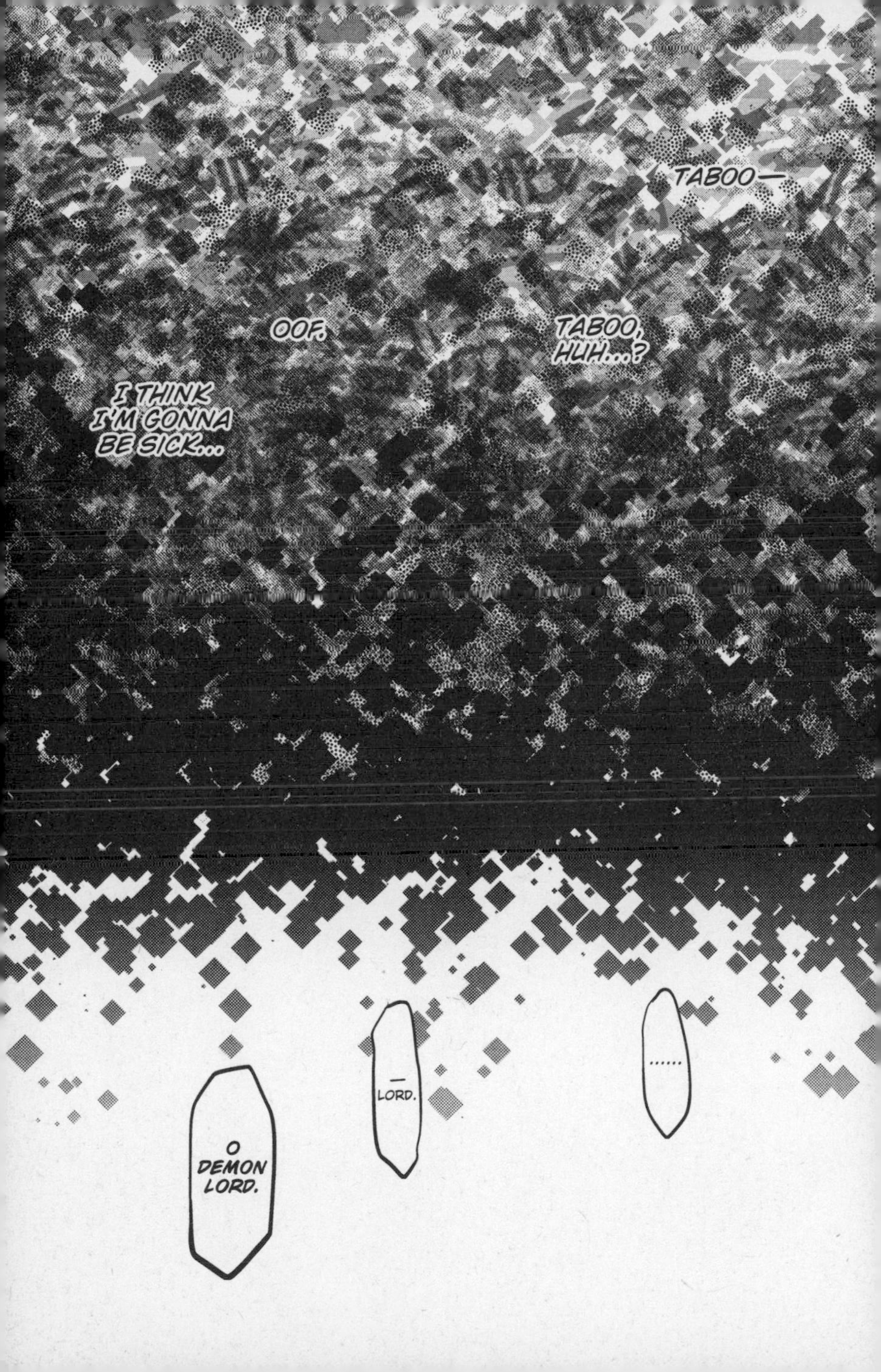
TABOO—
TABOO, HUH...?
OOF.
I THINK I'M GONNA BE SICK...
......
—LORD.
O DEMON LORD.

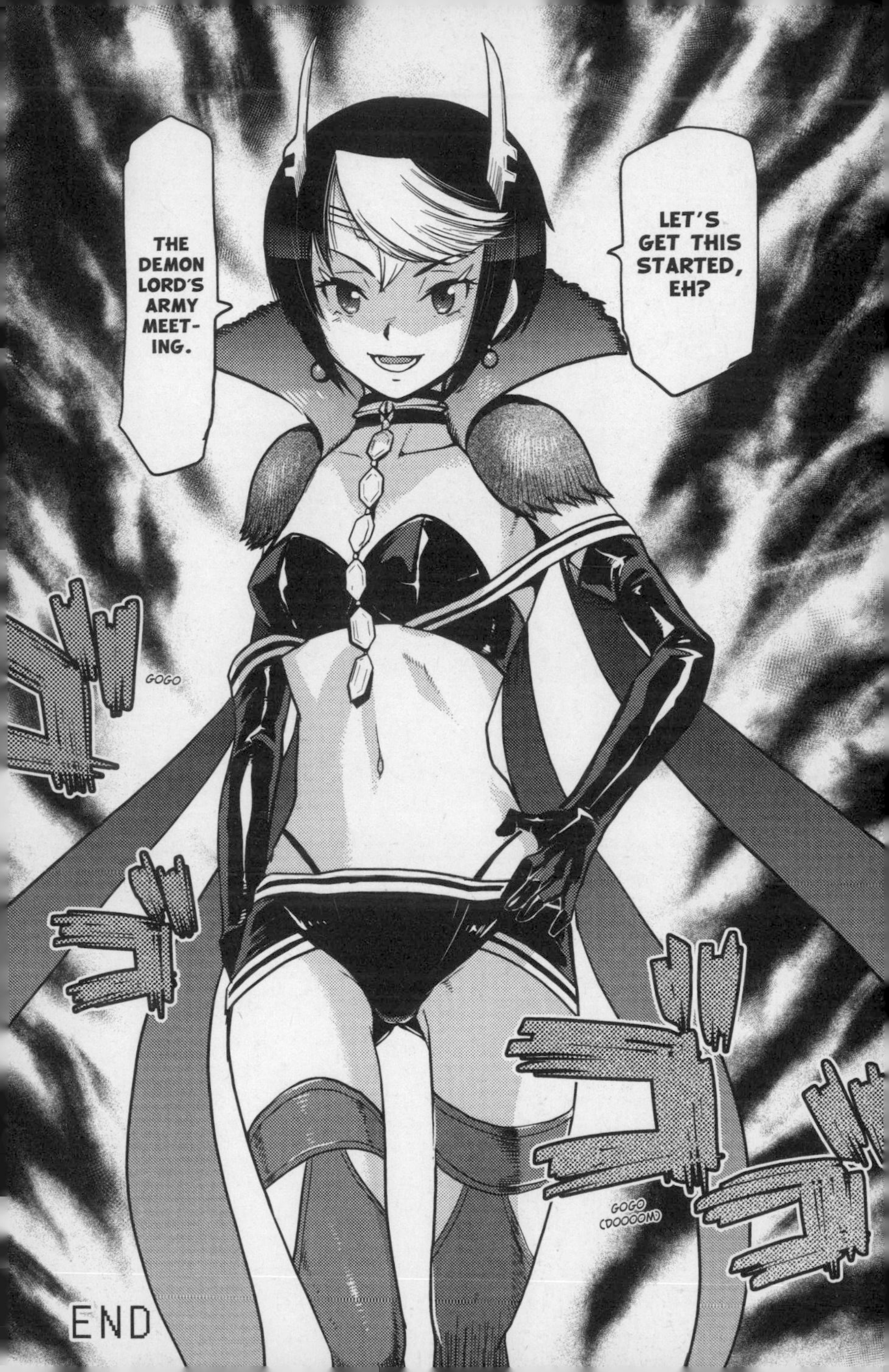
LET'S GET THIS STARTED, EH?
THE DEMON LORD'S ARMY MEET-ING.
GOGO
GOGO (DOOOOM)
END

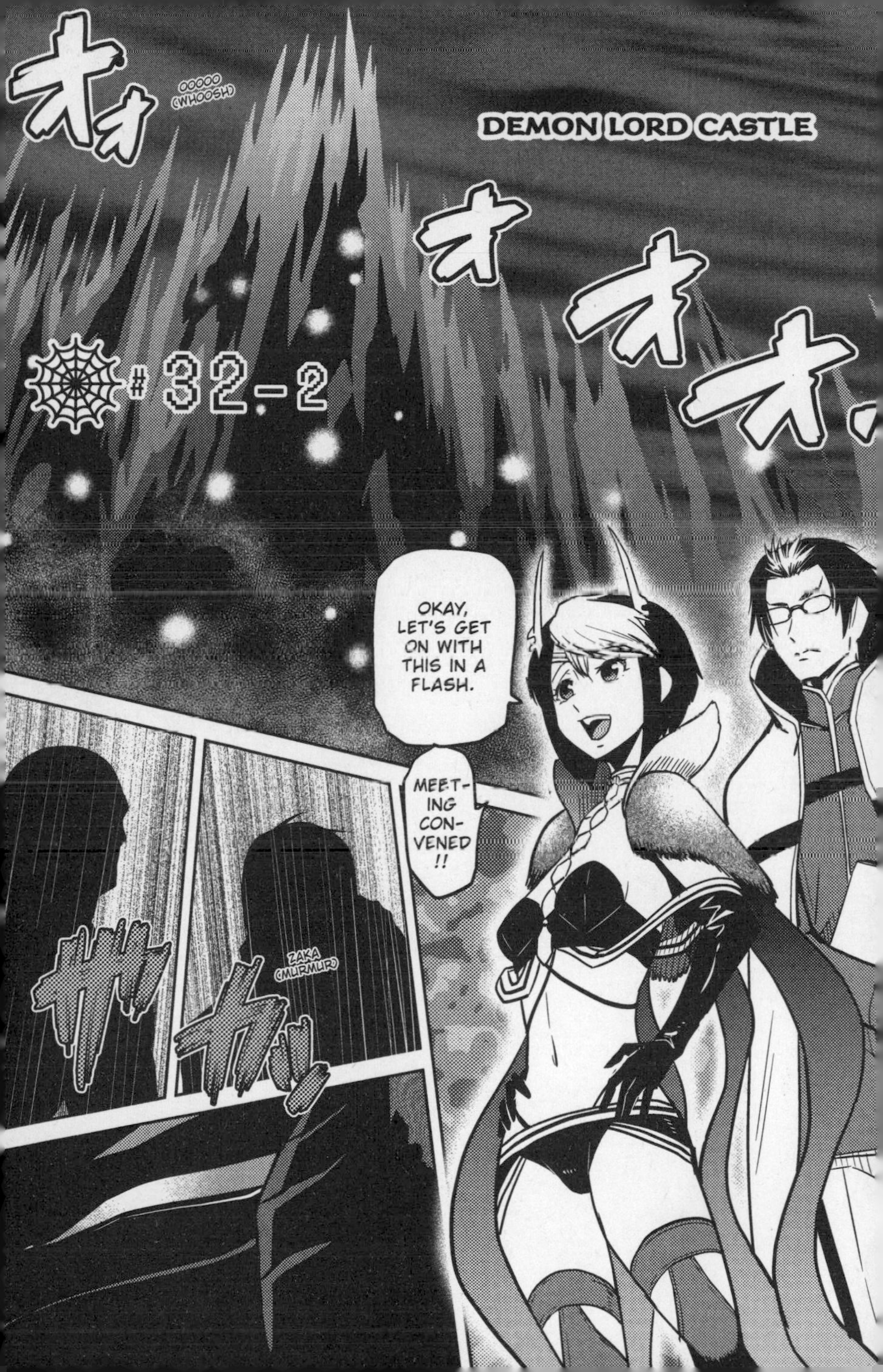
DEMON LORD CASTLE
OOOOO (WHOOSH)
#32-2
OKAY, LET'S GET ON WITH THIS IN A FLASH.
MEET-ING CON-VENED!!
ZAKA (MURMUR)

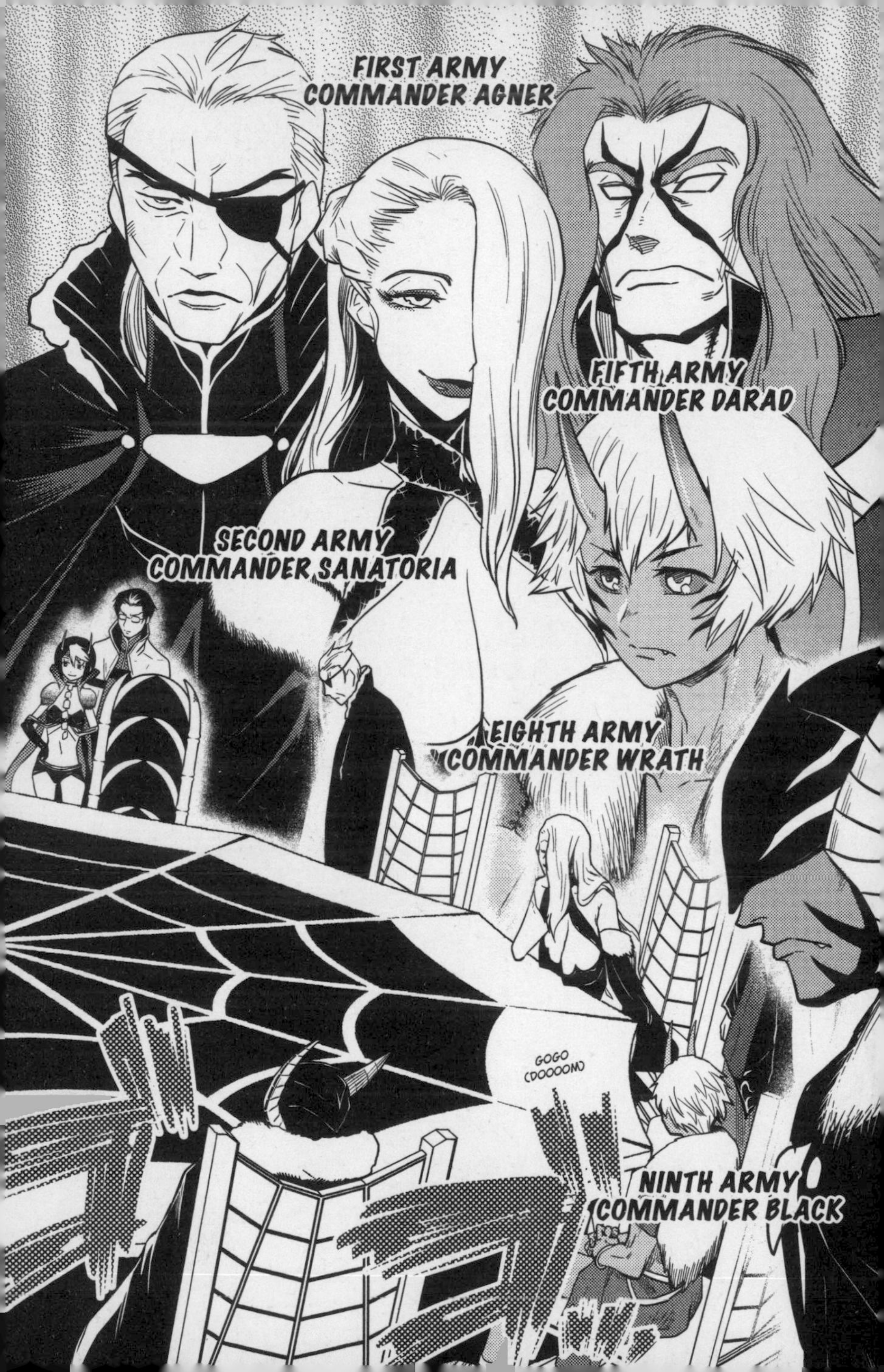
FIRST ARMY COMMANDER AGNER
FIFTH ARMY COMMANDER DARAD
SECOND ARMY COMMANDER SANATORIA
EIGHTH ARMY COMMANDER WRATH
GOGO (DOOOOM)
NINTH ARMY COMMANDER BLACK

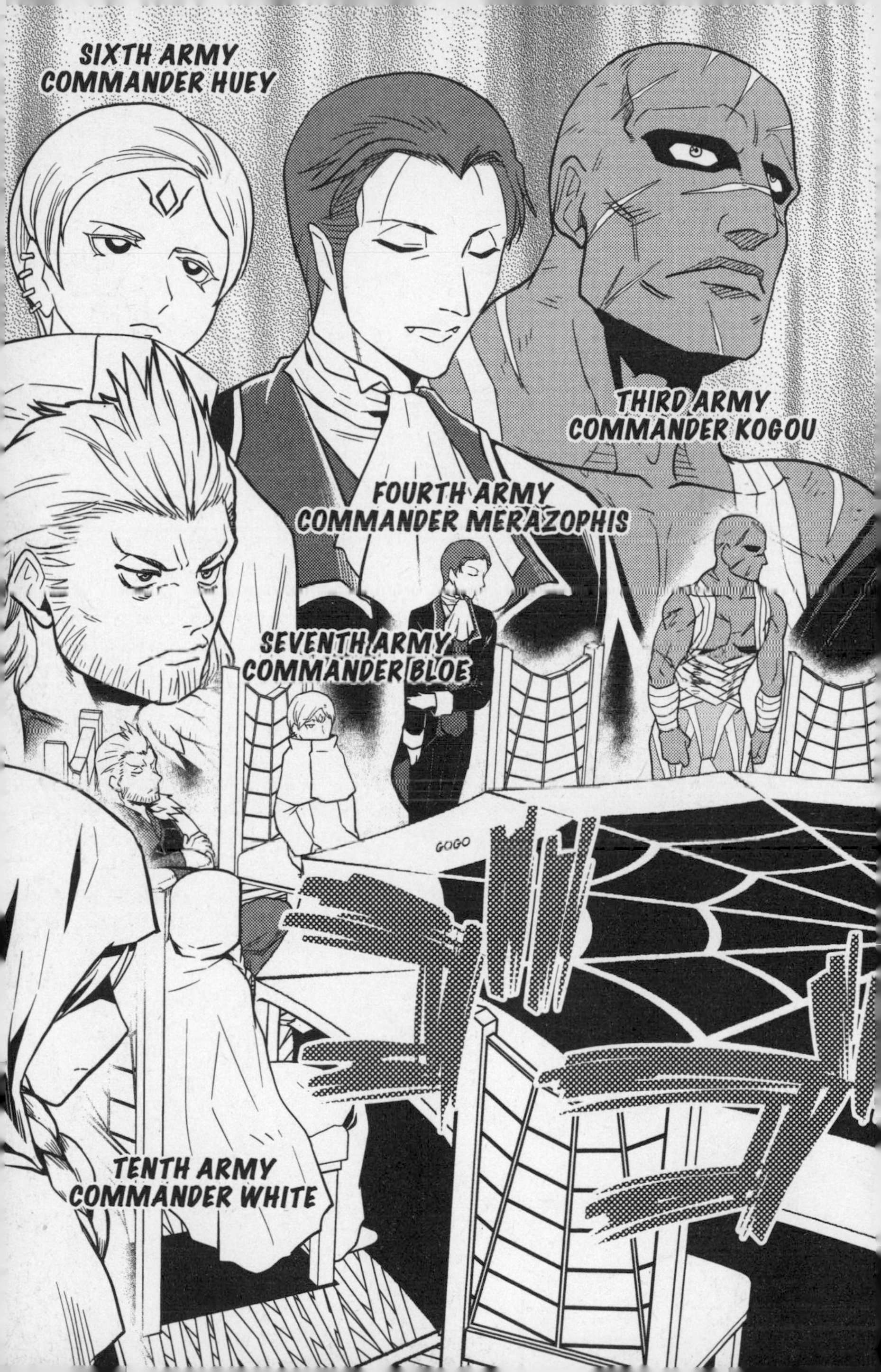
SIXTH ARMY COMMANDER HUEY
THIRD ARMY COMMANDER KOGOU
FOURTH ARMY COMMANDER MERAZOPHIS
SEVENTH ARMY COMMANDER BLOE
GOGO
TENTH ARMY COMMANDER WHITE

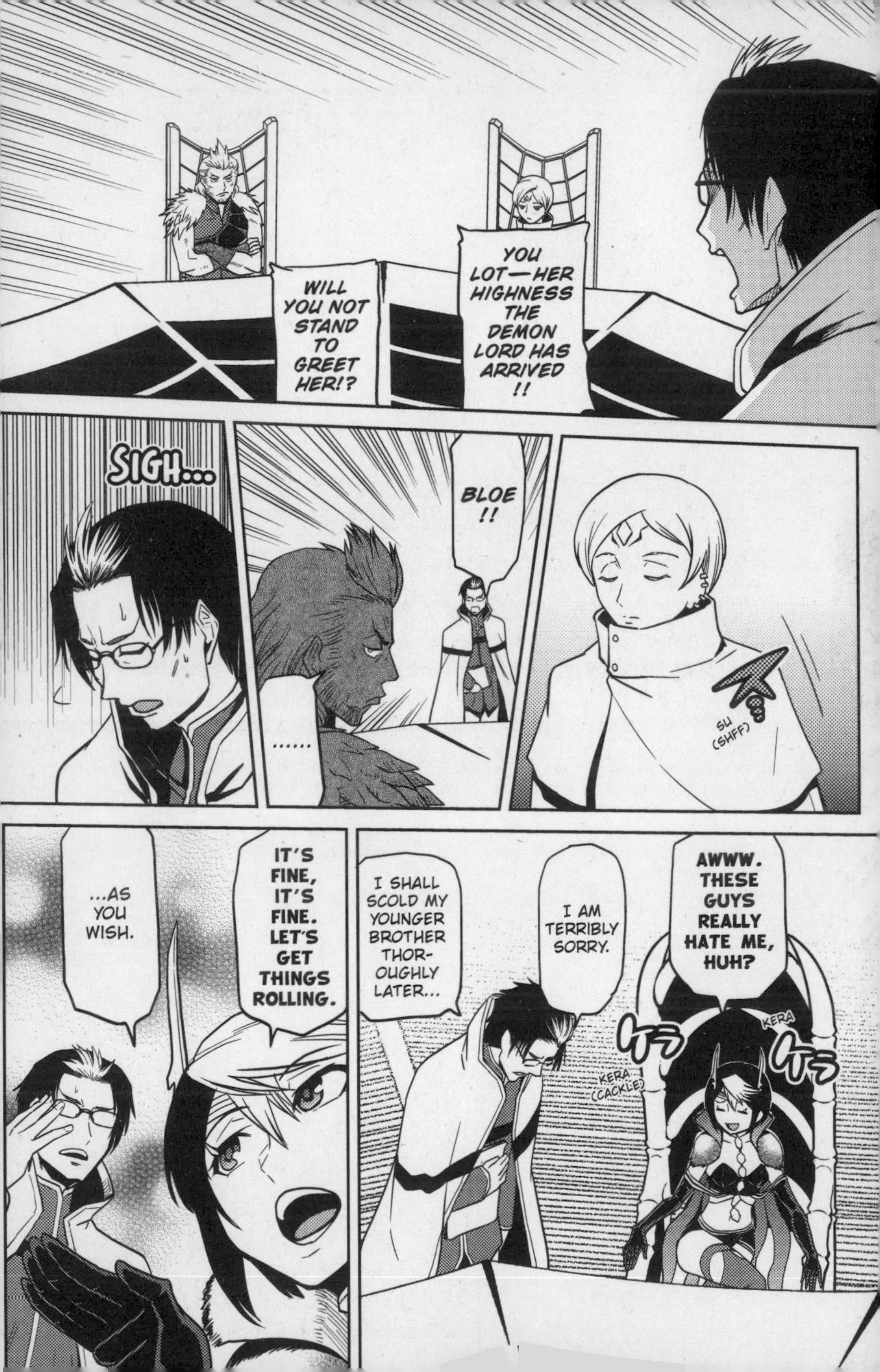
YOU LOT—HER HIGHNESS THE DEMON LORD HAS ARRIVED!!
WILL YOU NOT STAND TO GREET HER!?
SU (SHFF)
BLOE!!
......
SIGH...
AWWW. THESE GUYS REALLY HATE ME, HUH?
ケラ
KERA
ケラ
KERA (CACKLE)
I AM TERRIBLY SORRY.
I SHALL SCOLD MY YOUNGER BROTHER THOR-OUGHLY LATER...
IT'S FINE, IT'S FINE. LET'S GET THINGS ROLLING.
...AS YOU WISH.

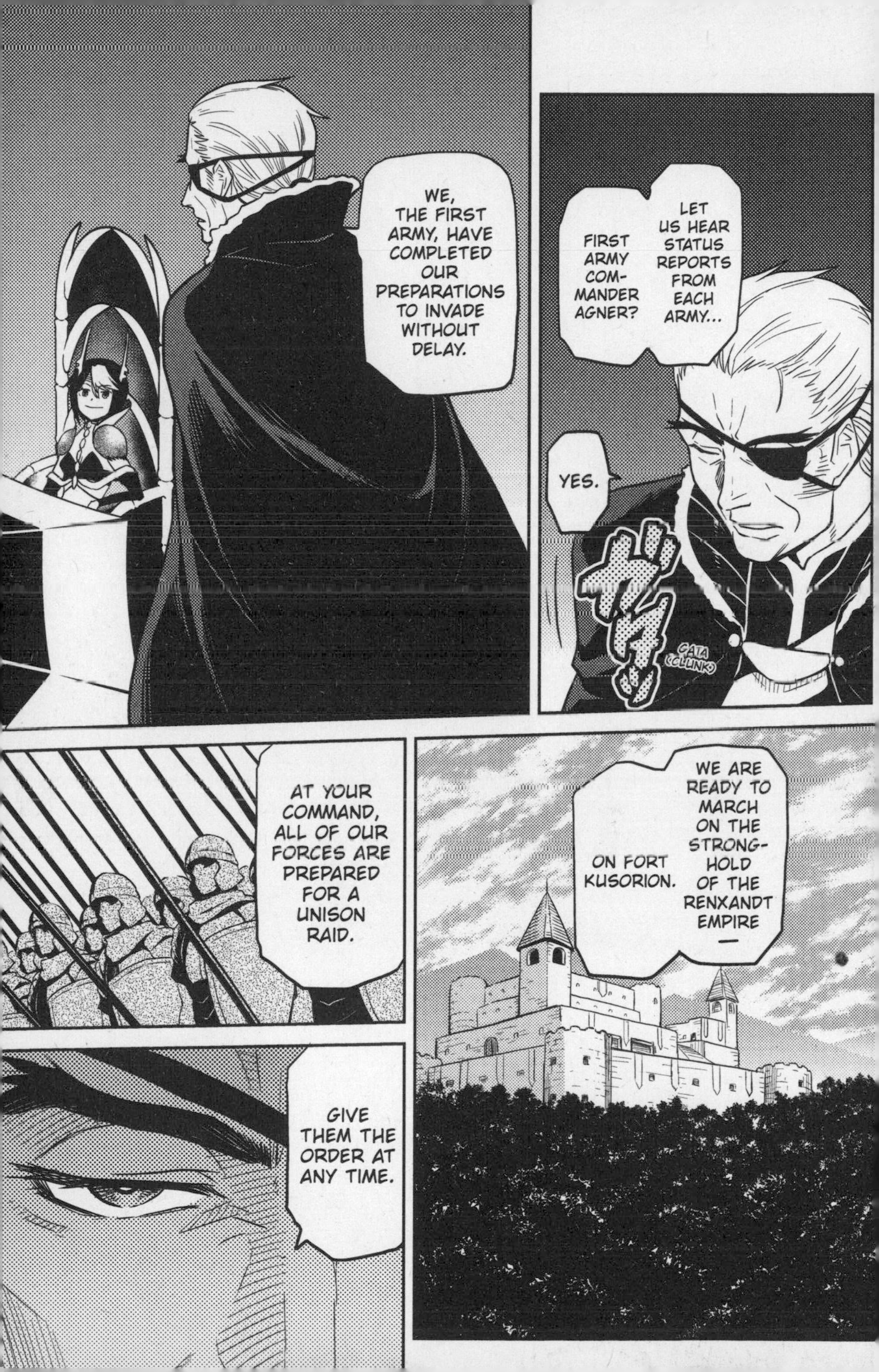
LET US HEAR STATUS REPORTS FROM EACH ARMY...
FIRST ARMY COM-MANDER AGNER?
YES.
GATA (CLUNK)
WE, THE FIRST ARMY, HAVE COMPLETED OUR PREPARATIONS TO INVADE WITHOUT DELAY.
WE ARE READY TO MARCH ON THE STRONG-HOLD OF THE RENXANDT EMPIRE —
ON FORT KUSORION.
AT YOUR COMMAND, ALL OF OUR FORCES ARE PREPARED FOR A UNISON RAID.
GIVE THEM THE ORDER AT ANY TIME.

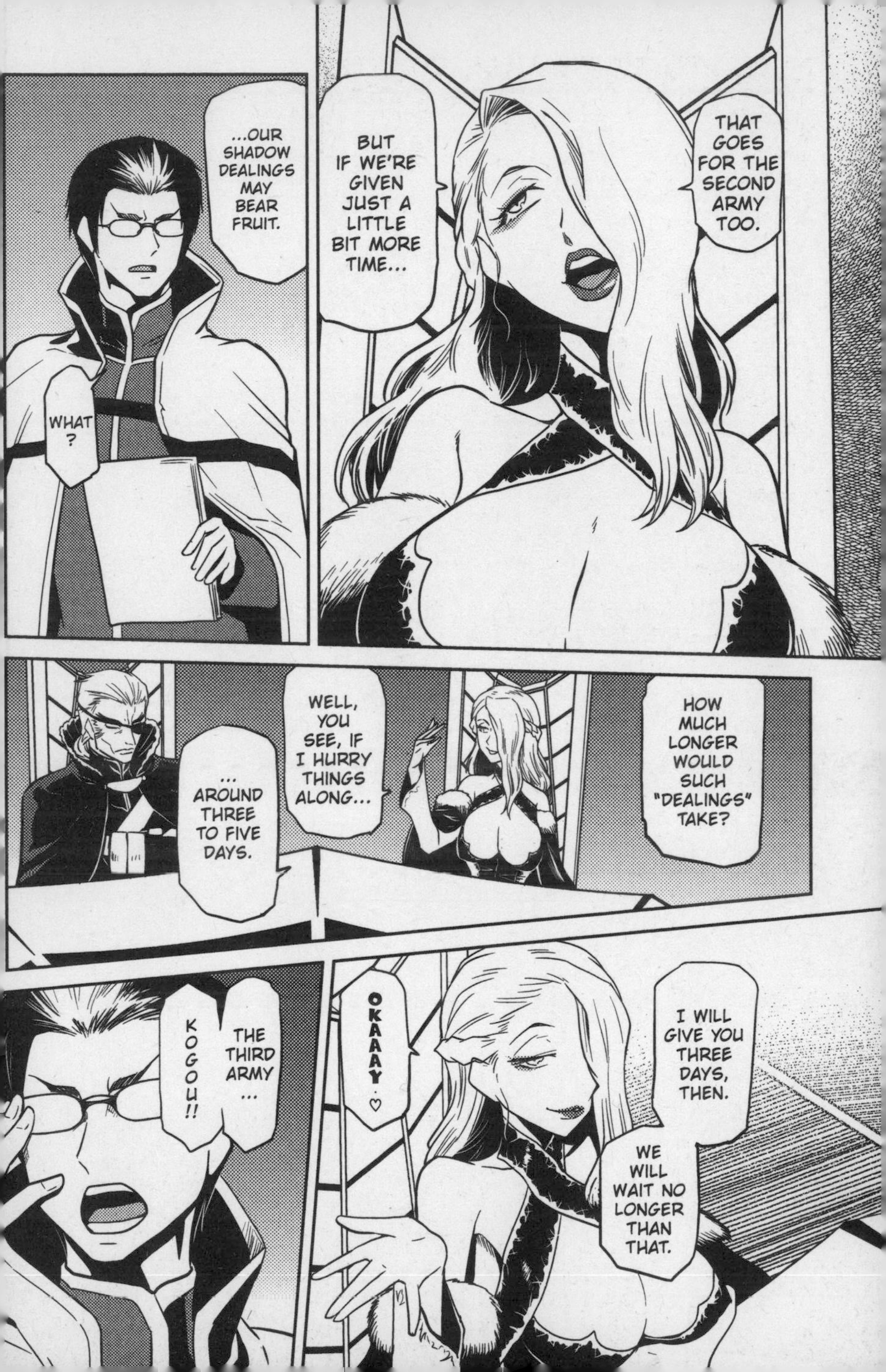
THAT GOES FOR THE SECOND ARMY TOO.
BUT IF WE'RE GIVEN JUST A LITTLE BIT MORE TIME...
...OUR SHADOW DEALINGS MAY BEAR FRUIT.
WHAT?
HOW MUCH LONGER WOULD SUCH "DEALINGS" TAKE?
WELL, YOU SEE, IF I HURRY THINGS ALONG...
...AROUND THREE TO FIVE DAYS.
I WILL GIVE YOU THREE DAYS, THEN.
WE WILL WAIT NO LONGER THAN THAT.
OKAAAY. ♡
THE THIRD ARMY...
KOGOU!!

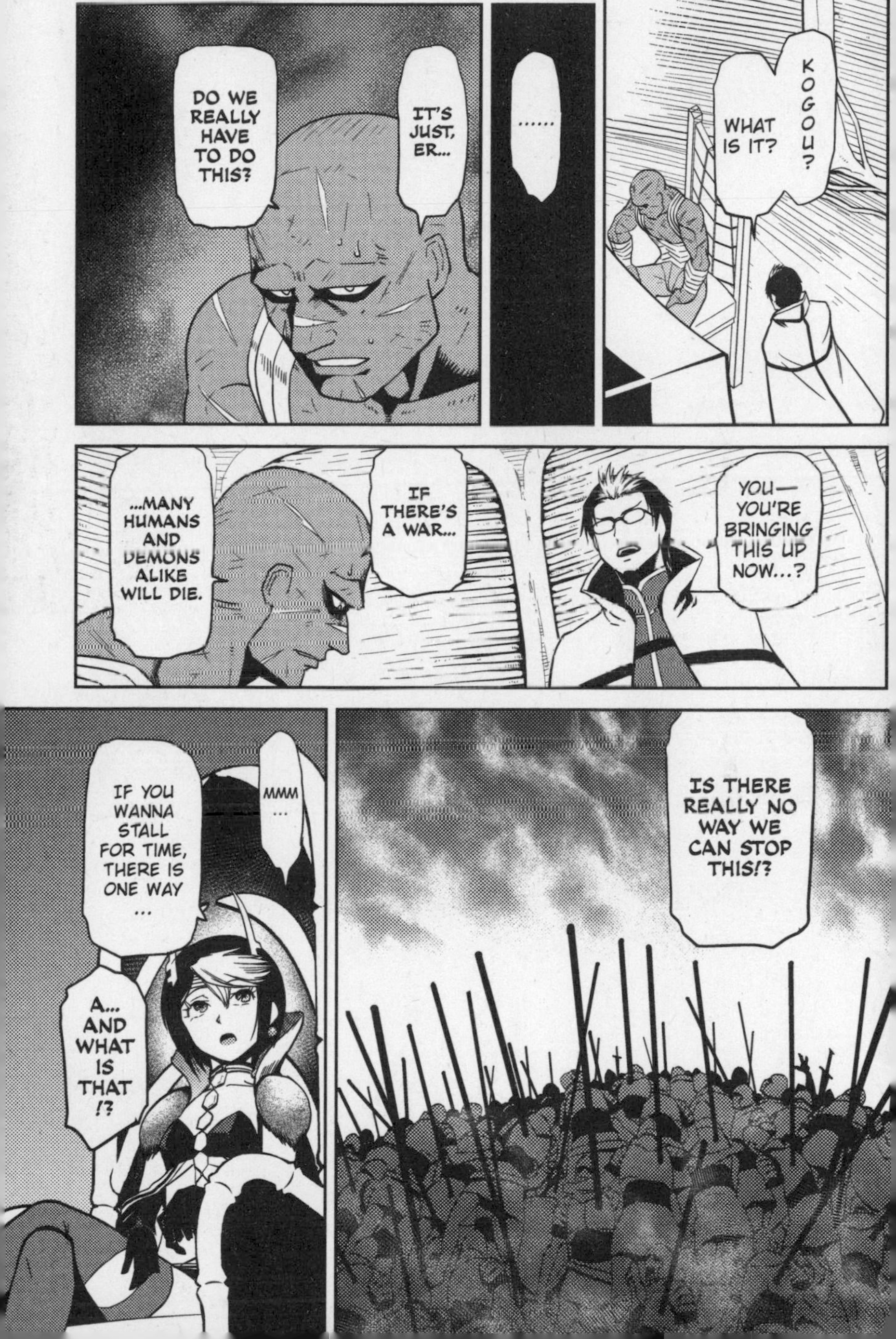
KOGOU?
WHAT IS IT?
......
IT'S JUST, ER...
DO WE REALLY HAVE TO DO THIS?
YOU— YOU'RE BRINGING THIS UP NOW...?
IF THERE'S A WAR...
...MANY HUMANS AND DEMONS ALIKE WILL DIE.
IS THERE REALLY NO WAY WE CAN STOP THIS!?
MMM...
IF YOU WANNA STALL FOR TIME, THERE IS ONE WAY...
A... AND WHAT IS THAT!?

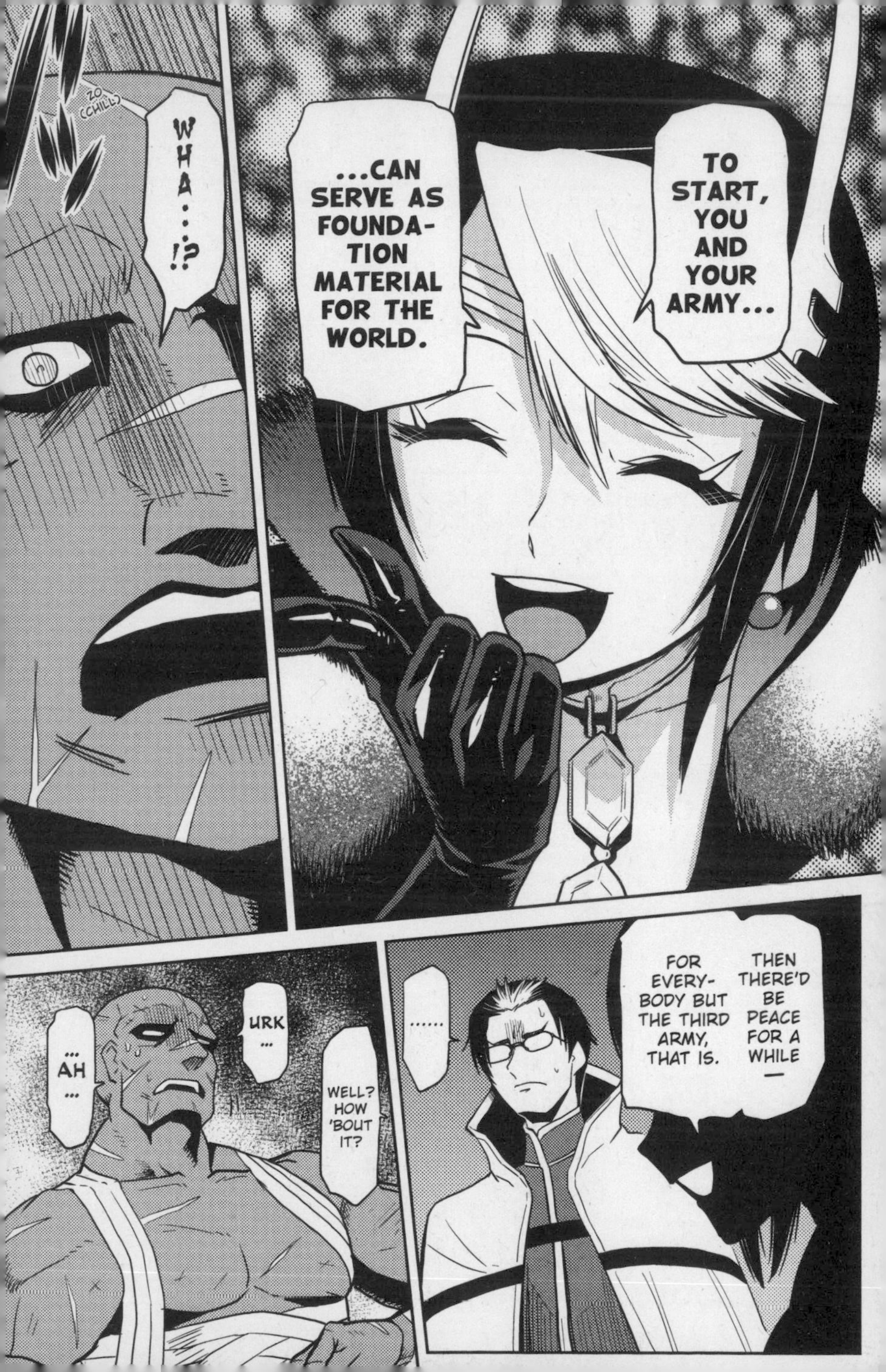
TO START, YOU AND YOUR ARMY...
...CAN SERVE AS FOUNDATION MATERIAL FOR THE WORLD.
ZO (CHILL)
WHA...!?
THEN THERE'D BE PEACE FOR A WHILE—
FOR EVERYBODY BUT THE THIRD ARMY, THAT IS.
......
WELL? HOW 'BOUT IT?
URK...
...AH...

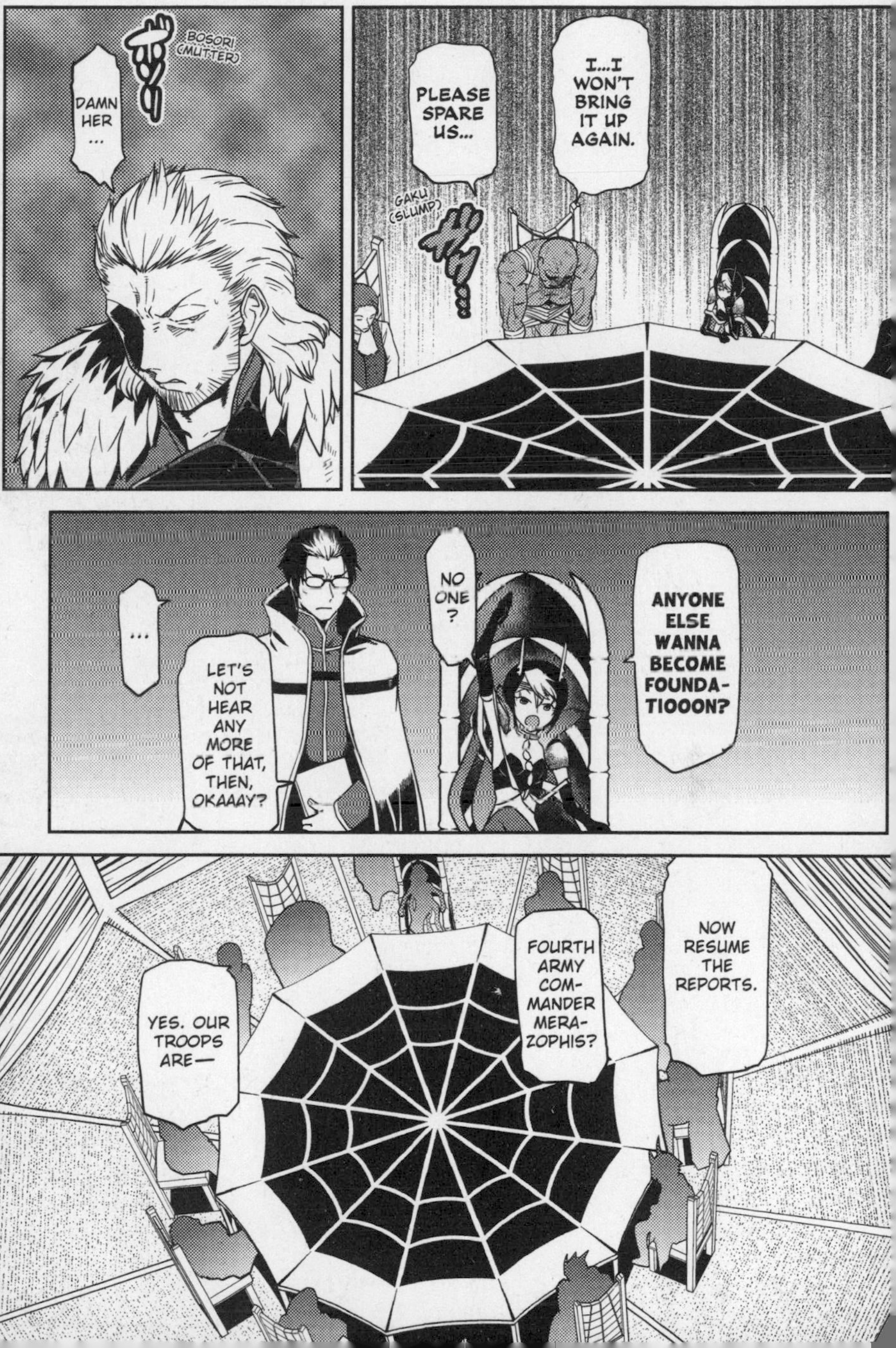
I...I WON'T BRING IT UP AGAIN.
PLEASE SPARE US...
GAKU (SLUMP)
BOSORI (MUTTER)
DAMN HER ...
ANYONE ELSE WANNA BECOME FOUNDA-TIOOON?
NO ONE?
LET'S NOT HEAR ANY MORE OF THAT, THEN, OKAAAY?
...
NOW RESUME THE REPORTS.
FOURTH ARMY COMMANDER MERA-ZOPHIS?
YES. OUR TROOPS ARE—

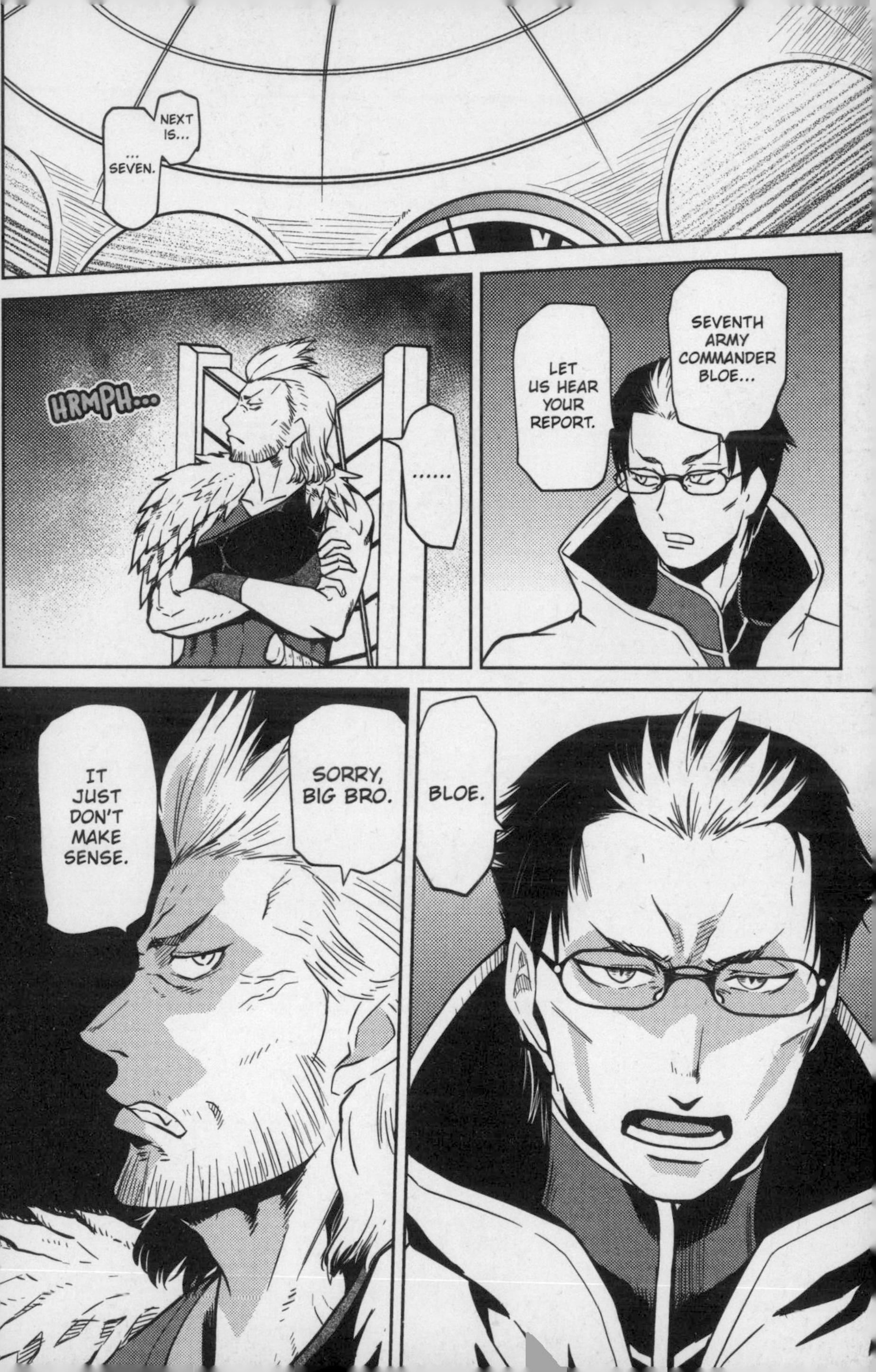
NEXT IS...
... SEVEN.
SEVENTH ARMY COMMANDER BLOE...
LET US HEAR YOUR REPORT.
......
HRMPH...
BLOE.
SORRY, BIG BRO.
IT JUST DON'T MAKE SENSE.

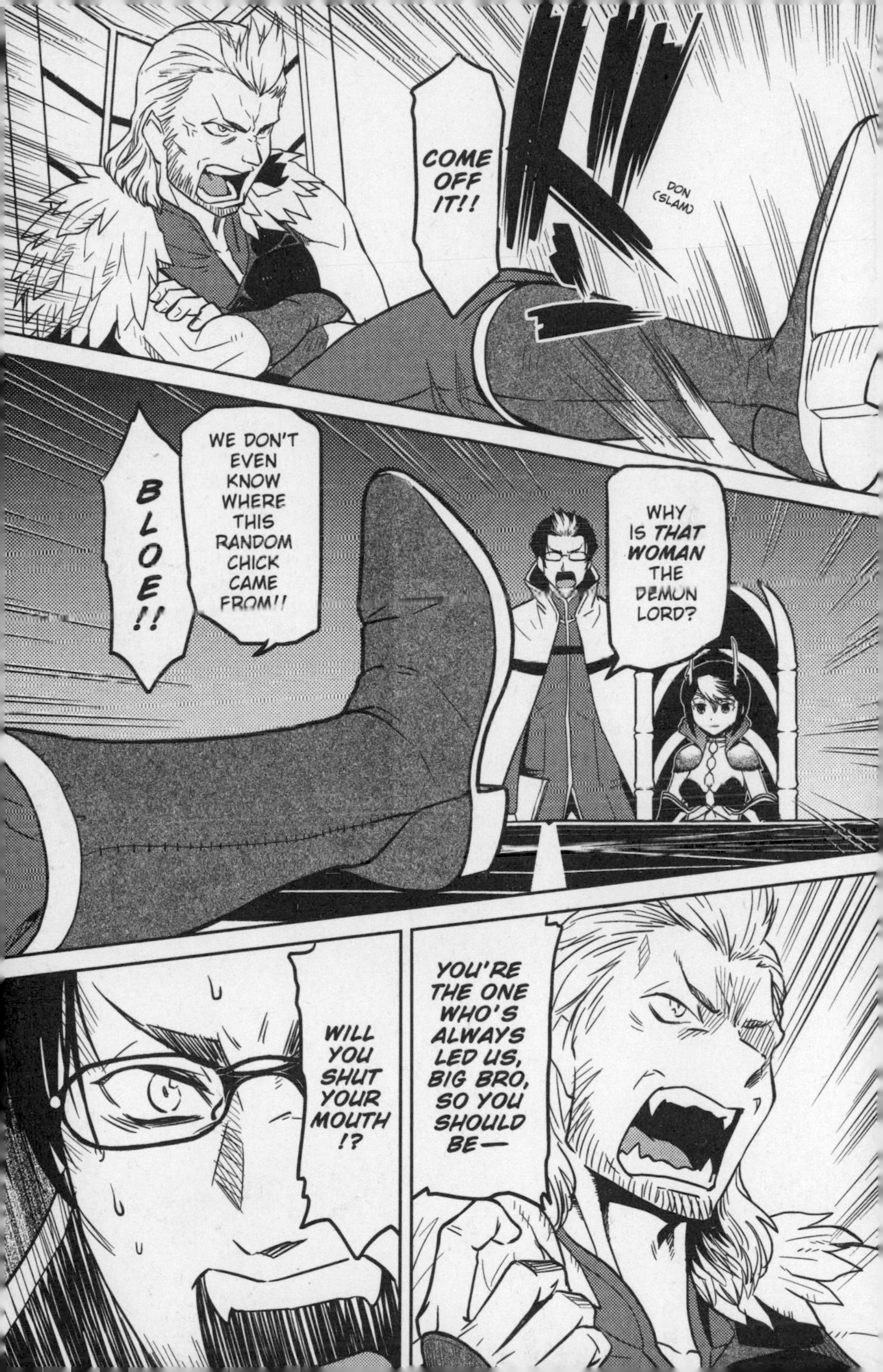
DON (SLAM)
COME OFF IT!!
WHY IS *THAT WOMAN* THE DEMON LORD?
WE DON'T EVEN KNOW WHERE THIS RANDOM CHICK CAME FROM!!
BLOE!!
YOU'RE THE ONE WHO'S ALWAYS LED US, BIG BRO, SO YOU SHOULD BE—
WILL YOU SHUT YOUR MOUTH!?

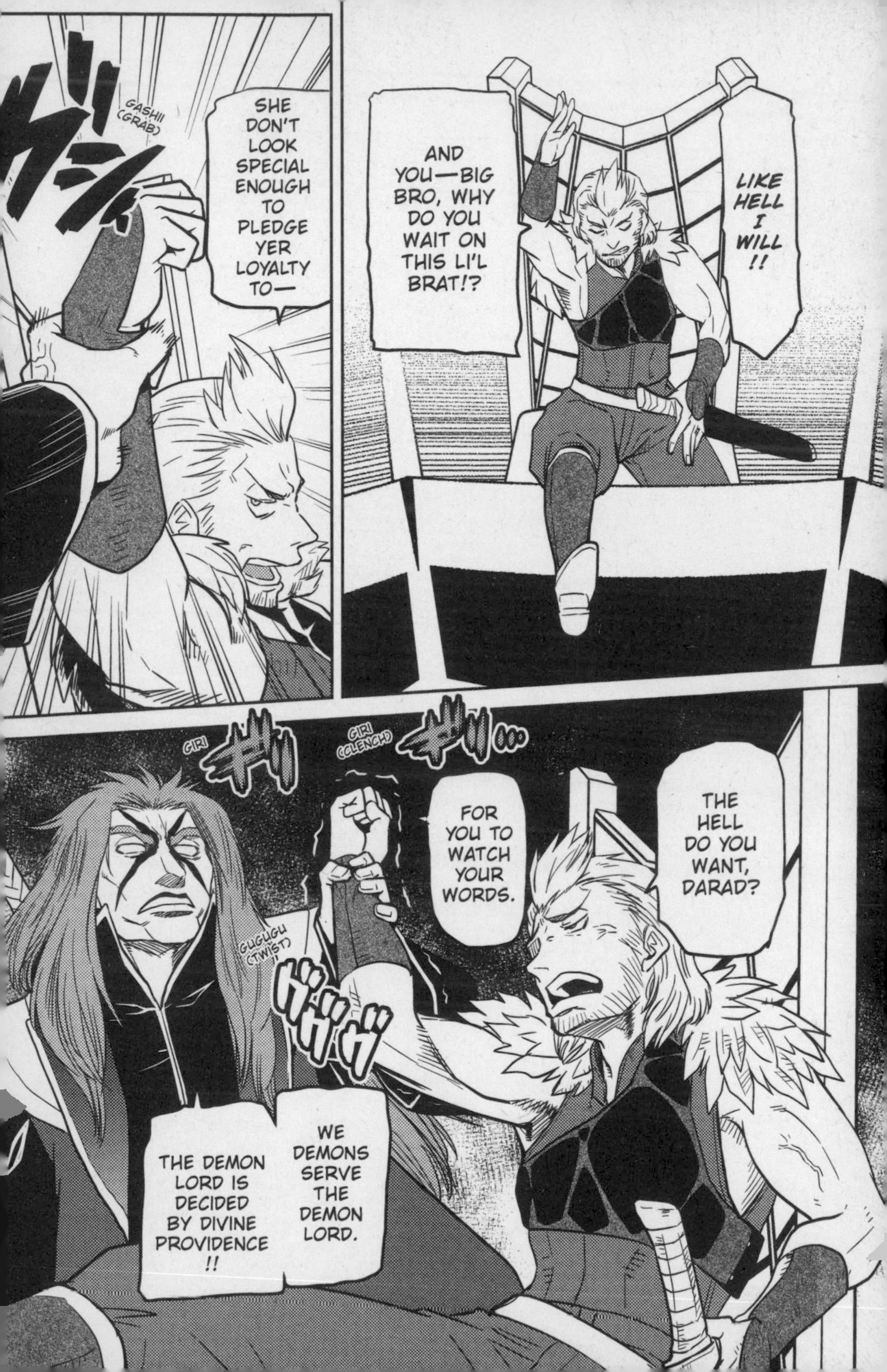
LIKE HELL I WILL!!
AND YOU—BIG BRO, WHY DO YOU WAIT ON THIS LI'L BRAT!?
SHE DON'T LOOK SPECIAL ENOUGH TO PLEDGE YER LOYALTY TO—
GASHIII (GRAB)
THE HELL DO YOU WANT, DARAD?
GIRI (CLENCH)
FOR YOU TO WATCH YOUR WORDS.
GIRI
GUGUGU (TWIST)
WE DEMONS SERVE THE DEMON LORD.
THE DEMON LORD IS DECIDED BY DIVINE PROVIDENCE!!

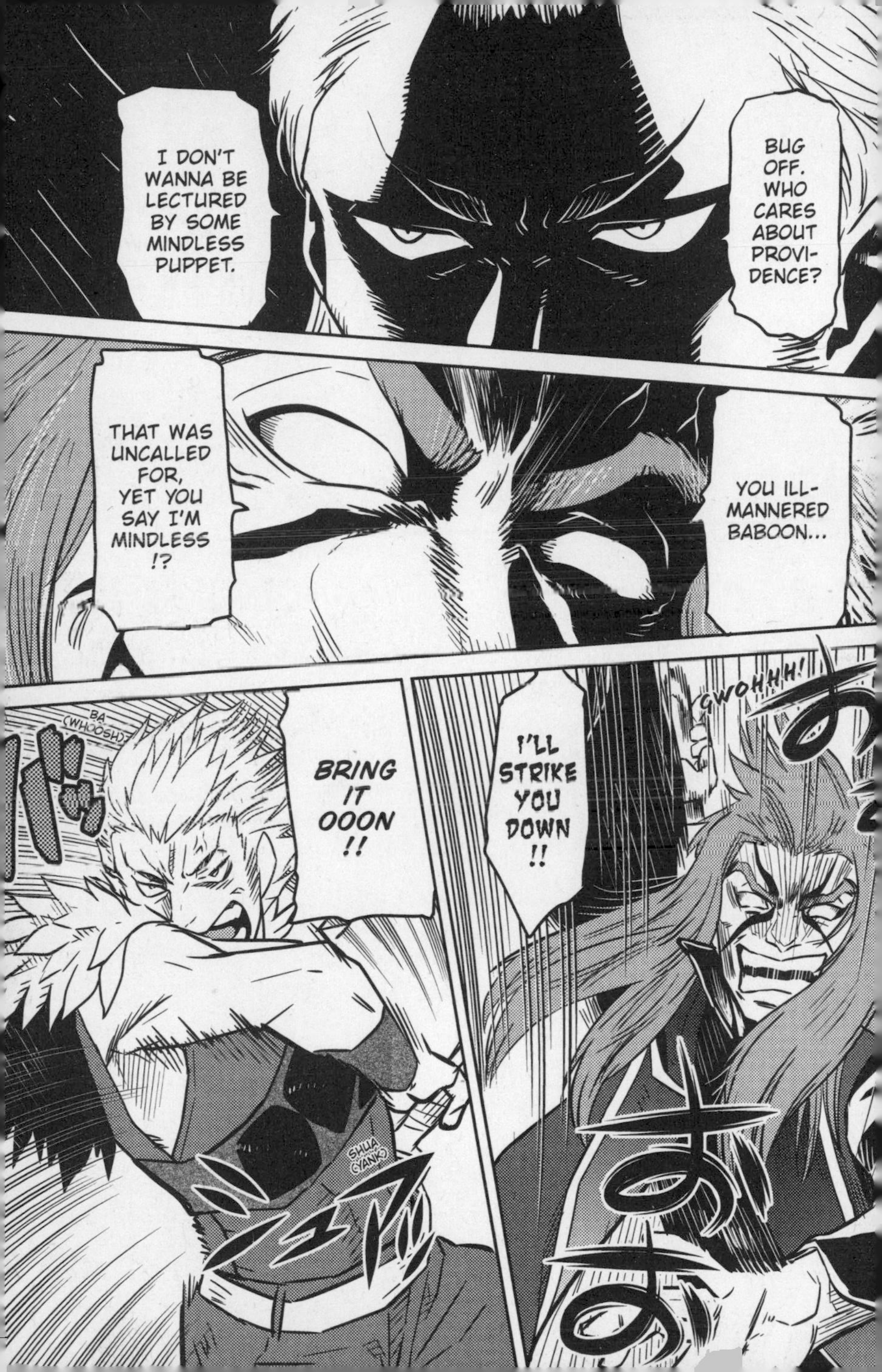
BUG OFF. WHO CARES ABOUT PROVIDENCE?
I DON'T WANNA BE LECTURED BY SOME MINDLESS PUPPET.
YOU ILL-MANNERED BABOON...
THAT WAS UNCALLED FOR, YET YOU SAY I'M MINDLESS!?
GWOHHHH!
I'LL STRIKE YOU DOWN!!
BRING IT OOON!!
BA (WHOOSH)
SHUA (YANK)

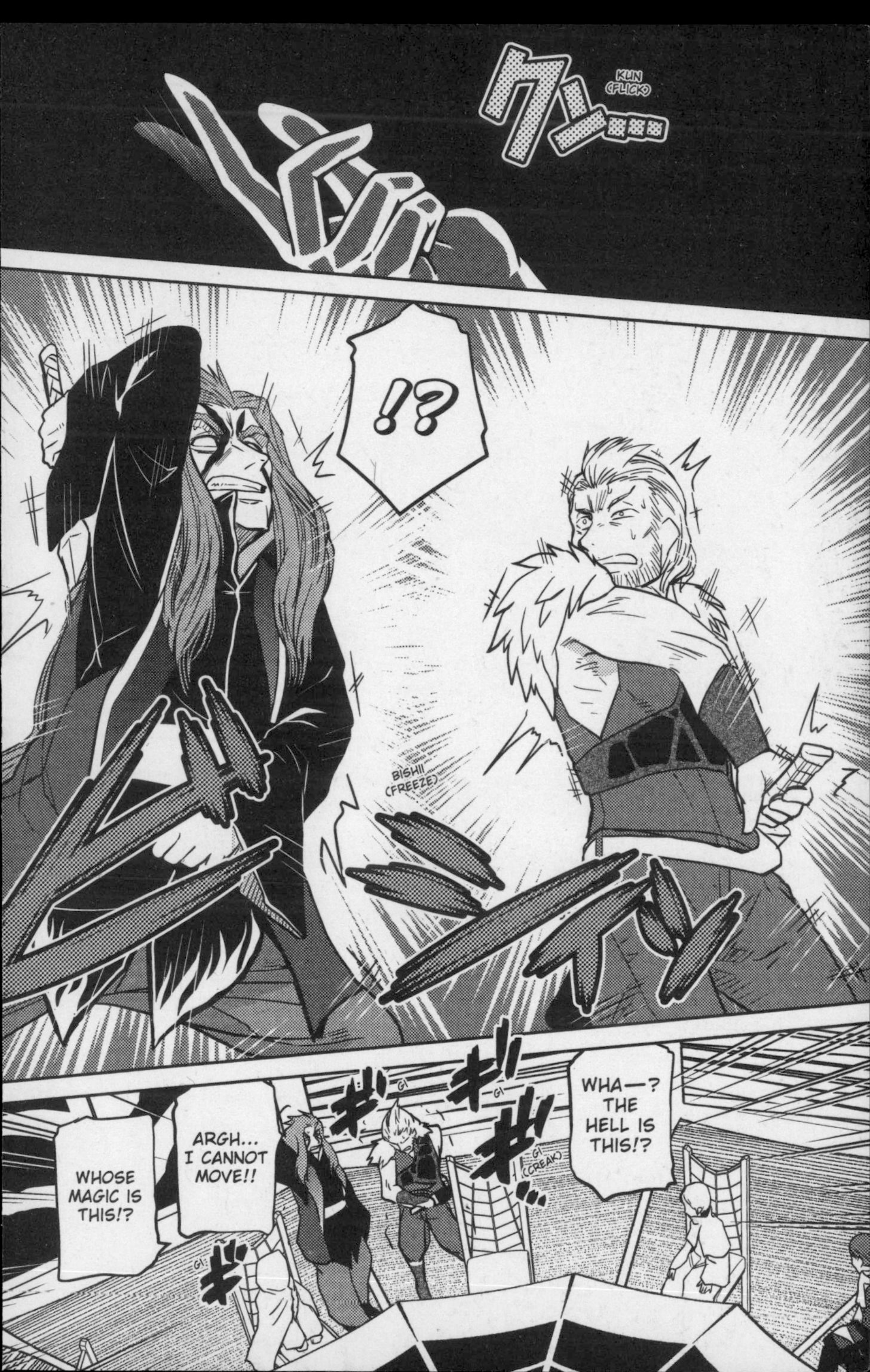
KUN (FLICK)
!?
BISHI! (FREEZE)
WHA—? THE HELL IS THIS!?
GI GI GI (CREAK)
ARGH... I CANNOT MOVE!!
WHOSE MAGIC IS THIS!?
GI

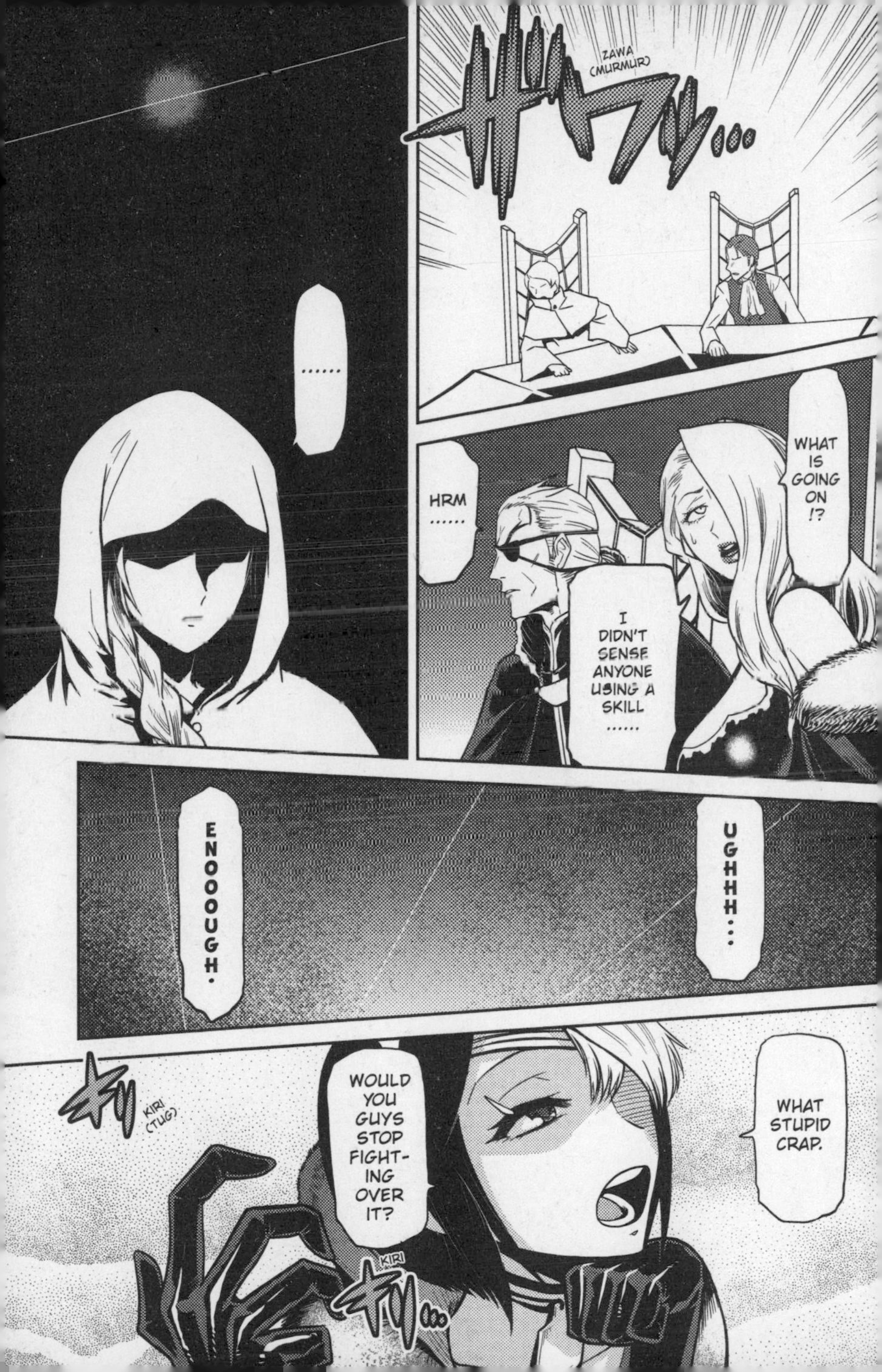
ZAWA (MURMUR)
WHAT IS GOING ON!?
HRM......
I DIDN'T SENSE ANYONE USING A SKILL......
......
UGHHH...
ENOOOUGH.
WHAT STUPID CRAP.
WOULD YOU GUYS STOP FIGHT-ING OVER IT?
KIRI (TUG)
KIRI

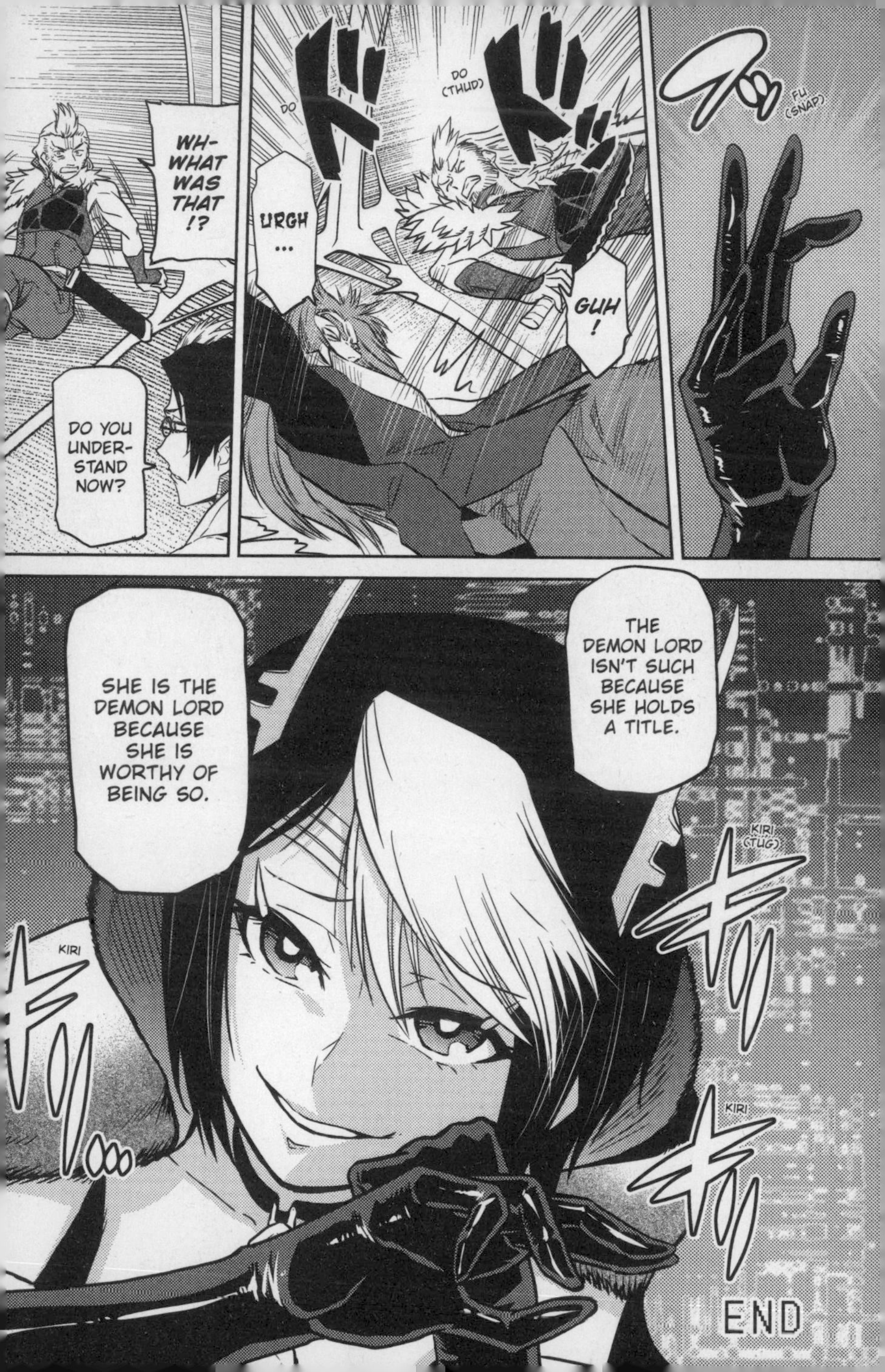

FU (SNAP)
DO (THUD)
DO
GUH!
URGH...
WH-WHAT WAS THAT!?
DO YOU UNDERSTAND NOW?
THE DEMON LORD ISN'T SUCH BECAUSE SHE HOLDS A TITLE.
SHE IS THE DEMON LORD BECAUSE SHE IS WORTHY OF BEING SO.
KIRI (TUG)
KIRI
KIRI
END

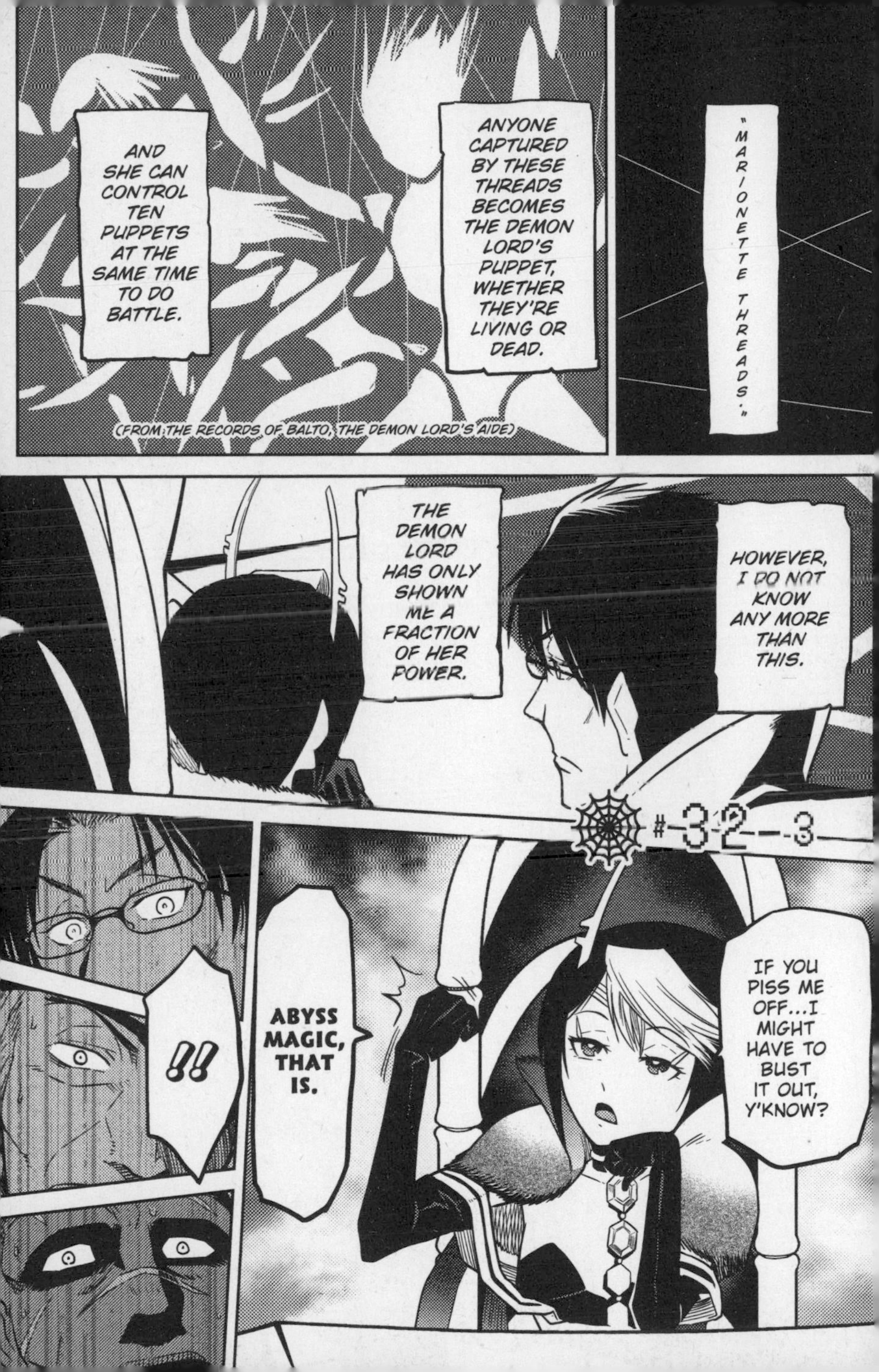
"MARIONETTE THREADS."
ANYONE CAPTURED BY THESE THREADS BECOMES THE DEMON LORD'S PUPPET, WHETHER THEY'RE LIVING OR DEAD.
AND SHE CAN CONTROL TEN PUPPETS AT THE SAME TIME TO DO BATTLE.
(FROM THE RECORDS OF BALTO, THE DEMON LORD'S AIDE)
HOWEVER, I DO NOT KNOW ANY MORE THAN THIS.
THE DEMON LORD HAS ONLY SHOWN ME A FRACTION OF HER POWER.
#32-3
IF YOU PISS ME OFF...I MIGHT HAVE TO BUST IT OUT, Y'KNOW?
ABYSS MAGIC, THAT IS.
!!

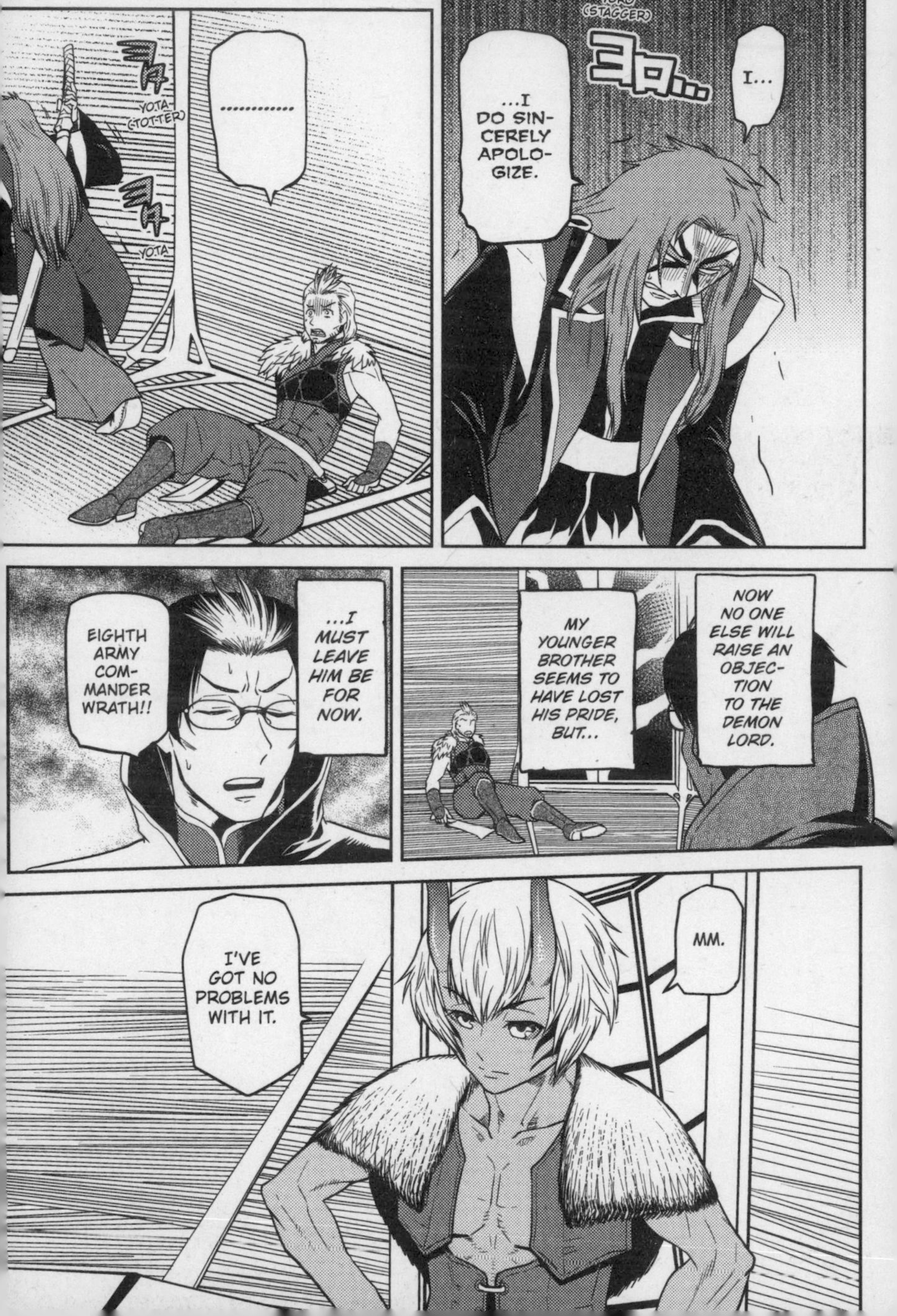
I...
YORO (STAGGER)
ヨロ...
...I DO SINCERELY APOLOGIZE.
ヨタ
YOTA (TOTTER)
ヨタ
YOTA
....
NOW NO ONE ELSE WILL RAISE AN OBJECTION TO THE DEMON LORD.
MY YOUNGER BROTHER SEEMS TO HAVE LOST HIS PRIDE, BUT...
...I MUST LEAVE HIM BE FOR NOW.
EIGHTH ARMY COMMANDER WRATH!!
MM.
I'VE GOT NO PROBLEMS WITH IT.

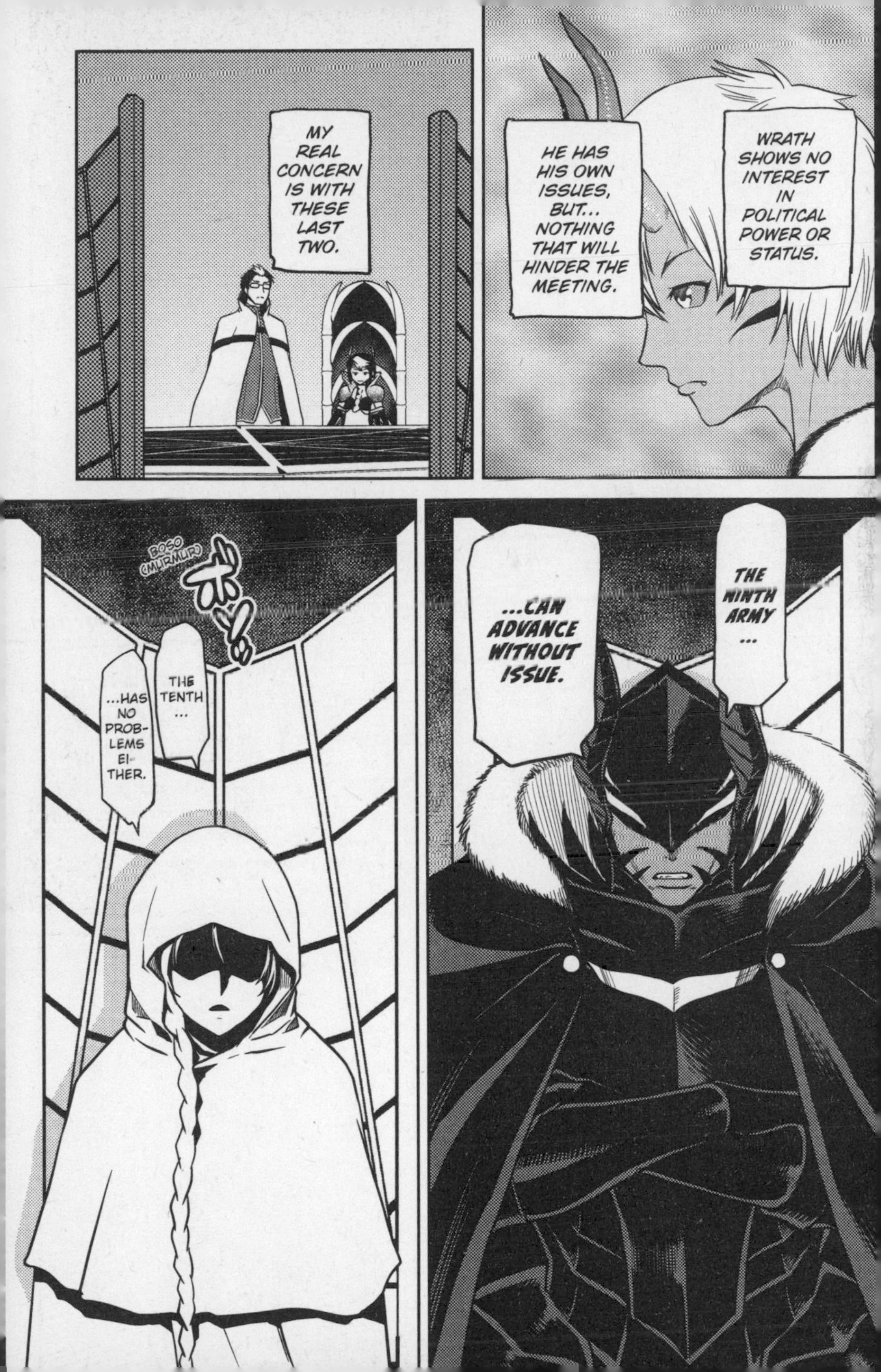
WRATH SHOWS NO INTEREST IN POLITICAL POWER OR STATUS.
HE HAS HIS OWN ISSUES, BUT... NOTHING THAT WILL HINDER THE MEETING.
MY REAL CONCERN IS WITH THESE LAST TWO.
THE NINTH ARMY...
...CAN ADVANCE WITHOUT ISSUE.
BOSO (MURMUR)
THE TENTH...
...HAS NO PROBLEMS EITHER.

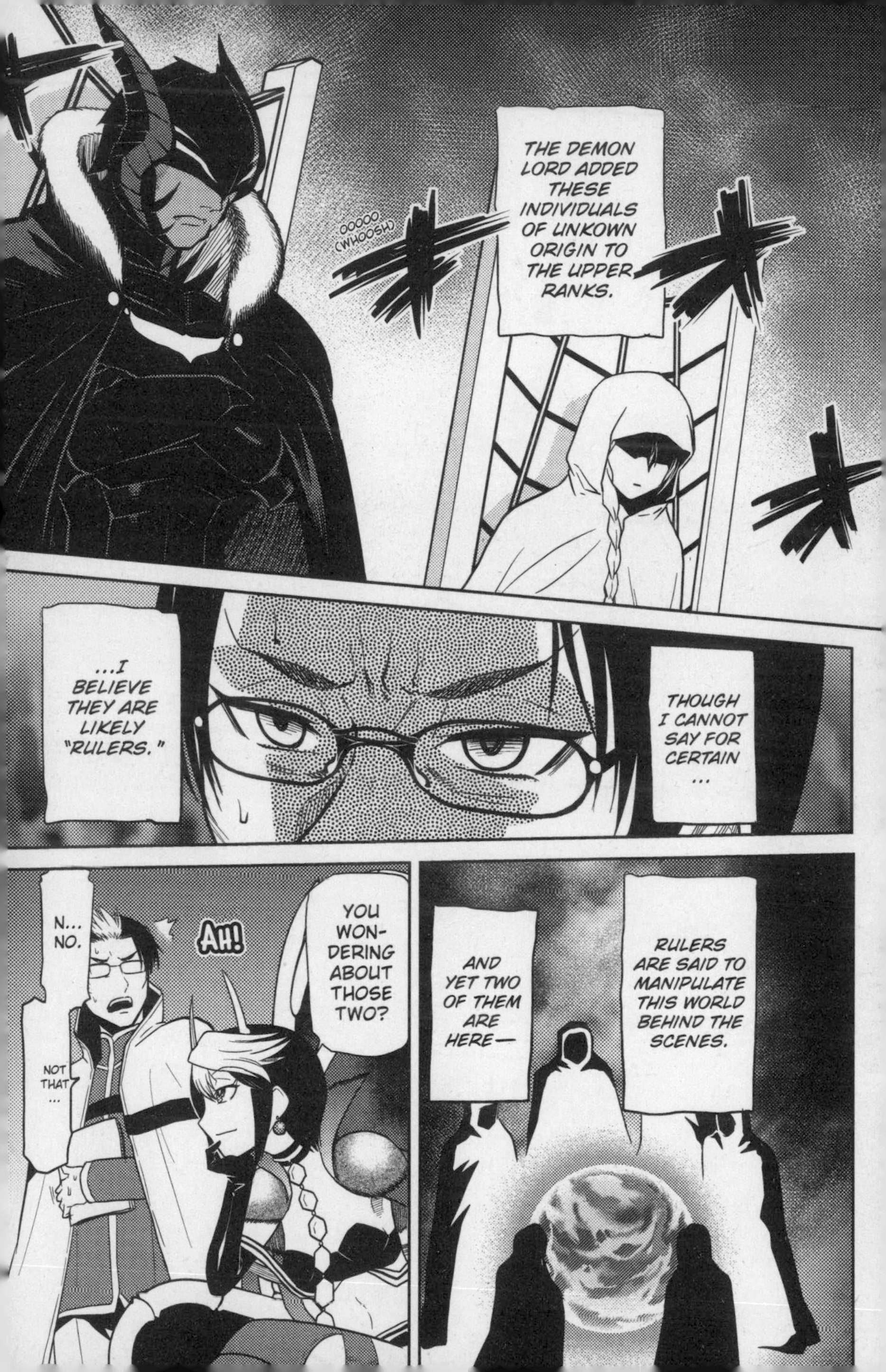
THE DEMON LORD ADDED THESE INDIVIDUALS OF UNKOWN ORIGIN TO THE UPPER RANKS.
OOOOO (WHOOSH)
THOUGH I CANNOT SAY FOR CERTAIN ...
...I BELIEVE THEY ARE LIKELY "RULERS."
RULERS ARE SAID TO MANIPULATE THIS WORLD BEHIND THE SCENES.
AND YET TWO OF THEM ARE HERE—
YOU WONDERING ABOUT THOSE TWO?
AH!
N... NO.
NOT THAT ...

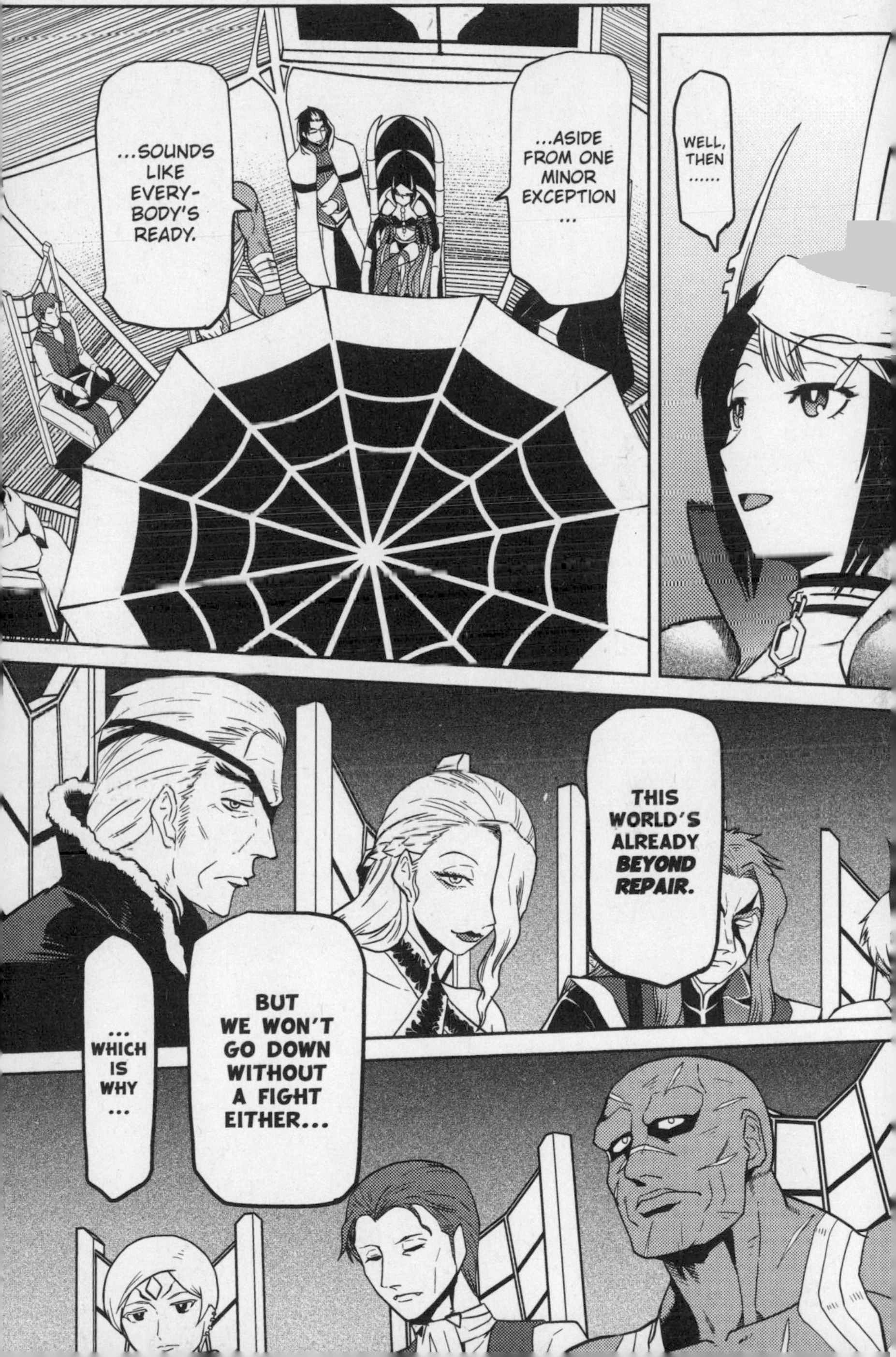
WELL, THEN ......
...ASIDE FROM ONE MINOR EXCEPTION ...
...SOUNDS LIKE EVERY-BODY'S READY.
THIS WORLD'S ALREADY *BEYOND REPAIR.*
BUT WE WON'T GO DOWN WITHOUT A FIGHT EITHER...
... WHICH IS WHY ...

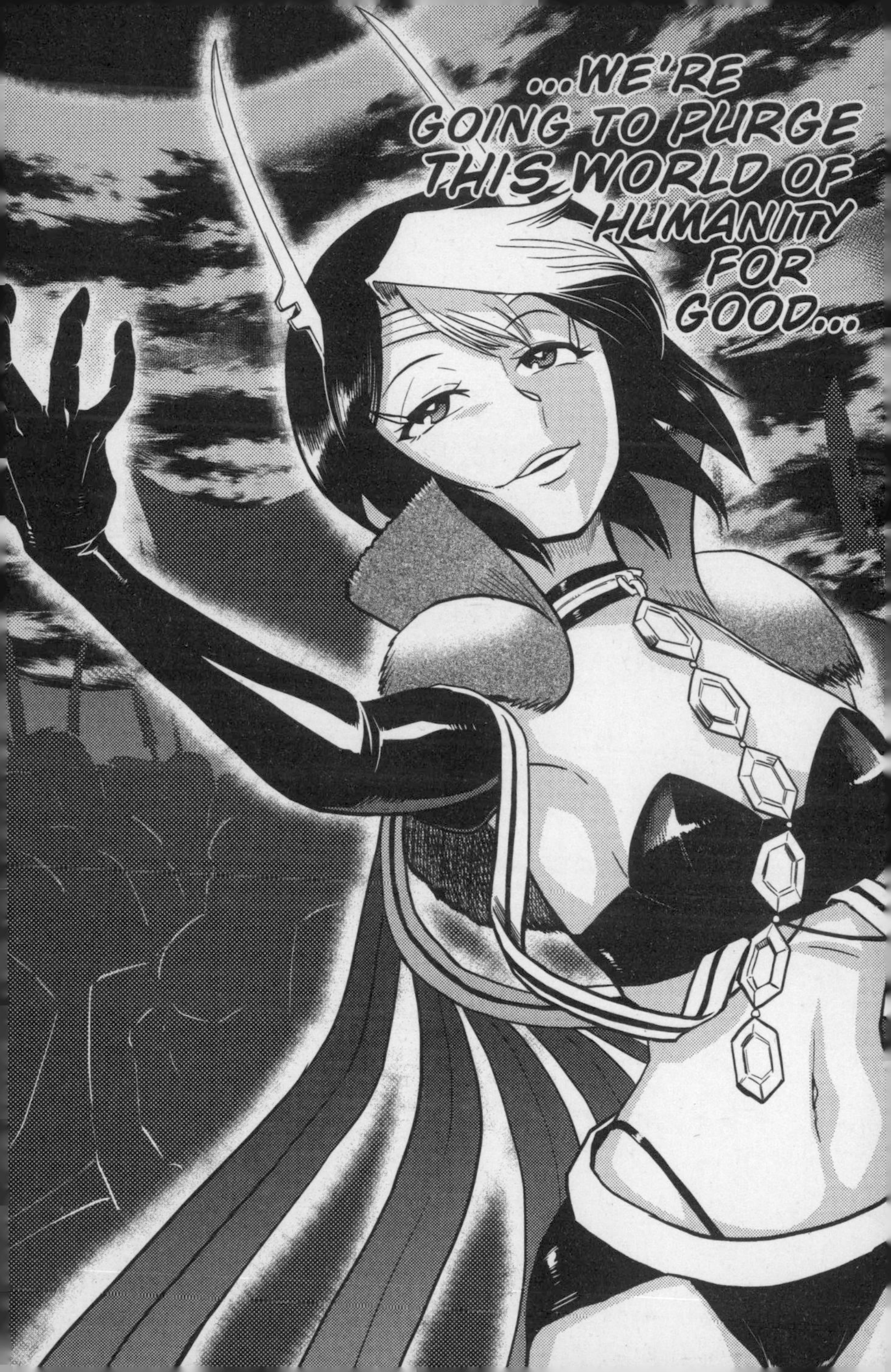
...WE'RE GOING TO PURGE THIS WORLD OF HUMANITY FOR GOOD...

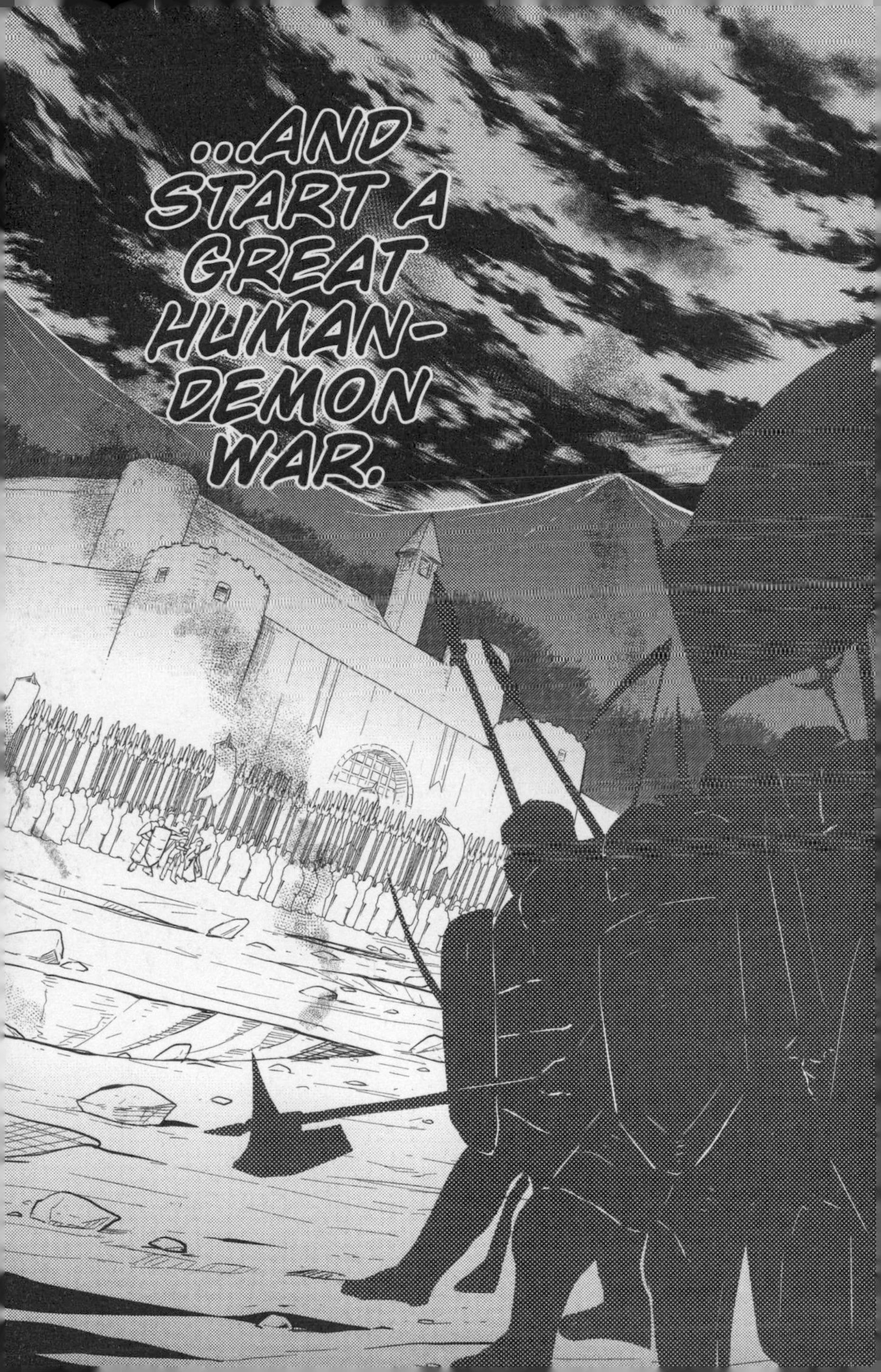
...AND START A GREAT HUMAN-DEMON WAR.

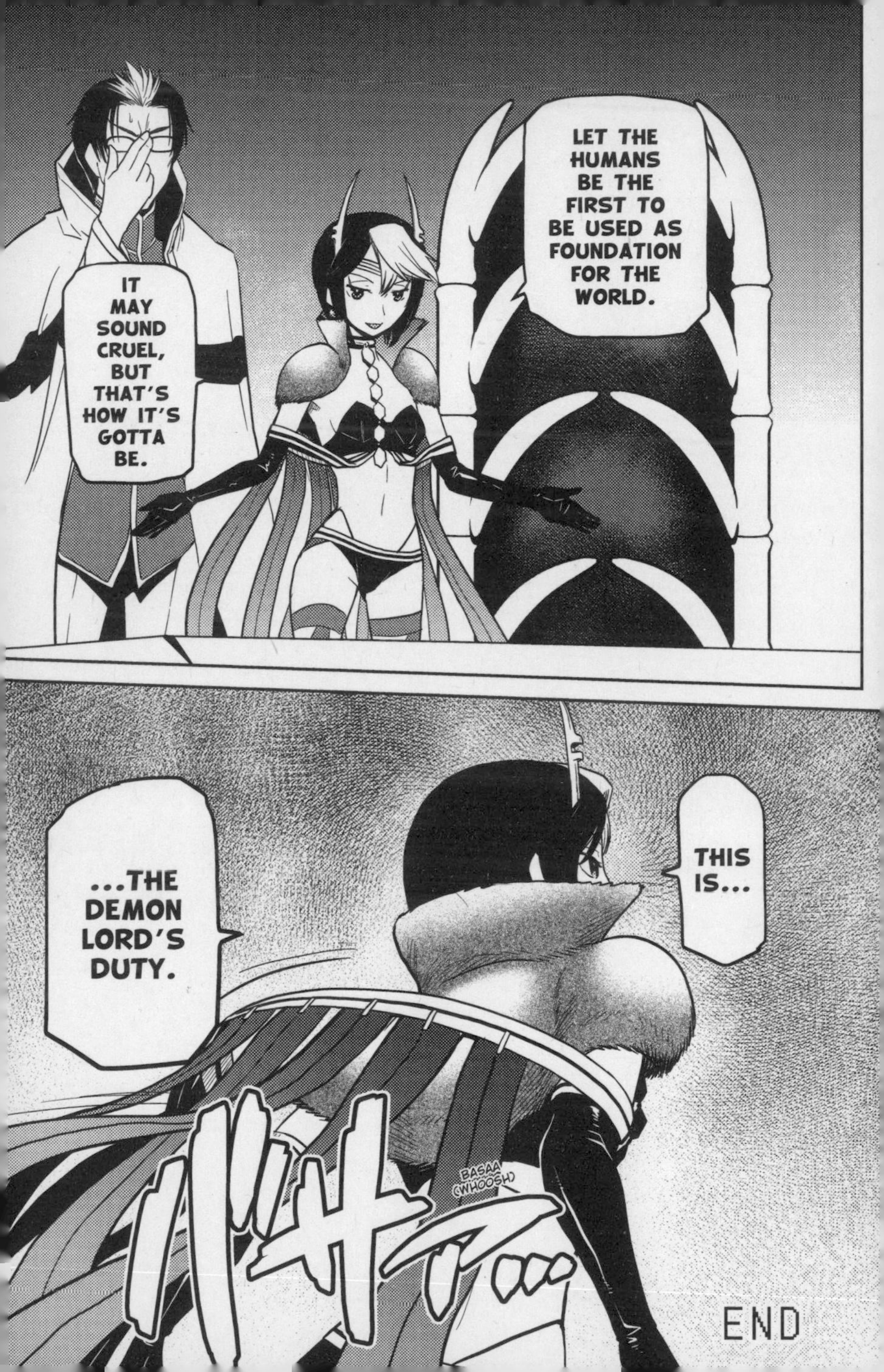
LET THE HUMANS BE THE FIRST TO BE USED AS FOUNDATION FOR THE WORLD.
IT MAY SOUND CRUEL, BUT THAT'S HOW IT'S GOTTA BE.
THIS IS...
...THE DEMON LORD'S DUTY.
BASAA (WHOOSH)
END

so I'm a Spider, so What?

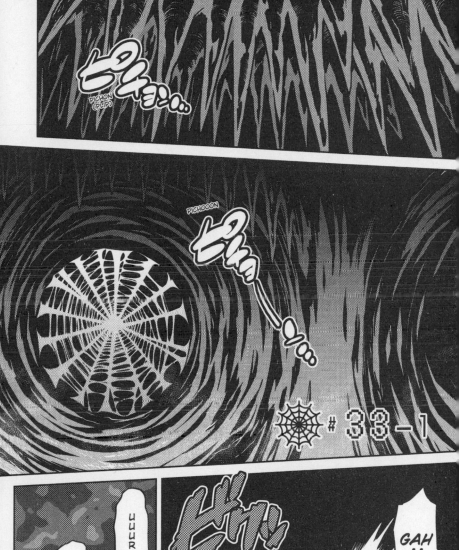

PICHON
(PLIP)

PICHOOON

✳ #33-1

UUURGH...

WHAT A HEAD-ACHE ......

BIKU
(TWITCH)

GAH!!

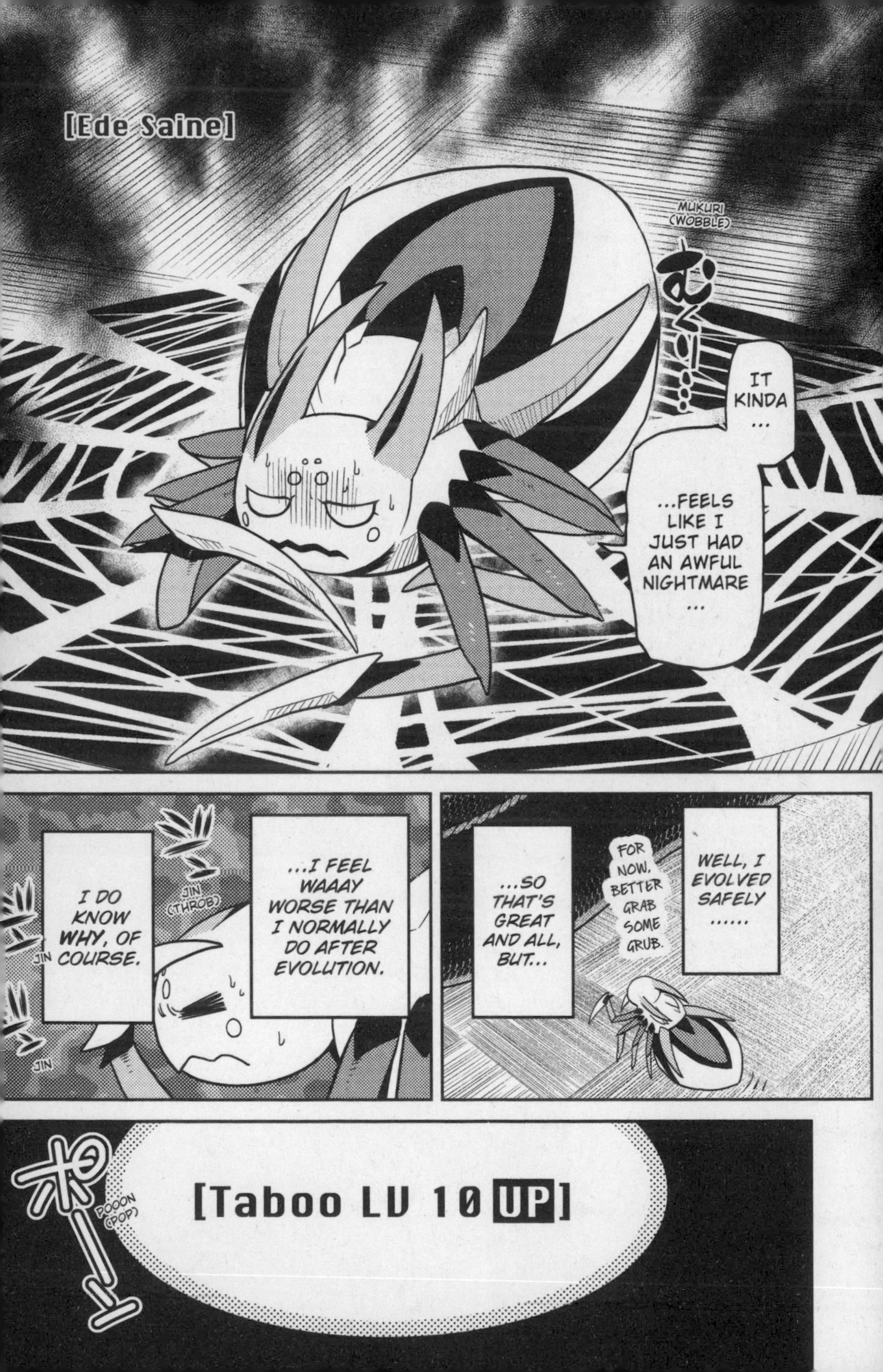
MUKURI (WOBBLE)
IT KINDA...
...FEELS LIKE I JUST HAD AN AWFUL NIGHTMARE...
[Ede Saine]
WELL, I EVOLVED SAFELY......
FOR NOW, BETTER GRAB SOME GRUB.
...SO THAT'S GREAT AND ALL, BUT...
...I FEEL WAAAY WORSE THAN I NORMALLY DO AFTER EVOLUTION.
JIN (THROB)
I DO KNOW WHY, OF COURSE.
JIN
JIN
POOON (POP)
[Taboo LV 10 UP]

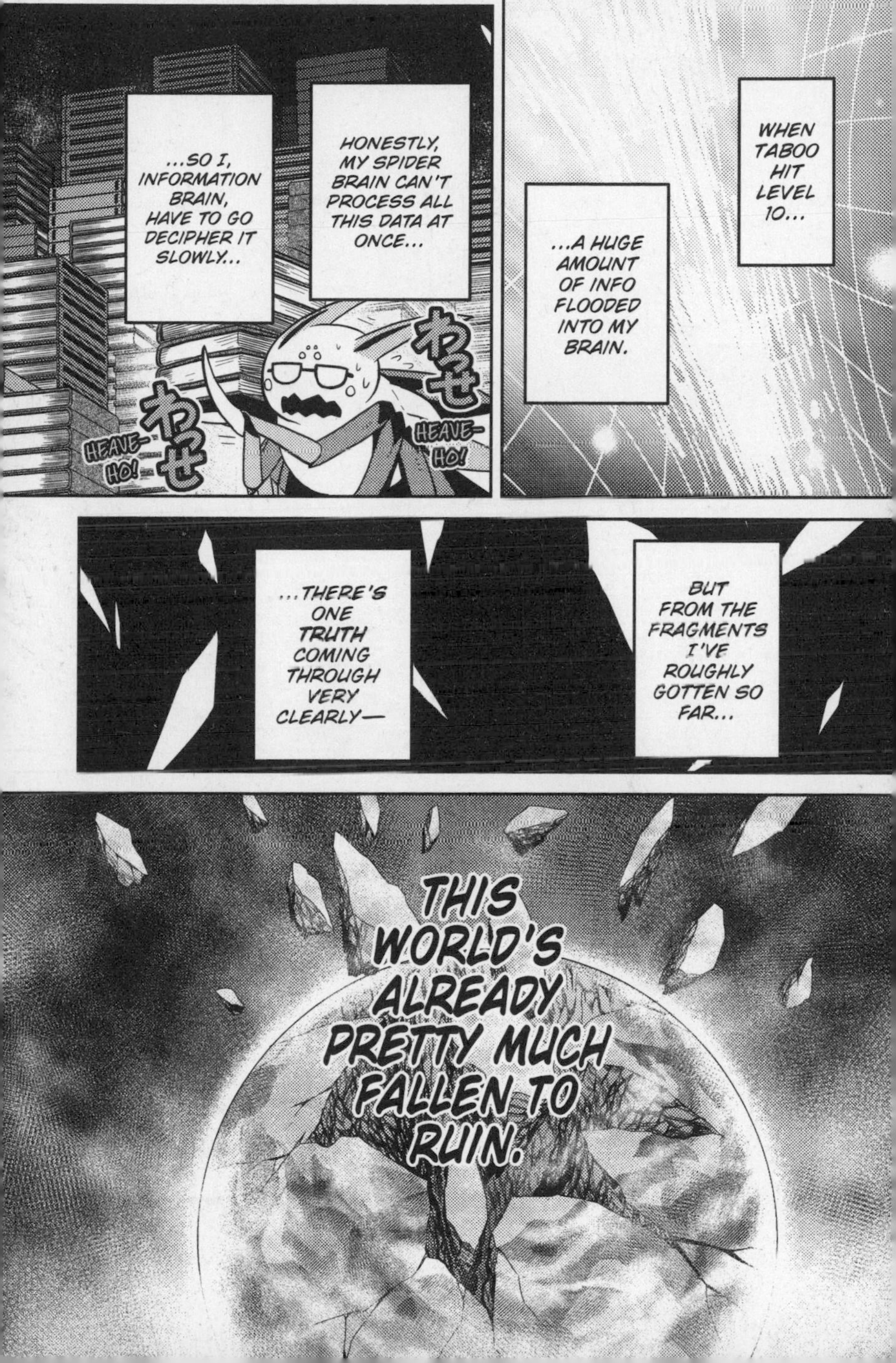
WHEN TABOO HIT LEVEL 10...
...A HUGE AMOUNT OF INFO FLOODED INTO MY BRAIN.
HONESTLY, MY SPIDER BRAIN CAN'T PROCESS ALL THIS DATA AT ONCE...
...SO I, INFORMATION BRAIN, HAVE TO GO DECIPHER IT SLOWLY...
わっせ
HEAVE-HO!
わっせ
HEAVE-HO!
BUT FROM THE FRAGMENTS I'VE ROUGHLY GOTTEN SO FAR...
...THERE'S ONE TRUTH COMING THROUGH VERY CLEARLY—
THIS WORLD'S ALREADY PRETTY MUCH FALLEN TO RUIN.

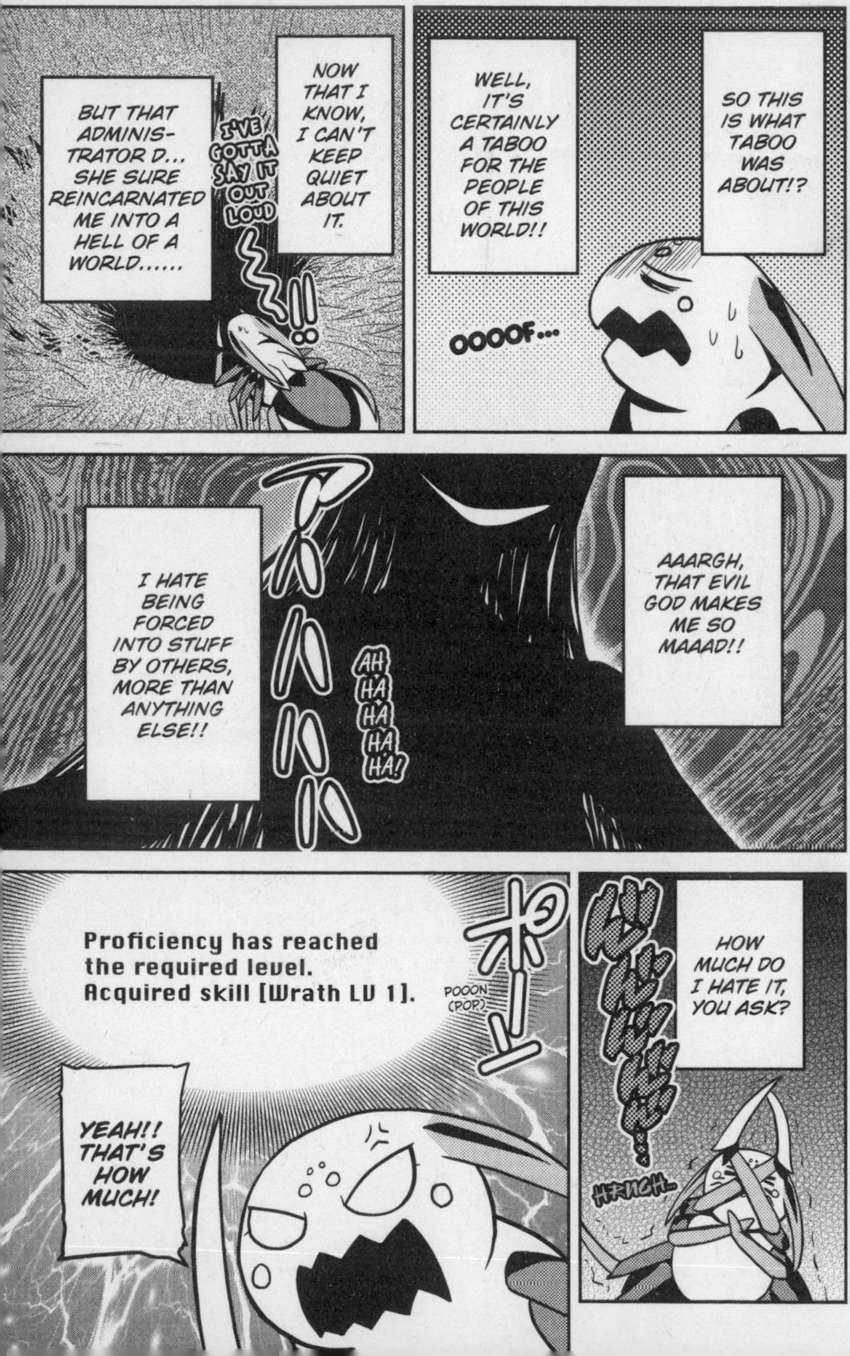
SO THIS IS WHAT TABOO WAS ABOUT!?
WELL, IT'S CERTAINLY A TABOO FOR THE PEOPLE OF THIS WORLD!!
OOOOF...
NOW THAT I KNOW, I CAN'T KEEP QUIET ABOUT IT.
I'VE GOTTA SAY IT OUT LOUD
BUT THAT ADMINIS-TRATOR D... SHE SURE REINCARNATED ME INTO A HELL OF A WORLD......
AAARGH, THAT EVIL GOD MAKES ME SO MAAAD!!
AH HA HA HA HA!
I HATE BEING FORCED INTO STUFF BY OTHERS, MORE THAN ANYTHING ELSE!!
HOW MUCH DO I HATE IT, YOU ASK?
HRNGH...
POOON (POP.)
Proficiency has reached the required level. Acquired skill [Wrath LV 1].
YEAH!! THAT'S HOW MUCH!

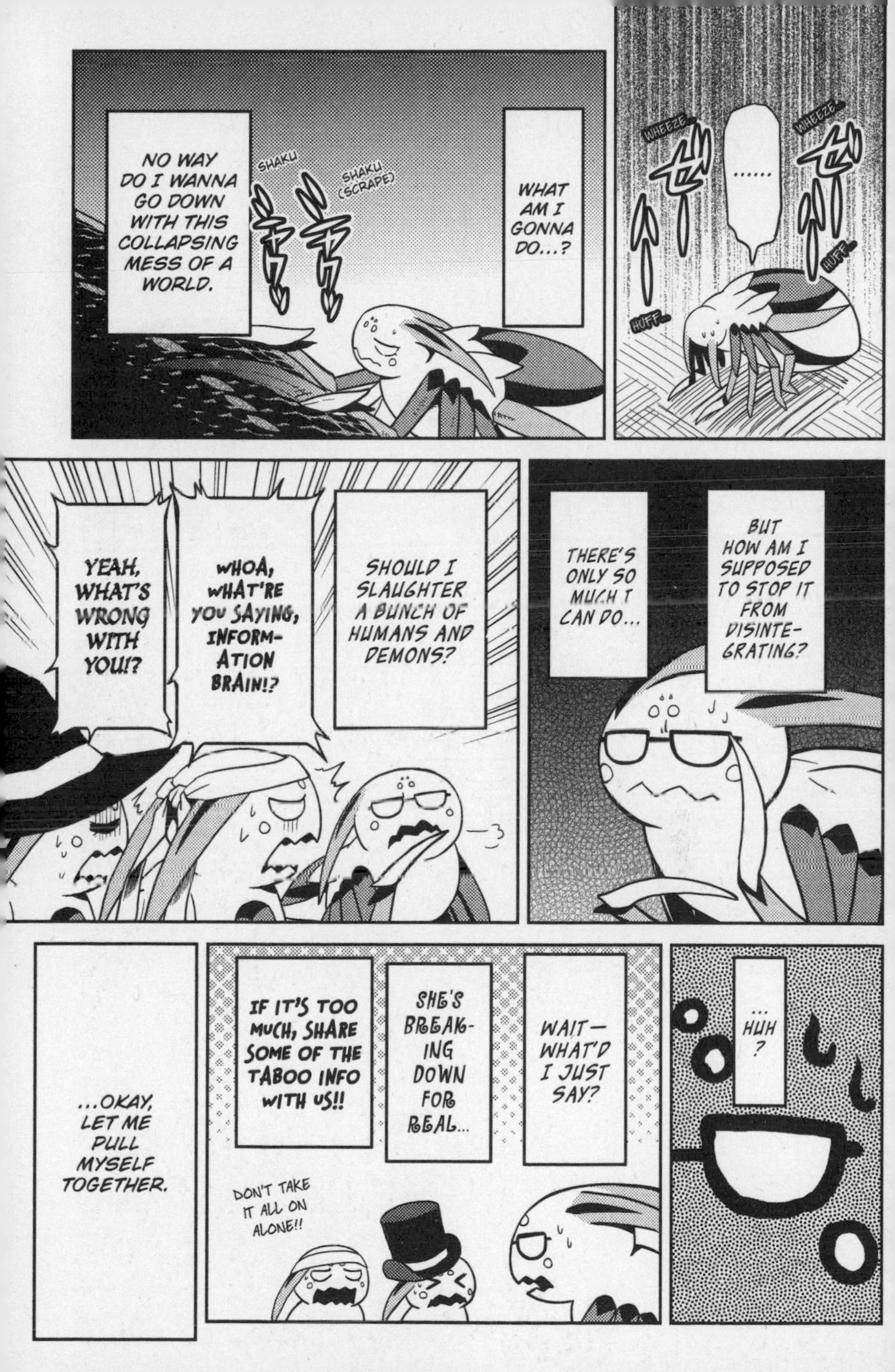
WHEEZE...
......
WHEEZE...
HUFF...
HUFF...
WHAT AM I GONNA DO...?
SHAKU (SCRAPE)
SHAKU
NO WAY DO I WANNA GO DOWN WITH THIS COLLAPSING MESS OF A WORLD.
BUT HOW AM I SUPPOSED TO STOP IT FROM DISINTEGRATING?
THERE'S ONLY SO MUCH I CAN DO...
SHOULD I SLAUGHTER A BUNCH OF HUMANS AND DEMONS?
WHOA, WHAT'RE YOU SAYING, INFORMATION BRAIN!?
YEAH, WHAT'S WRONG WITH YOU!?
...HUH?
WAIT—WHAT'D I JUST SAY?
SHE'S BREAKING DOWN FOR REAL...
IF IT'S TOO MUCH, SHARE SOME OF THE TABOO INFO WITH US!!
DON'T TAKE IT ALL ON ALONE!!
...OKAY, LET ME PULL MYSELF TOGETHER.

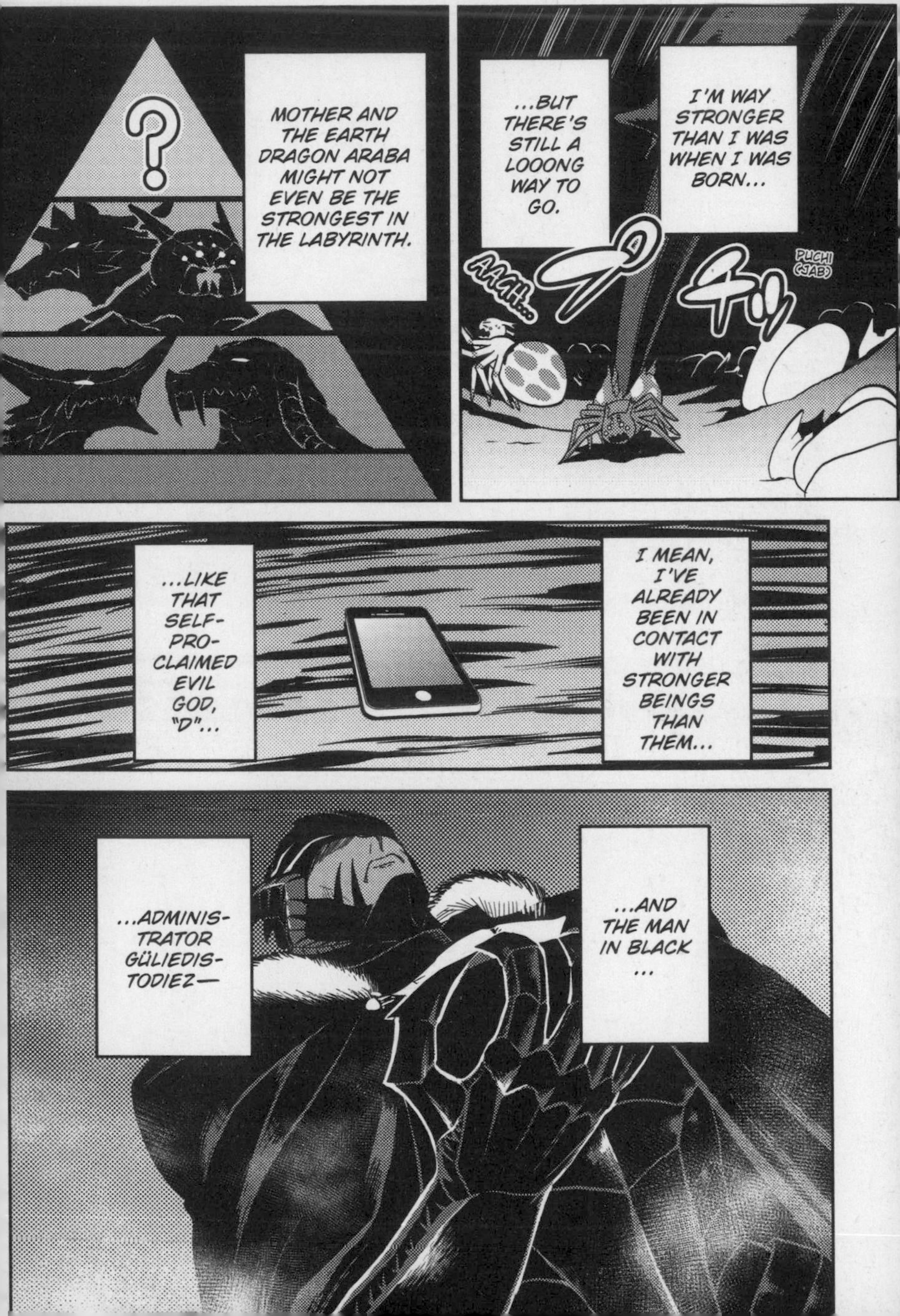
I'M WAY STRONGER THAN I WAS WHEN I WAS BORN...
...BUT THERE'S STILL A LOOONG WAY TO GO.
PUCHI (JAB)
AAAH...
MOTHER AND THE EARTH DRAGON ARABA MIGHT NOT EVEN BE THE STRONGEST IN THE LABYRINTH.
I MEAN, I'VE ALREADY BEEN IN CONTACT WITH STRONGER BEINGS THAN THEM...
...LIKE THAT SELF-PROCLAIMED EVIL GOD, "D"...
...AND THE MAN IN BLACK...
...ADMINISTRATOR GÜLIEDISTODIEZ—

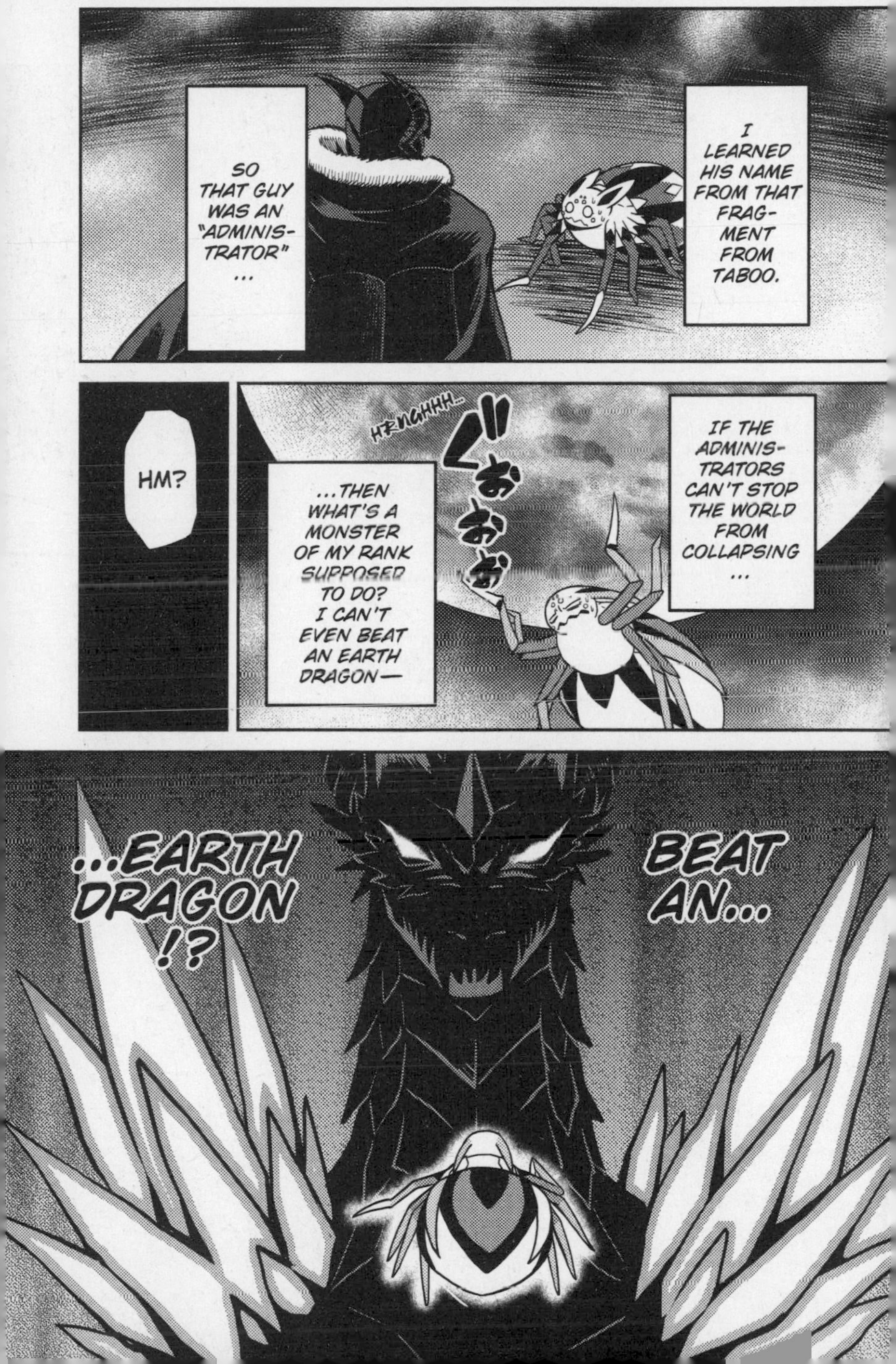
I LEARNED HIS NAME FROM THAT FRAG-MENT FROM TABOO.
SO THAT GUY WAS AN "ADMINIS-TRATOR"...
IF THE ADMINIS-TRATORS CAN'T STOP THE WORLD FROM COLLAPSING...
HRNGHHH...
...THEN WHAT'S A MONSTER OF MY RANK SUPPOSED TO DO? I CAN'T EVEN BEAT AN EARTH DRAGON—
HM?
BEAT AN...
...EARTH DRAGON!?

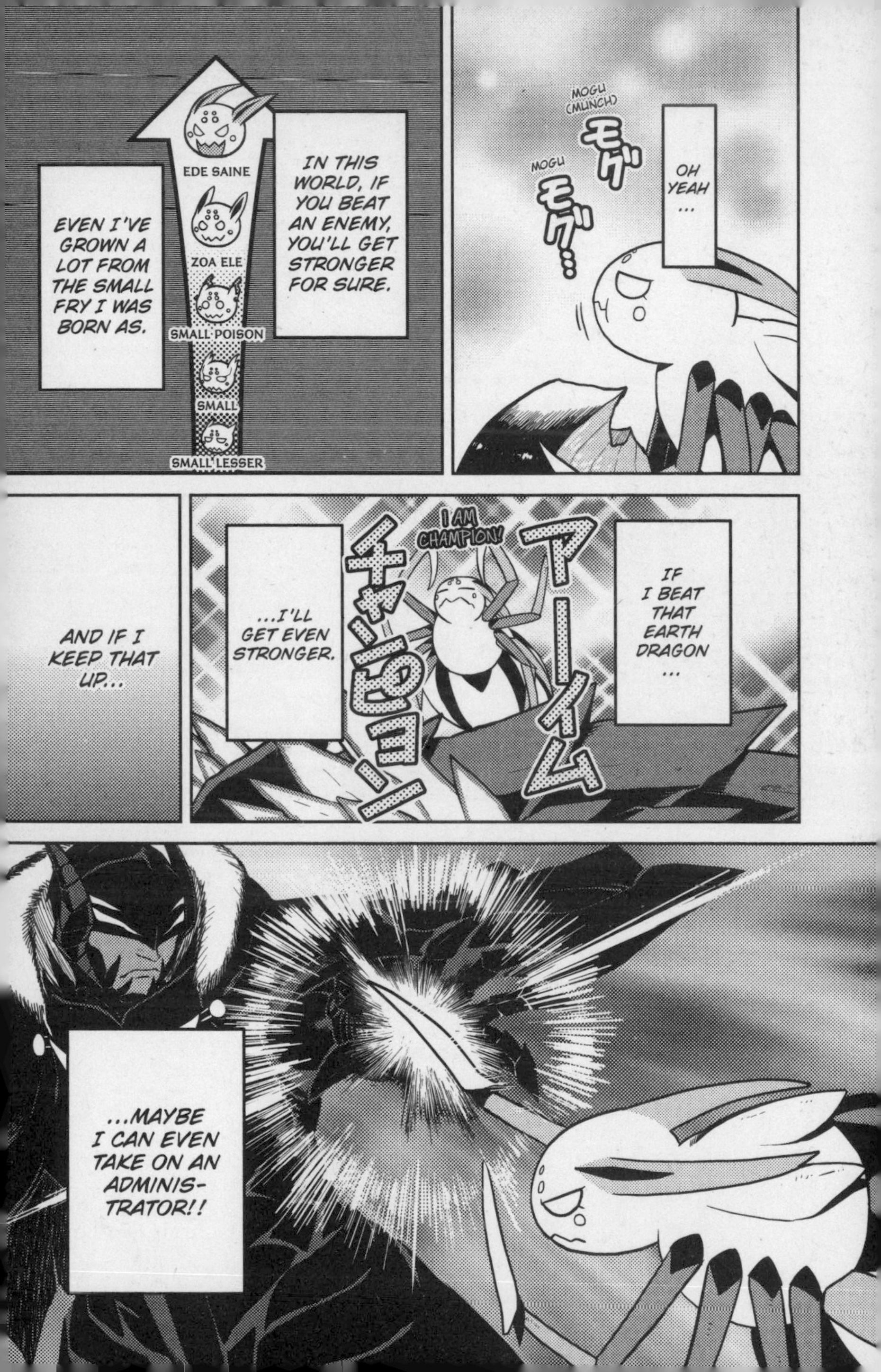
MOGU (MUNCH)
モグ
MOGU
モグ…
OH YEAH…
IN THIS WORLD, IF YOU BEAT AN ENEMY, YOU'LL GET STRONGER FOR SURE.
EDE SAINE
ZOA ELE
SMALL POISON
SMALL
SMALL LESSER
EVEN I'VE GROWN A LOT FROM THE SMALL FRY I WAS BORN AS.
IF I BEAT THAT EARTH DRAGON…
I AM CHAMPION!
アーイム
チャンピョーン
…I'LL GET EVEN STRONGER.
AND IF I KEEP THAT UP…
…MAYBE I CAN EVEN TAKE ON AN ADMINISTRATOR!!

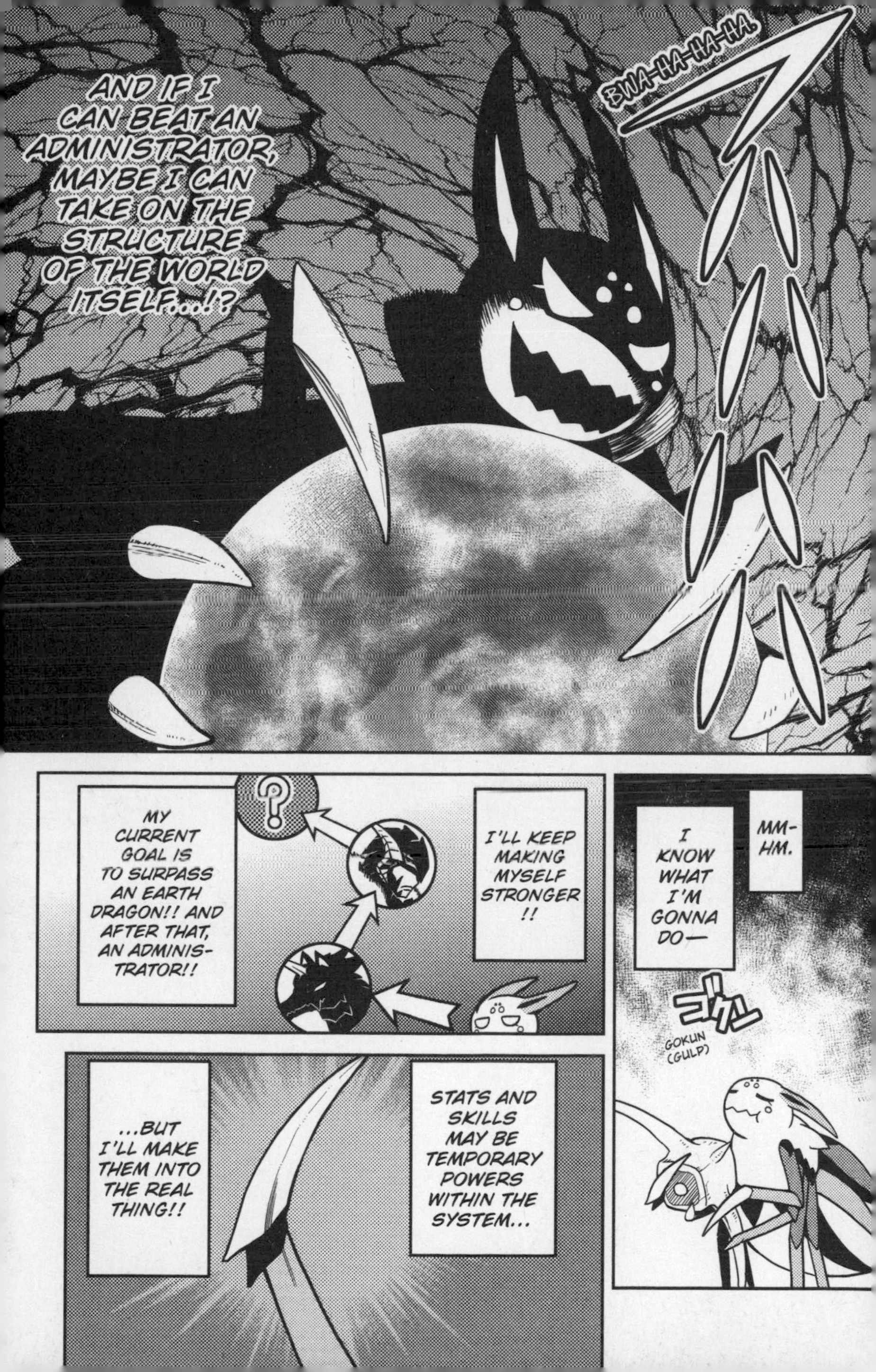
BWA-HA-HA-HA
AND IF I CAN BEAT AN ADMINISTRATOR, MAYBE I CAN TAKE ON THE STRUCTURE OF THE WORLD ITSELF...!?
MM-HM.
I KNOW WHAT I'M GONNA DO—
ゴクン
GOKUN (GULP)
I'LL KEEP MAKING MYSELF STRONGER!!
?
MY CURRENT GOAL IS TO SURPASS AN EARTH DRAGON!! AND AFTER THAT, AN ADMINISTRATOR!!
STATS AND SKILLS MAY BE TEMPORARY POWERS WITHIN THE SYSTEM...
...BUT I'LL MAKE THEM INTO THE REAL THING!!

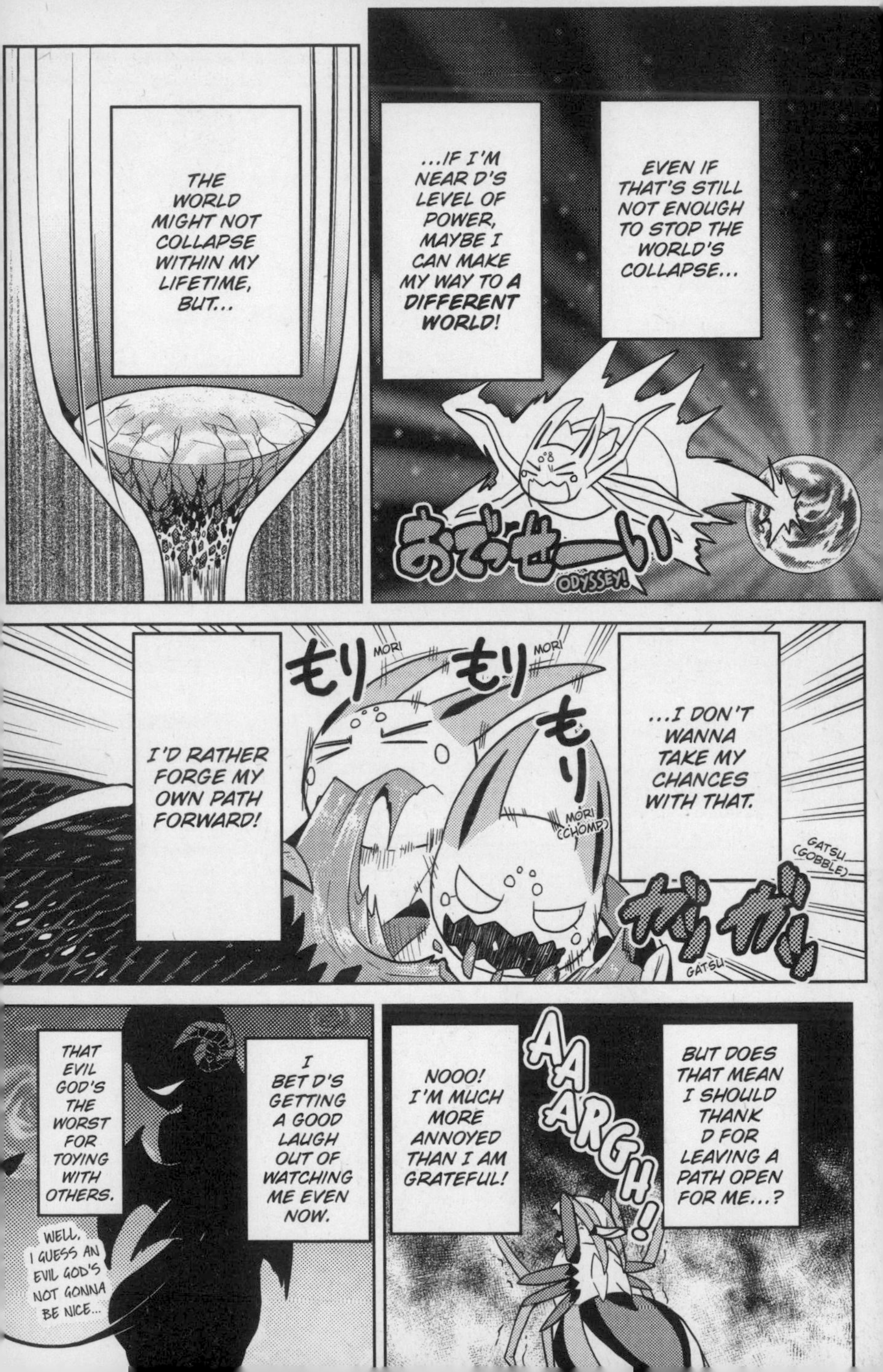
EVEN IF THAT'S STILL NOT ENOUGH TO STOP THE WORLD'S COLLAPSE...
...IF I'M NEAR D'S LEVEL OF POWER, MAYBE I CAN MAKE MY WAY TO A DIFFERENT WORLD!
おでっせーい
ODYSSEY!
THE WORLD MIGHT NOT COLLAPSE WITHIN MY LIFETIME, BUT...
...I DON'T WANNA TAKE MY CHANCES WITH THAT.
GATSU (GOBBLE)
ガッ
ガッ
GATSU
もり
MORI (CHOMP)
もり
MORI
もり
MORI
I'D RATHER FORGE MY OWN PATH FORWARD!
BUT DOES THAT MEAN I SHOULD THANK D FOR LEAVING A PATH OPEN FOR ME...?
AAARGH!
NOOO! I'M MUCH MORE ANNOYED THAN I AM GRATEFUL!
I BET D'S GETTING A GOOD LAUGH OUT OF WATCHING ME EVEN NOW.
THAT EVIL GOD'S THE WORST FOR TOYING WITH OTHERS.
WELL, I GUESS AN EVIL GOD'S NOT GONNA BE NICE...

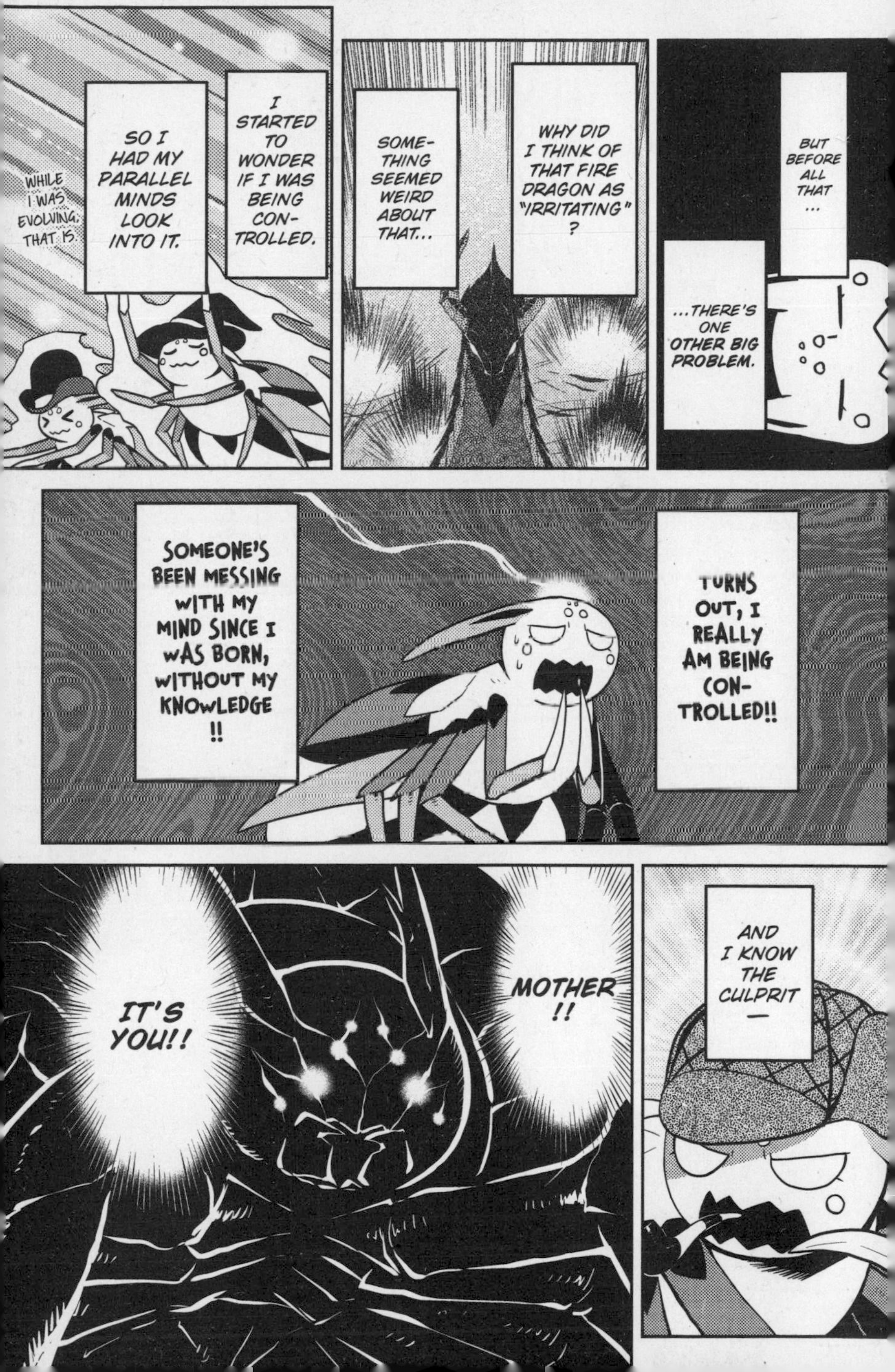
BUT BEFORE ALL THAT ...
...THERE'S ONE OTHER BIG PROBLEM.
WHY DID I THINK OF THAT FIRE DRAGON AS "IRRITATING"?
SOME-THING SEEMED WEIRD ABOUT THAT...
I STARTED TO WONDER IF I WAS BEING CON-TROLLED.
SO I HAD MY PARALLEL MINDS LOOK INTO IT.
WHILE I WAS EVOLVING, THAT IS.
TURNS OUT, I REALLY AM BEING CON-TROLLED!!
SOMEONE'S BEEN MESSING WITH MY MIND SINCE I WAS BORN, WITHOUT MY KNOWLEDGE!!
AND I KNOW THE CULPRIT—
MOTHER!!
IT'S YOU!!

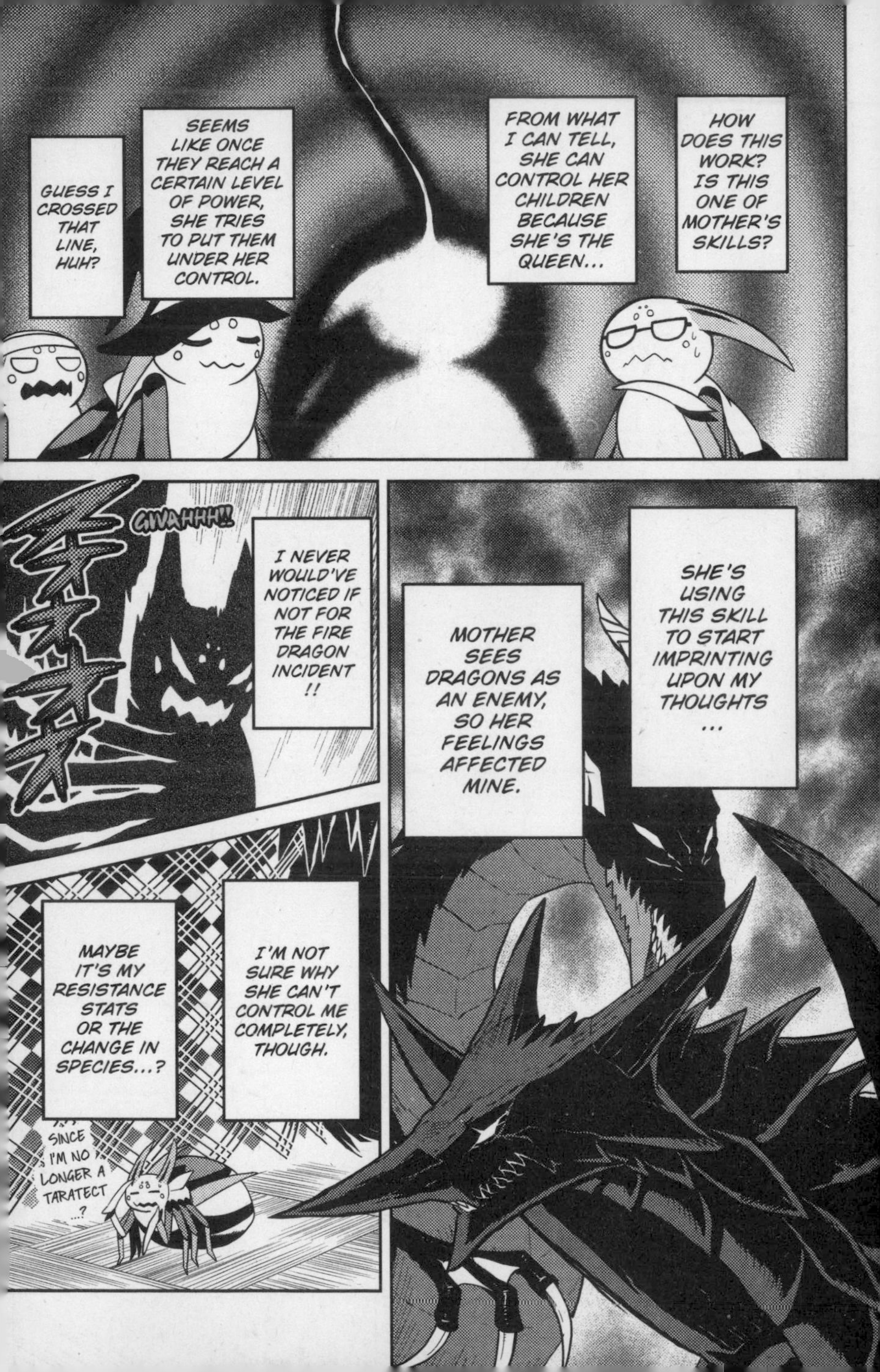
HOW DOES THIS WORK? IS THIS ONE OF MOTHER'S SKILLS?
FROM WHAT I CAN TELL, SHE CAN CONTROL HER CHILDREN BECAUSE SHE'S THE QUEEN...
SEEMS LIKE ONCE THEY REACH A CERTAIN LEVEL OF POWER, SHE TRIES TO PUT THEM UNDER HER CONTROL.
GUESS I CROSSED THAT LINE, HUH?
SHE'S USING THIS SKILL TO START IMPRINTING UPON MY THOUGHTS...
MOTHER SEES DRAGONS AS AN ENEMY, SO HER FEELINGS AFFECTED MINE.
GIWAHHH!!
I NEVER WOULD'VE NOTICED IF NOT FOR THE FIRE DRAGON INCIDENT!!
I'M NOT SURE WHY SHE CAN'T CONTROL ME COMPLETELY, THOUGH.
MAYBE IT'S MY RESISTANCE STATS OR THE CHANGE IN SPECIES...?
SINCE I'M NO LONGER A TARATECT ...?

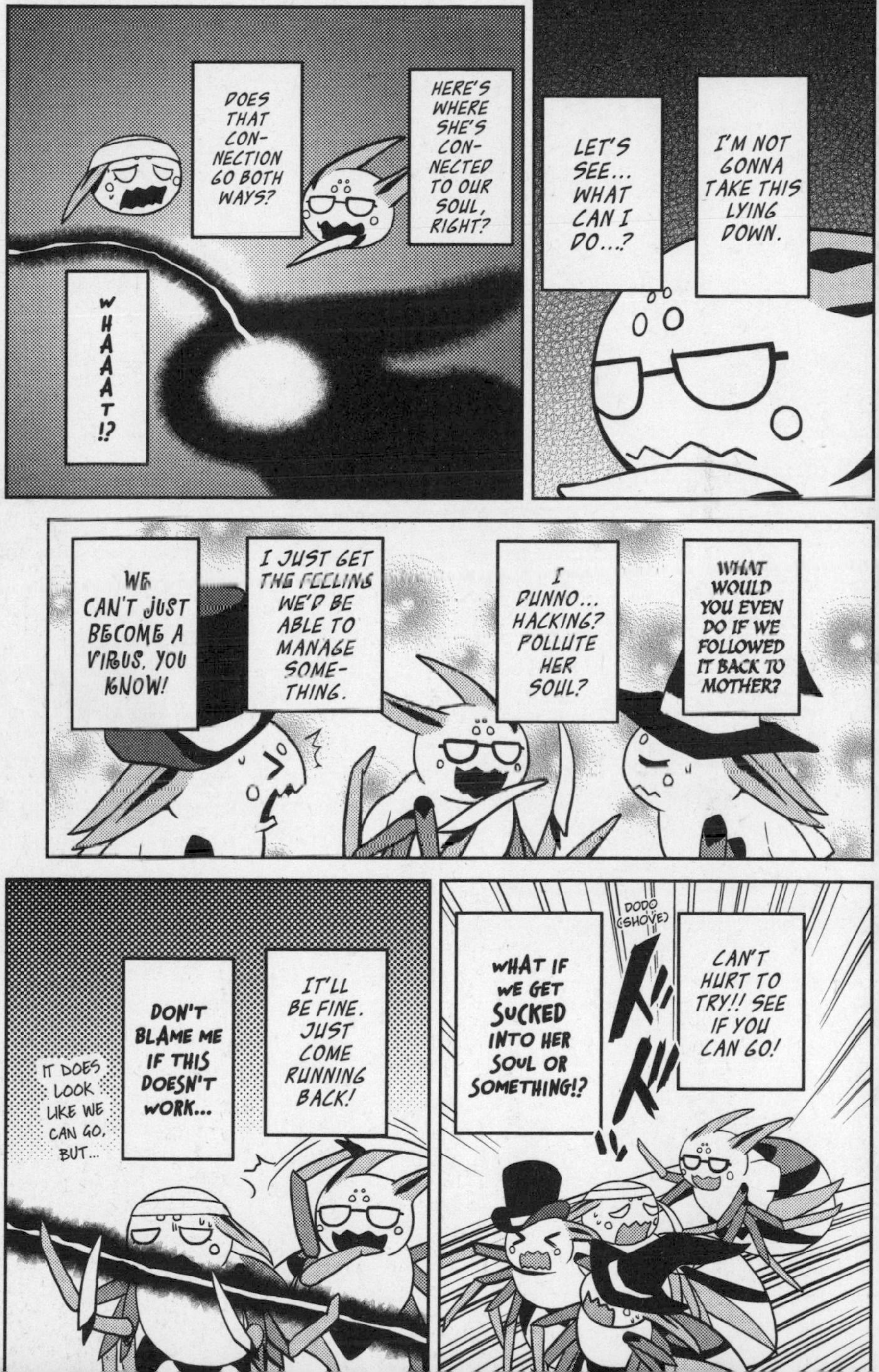
I'M NOT GONNA TAKE THIS LYING DOWN.
LET'S SEE... WHAT CAN I DO...?
HERE'S WHERE SHE'S CON-NECTED TO OUR SOUL, RIGHT?
DOES THAT CON-NECTION GO BOTH WAYS?
WHAAAAT!?
WHAT WOULD YOU EVEN DO IF WE FOLLOWED IT BACK TO MOTHER?
I DUNNO... HACKING? POLLUTE HER SOUL?
I JUST GET THE FEELING WE'D BE ABLE TO MANAGE SOME-THING.
WE CAN'T JUST BECOME A VIRUS, YOU KNOW!
DODO (SHOVE)
CAN'T HURT TO TRY!! SEE IF YOU CAN GO!
WHAT IF WE GET SUCKED INTO HER SOUL OR SOMETHING!?
IT'LL BE FINE. JUST COME RUNNING BACK!
DON'T BLAME ME IF THIS DOESN'T WORK...
IT DOES LOOK LIKE WE CAN GO, BUT...

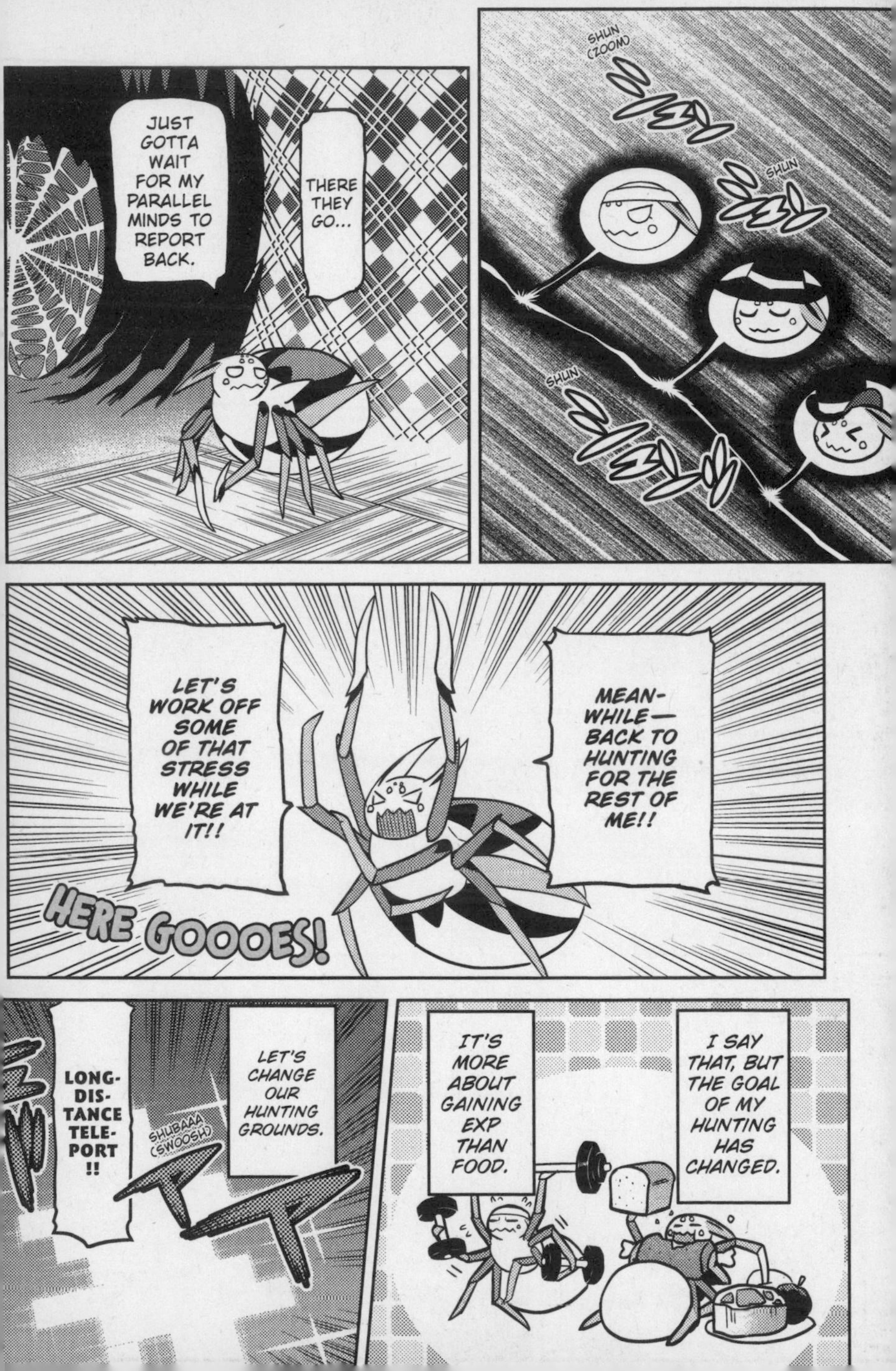
SHUN (ZOOM)
SHUN
SHUN
THERE THEY GO...
JUST GOTTA WAIT FOR MY PARALLEL MINDS TO REPORT BACK.
MEAN-WHILE—BACK TO HUNTING FOR THE REST OF ME!!
LET'S WORK OFF SOME OF THAT STRESS WHILE WE'RE AT IT!!
HERE GOOOES!
I SAY THAT, BUT THE GOAL OF MY HUNTING HAS CHANGED.
IT'S MORE ABOUT GAINING EXP THAN FOOD.
LET'S CHANGE OUR HUNTING GROUNDS.
SHUBAAA (SWOOSH)
LONG-DISTANCE TELEPORT!!

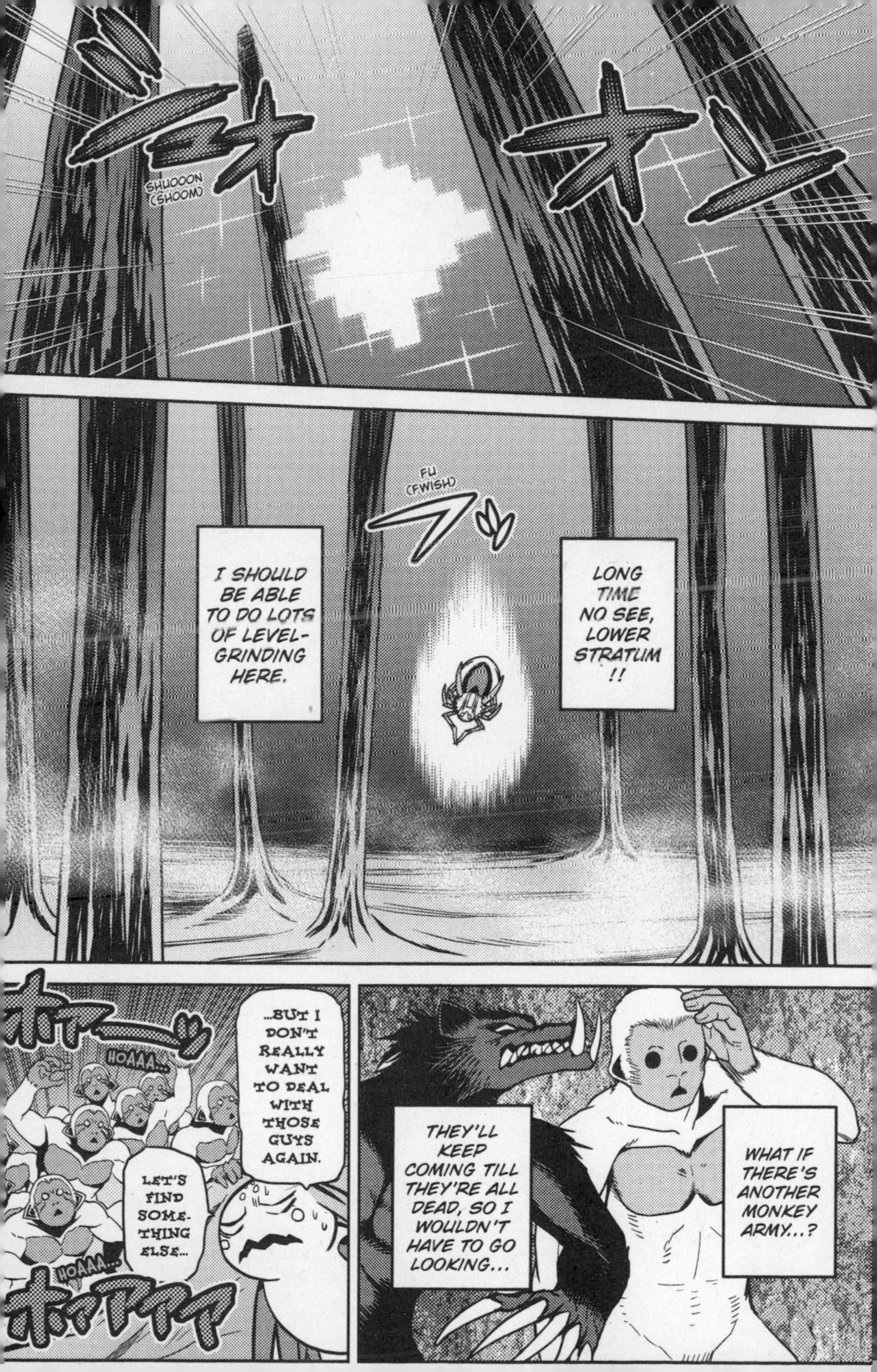
SHUOOON (SHOOM)
FU (FWISH)
LONG TIME NO SEE, LOWER STRATUM!!
I SHOULD BE ABLE TO DO LOTS OF LEVEL-GRINDING HERE.
WHAT IF THERE'S ANOTHER MONKEY ARMY...?
THEY'LL KEEP COMING TILL THEY'RE ALL DEAD, SO I WOULDN'T HAVE TO GO LOOKING...
HOAAA...
...BUT I DON'T REALLY WANT TO DEAL WITH THOSE GUYS AGAIN.
LET'S FIND SOME-THING ELSE...
HOAAA...

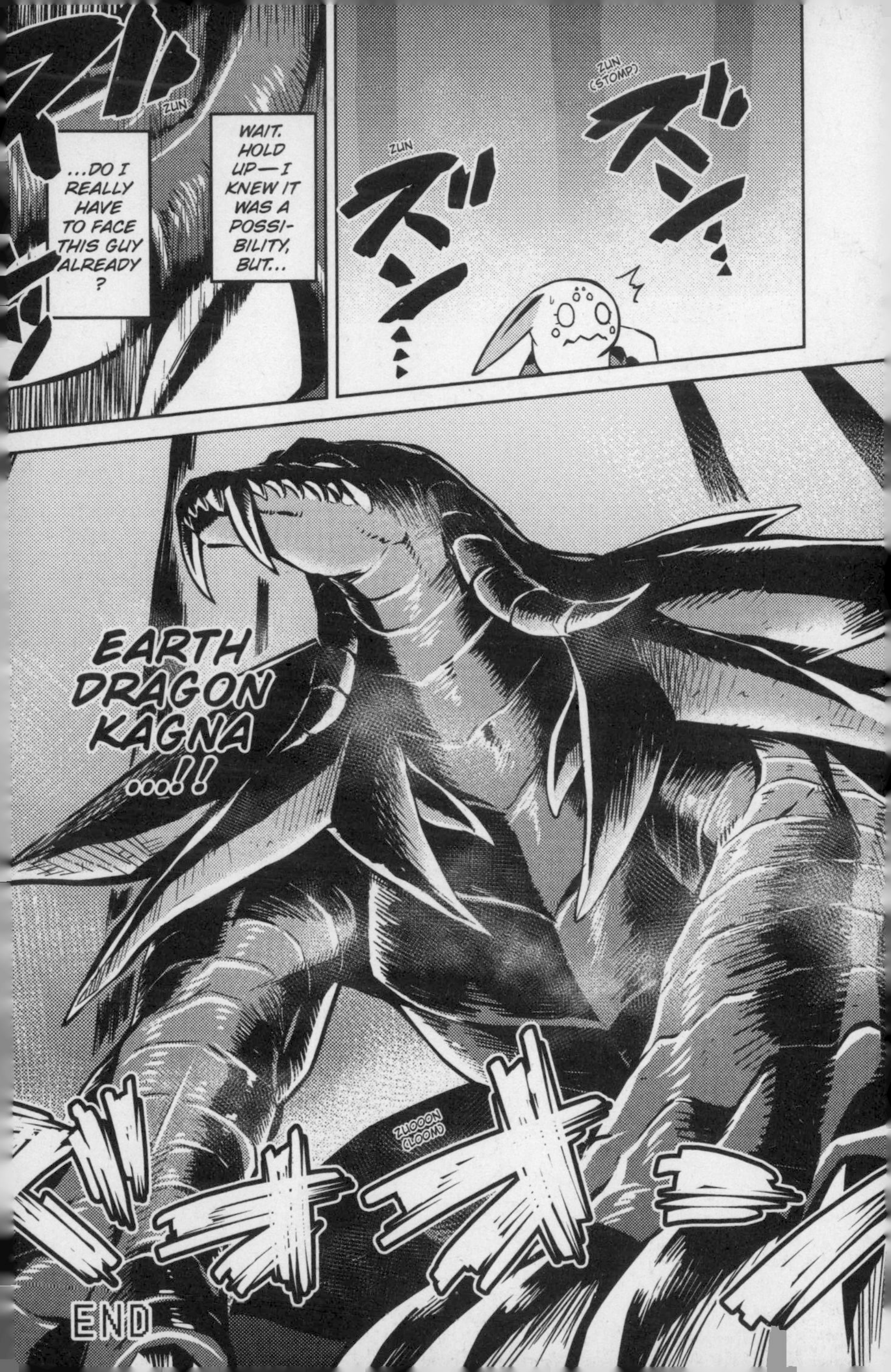
ZUN (STOMP)
ZUN
ZUN
WAIT. HOLD UP—I KNEW IT WAS A POSSI-BILITY, BUT...
...DO I REALLY HAVE TO FACE THIS GUY ALREADY?
EARTH DRAGON KAGNA...!!
ZUOOON (LOON)
END

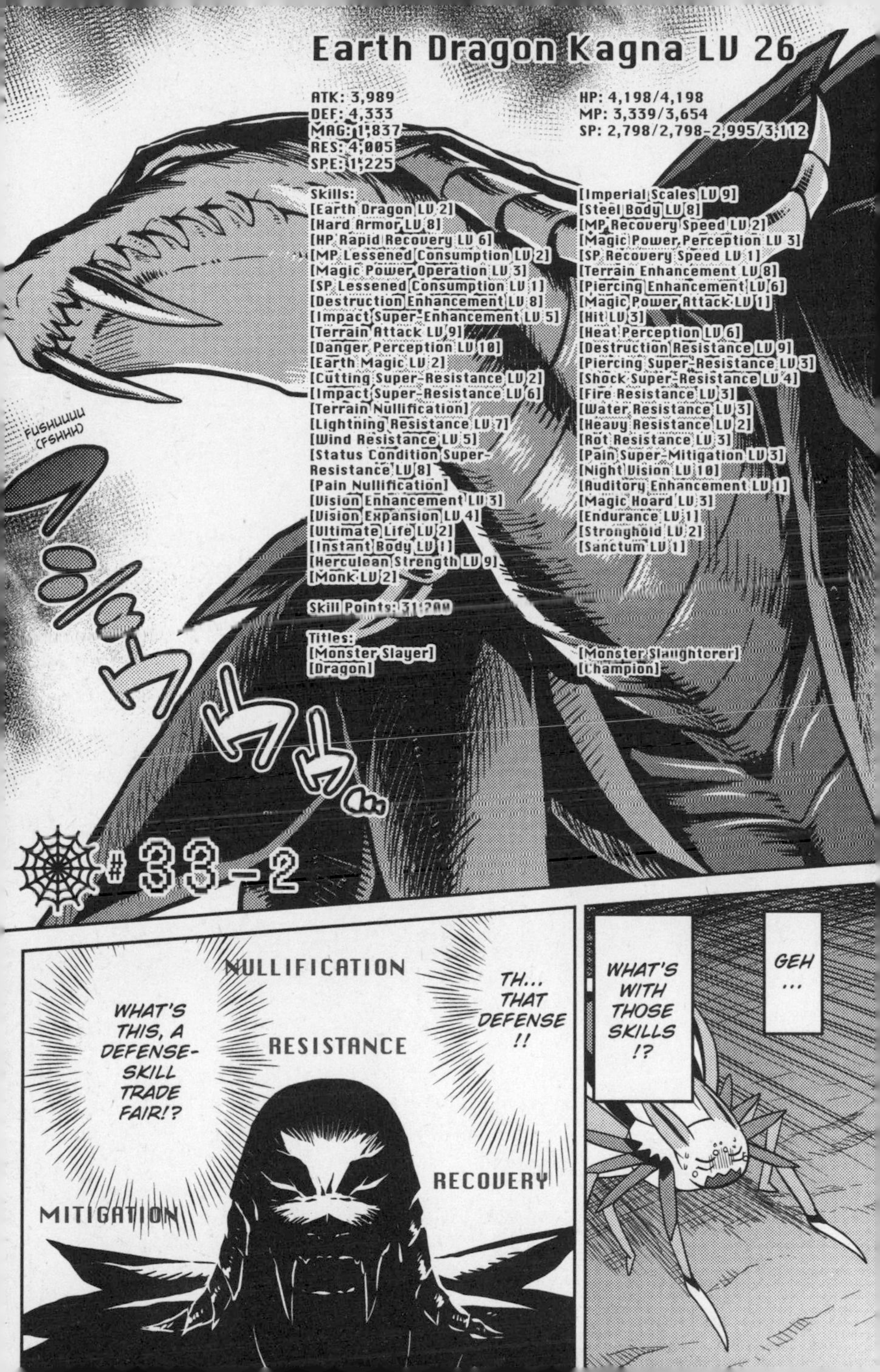
Earth Dragon Kagna LV 26
ATK: 3,989
DEF: 4,333
MAG: 1,837
RES: 4,005
SPE: 1,225
HP: 4,198/4,198
MP: 3,339/3,654
SP: 2,798/2,798-2,995/3,112
Skills:
[Earth Dragon LV 2]
[Hard Armor LV 8]
[HP Rapid Recovery LV 6]
[MP Lessened Consumption LV 2]
[Magic Power Operation LV 3]
[SP Lessened Consumption LV 1]
[Destruction Enhancement LV 8]
[Impact Super-Enhancement LV 5]
[Terrain Attack LV 9]
[Danger Perception LV 10]
[Earth Magic LV 2]
[Cutting Super-Resistance LV 2]
[Impact Super-Resistance LV 6]
[Terrain Nullification]
[Lightning Resistance LV 7]
[Wind Resistance LV 5]
[Status Condition Super-Resistance LV 8]
[Pain Nullification]
[Vision Enhancement LV 3]
[Vision Expansion LV 4]
[Ultimate Life LV 2]
[Instant Body LV 1]
[Herculean Strength LV 9]
[Monk LV 2]
[Imperial Scales LV 9]
[Steel Body LV 8]
[MP Recovery Speed LV 2]
[Magic Power Perception LV 3]
[SP Recovery Speed LV 1]
[Terrain Enhancement LV 8]
[Piercing Enhancement LV 6]
[Magic Power Attack LV 1]
[Hit LV 3]
[Heat Perception LV 6]
[Destruction Resistance LV 9]
[Piercing Super-Resistance LV 3]
[Shock Super-Resistance LV 4]
[Fire Resistance LV 3]
[Water Resistance LV 3]
[Heavy Resistance LV 2]
[Rot Resistance LV 3]
[Pain Super-Mitigation LV 3]
[Night Vision LV 10]
[Auditory Enhancement LV 1]
[Magic Hoard LV 3]
[Endurance LV 1]
[Stronghold LV 2]
[Sanctum LV 1]
Skill Points: 31,200
Titles:
[Monster Slayer]
[Dragon]
[Monster Slaughterer]
[Champion]
FUSHUUUU (FSHHH)
#33-2
GEH...
WHAT'S WITH THOSE SKILLS!?
TH... THAT DEFENSE!!
NULLIFICATION
RESISTANCE
RECOVERY
MITIGATION
WHAT'S THIS, A DEFENSE-SKILL TRADE FAIR!?

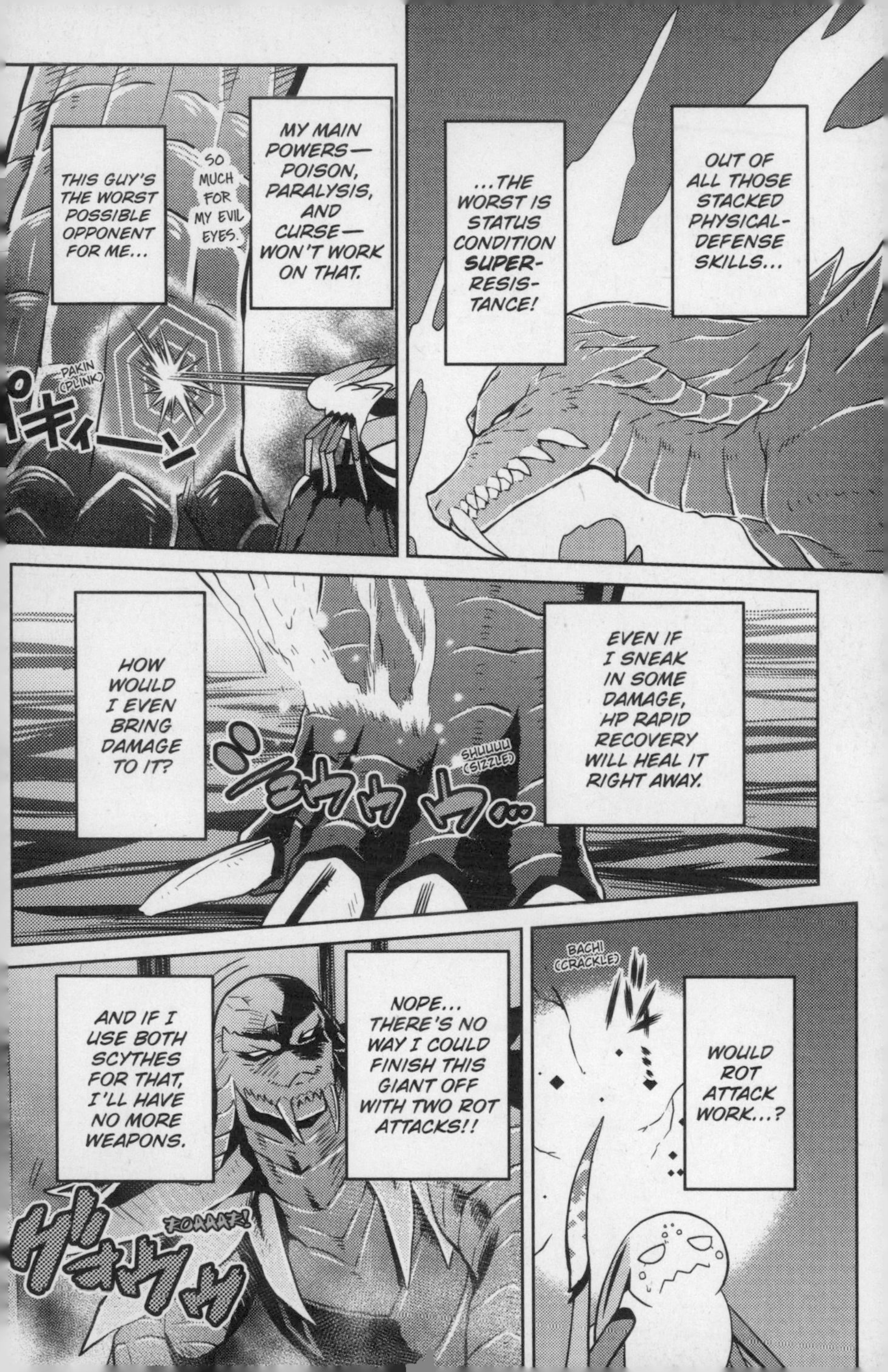
OUT OF ALL THOSE STACKED PHYSICAL-DEFENSE SKILLS...
...THE WORST IS STATUS CONDITION SUPER-RESISTANCE!
MY MAIN POWERS—POISON, PARALYSIS, AND CURSE—WON'T WORK ON THAT.
SO MUCH FOR MY EVIL EYES.
THIS GUY'S THE WORST POSSIBLE OPPONENT FOR ME...
PAKIN (PLINK)
EVEN IF I SNEAK IN SOME DAMAGE, HP RAPID RECOVERY WILL HEAL IT RIGHT AWAY.
SHUUUU (SIZZLE)
HOW WOULD I EVEN BRING DAMAGE TO IT?
BACHI (CRACKLE)
WOULD ROT ATTACK WORK...?
NOPE... THERE'S NO WAY I COULD FINISH THIS GIANT OFF WITH TWO ROT ATTACKS!!
AND IF I USE BOTH SCYTHES FOR THAT, I'LL HAVE NO MORE WEAPONS.
ROAAAR!

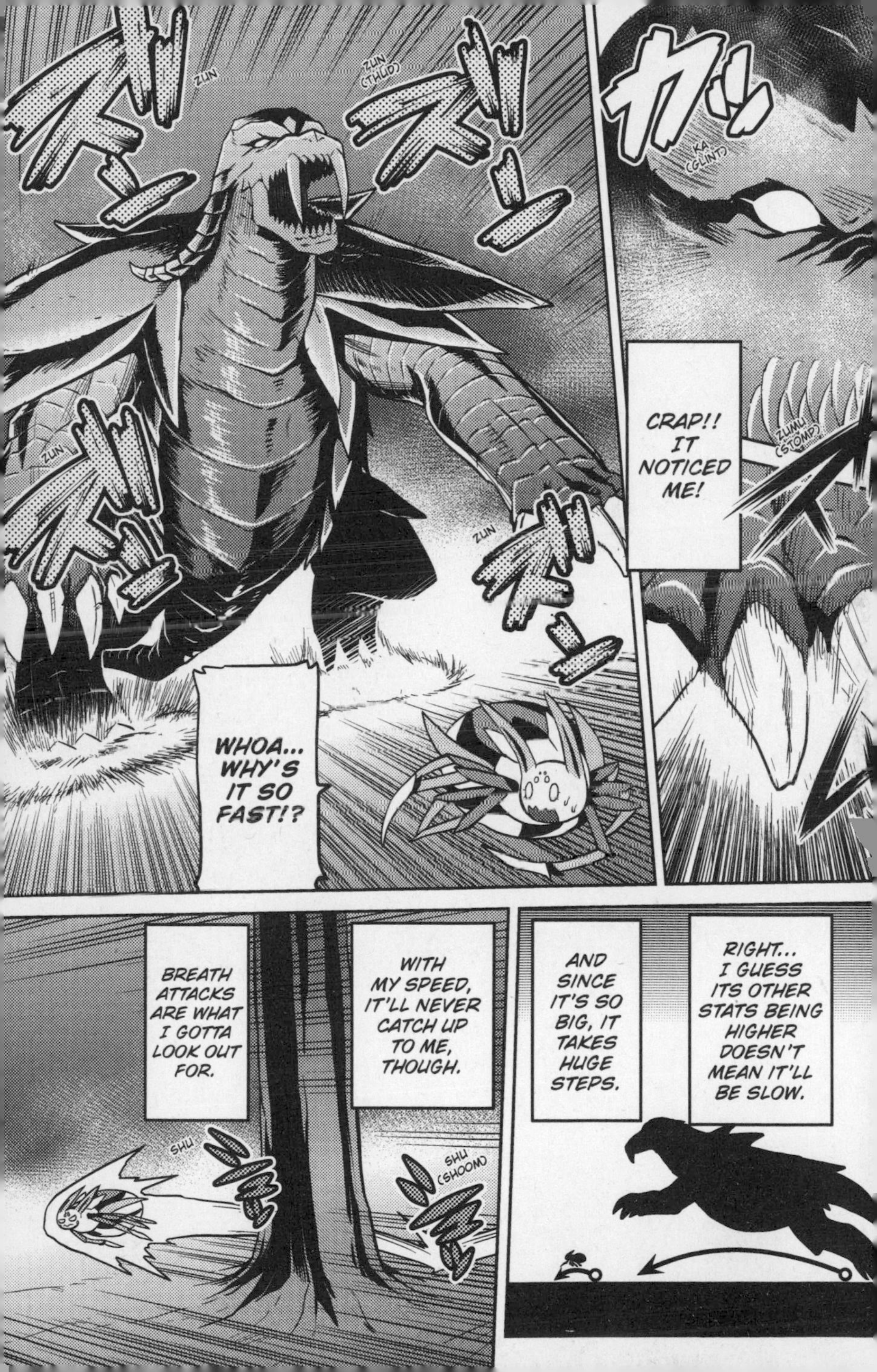
KA (GLINT)
CRAP!! IT NOTICED ME!
ZUMU (STOMP)
ZUN (THUD)
ZUN
ZUN
ZUN
WHOA... WHY'S IT SO FAST!?
RIGHT... I GUESS ITS OTHER STATS BEING HIGHER DOESN'T MEAN IT'LL BE SLOW.
AND SINCE IT'S SO BIG, IT TAKES HUGE STEPS.
WITH MY SPEED, IT'LL NEVER CATCH UP TO ME, THOUGH.
BREATH ATTACKS ARE WHAT I GOTTA LOOK OUT FOR.
SHU (SHOOM)
SHU

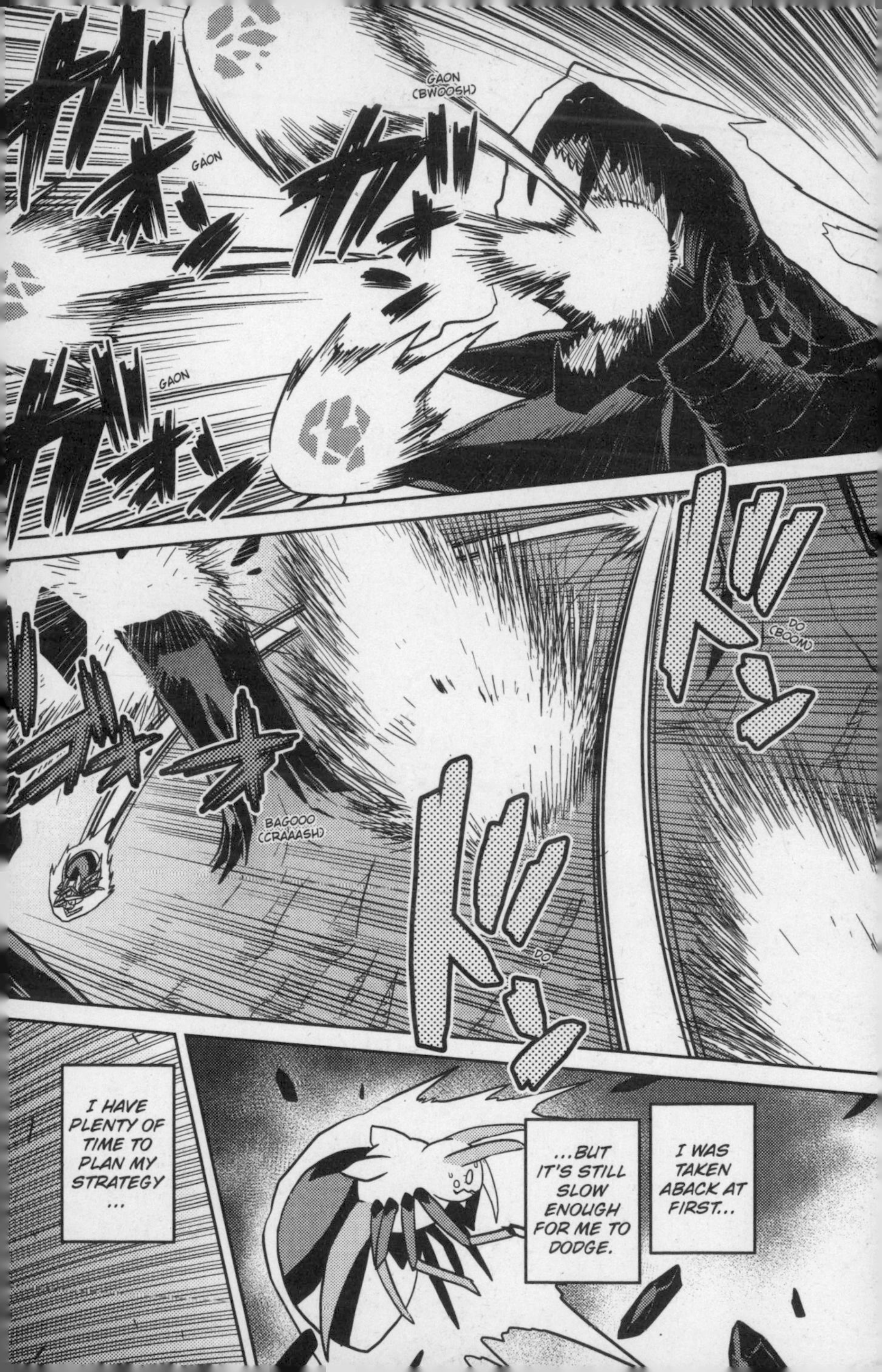
GAON
(BWOOSH)
GAON
GAON
DO
(BOOM)
BAGOOO
(CRAAASH)
DO
I WAS TAKEN ABACK AT FIRST...
...BUT IT'S STILL SLOW ENOUGH FOR ME TO DODGE.
I HAVE PLENTY OF TIME TO PLAN MY STRATEGY...

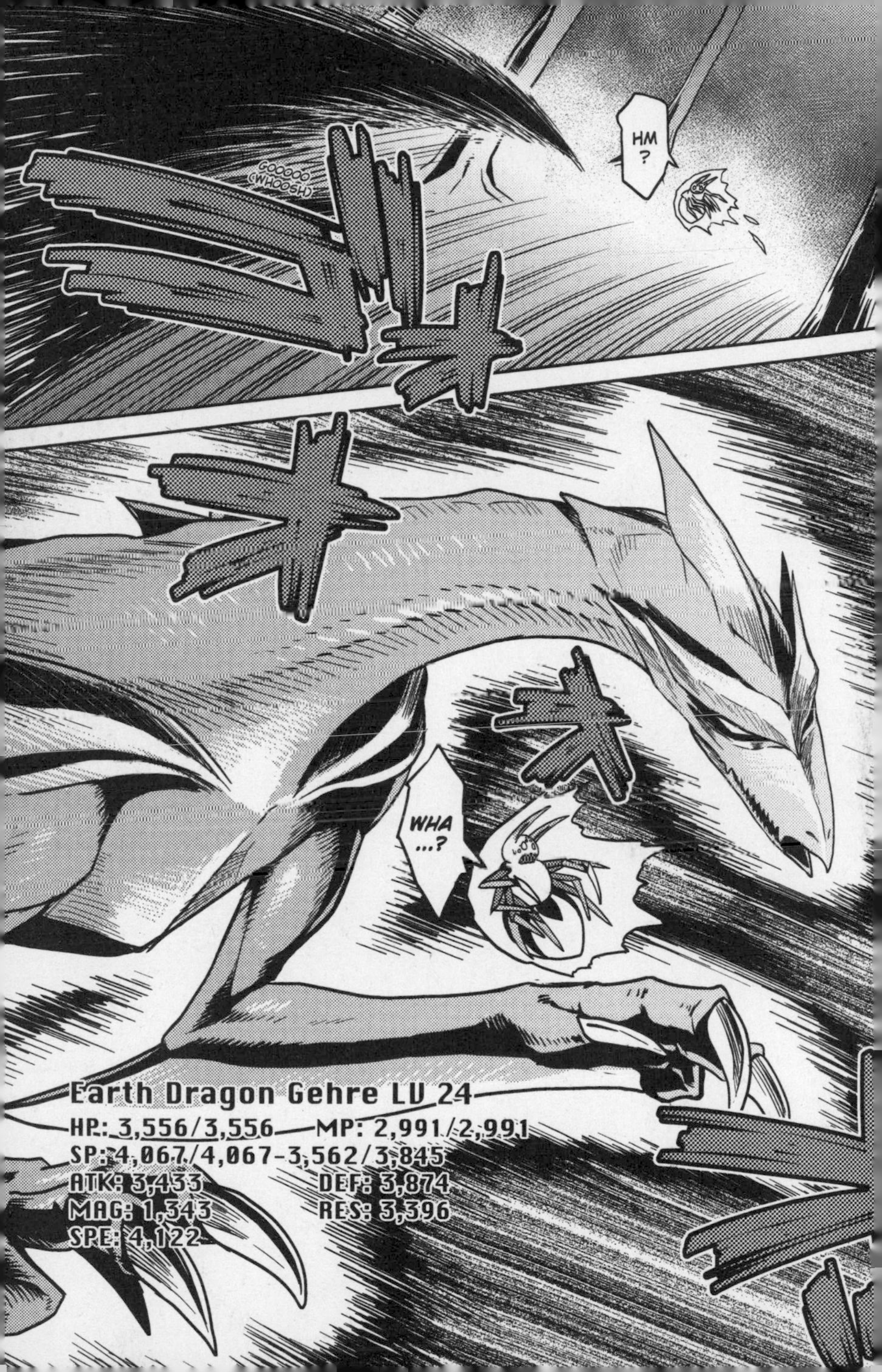
HM ?
GOOOOO (WHOOSH)
WHA ...?
Earth Dragon Gehre LV 24
HP: 3,556/3,556 MP: 2,991/2,991
SP: 4,067/4,067-3,562/3,845
ATK: 3,433 DEF: 3,874
MAG: 1,343 RES: 3,396
SPE: 4,122

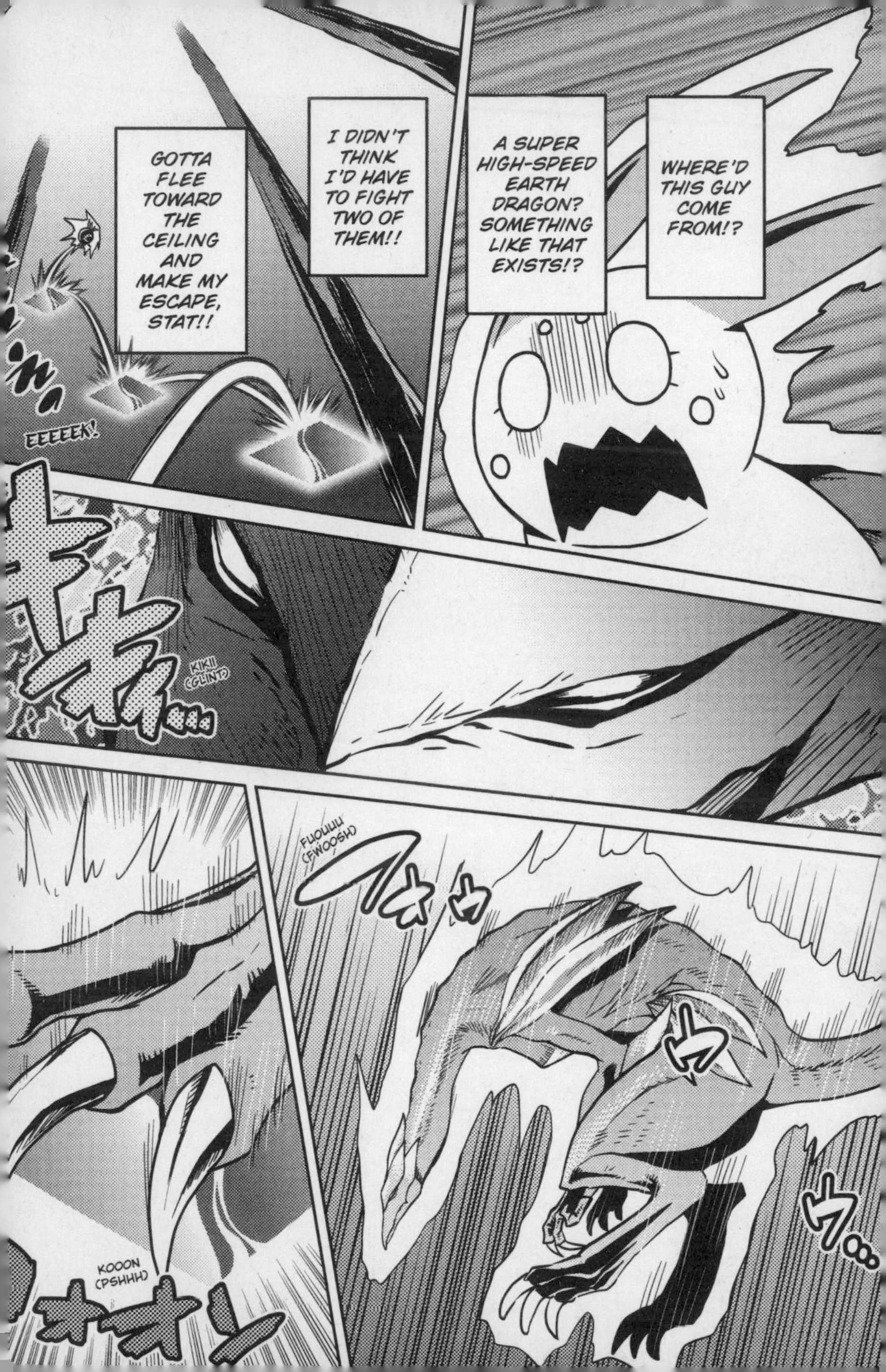
WHERE'D THIS GUY COME FROM!?
A SUPER HIGH-SPEED EARTH DRAGON? SOMETHING LIKE THAT EXISTS!?
I DIDN'T THINK I'D HAVE TO FIGHT TWO OF THEM!!
GOTTA FLEE TOWARD THE CEILING AND MAKE MY ESCAPE, STAT!!
EEEEEK!
KIKII (GLINT)
FUOUUU (FWOOSH)
KOOON (PSHHH)

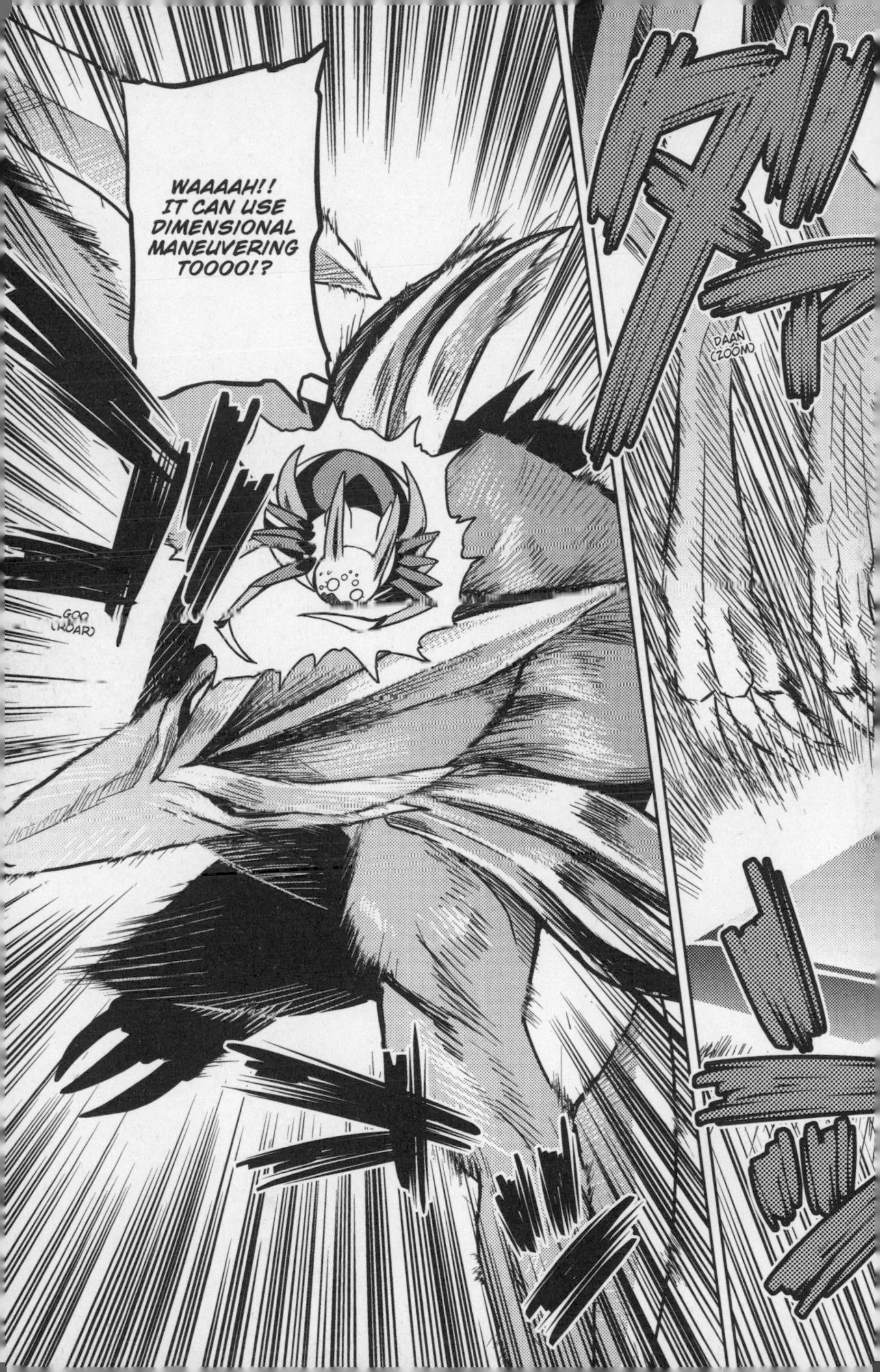
DAAN (ZOOM)
WAAAAH!! IT CAN USE DIMENSIONAL MANEUVERING TOOOO!?
GOO (ROAR)

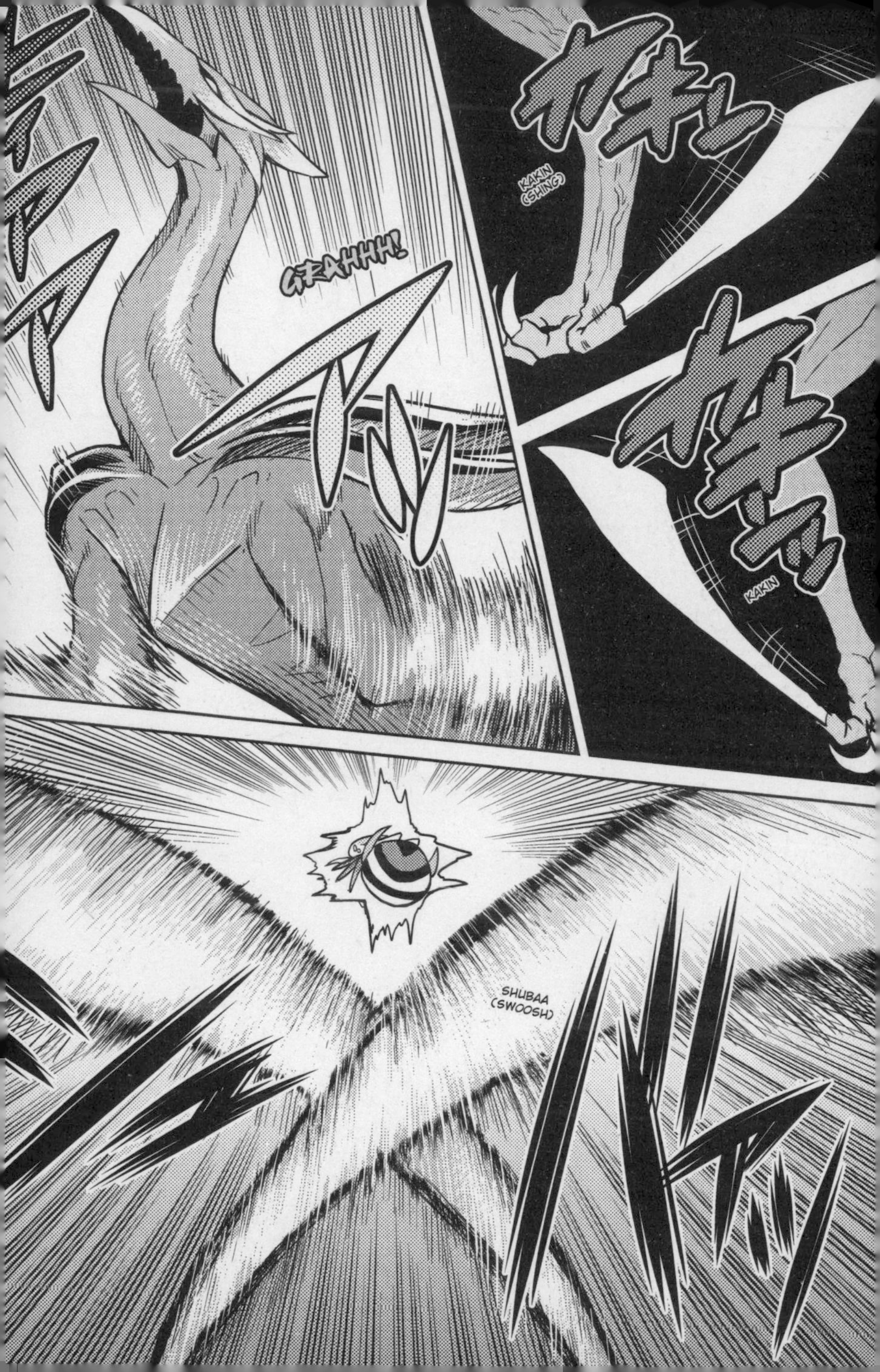
KAKIN (SHING)
KAKIN
GRAHHH!
SHUBAA (SWOOSH)

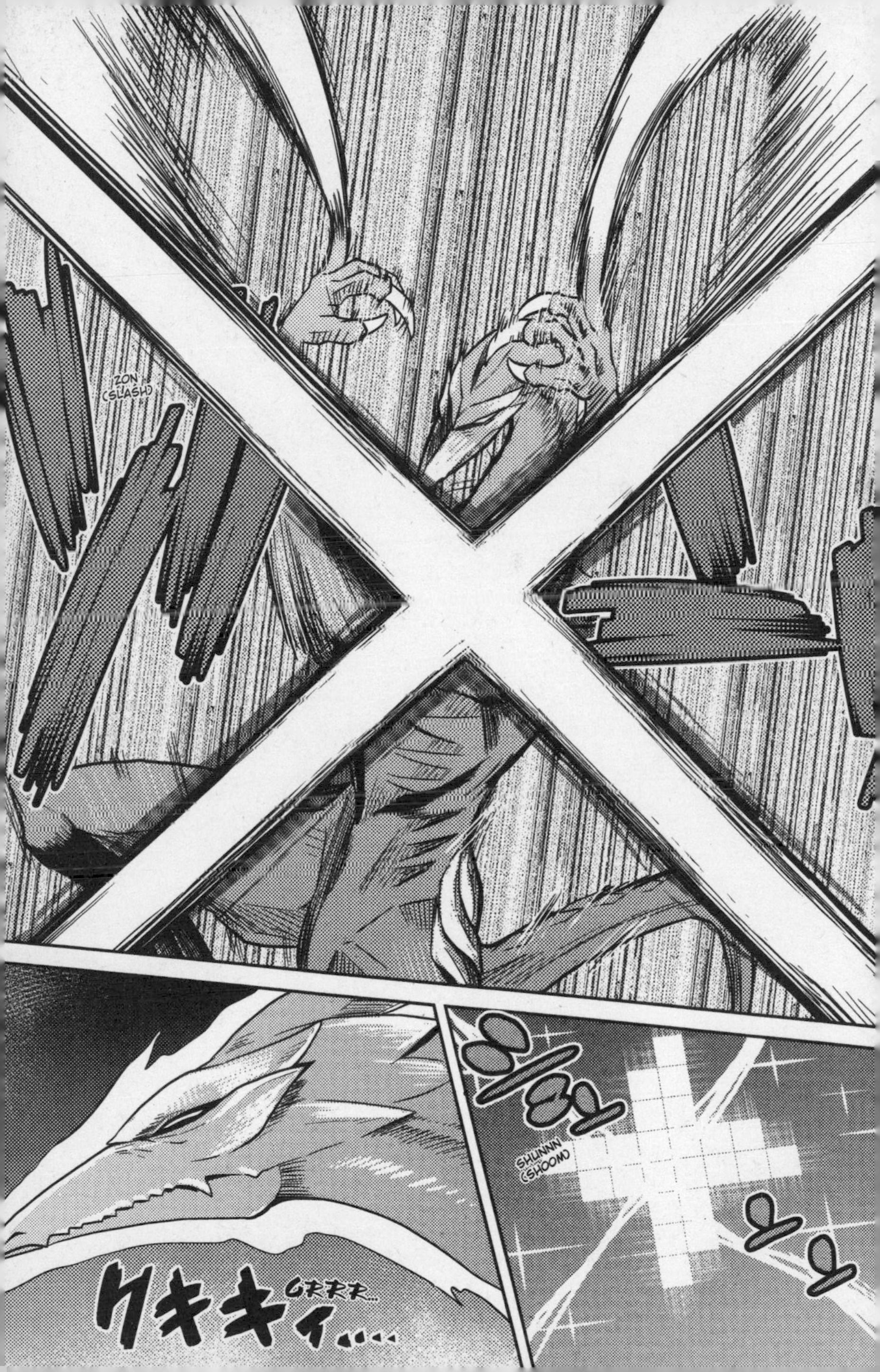
ZON (SLASH)
SHUNNN (SHOOM)
クキキィ...
GRRR...

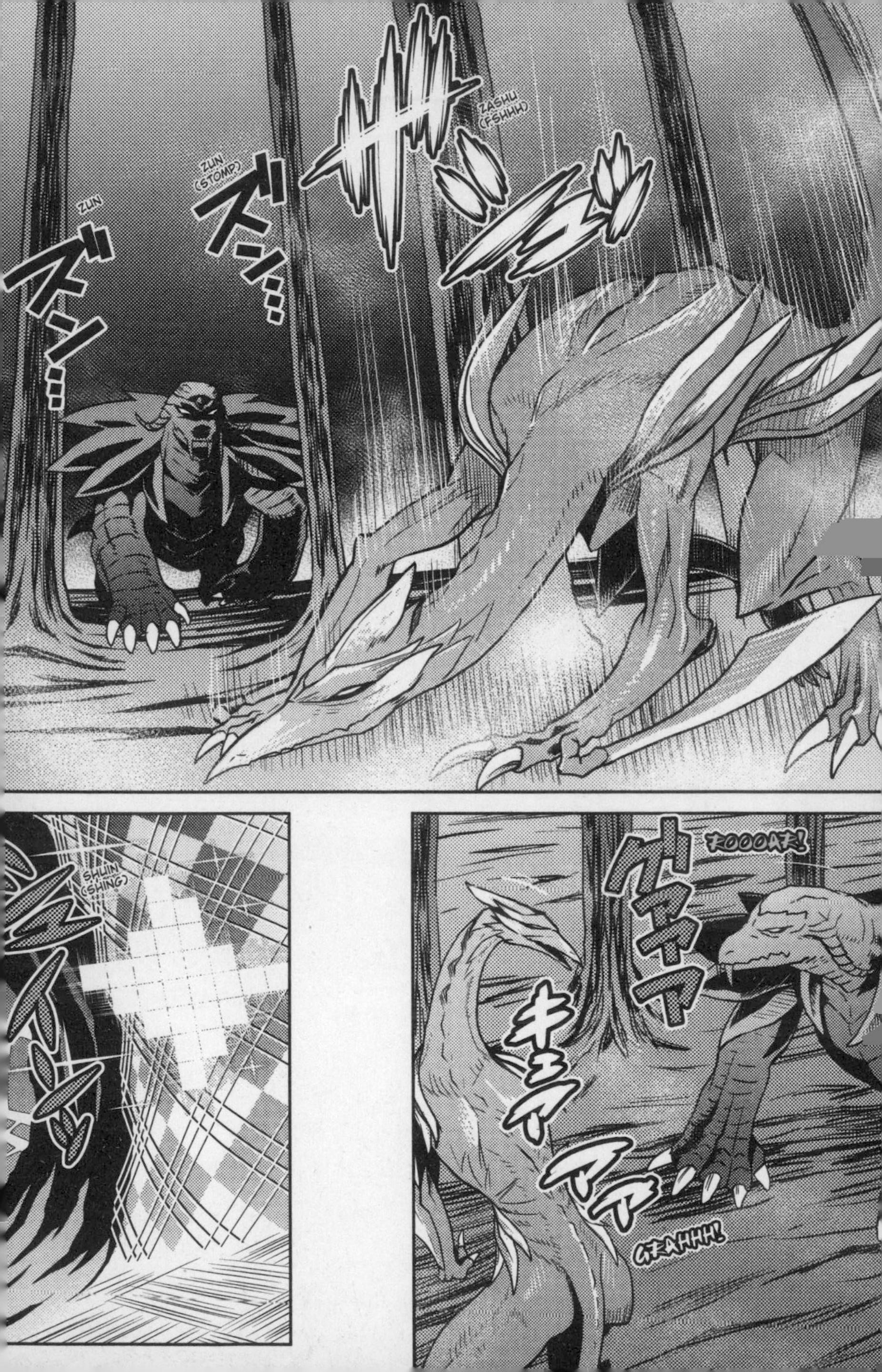
ZASHU
(FSHHH)
ZUN
(STOMP)
ZUN
ROOOAR!
GRAHHH!
SHUIN
(SHING)

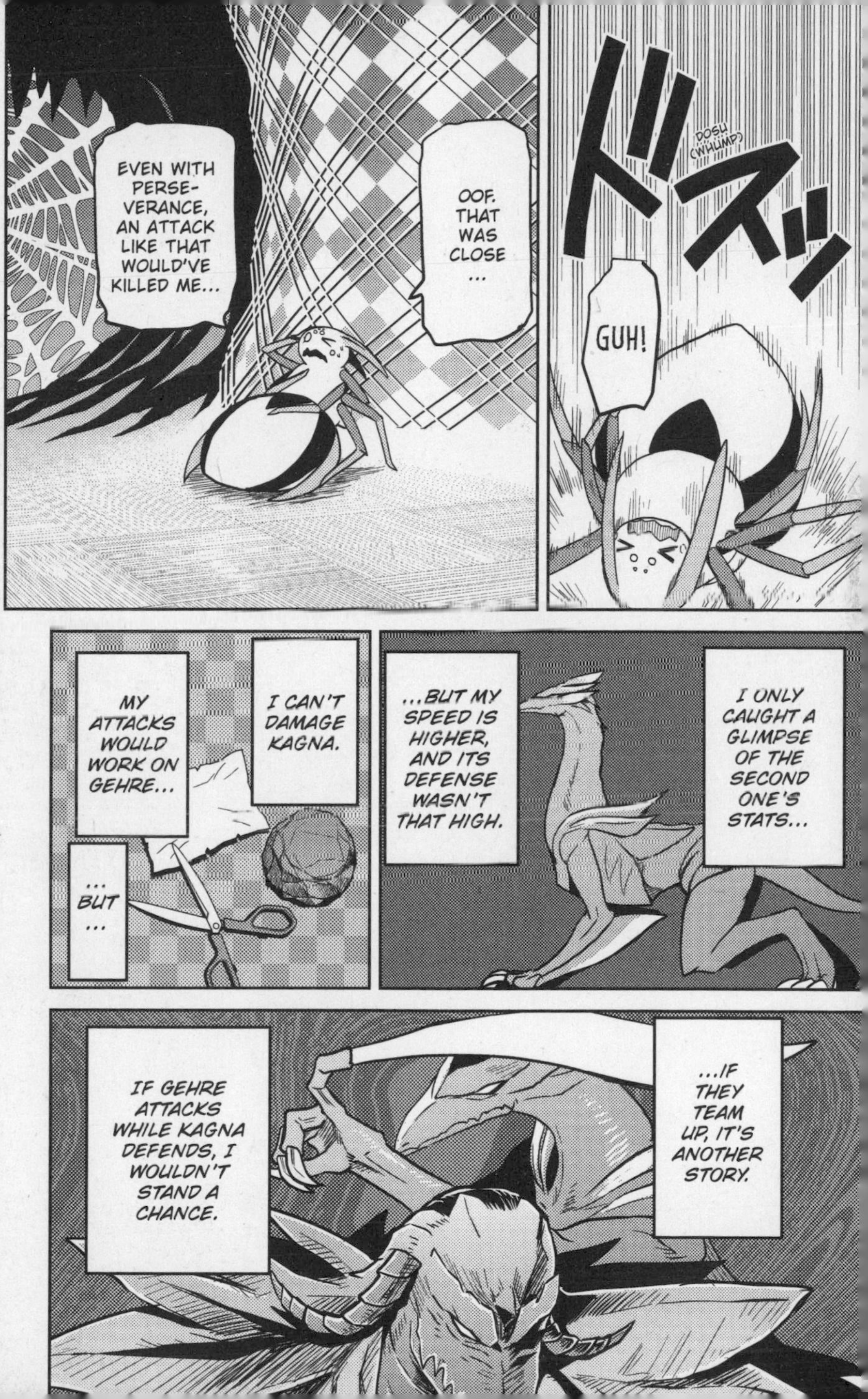
ドスッ
DOSH (WHUMP)
GUH!
OOF. THAT WAS CLOSE...
EVEN WITH PERSE-VERANCE, AN ATTACK LIKE THAT WOULD'VE KILLED ME...
I ONLY CAUGHT A GLIMPSE OF THE SECOND ONE'S STATS...
...BUT MY SPEED IS HIGHER, AND ITS DEFENSE WASN'T THAT HIGH.
I CAN'T DAMAGE KAGNA.
MY ATTACKS WOULD WORK ON GEHRE...
...BUT...
...IF THEY TEAM UP, IT'S ANOTHER STORY.
IF GEHRE ATTACKS WHILE KAGNA DEFENDS, I WOULDN'T STAND A CHANCE.

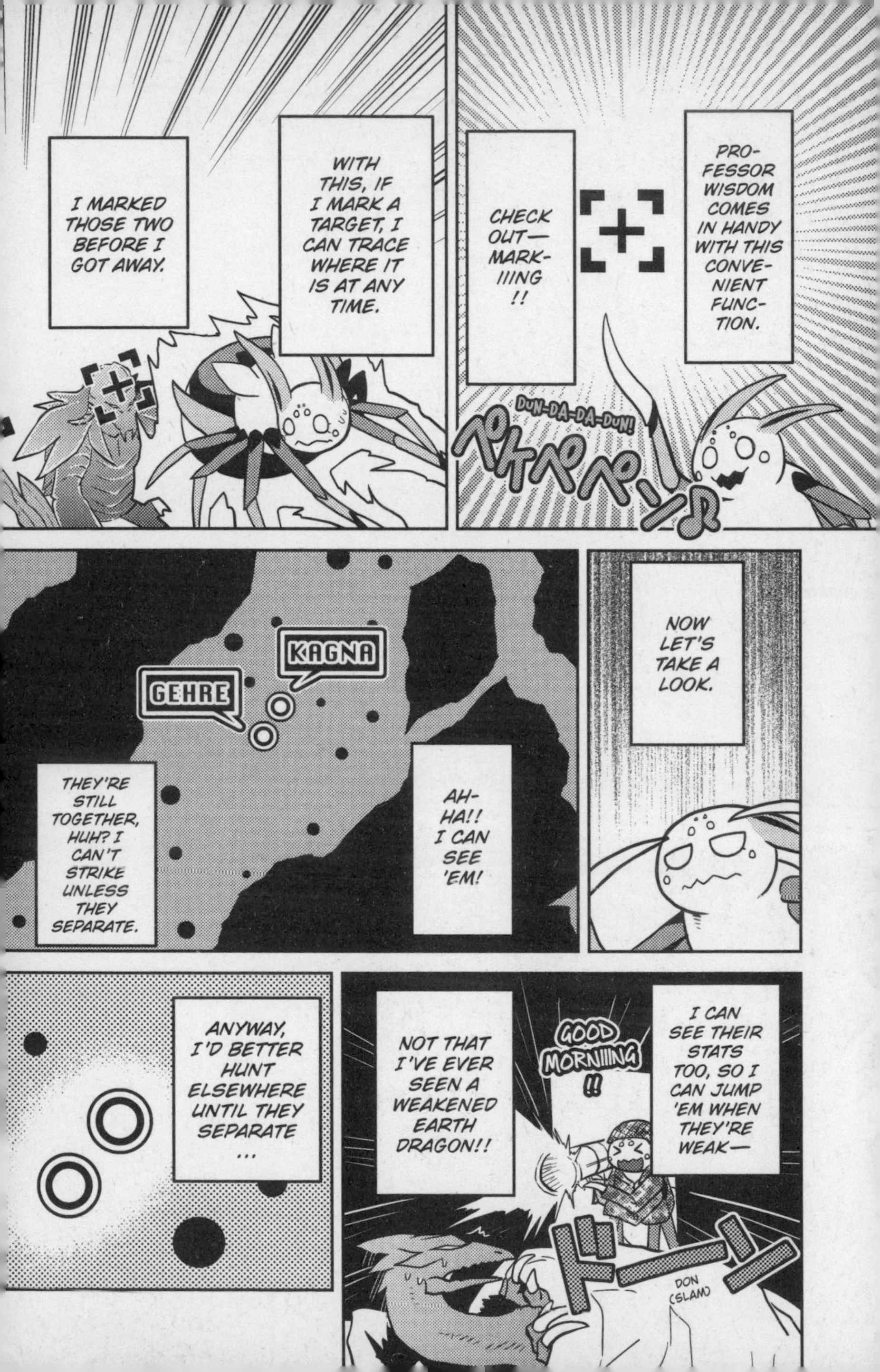
PRO-FESSOR WISDOM COMES IN HANDY WITH THIS CONVE-NIENT FUNC-TION.
CHECK OUT—MARK-IIING !!
DUN-DA-DA-DUN!
ペケペペー♪
WITH THIS, IF I MARK A TARGET, I CAN TRACE WHERE IT IS AT ANY TIME.
I MARKED THOSE TWO BEFORE I GOT AWAY.
NOW LET'S TAKE A LOOK.
AH-HA!! I CAN SEE 'EM!
KAGNA
GEHRE
THEY'RE STILL TOGETHER, HUH? I CAN'T STRIKE UNLESS THEY SEPARATE.
I CAN SEE THEIR STATS TOO, SO I CAN JUMP 'EM WHEN THEY'RE WEAK—
GOOD MORNIIING !!
NOT THAT I'VE EVER SEEN A WEAKENED EARTH DRAGON!!
ドーン
DON (SLAM)
ANYWAY, I'D BETTER HUNT ELSEWHERE UNTIL THEY SEPARATE ...

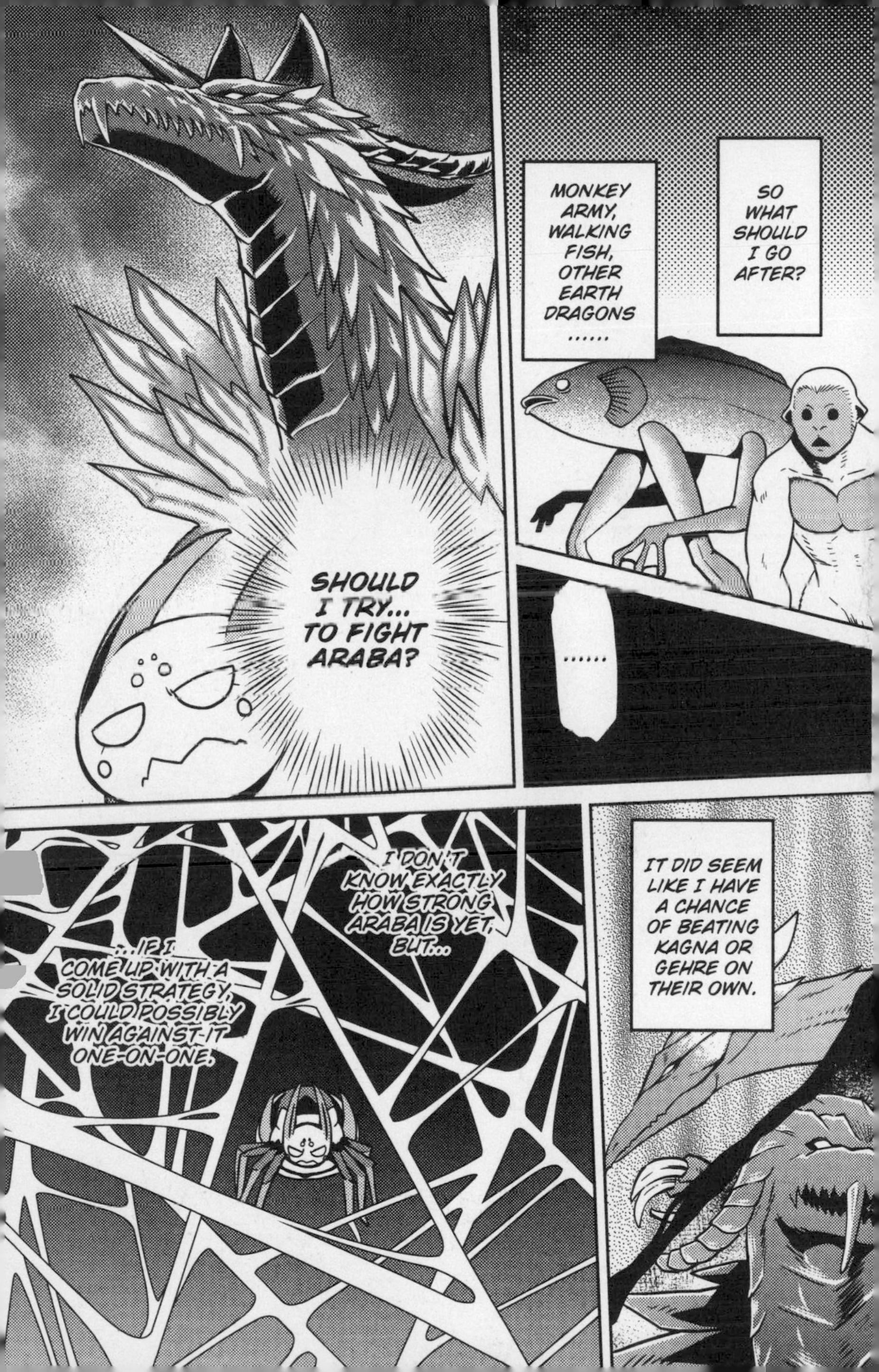
SO WHAT SHOULD I GO AFTER?
MONKEY ARMY, WALKING FISH, OTHER EARTH DRAGONS ......
......
SHOULD I TRY... TO FIGHT ARABA?
IT DID SEEM LIKE I HAVE A CHANCE OF BEATING KAGNA OR GEHRE ON THEIR OWN.
I DON'T KNOW EXACTLY HOW STRONG ARABA IS YET, BUT...
...IF I COME UP WITH A SOLID STRATEGY, I COULD POSSIBLY WIN AGAINST IT ONE-ON-ONE.

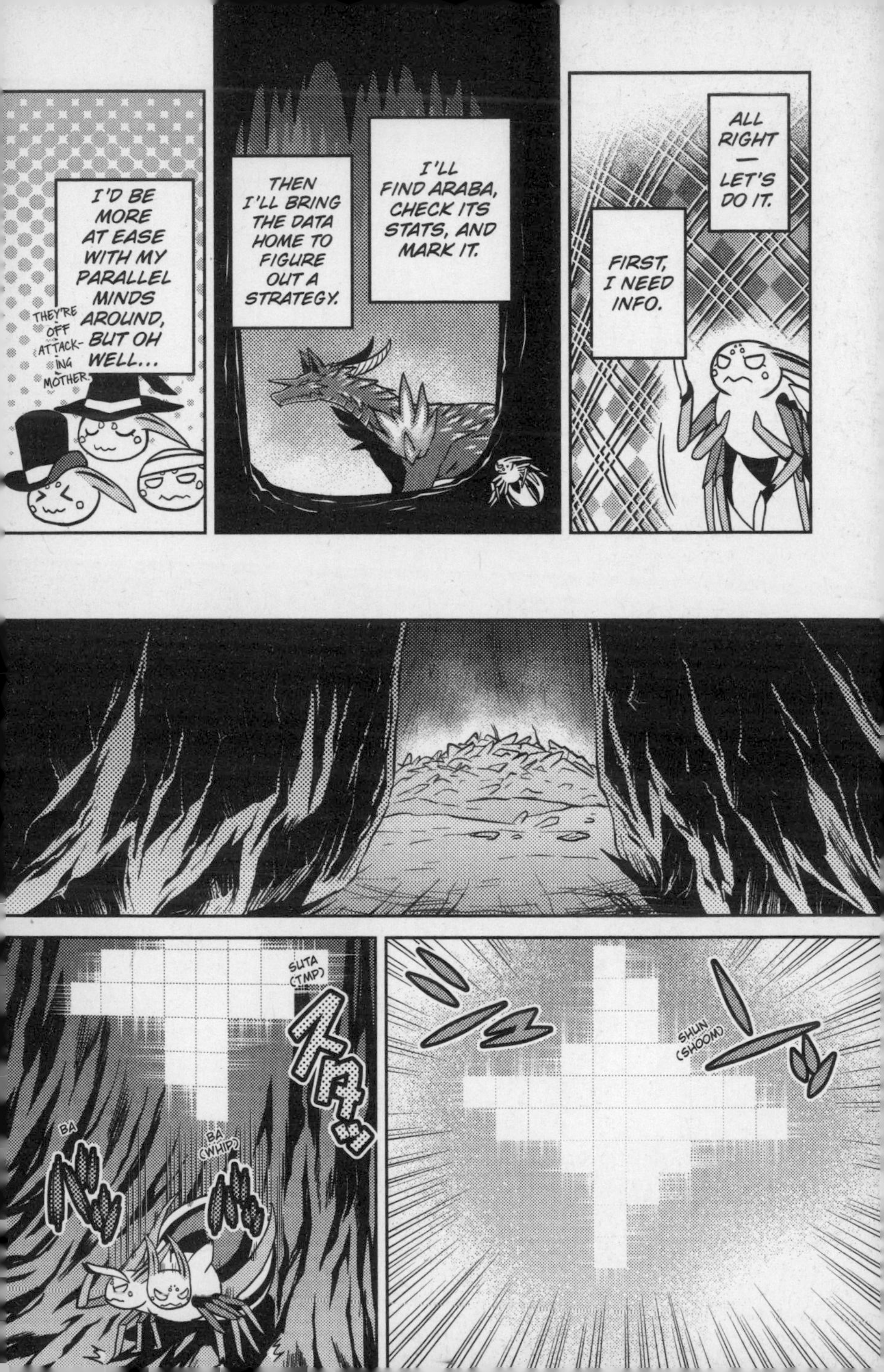
ALL RIGHT — LET'S DO IT.
FIRST, I NEED INFO.
I'LL FIND ARABA, CHECK ITS STATS, AND MARK IT.
THEN I'LL BRING THE DATA HOME TO FIGURE OUT A STRATEGY.
I'D BE MORE AT EASE WITH MY PARALLEL MINDS AROUND, BUT OH WELL...
THEY'RE OFF ATTACK-ING MOTHER.
SHUN (SHOOM)
SUTA (TMP)
BA
BA (WHIP)

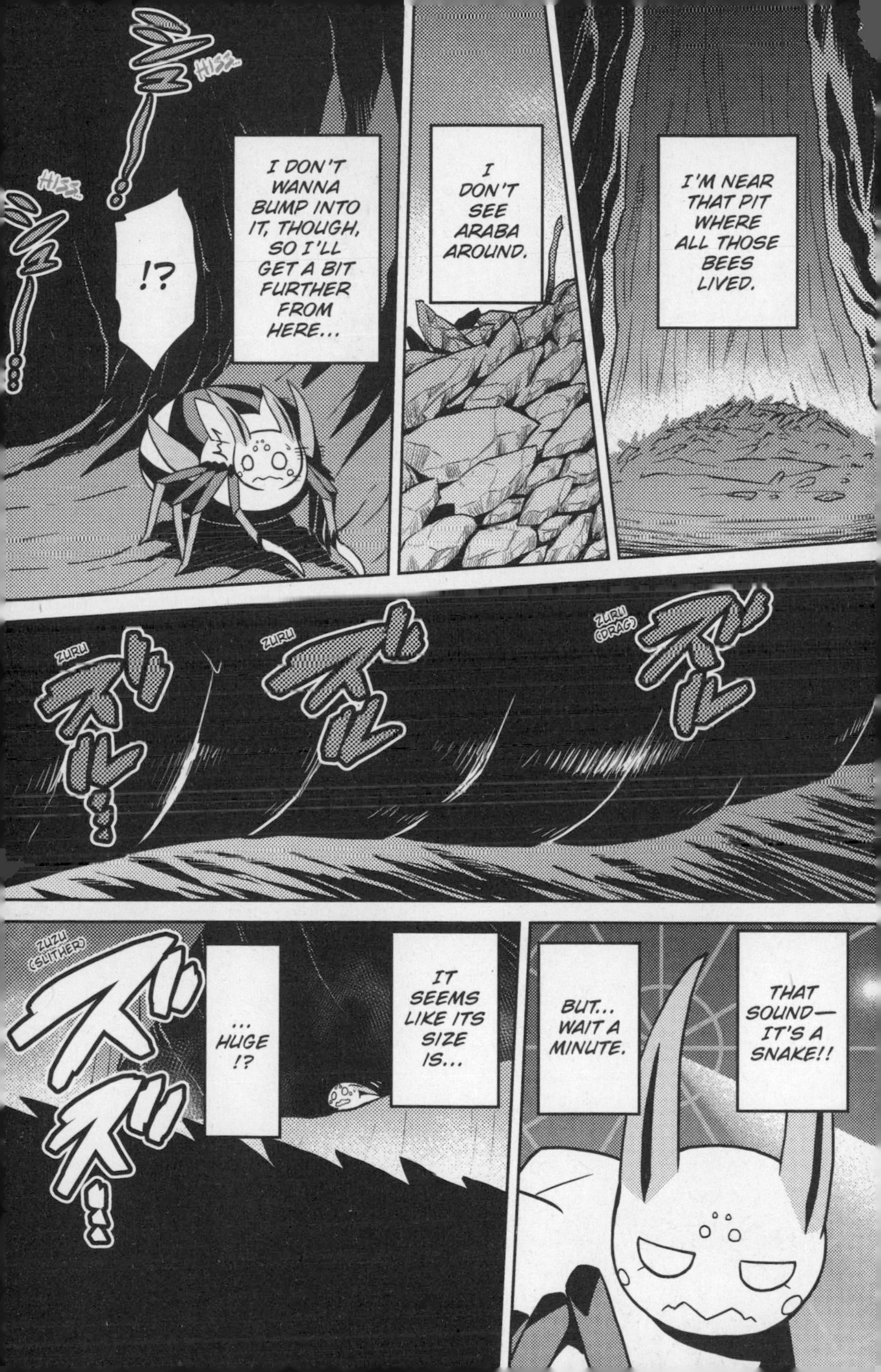
I'M NEAR THAT PIT WHERE ALL THOSE BEES LIVED.
I DON'T SEE ARABA AROUND.
HISS...
I DON'T WANNA BUMP INTO IT, THOUGH, SO I'LL GET A BIT FURTHER FROM HERE...
HISS...
!?
ZURU (DRAG)
ZURU
ZURU
THAT SOUND—IT'S A SNAKE!!
BUT... WAIT A MINUTE.
IT SEEMS LIKE ITS SIZE IS...
...HUGE!?
ZUZU (SLITHER)

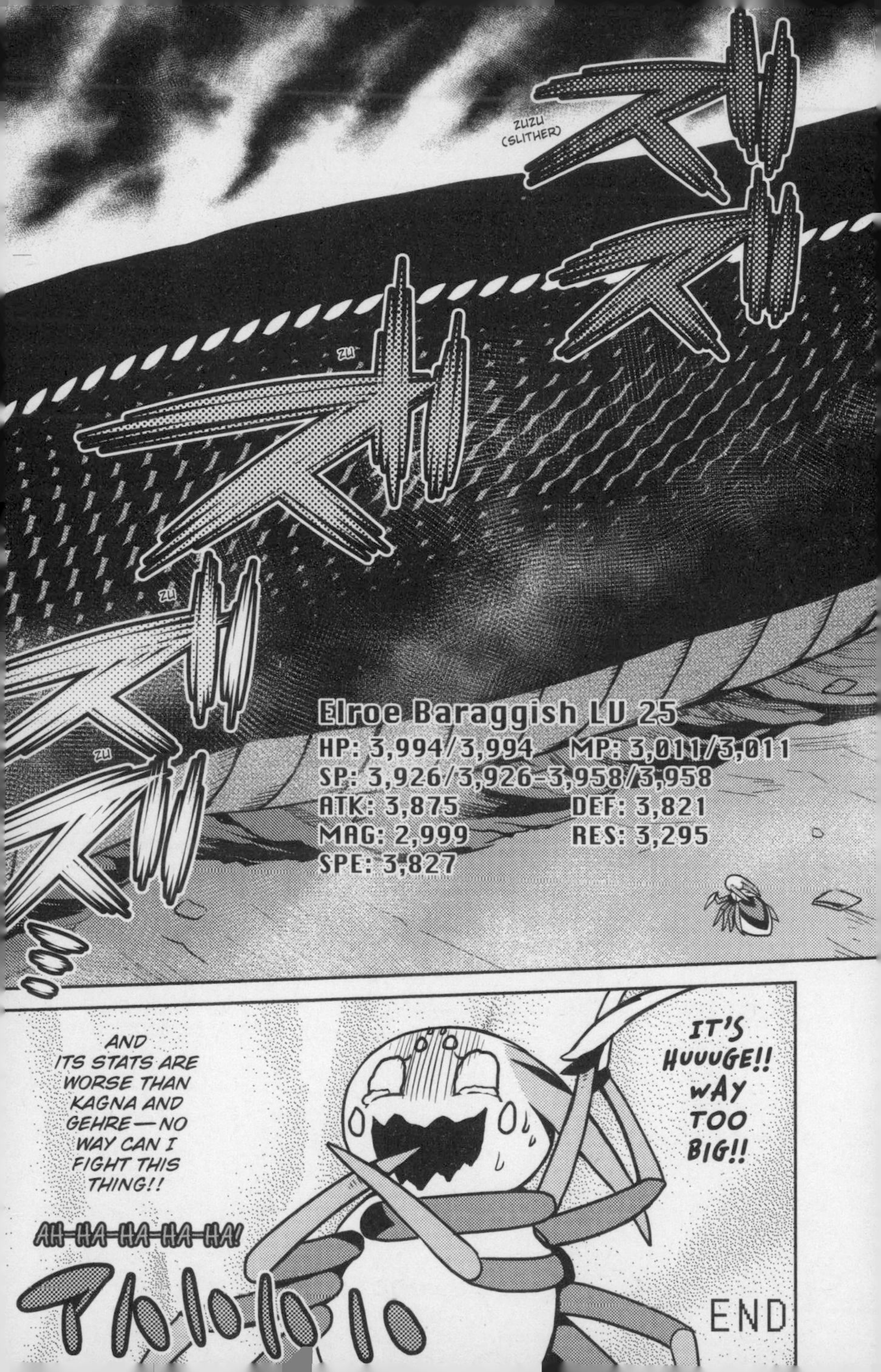
ZUZU (SLITHER)
ZU
ZU
ZU
Elroe Baraggish LV 25
HP: 3,994/3,994 MP: 3,011/3,011
SP: 3,926/3,926-3,958/3,958
ATK: 3,875 DEF: 3,821
MAG: 2,999 RES: 3,295
SPE: 3,827
IT'S HUUUGE!! WAY TOO BIG!!
AND ITS STATS ARE WORSE THAN KAGNA AND GEHRE—NO WAY CAN I FIGHT THIS THING!!
AH-HA-HA-HA-HA!
END

So I'm a Spider, So What?

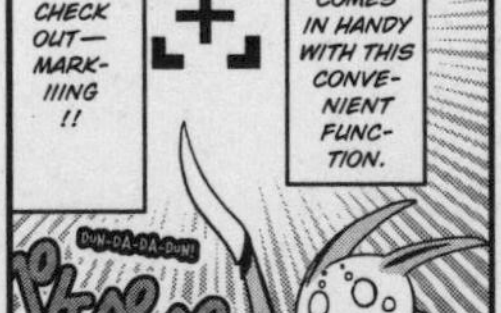
PROFESSOR WISDOM COMES IN HANDY WITH THIS CONVENIENT FUNCTION.
CHECK OUT—MARKIIING!!
DUN-DA-DA-DUN!

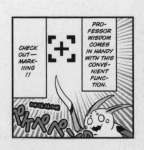

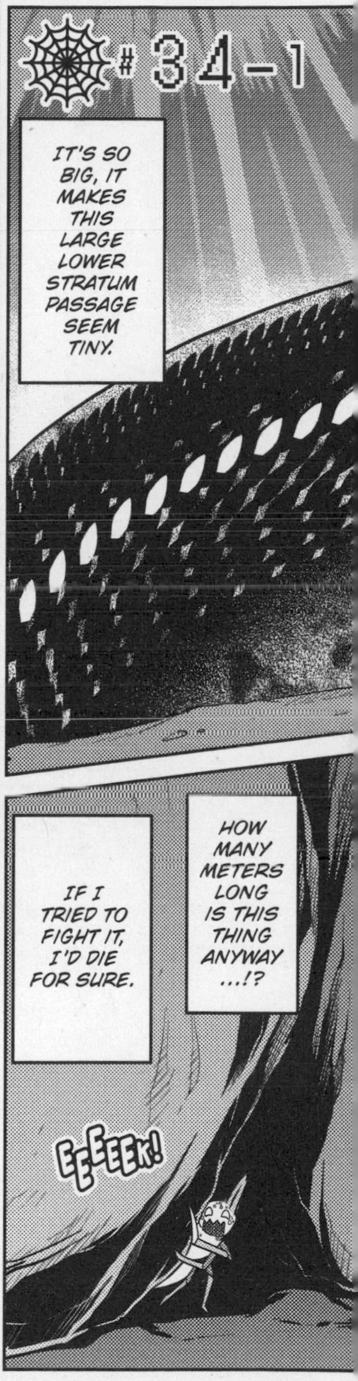
#34-1
IT'S SO BIG, IT MAKES THIS LARGE LOWER STRATUM PASSAGE SEEM TINY.
HOW MANY METERS LONG IS THIS THING ANYWAY ...!?
IF I TRIED TO FIGHT IT, I'D DIE FOR SURE.
EEEEEK!

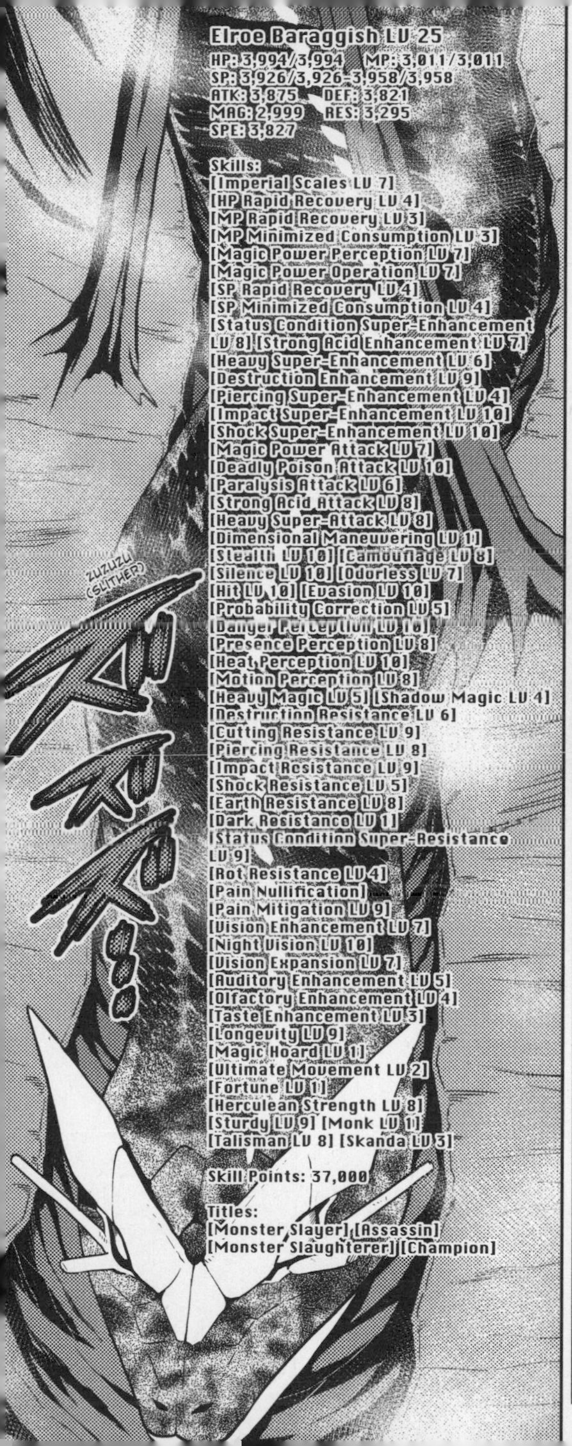
Elroe Baraggish LV 25
HP: 3,994/3,994 MP: 3,011/3,011
SP: 3,926/3,926-3,958/3,958
ATK: 3,875 DEF: 3,821
MAG: 2,999 RES: 3,295
SPE: 3,827
Skills:
[Imperial Scales LV 7]
[HP Rapid Recovery LV 4]
[MP Rapid Recovery LV 3]
[MP Minimized Consumption LV 3]
[Magic Power Perception LV 7]
[Magic Power Operation LV 7]
[SP Rapid Recovery LV 4]
[SP Minimized Consumption LV 4]
[Status Condition Super-Enhancement LV 8] [Strong Acid Enhancement LV 7]
[Heavy Super-Enhancement LV 6]
[Destruction Enhancement LV 9]
[Piercing Super-Enhancement LV 4]
[Impact Super-Enhancement LV 10]
[Shock Super-Enhancement LV 10]
[Magic Power Attack LV 7]
[Deadly Poison Attack LV 10]
[Paralysis Attack LV 6]
[Strong Acid Attack LV 8]
[Heavy Super-Attack LV 8]
[Dimensional Maneuvering LV 1]
[Stealth LV 10] [Camouflage LV 8]
[Silence LV 10] [Odorless LV 7]
[Hit LV 10] [Evasion LV 10]
[Probability Correction LV 5]
[Danger Perception LV 10]
[Presence Perception LV 8]
[Heat Perception LV 10]
[Motion Perception LV 8]
[Heavy Magic LV 5] [Shadow Magic LV 4]
[Destruction Resistance LV 6]
[Cutting Resistance LV 9]
[Piercing Resistance LV 8]
[Impact Resistance LV 9]
[Shock Resistance LV 5]
[Earth Resistance LV 8]
[Dark Resistance LV 1]
[Status Condition Super-Resistance LV 9]
[Rot Resistance LV 4]
[Pain Nullification]
[Pain Mitigation LV 9]
[Vision Enhancement LV 7]
[Night Vision LV 10]
[Vision Expansion LV 7]
[Auditory Enhancement LV 5]
[Olfactory Enhancement LV 4]
[Taste Enhancement LV 3]
[Longevity LV 9]
[Magic Hoard LV 1]
[Ultimate Movement LV 2]
[Fortune LV 1]
[Herculean Strength LV 8]
[Sturdy LV 9] [Monk LV 1]
[Talisman LV 8] [Skanda LV 3]
Skill Points: 37,000
Titles:
[Monster Slayer] [Assassin]
[Monster Slaughterer] [Champion]
ZUZUZU (SLITHER)

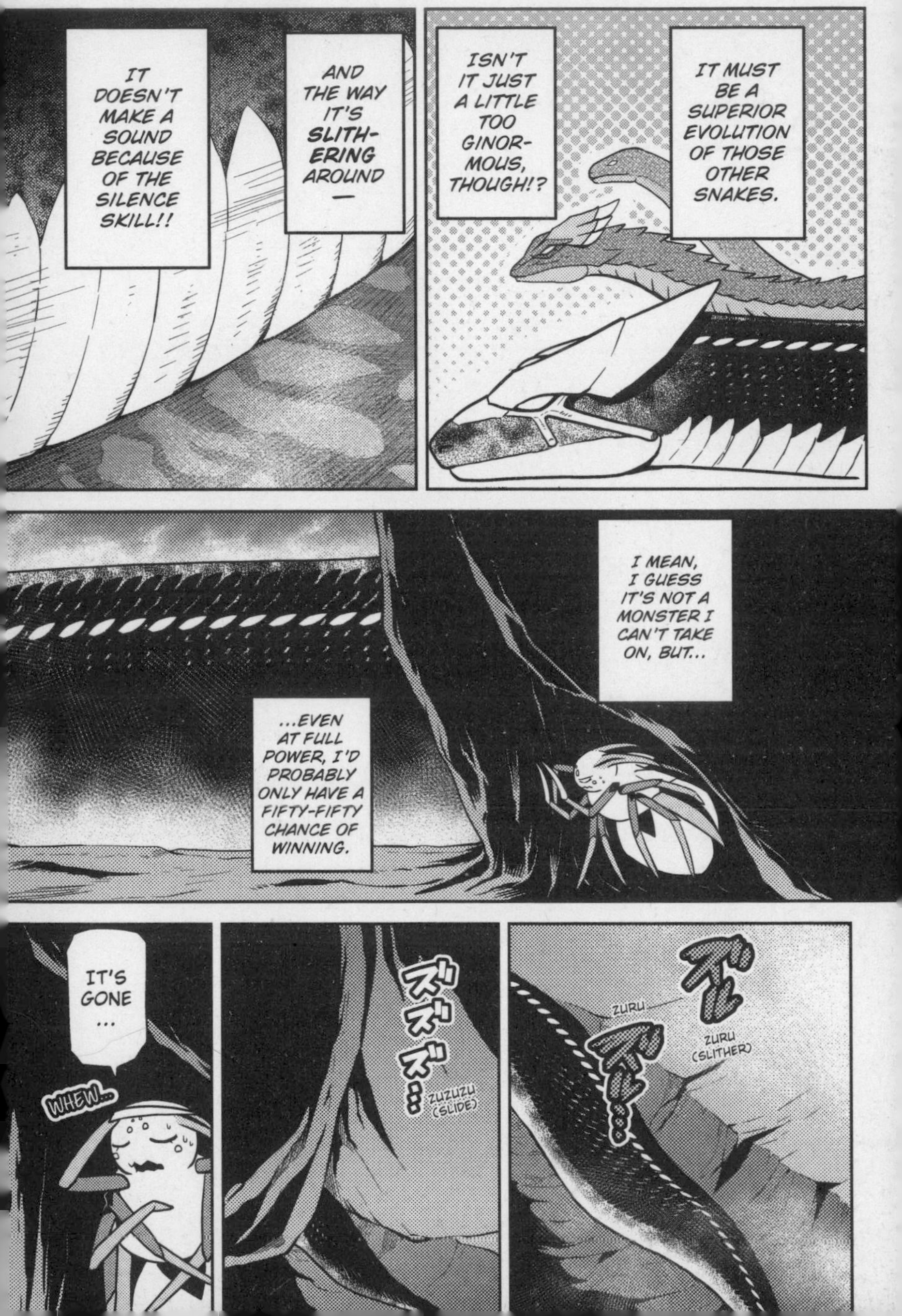
IT MUST BE A SUPERIOR EVOLUTION OF THOSE OTHER SNAKES.
ISN'T IT JUST A LITTLE TOO GINORMOUS, THOUGH!?
AND THE WAY IT'S SLITHERING AROUND —
IT DOESN'T MAKE A SOUND BECAUSE OF THE SILENCE SKILL!!
I MEAN, I GUESS IT'S NOT A MONSTER I CAN'T TAKE ON, BUT...
...EVEN AT FULL POWER, I'D PROBABLY ONLY HAVE A FIFTY-FIFTY CHANCE OF WINNING.
ZURU
ZURU (SLITHER)
ZUZUZU (SLIDE)
IT'S GONE...
WHEW...

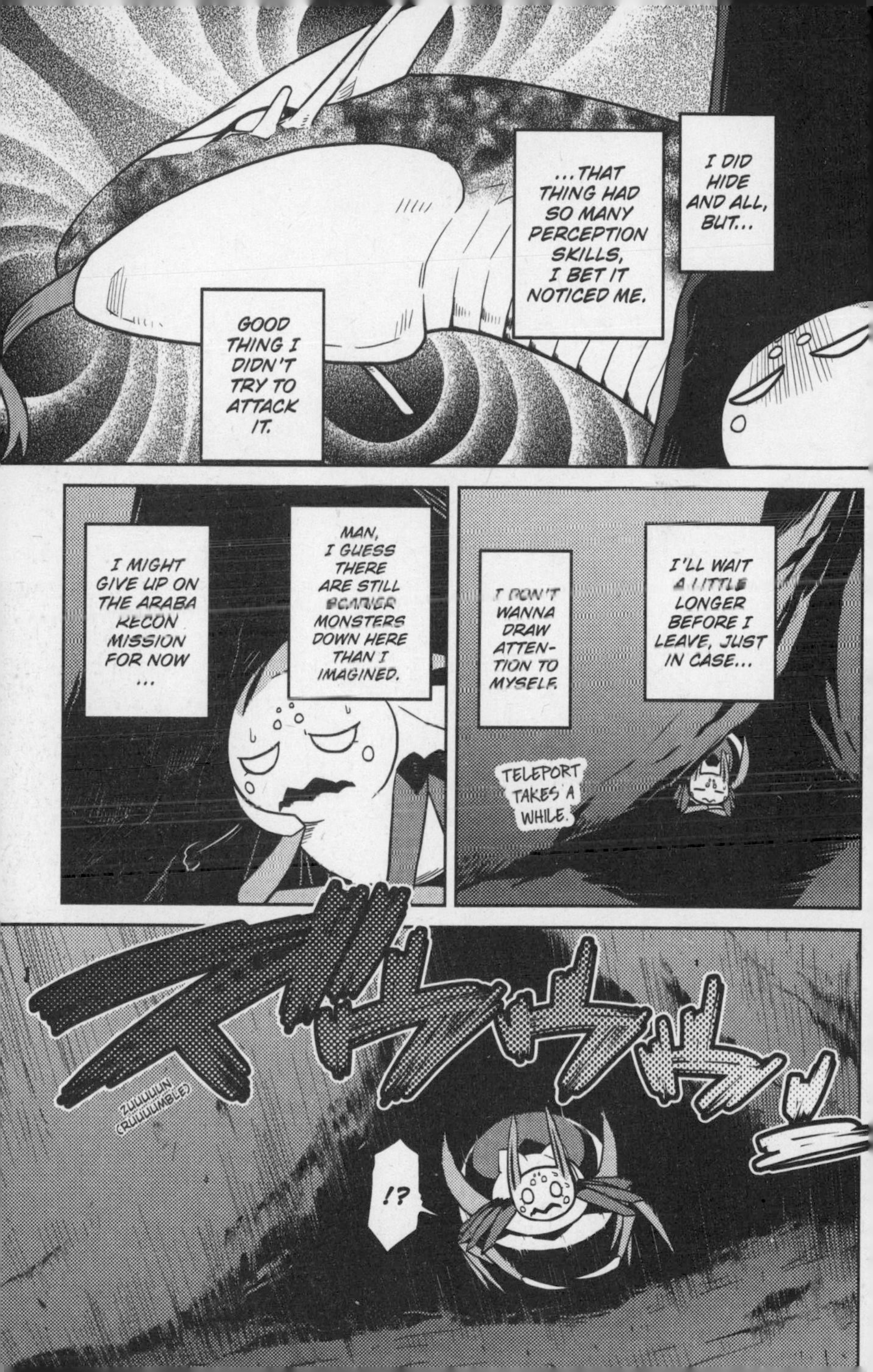

I DID HIDE AND ALL, BUT...
...THAT THING HAD SO MANY PERCEPTION SKILLS, I BET IT NOTICED ME.
GOOD THING I DIDN'T TRY TO ATTACK IT.
I'LL WAIT A LITTLE LONGER BEFORE I LEAVE, JUST IN CASE...
I DON'T WANNA DRAW ATTEN-TION TO MYSELF.
TELEPORT TAKES A WHILE.
MAN, I GUESS THERE ARE STILL SCARIER MONSTERS DOWN HERE THAN I IMAGINED.
I MIGHT GIVE UP ON THE ARABA RECON MISSION FOR NOW...
ZUUUUUN (RUUUUMBLE)
!?

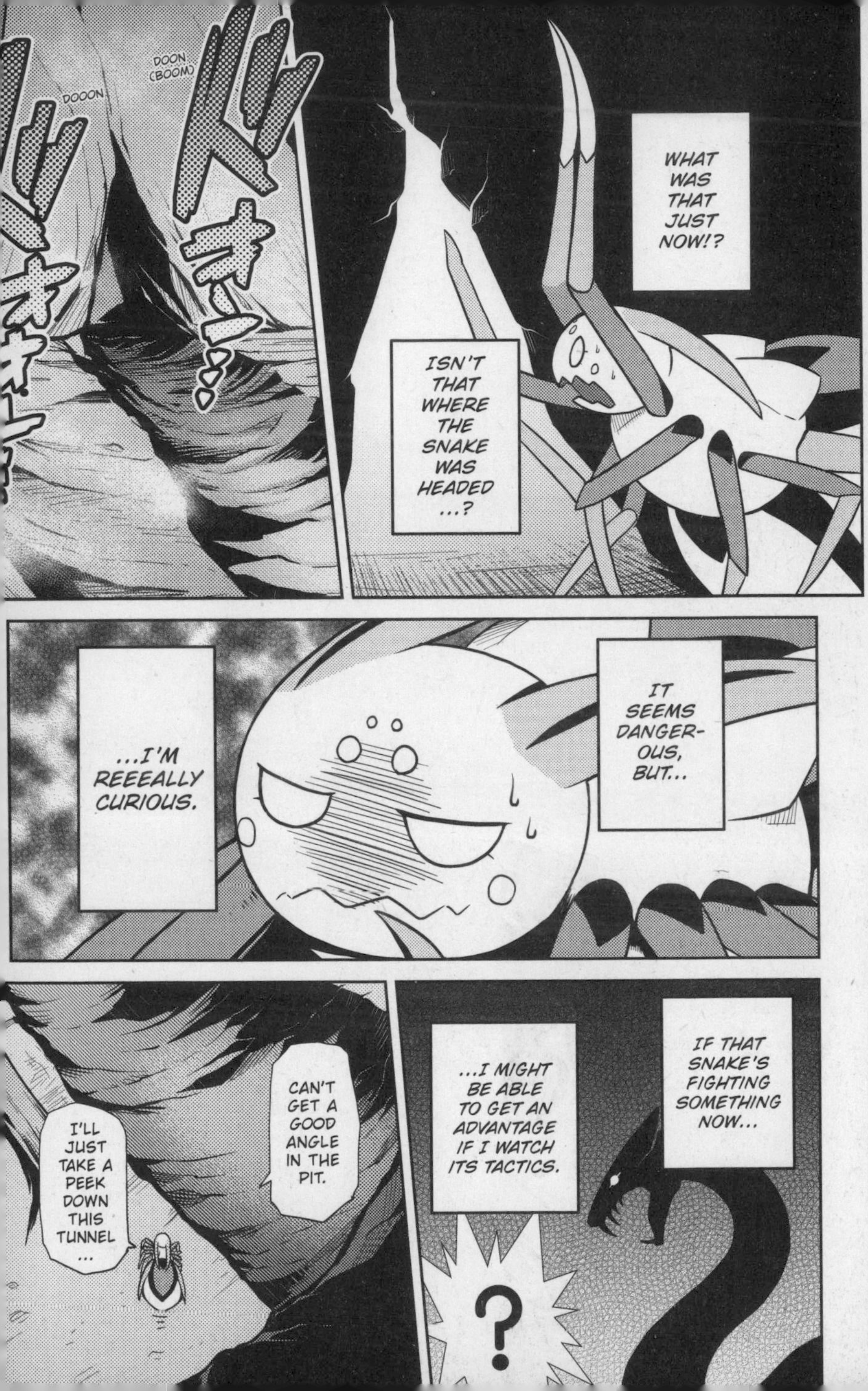
WHAT WAS THAT JUST NOW!?
ISN'T THAT WHERE THE SNAKE WAS HEADED ...?
DOON (BOOM)
DOOON
IT SEEMS DANGER-OUS, BUT...
...I'M REEEALLY CURIOUS.
IF THAT SNAKE'S FIGHTING SOMETHING NOW...
...I MIGHT BE ABLE TO GET AN ADVANTAGE IF I WATCH ITS TACTICS.
?
CAN'T GET A GOOD ANGLE IN THE PIT.
I'LL JUST TAKE A PEEK DOWN THIS TUNNEL ...

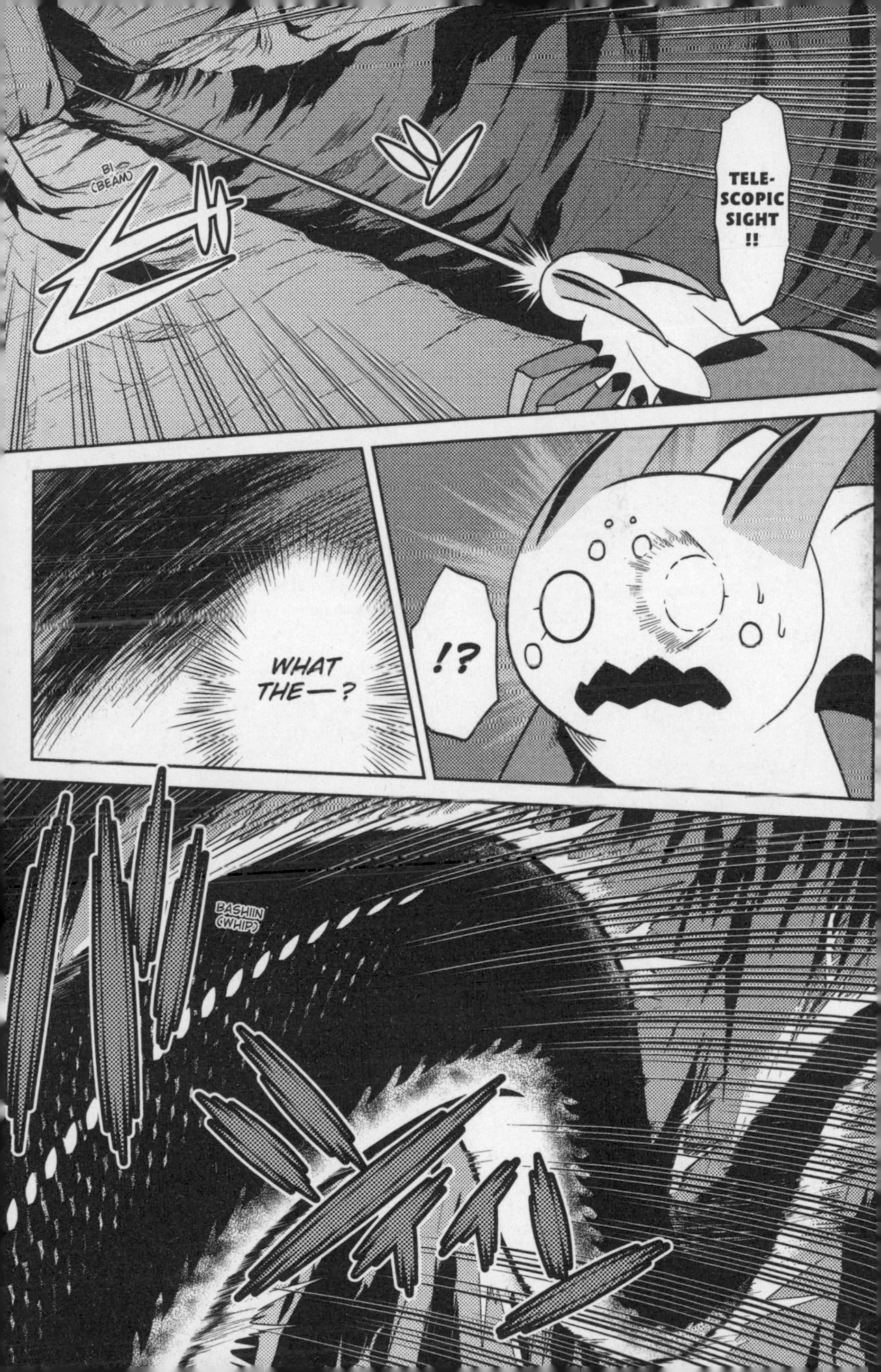
TELE-
SCOPIC
SIGHT
!!
BI
(BEAM)
!?
WHAT
THE—?
BASHIIN
(WHIP)

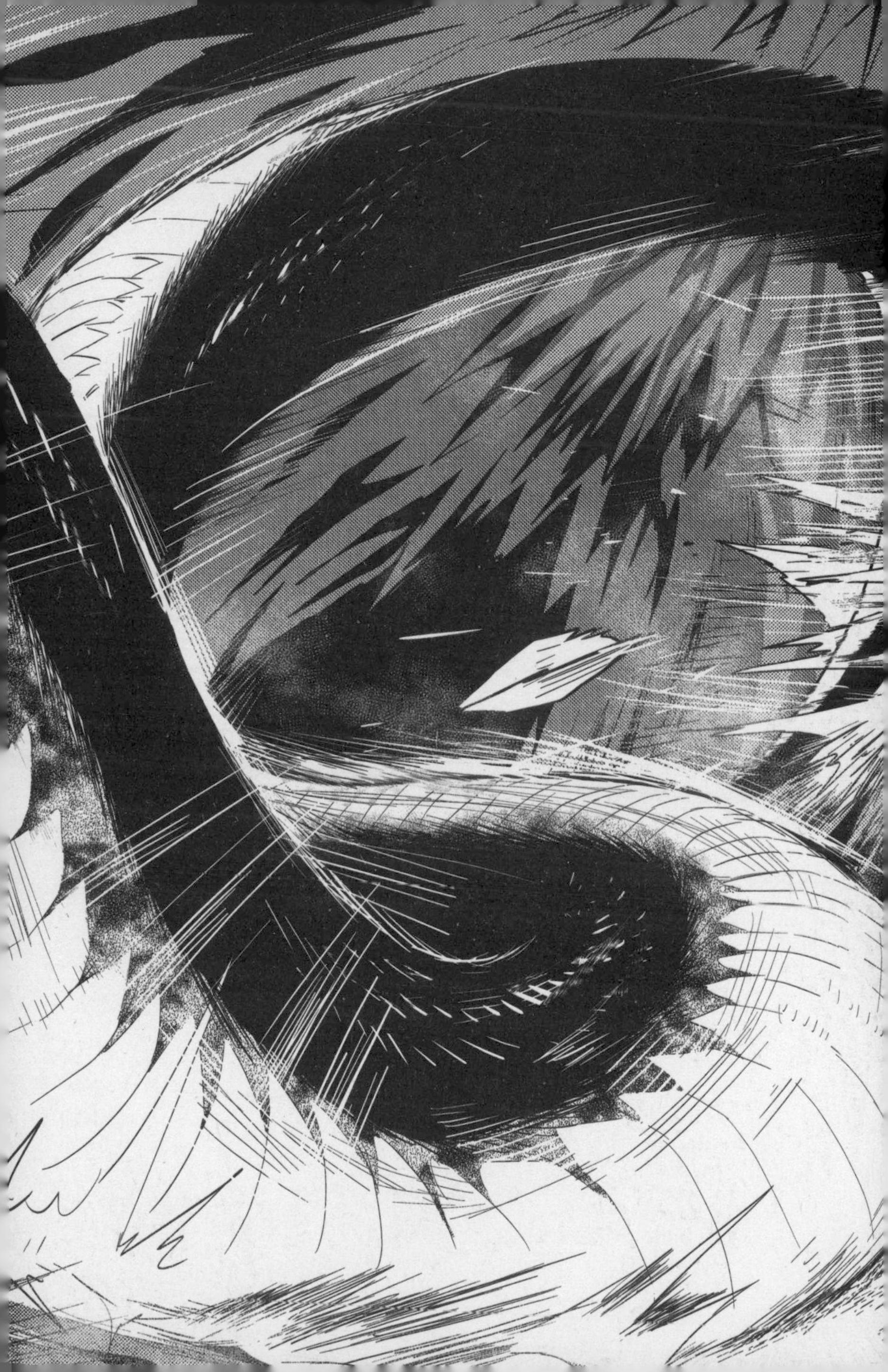

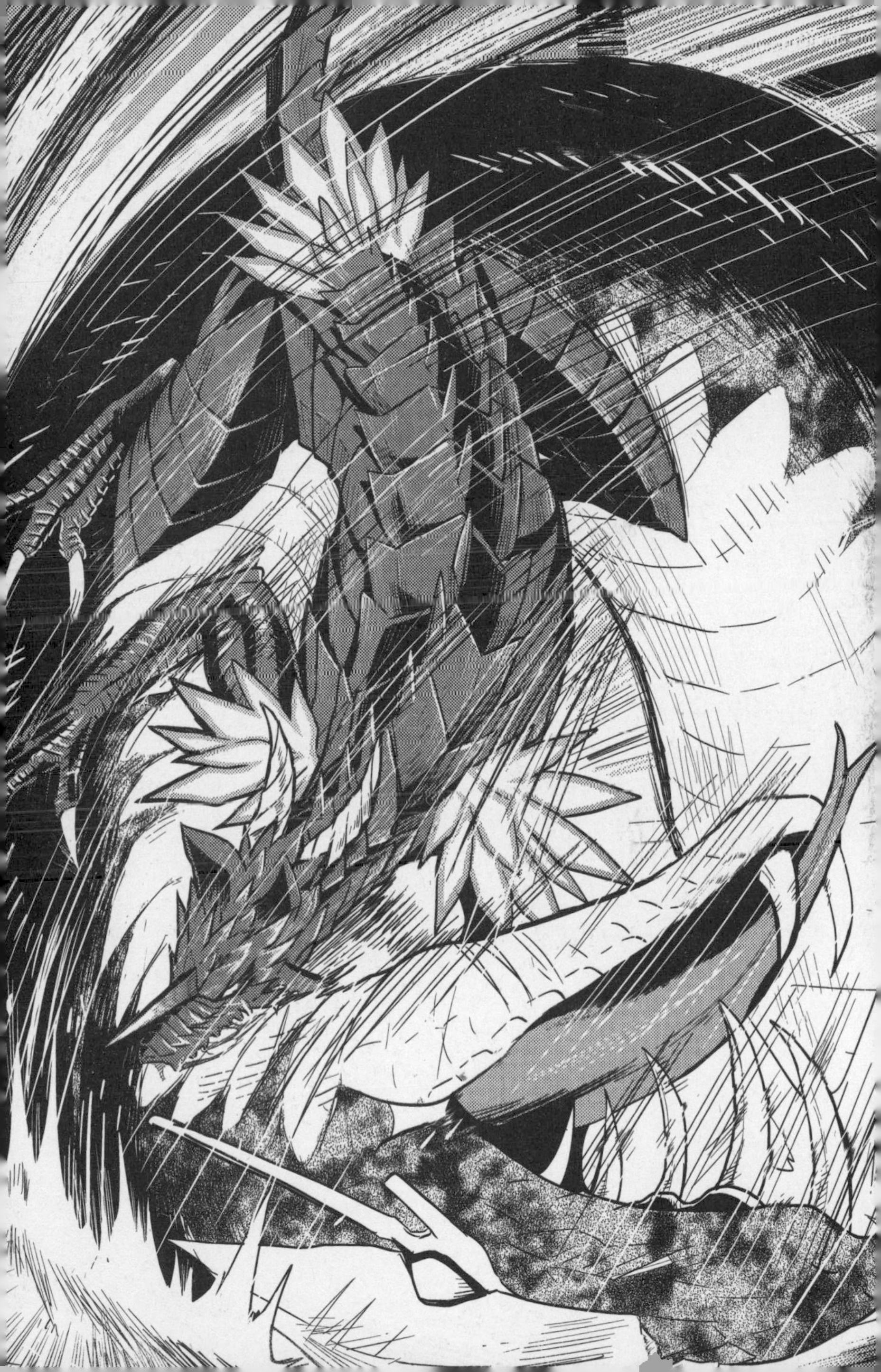

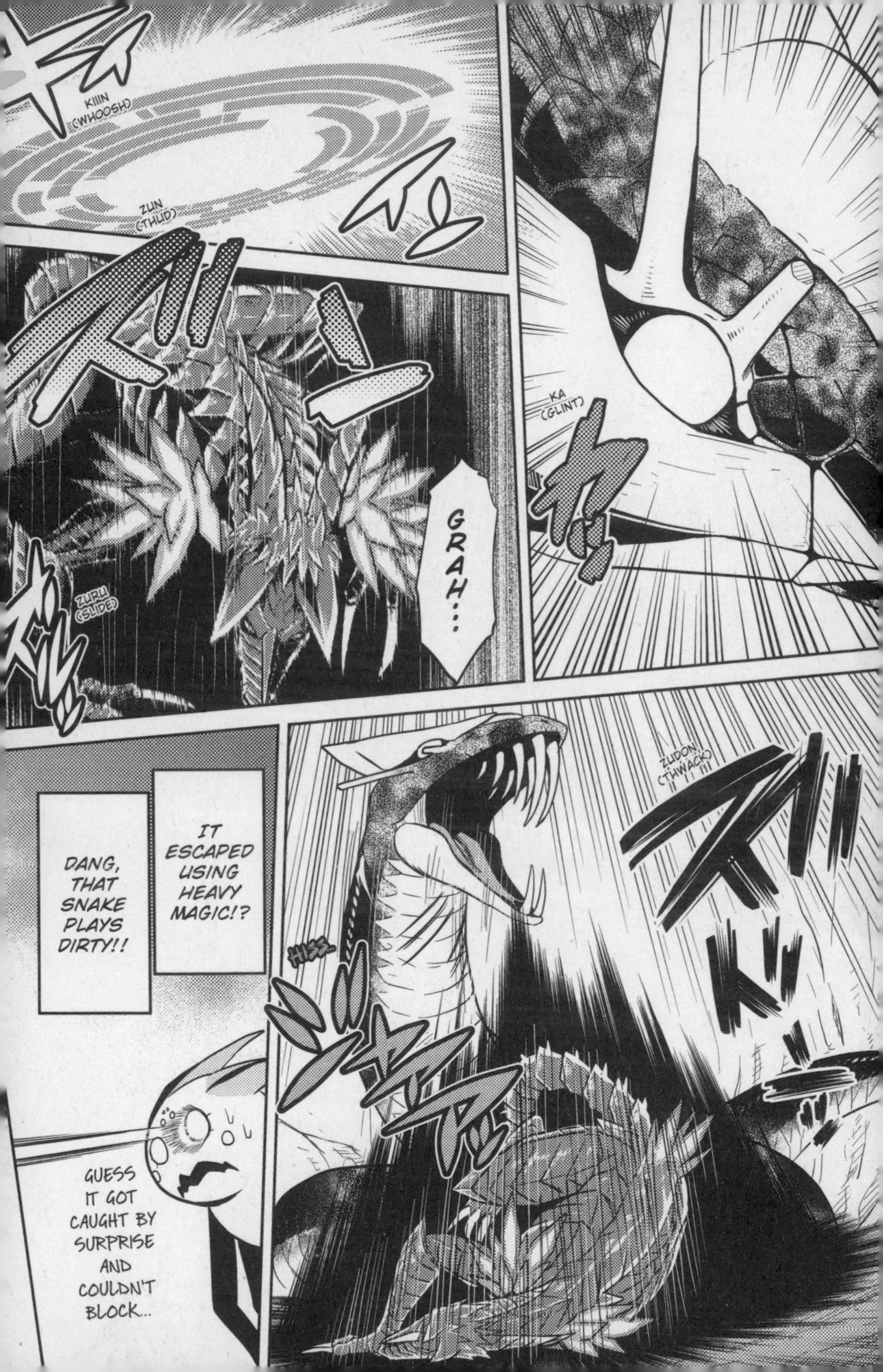
KA (GLINT)
KIIN (WHOOSH)
ZUN (THUD)
GRAH...
ZURU (SLIDE)
ZUDON (THWACK)
HISS...
IT ESCAPED USING HEAVY MAGIC!?
DANG, THAT SNAKE PLAYS DIRTY!!
GUESS IT GOT CAUGHT BY SURPRISE AND COULDN'T BLOCK...

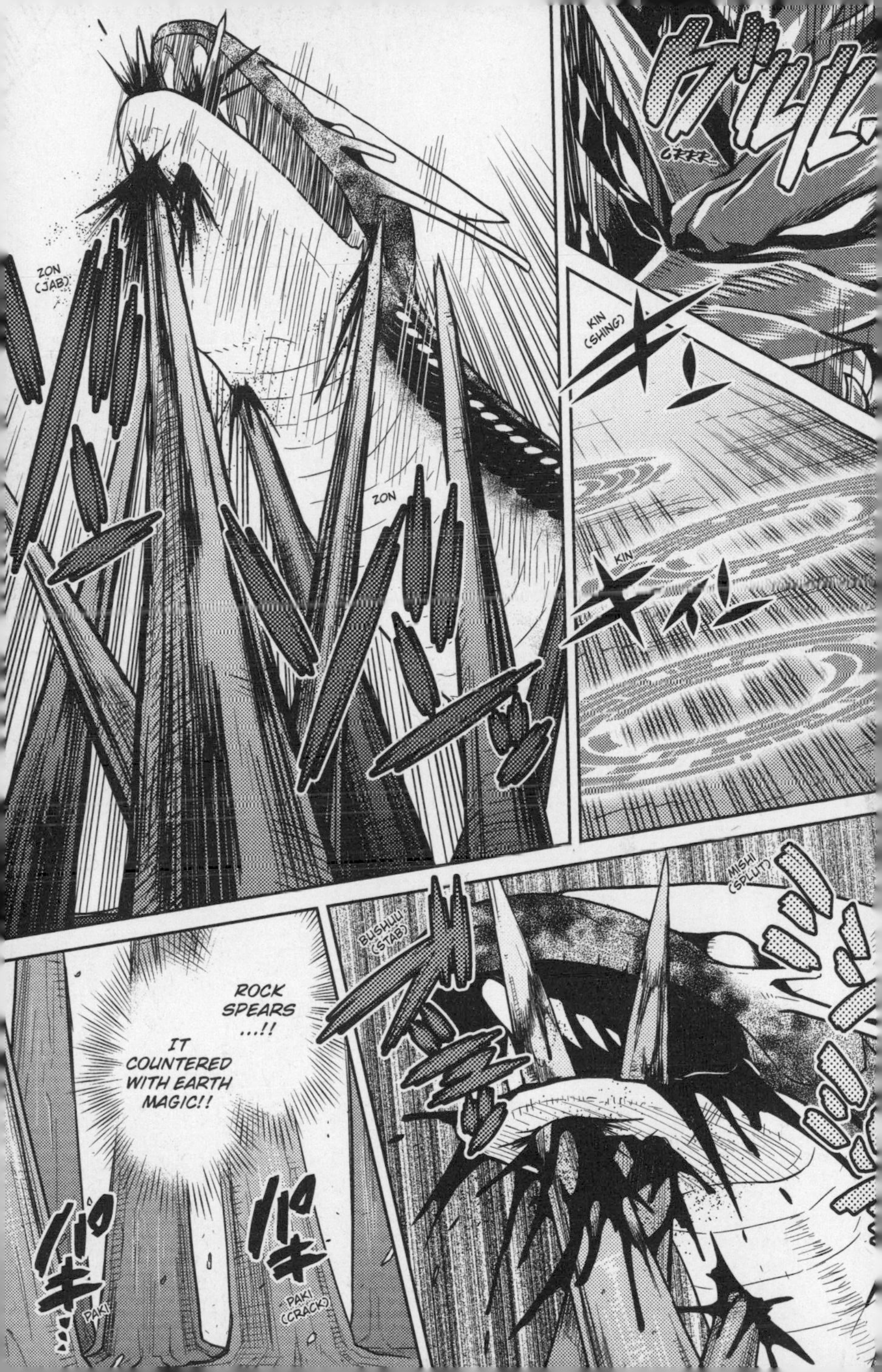
GRRR...
KIN (SHING)
KIN
ZON (JAB)
ZON
MISHI (SPLUT)
BUSHUU (STAB)
ROCK SPEARS ...!!
IT COUNTERED WITH EARTH MAGIC!!
PAKI (CRACK)
PAKI

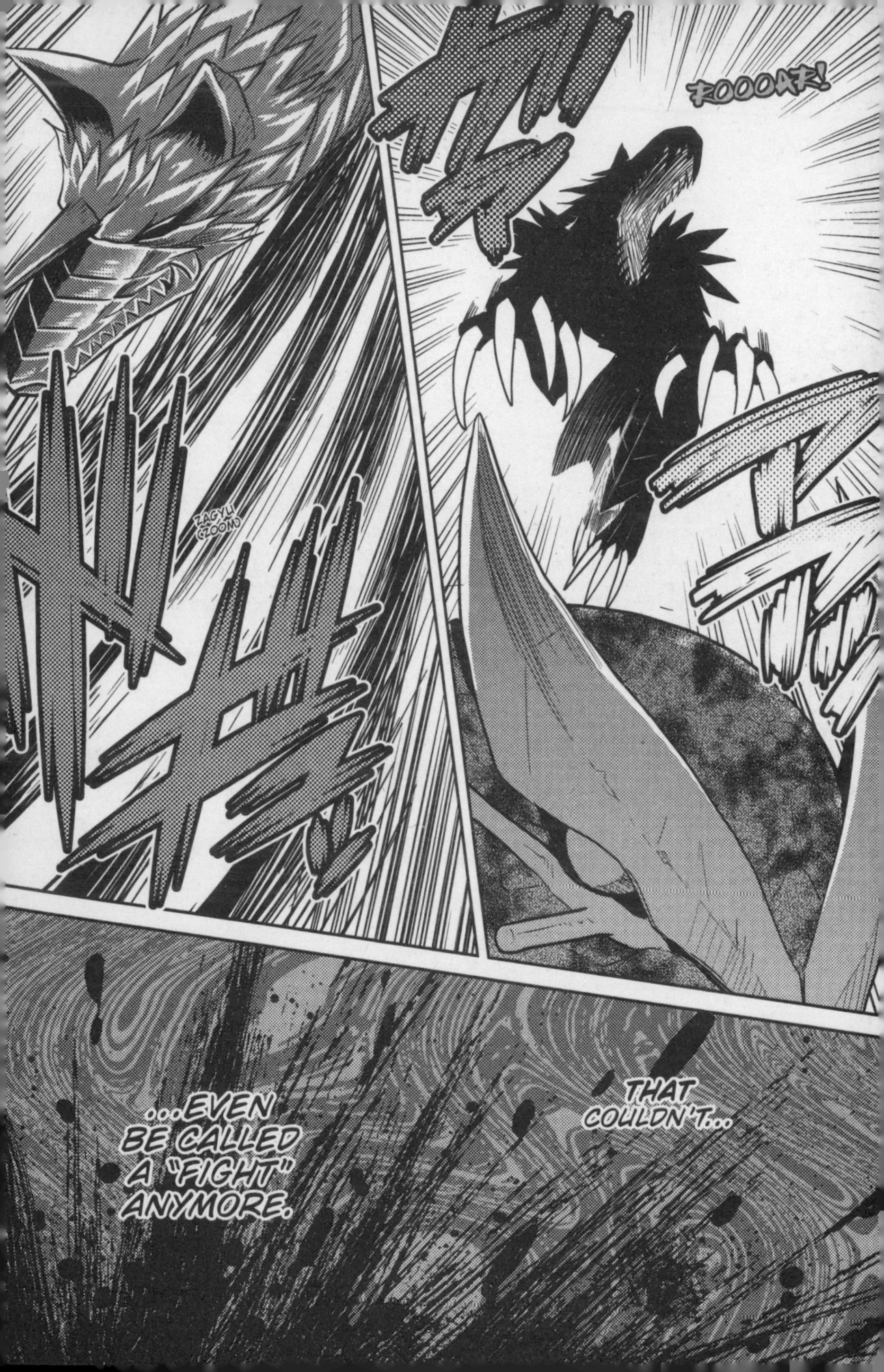
ROOOAR!
ZAGYU
(ZOOM)
THAT COULDN'T...
...EVEN BE CALLED A "FIGHT" ANYMORE.

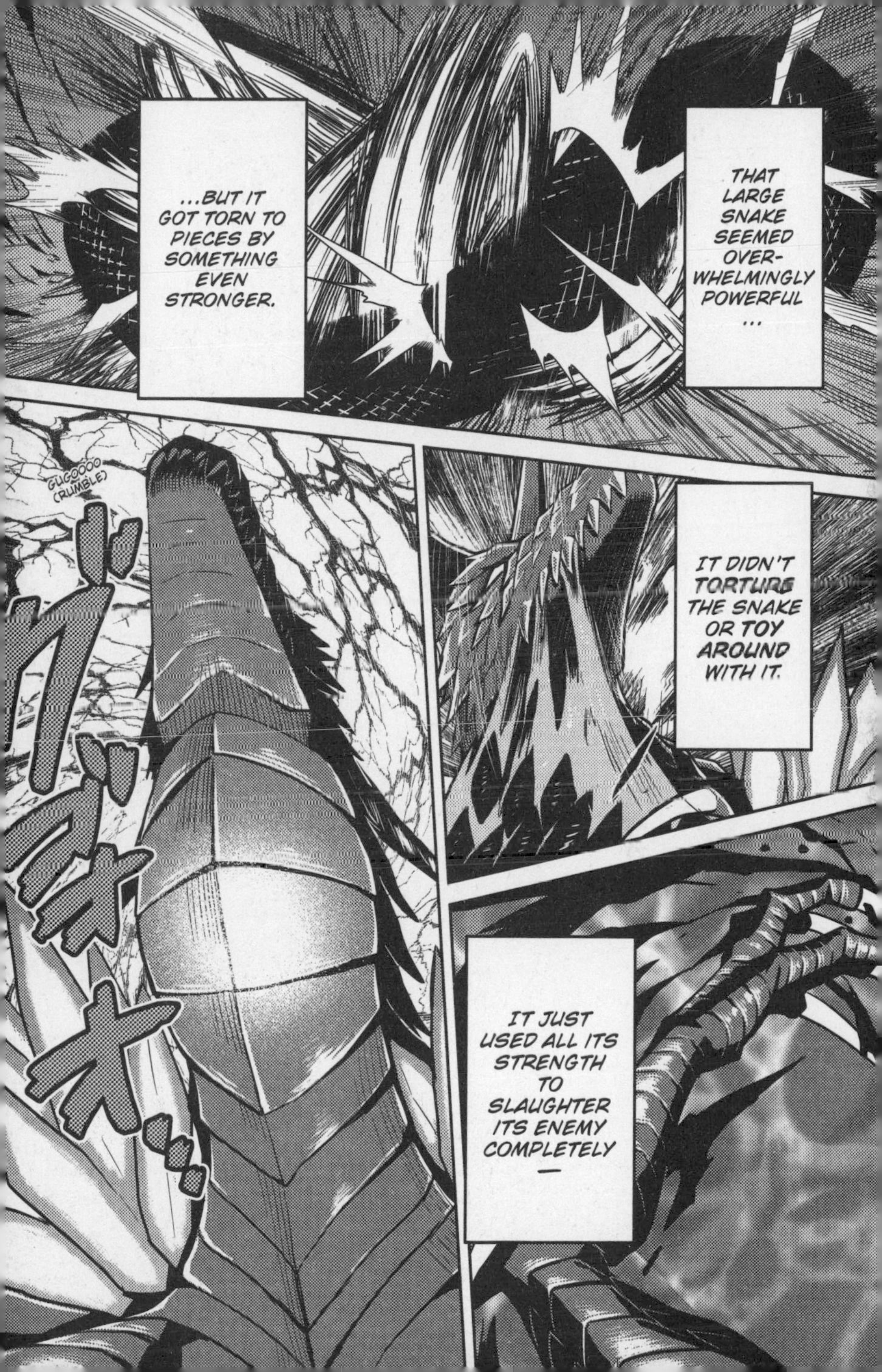
THAT LARGE SNAKE SEEMED OVER-WHELMINGLY POWERFUL ...
...BUT IT GOT TORN TO PIECES BY SOMETHING EVEN STRONGER.
IT DIDN'T TORTURE THE SNAKE OR TOY AROUND WITH IT.
GUGOOOO (RUMBLE)
IT JUST USED ALL ITS STRENGTH TO SLAUGHTER ITS ENEMY COMPLETELY —

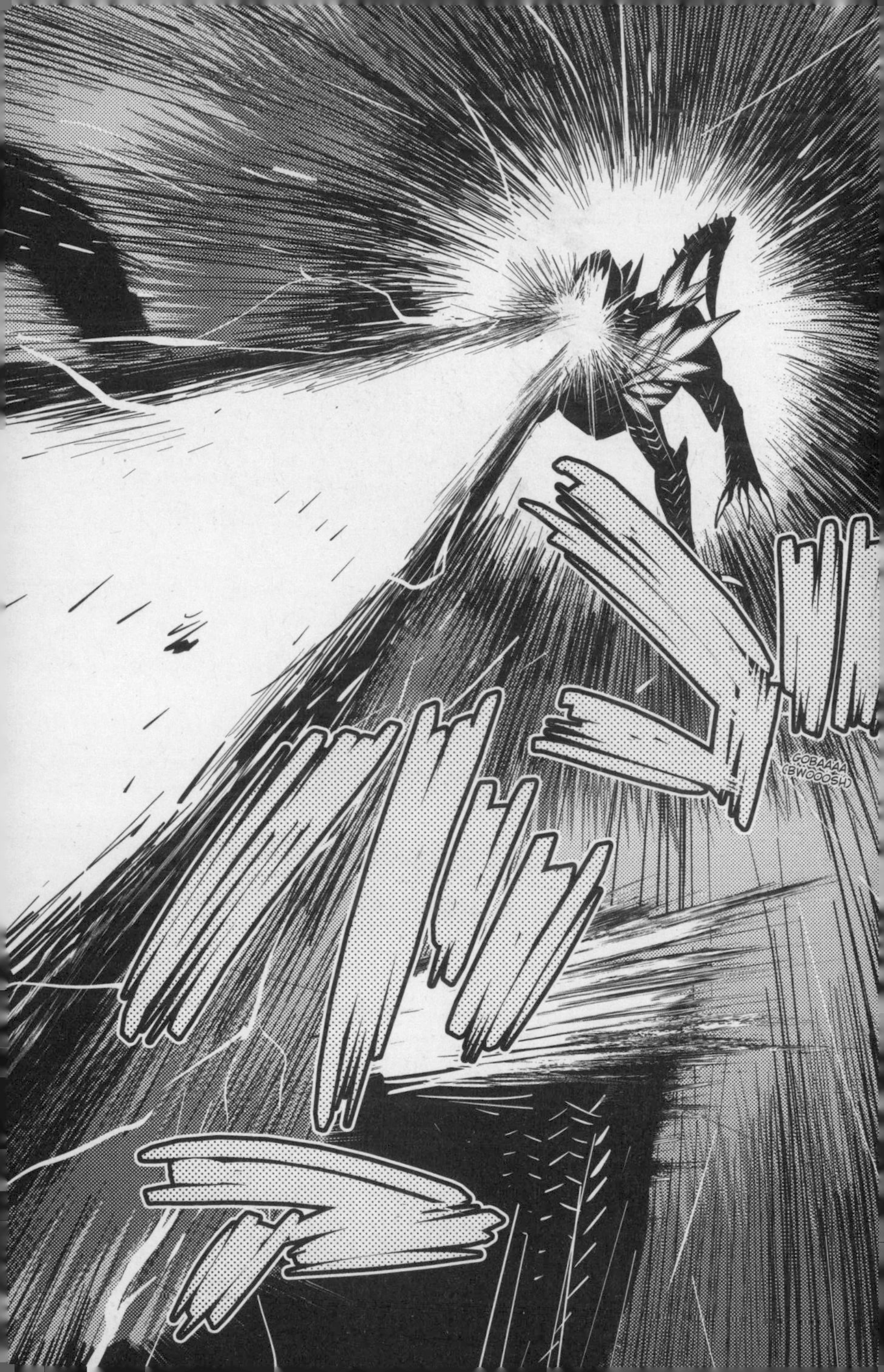
GOBAAAA
(BWOOOSH)

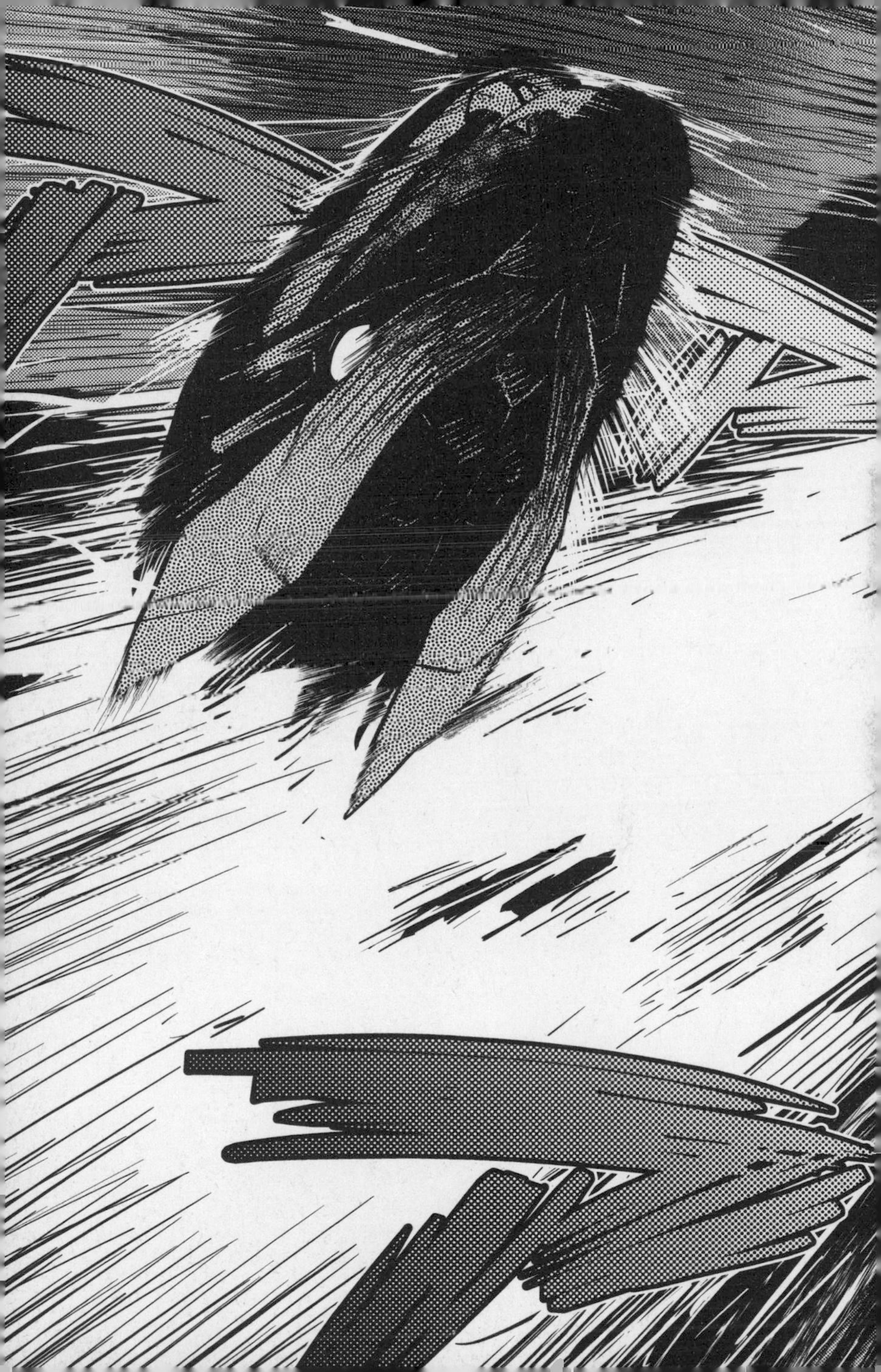

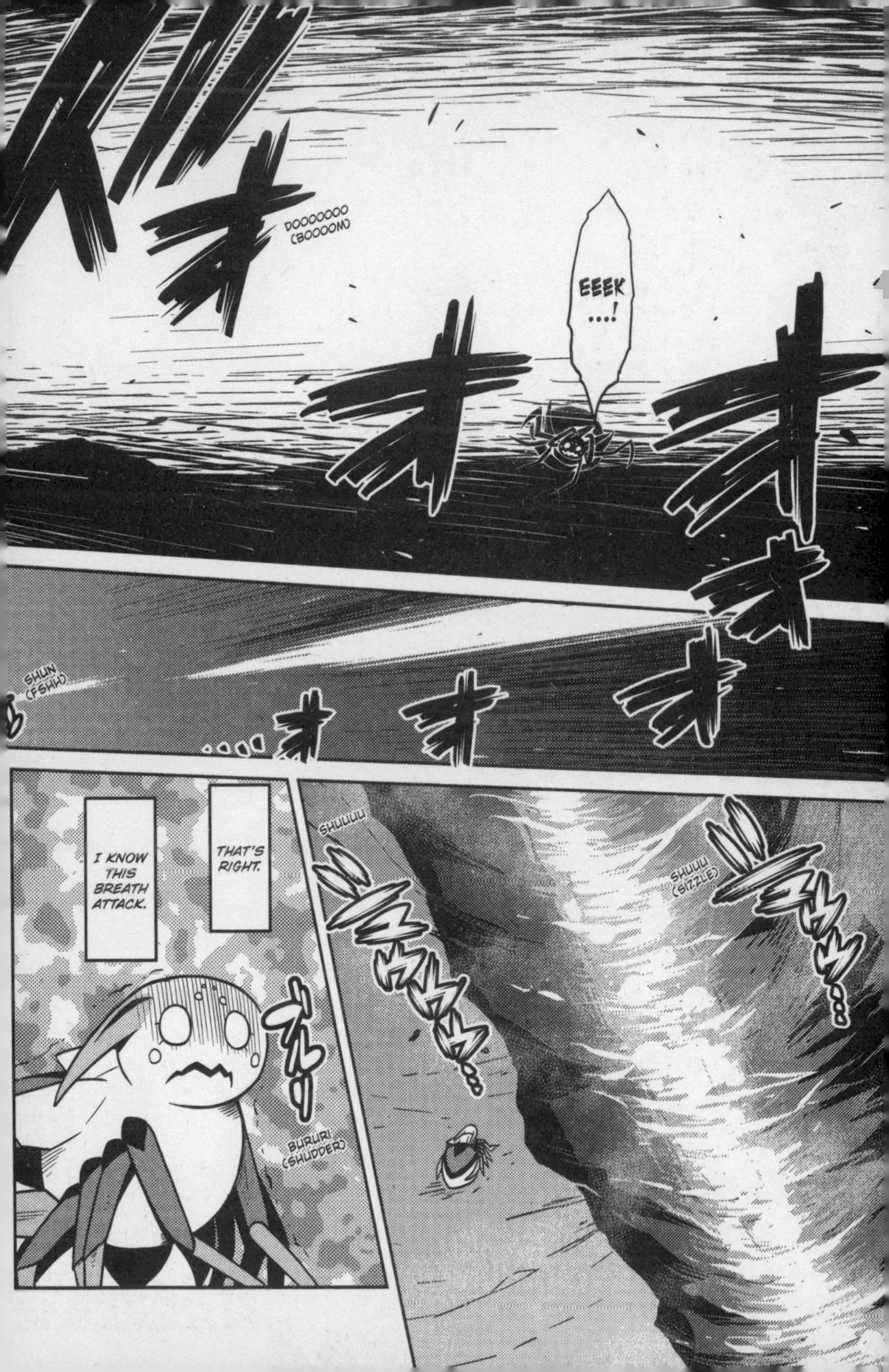
DOOOOOOO (BOOOOM)
EEEK ...!
SHUN (FSHH)
SHUUUU
SHUUU (SIZZLE)
THAT'S RIGHT.
I KNOW THIS BREATH ATTACK.
BURURI (SHUDDER)

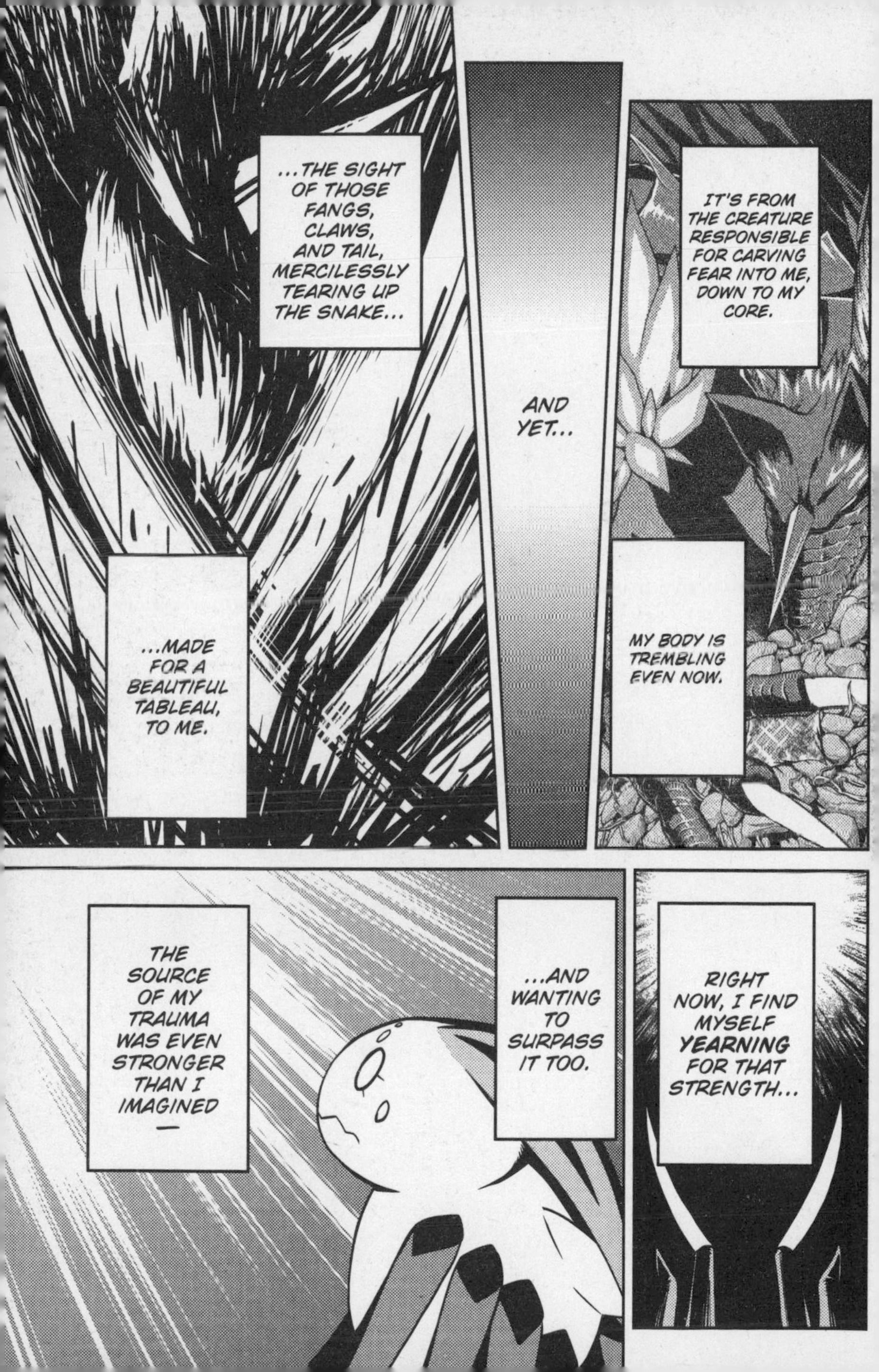
IT'S FROM THE CREATURE RESPONSIBLE FOR CARVING FEAR INTO ME, DOWN TO MY CORE.
MY BODY IS TREMBLING EVEN NOW.
AND YET...
...THE SIGHT OF THOSE FANGS, CLAWS, AND TAIL, MERCILESSLY TEARING UP THE SNAKE...
...MADE FOR A BEAUTIFUL TABLEAU, TO ME.
RIGHT NOW, I FIND MYSELF **YEARNING** FOR THAT STRENGTH...
...AND WANTING TO SURPASS IT TOO.
THE SOURCE OF MY TRAUMA WAS EVEN STRONGER THAN I IMAGINED —

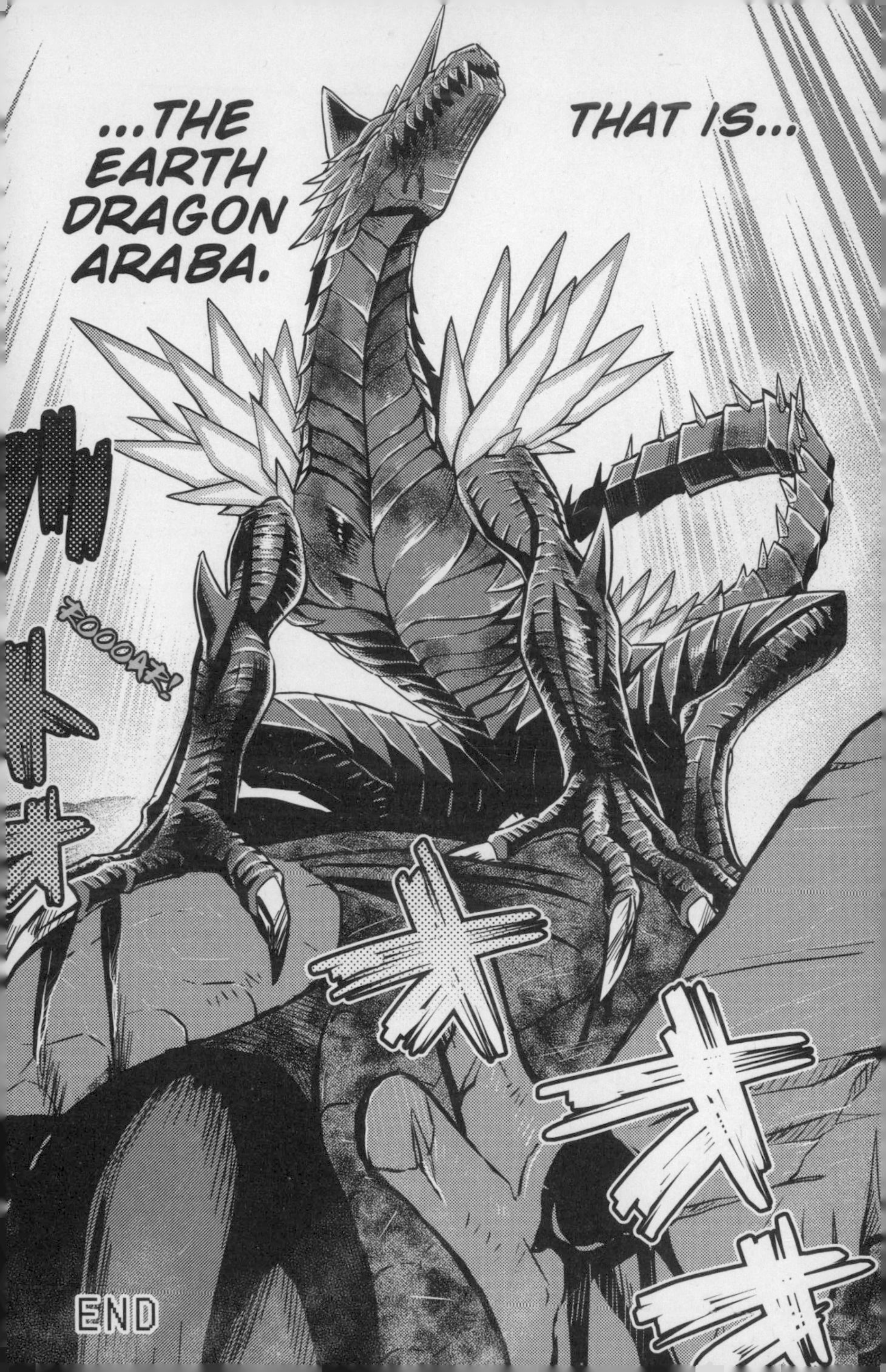
THAT IS...
...THE EARTH DRAGON ARABA.
ROOOAR!
END

So I'm a Spider, So What?

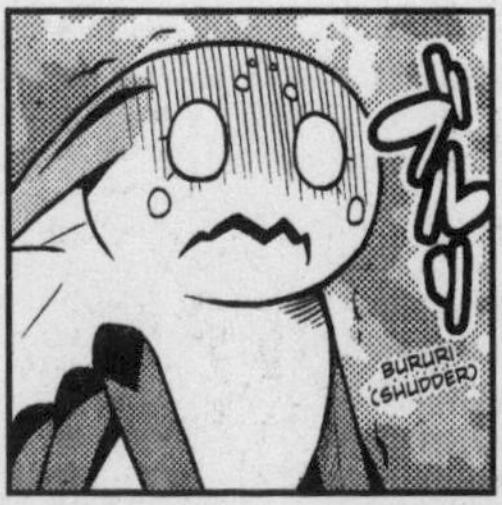
BURURI
(SHUDDER)

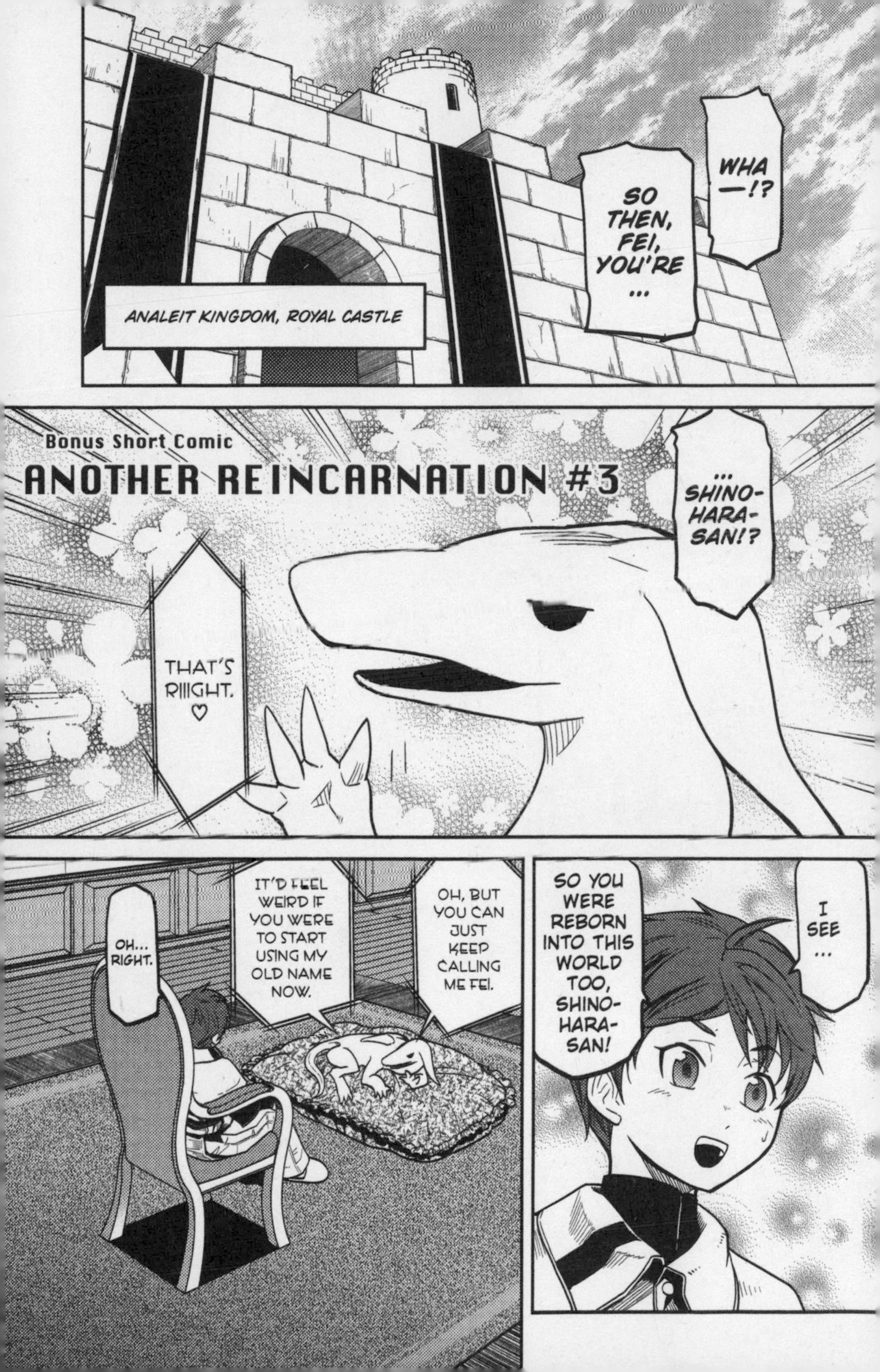
WHA—!?
SO THEN, FEI, YOU'RE ...
ANALEIT KINGDOM, ROYAL CASTLE
... SHINOHARA-SAN!?
Bonus Short Comic
ANOTHER REINCARNATION #3
THAT'S RIIIGHT. ♡
I SEE ...
SO YOU WERE REBORN INTO THIS WORLD TOO, SHINOHARA-SAN!
OH, BUT YOU CAN JUST KEEP CALLING ME FEI.
IT'D FEEL WEIRD IF YOU WERE TO START USING MY OLD NAME NOW.
OH... RIGHT.

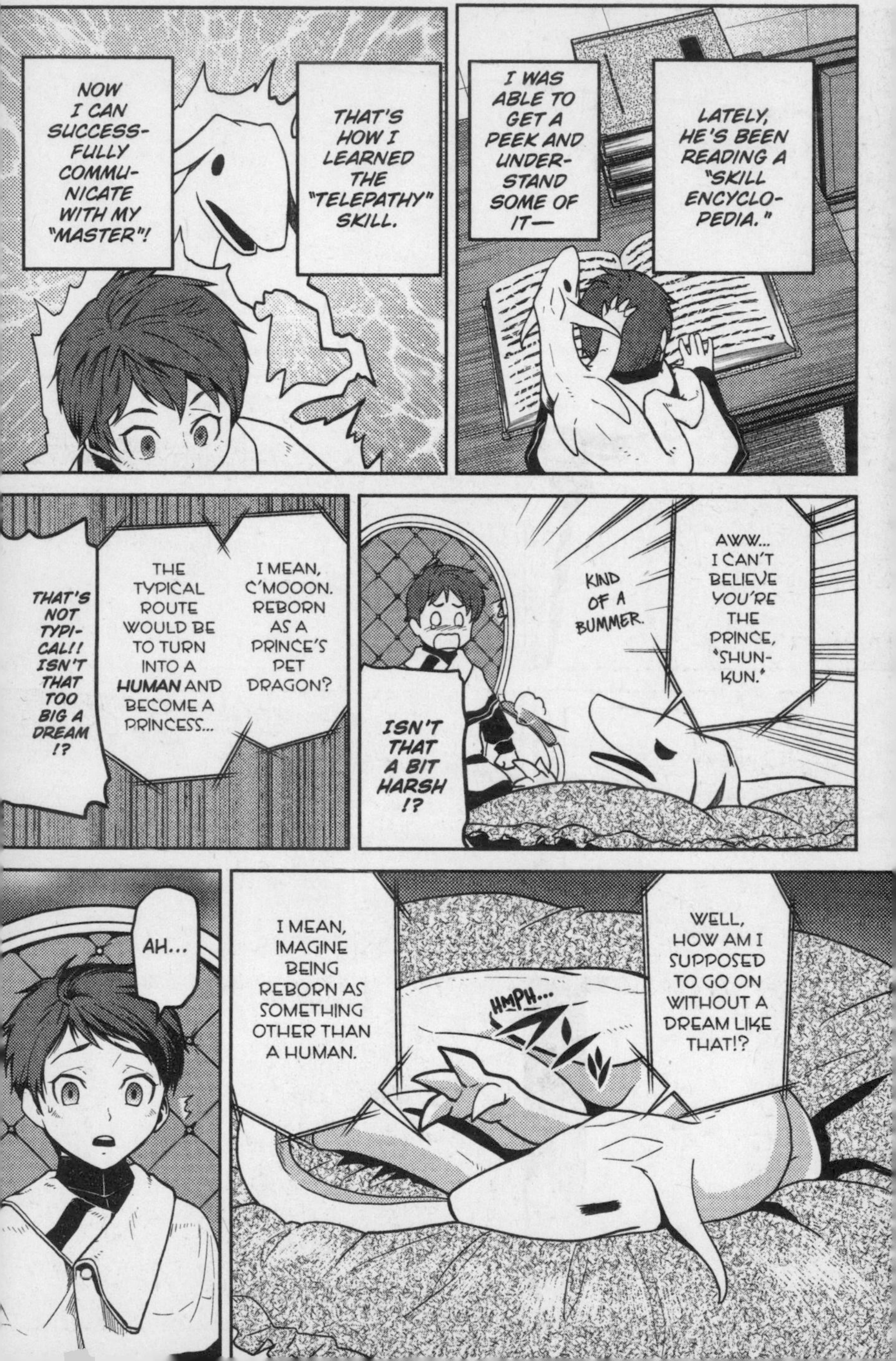
LATELY, HE'S BEEN READING A "SKILL ENCYCLOPEDIA."
I WAS ABLE TO GET A PEEK AND UNDERSTAND SOME OF IT—
THAT'S HOW I LEARNED THE "TELEPATHY" SKILL.
NOW I CAN SUCCESSFULLY COMMUNICATE WITH MY "MASTER"!
AWW... I CAN'T BELIEVE YOU'RE THE PRINCE, "SHUN-KUN."
KIND OF A BUMMER.
ISN'T THAT A BIT HARSH!?
I MEAN, C'MOOON. REBORN AS A PRINCE'S PET DRAGON?
THE TYPICAL ROUTE WOULD BE TO TURN INTO A **HUMAN** AND BECOME A PRINCESS...
THAT'S NOT TYPICAL!! ISN'T THAT TOO BIG A DREAM!?
WELL, HOW AM I SUPPOSED TO GO ON WITHOUT A DREAM LIKE THAT!?
HMPH...
I MEAN, IMAGINE BEING REBORN AS SOMETHING OTHER THAN A HUMAN.
AH...

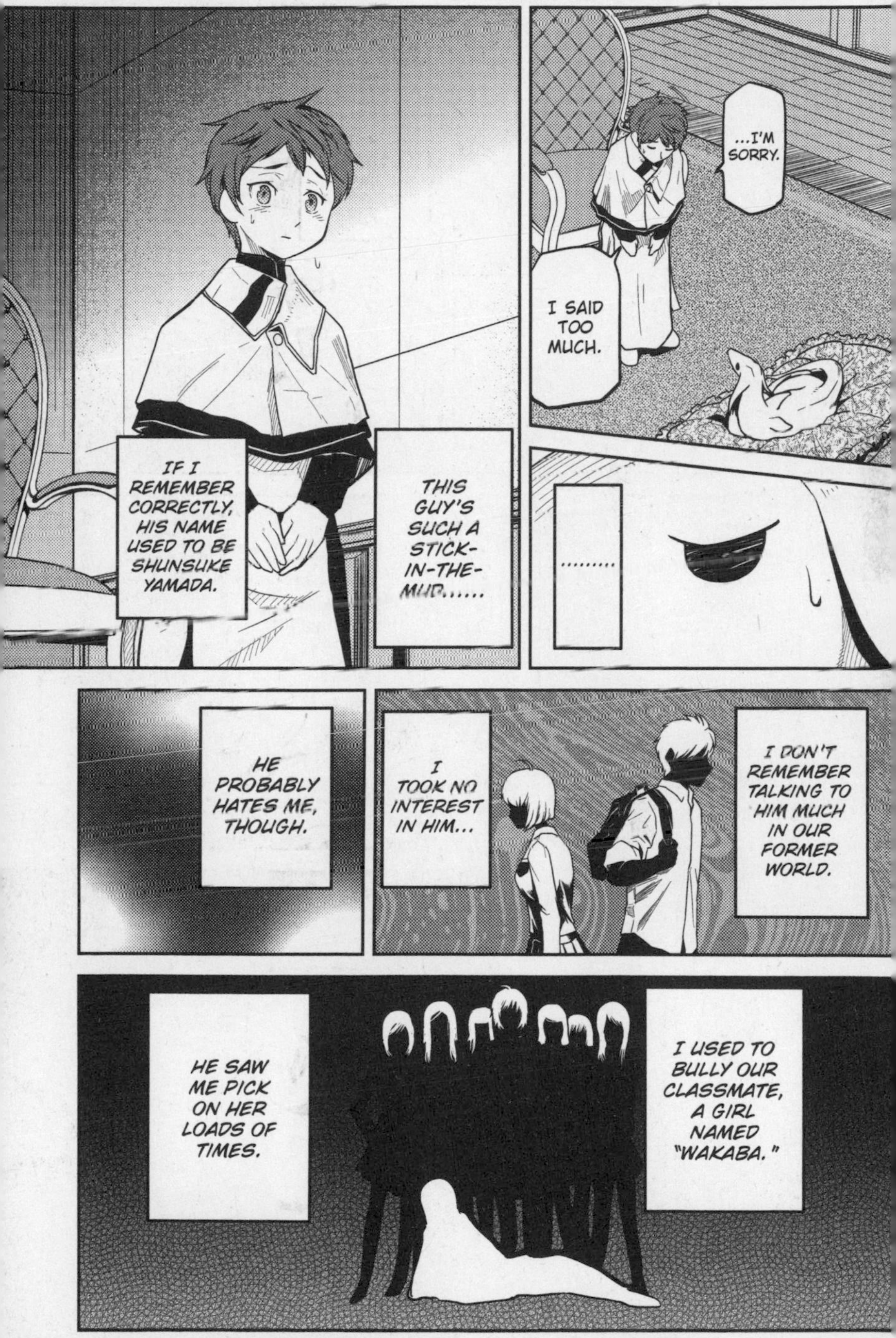
...I'M SORRY.
I SAID TOO MUCH.
....
THIS GUY'S SUCH A STICK-IN-THE-MUD......
IF I REMEMBER CORRECTLY, HIS NAME USED TO BE SHUNSUKE YAMADA.
I DON'T REMEMBER TALKING TO HIM MUCH IN OUR FORMER WORLD.
I TOOK NO INTEREST IN HIM...
HE PROBABLY HATES ME, THOUGH.
I USED TO BULLY OUR CLASSMATE, A GIRL NAMED "WAKABA."
HE SAW ME PICK ON HER LOADS OF TIMES.

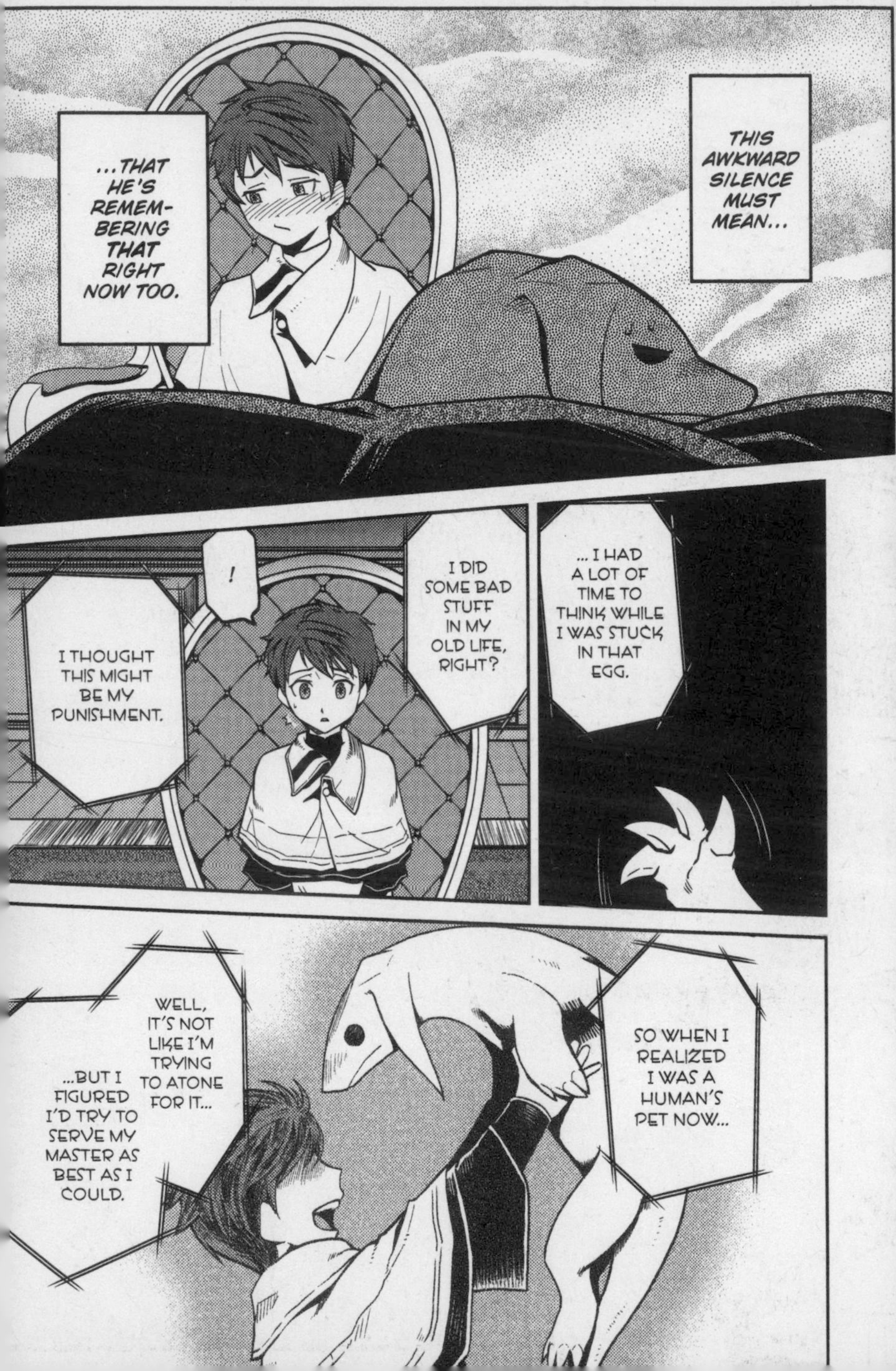
THIS AWKWARD SILENCE MUST MEAN...
...THAT HE'S REMEMBERING THAT RIGHT NOW TOO.
...I HAD A LOT OF TIME TO THINK WHILE I WAS STUCK IN THAT EGG.
I DID SOME BAD STUFF IN MY OLD LIFE, RIGHT?
!
I THOUGHT THIS MIGHT BE MY PUNISHMENT.
SO WHEN I REALIZED I WAS A HUMAN'S PET NOW...
WELL, IT'S NOT LIKE I'M TRYING TO ATONE FOR IT...
...BUT I FIGURED I'D TRY TO SERVE MY MASTER AS BEST AS I COULD.

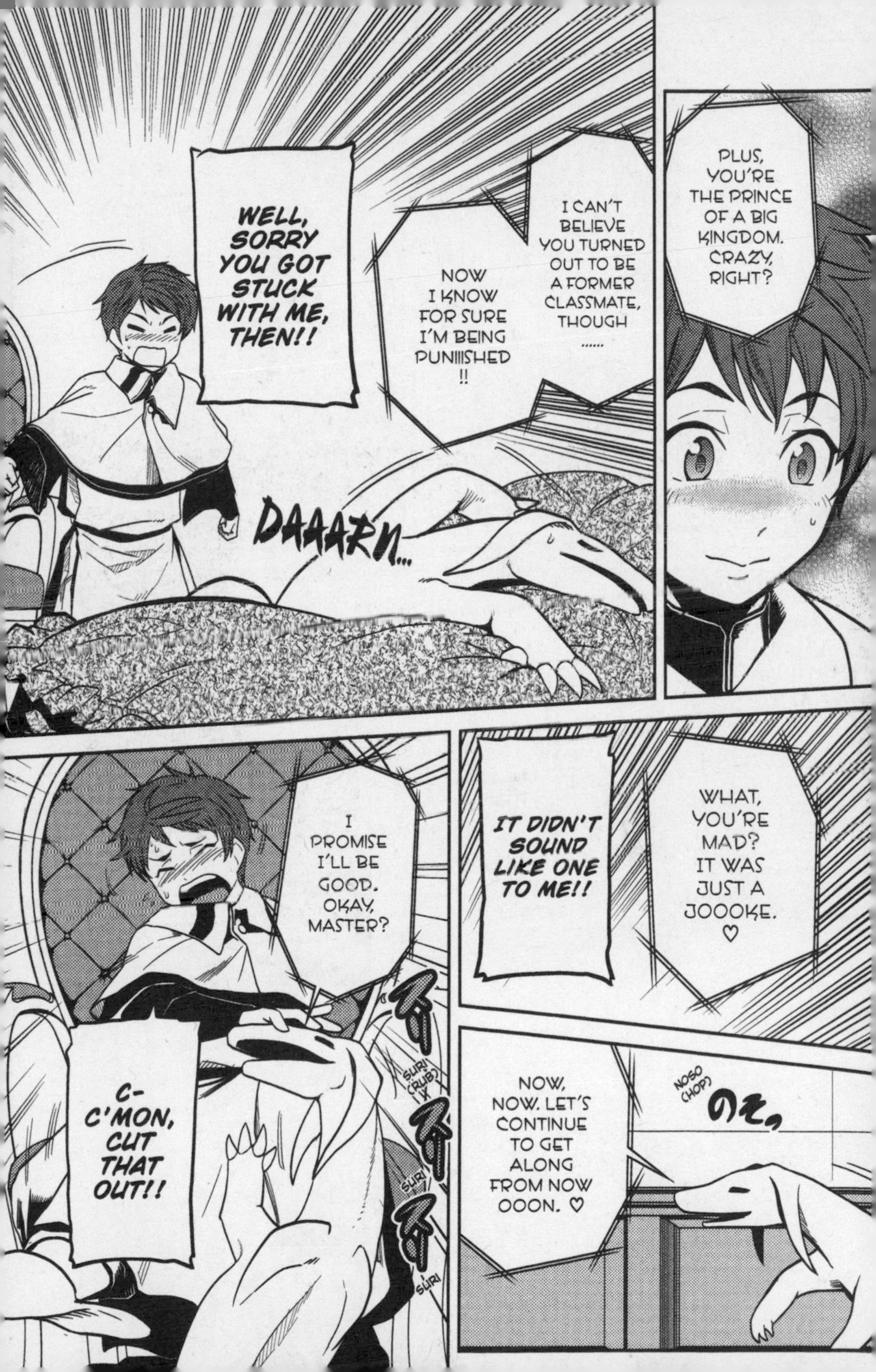
PLUS, YOU'RE THE PRINCE OF A BIG KINGDOM. CRAZY, RIGHT?
I CAN'T BELIEVE YOU TURNED OUT TO BE A FORMER CLASSMATE, THOUGH ......
NOW I KNOW FOR SURE I'M BEING PUNIIISHED !!
WELL, SORRY YOU GOT STUCK WITH ME, THEN!!
DAAARN...
WHAT, YOU'RE MAD? IT WAS JUST A JOOOKE. ♡
IT DIDN'T SOUND LIKE ONE TO ME!!
NOSO (HOP)
NOW, NOW. LET'S CONTINUE TO GET ALONG FROM NOW OOON. ♡
I PROMISE I'LL BE GOOD. OKAY, MASTER?
SURI (RUB)
SURI
SURI
C-C'MON, CUT THAT OUT!!

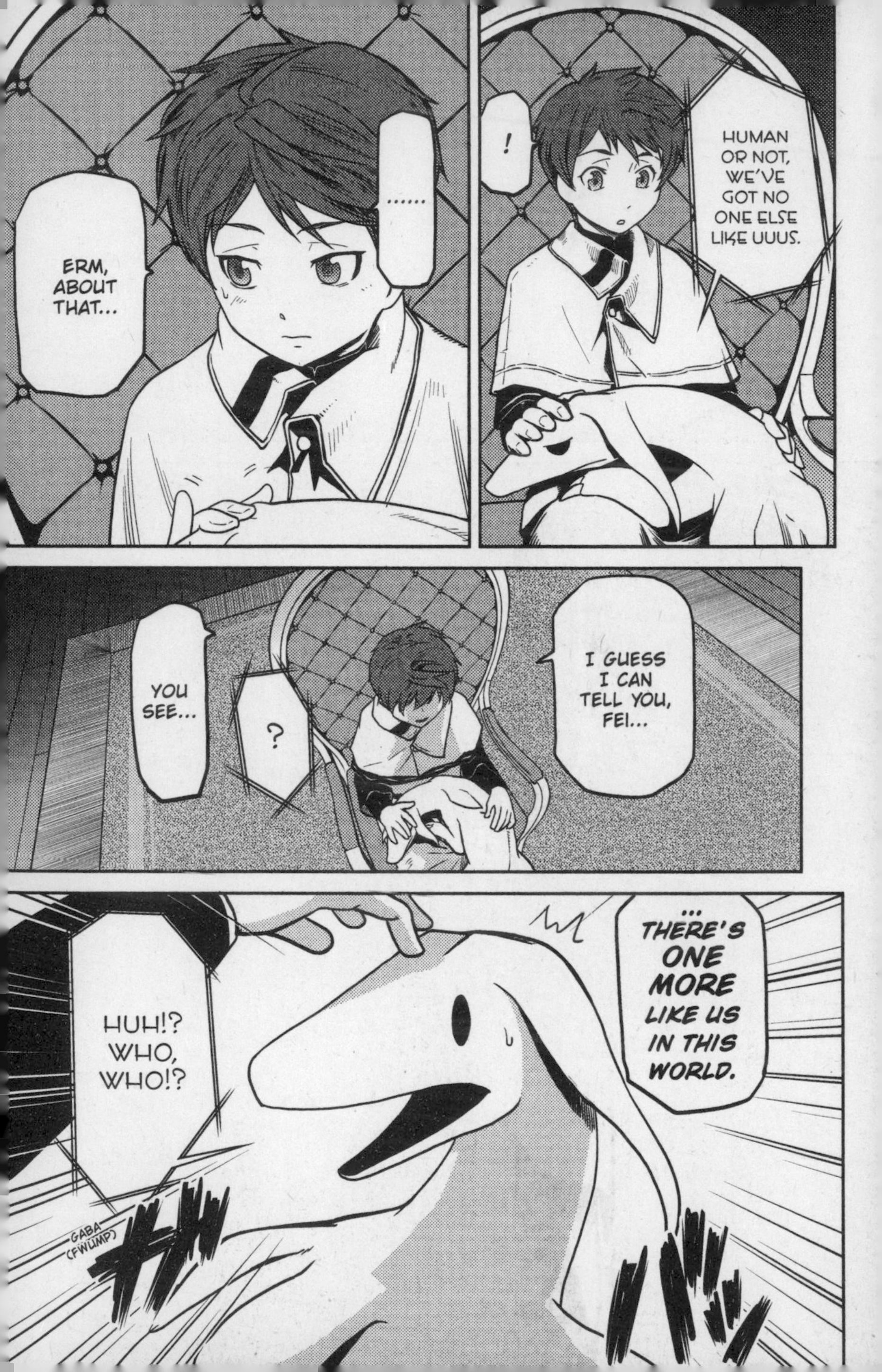
HUMAN OR NOT, WE'VE GOT NO ONE ELSE LIKE UUUS.
!
......
ERM, ABOUT THAT...
I GUESS I CAN TELL YOU, FEI...
?
YOU SEE...
... THERE'S ONE MORE LIKE US IN THIS WORLD.
HUH!? WHO, WHO!?
GABA (FWUMP)

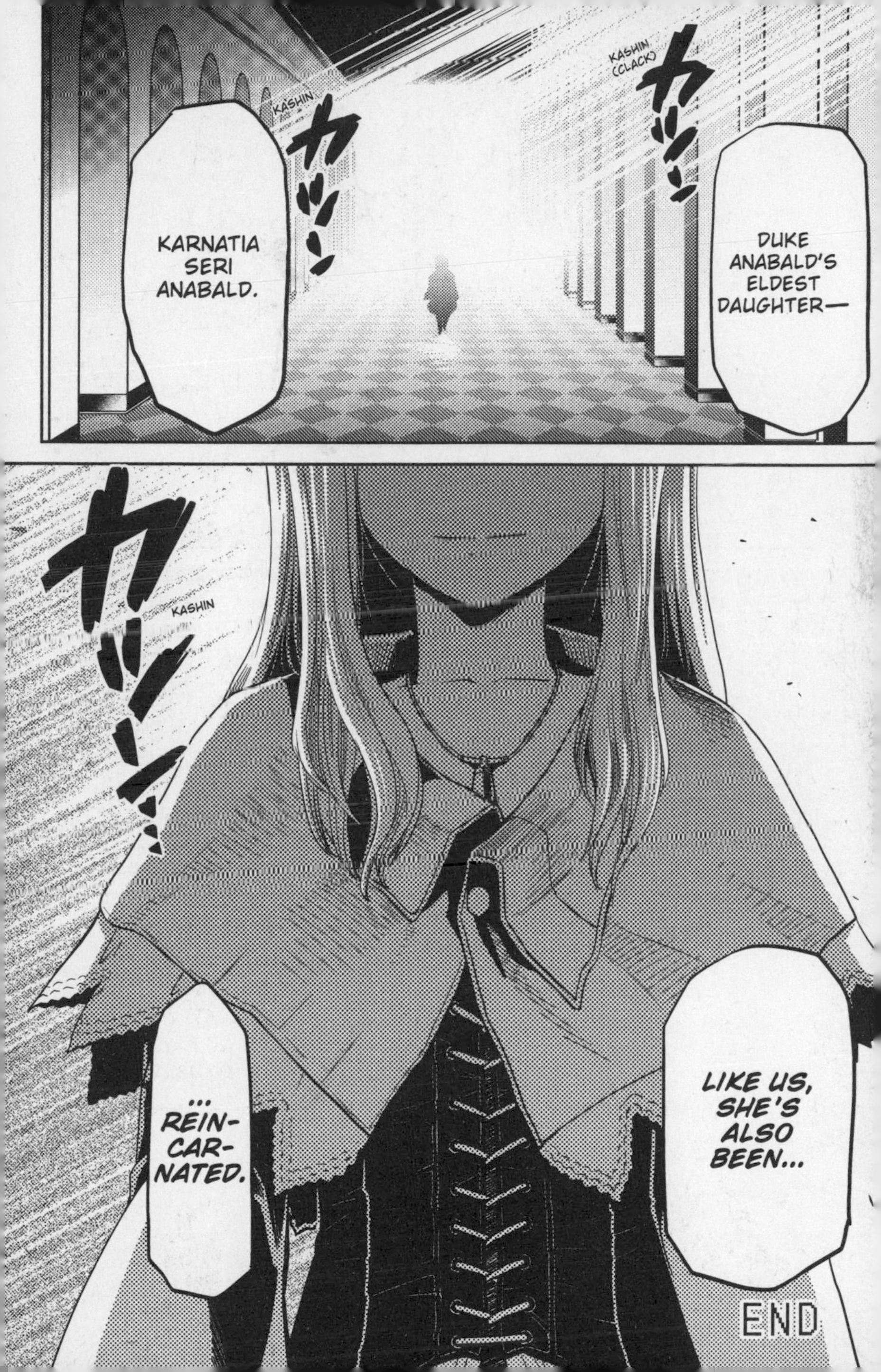
KASHIN (CLACK)
DUKE ANABALD'S ELDEST DAUGHTER—
KASHIN
KARNATIA SERI ANABALD.
KASHIN
LIKE US, SHE'S ALSO BEEN...
... REIN-CAR-NATED.
END

AFTERWORD

ORIGINAL CREATOR: OKINA BABA

WHO THE HELL AM I? WHY, I'M THE ORIGINAL CREATOR, OKINA BABA!

LOOK AT THAT. WE'RE ALREADY AT THE SIXTH VOLUME!

THERE ARE A LOT OF BIG EVENTS IN THIS VOLUME.

AND I'M SURE THE MANGA FANS WHO DON'T READ THE NOVELS ARE THINKING, "WHO THE HELL ARE THESE GUYS?"

A WHOLE LOT OF NEW PEOPLE SHOWED UP AT ONCE!

PEOPLE. THAT'S RIGHT—PEOPLE!

PEOPLE, IN A SERIES THAT'S ONLY BEEN ABOUT MONSTERS SO FAR!

AND A WHOLE BUNCH OF THEM TOO!

WHO IN THE WORLD COULD THIS DEMON LORD BE? *SARCASM*

BY THE WAY, THE PEOPLE WHO APPEARED IN THIS VOLUME PREVIOUSLY DESIGNED BY THE NOVEL ILLUSTRATOR, KIRYU-SENSEI, ARE ALL CLOSE TO THEIR ORIGINAL DESIGNS.

THE REST OF THEM ARE ORIGINAL DESIGNS BY KAKASHI-SENSEI.

THE ONE WHO SURPRISED ME THE MOST WAS DARAD.

A KABUKI-LOOKING SAMURAI TYPE? I REALLY HAVE TO TIP MY HAT TO THAT IDEA.

KAKASHI-SENSEI'S WAY TOO GOOD AT IMPROVISING.

AS SUCH, I HOPE YOU'LL KEEP SUPPORTING KAKASHI-SENSEI'S MANGA IN THE FUTURE!

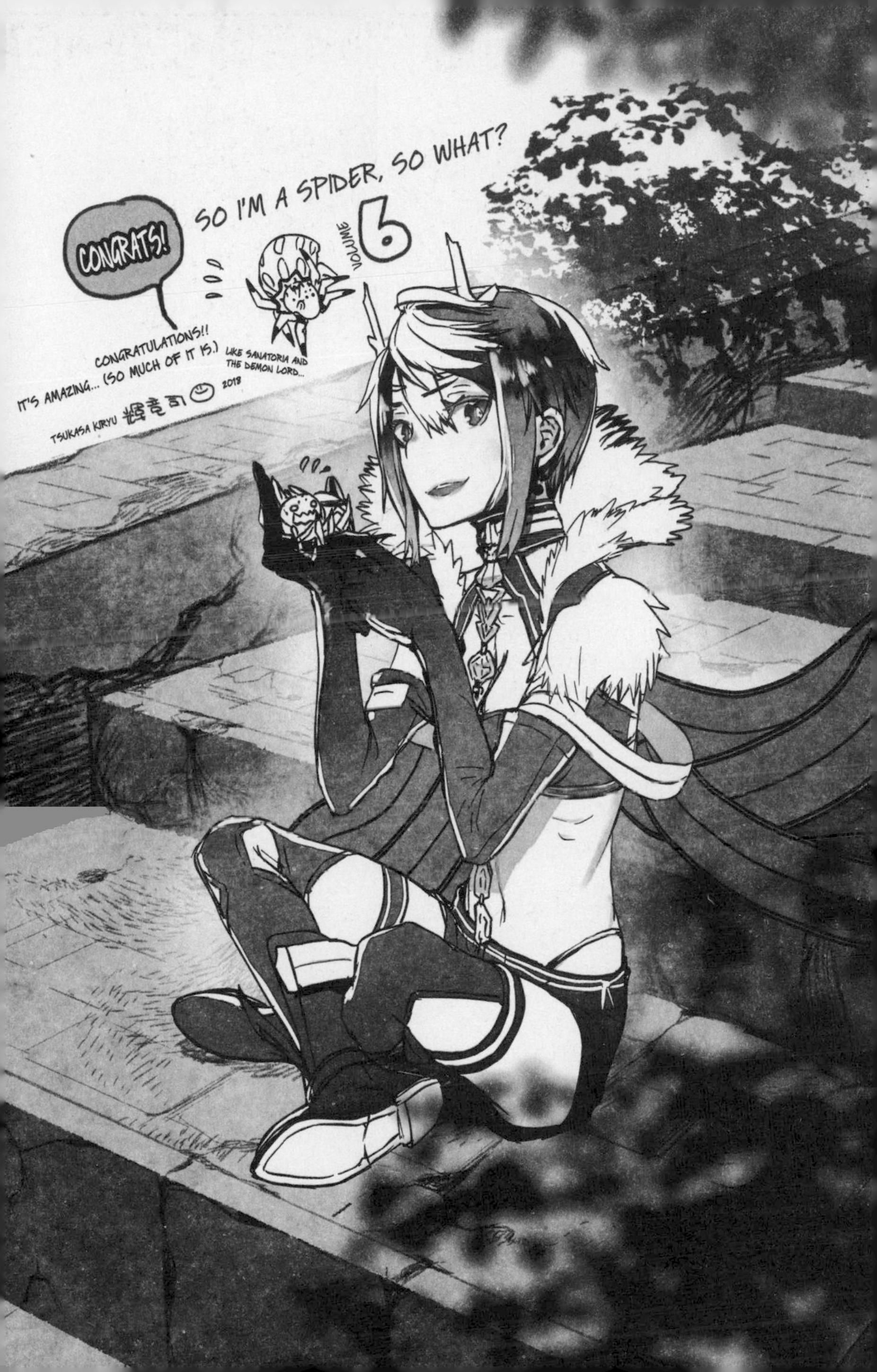

SO I'M A SPIDER, SO WHAT?
VOLUME 6
CONGRATS!
CONGRATULATIONS!!
IT'S AMAZING... (SO MUCH OF IT IS.)
LIKE SANATORIA AND THE DEMON LORD...
TSUKASA KIRYU 輝竜司 2018

STAFF LIST

The author
ASAHIRO KAKASHI

Assistant

TERUO HATANAKA

Design
R design studio
(Shinji Yamaguchi)

You're reading
the wrong way!
Turn the page to read
a bonus short story by
So I'm a Spider, So What?
original creator
Okina Baba!

If you're wondering why I was mulling over this stuff in the first place, it's 'cause I've run into so many people.

I'd seen some humans from this world before, of course, like the one who got caught in my web with that giant egg or those bastards who burned down my home.

But in those instances, I didn't have time to wonder about stupid stuff like this.

Though now that I mention it, I just realized that the people of this world look exactly like earthlings.

Which has got me thinking.

I'm glad they weren't octopus monsters or anything freaky like that.

I mean, can you say I'm wrong?

Imagine being reborn and meeting a bunch of tentacle-y aliens. How are you supposed to communicate?

I know I wouldn't be able to act natural in that situation!

"Yay, a parallel world! I bet I'll get a harem! Oh, wait—it's an octopus harem."

Who'd be into that?

When you consider the fact that otherworlders are technically aliens, it wouldn't be that surprising if things turned out that way.

Better not to have high expectations about a parallel world.

Actually, the fact that I was reincarnated here as a SPIDER should be proof enough of that!

In a way, this is worse than the octopus thing!

It's great that the people in this world resemble normal earthlings and all, but that doesn't do me much good if I'm a freaking spider!

Why couldn't I be reborn as a human?!

I was lucky enough to wind up in a place where the people are basically just like earthlings, but what does that matter if I'm gonna be reborn as a spider anyway?!

Huh? Then would I prefer the people here looked like octopuses, you ask?

Listen, I don't think I like your attitude, pal.

[The end]

So I'm a Spider, So What?

Alien

Okina Baba

I just realized something totally crazy!

So this place isn't Earth, right?

Which means, from an earthling's perspective, the people who live in this world are aliens!

Huh? What do you mean, it's a little late for that now?

I mean, yeah, it's super old news that this place isn't Earth. But I was thinking that, by phrasing things in a slightly different way, it can have a completely new impact, that's all.

I don't know if this place is a planet somewhere else in space or if it's actually a parallel world in a separate dimension from Earth altogether.

But it's not Earth, that's for sure.

I guess it could be that old plot twist where this turns out to be Earth in the super-distant future, but let's just assume that's not the case for now.

So if they're not earthlings, they're either aliens or uh... otherworlders?

The latter kinda makes you picture something more or less the same as earthlings, but *aliens* conjures up a totally different image.

Say the word "alien" and people start imagining little gray dudes, or octopus-looking creatures, or some other crazy thing that probably still walks on two legs.

Either way, they're obviously nothing close to humans.

Otherworlders and aliens... Both words describe someone who's not from Earth, but for some reason, what they bring to mind are totally different.

So I'm a Spider, So What?

 6

Art: **Asahiro Kakashi**

Original Story: **Okina Baba**

Character Design: **Tsukasa Kiryu**

Translation: Jenny McKeon Lettering: Bianca Pistillo

This book is a work of fiction. Names, characters, places, and incidents are the product of the author's imagination or are used fictitiously. Any resemblance to actual events, locales, or persons, living or dead, is coincidental.

Kumo desuga, nanika? Volume 6
© Asahiro KAKASHI 2019
© Okina Baba, Tsukasa Kiryu 2019
First published in Japan in 2019 by KADOKAWA CORPORATION, Tokyo.
English translation rights arranged with KADOKAWA CORPORATION, Tokyo,
through TUTTLE-MORI AGENCY, INC.

English translation © 2019 by Yen Press, LLC

Yen Press, LLC supports the right to free expression and the value of copyright.
The purpose of copyright is to encourage writers and artists to produce the creative
works that enrich our culture.

The scanning, uploading, and distribution of this book without permission is a theft
of the author's intellectual property. If you would like permission to use material from
the book (other than for review purposes), please contact the publisher. Thank you
for your support of the author's rights.

Yen Press
150 West 30th Street, 19th Floor
New York, NY 10001

Visit us at yenpress.com
facebook.com/yenpress
twitter.com/yenpress
yenpress.tumblr.com
instagram.com/yenpress

First Yen Press Edition: July 2019

Yen Press is an imprint of Yen Press, LLC.
The Yen Press name and logo are trademarks of Yen Press, LLC.

The publisher is not responsible for websites (or their content)
that are not owned by the publisher.

Library of Congress Control Number: 2017954138

ISBNs: 978-1-9753-5826-6 (paperback)
978-1-9753-3149-8 (ebook)

10 9 8 7 6 5 4 3 2 1

WOR

Printed in the United States of America

BUNGO STRAY DOGS

Volumes 1–10
available now

BUNGO STRAY DOGS 01
Story by KAFKA ASAGIRI · Art by SANGO HARUKAWA

If you've already seen the anime, it's time to read the manga!

Having been kicked out of the orphanage, Atsushi Nakajima rescues a strange man from a suicide attempt— Osamu Dazai. Turns out that Dazai is part of a detective agency staffed by individuals whose supernatural powers take on a literary bent!

BUNGO STRAY DOGS © Kafka ASAGIRI 2013
© Sango HARUKAWA 2013
KADOKAWA CORPORATION

www.yenpress.com

Yen Press

PRESS "SNOOZE" TO BEGIN.

DEATH MARCH TO THE PARALLEL WORLD RHAPSODY

MANGA

After a long night, programmer Suzuki nods off and finds himself having a surprisingly vivid dream about the RPG he's working on...only thing is, he can't seem to wake up.

LIGHT NOVEL

YEN ON

www.yenpress.com

Death March to the Parallel World Rhapsody (novel) © Hiro Ainana, shri 2014 / KADOKAWA CORPORATION
Death March to the Parallel World Rhapsody (manga) © AYAMEGUMU 2015 © HIRO AINANA, shri 2015/KADOKAWA CORPORATION